Grading Justice

Critical Communication Pedagogy

Series Editors
Ahmet Atay, The College of Wooster
Deanna L. Fassett, San José State University

Critical pedagogy, as Cooks (2010), Freire (1970), and Lovaas, Baroudi and Collins (2002) argue, aims to empower and liberate individuals to achieve social change and transform oppressive and unequal social structures. This book series aims to contribute to the discourse of critical communication pedagogy by featuring works that utilize different dimensions of critical communication pedagogy to foster dialogue, to encourage self-reflexivity, and to promote social justice by allowing marginalized voices to be heard. Even though projects that focus on dynamics between teachers and students and their issues within classroom settings are crucial, this series aims to focus on works that utilize critical and cultural theories to interrogate the role of larger structures as they influence these relationships in higher education. Hence, in this proposed series we will feature works that are built on critical communication pedagogy—works that function within a critical/cultural studies framework, and works that interrogate the notion of power, agency, dialogue and "voice" within the context of higher education and beyond. We argue that the work of educators and their educational philosophies are not limited to the classroom; hence, critical communication scholars are interested in connecting classroom pedagogy with its real life applications. Therefore, this series is interested in publishing work that captures these facets.

Titles in the series

Mediated Critical Communication Pedagogy edited by Ahmet Atay and Deanna L. Fassett

Critical Administration in Higher Education: Negotiating Political Commitment and Managerial Practice edited by Jay Brower and W. Benjamin Myers

Grading Justice: Teacher-Scholar-Activist Approaches to Assessment edited by Kristen C. Blinne

Grading Justice

Teacher-Activist Approaches to Assessment

Edited by
Kristen C. Blinne

LEXINGTON BOOKS
Lanham • Boulder • New York • London

Published by Lexington Books
An imprint of The Rowman & Littlefield Publishing Group, Inc.
4501 Forbes Boulevard, Suite 200, Lanham, Maryland 20706
www.rowman.com

6 Tinworth Street, London SE11 5AL, United Kingdom

Copyright © 2021 by The Rowman & Littlefield Publishing Group, Inc.

All rights reserved. No part of this book may be reproduced in any form or by
any electronic or mechanical means, including information storage and retrieval
systems, without written permission from the publisher, except by a reviewer who
may quote passages in a review.

British Library Cataloguing in Publication Information Available

Library of Congress Cataloging-in-Publication Data

Library of Congress Control Number: 2020946396
ISBN 978-1-7936-0955-7 (cloth)
ISBN 978-1-7936-0956-4 (electronic)

Contents

List of Tables and Figures		vii
Acknowledgments		ix
Preface		xi
Introduction: Grieving (Un)Grading (In)Justices		1
	Kristen C. Blinne	
1	Rhetoric of Grades: Evaluating Student Work and Its Consequences	43
	David Deifell	
2	Mobilizing a Critical Universal Design for Learning Framework for Justice Minded Course Design and Assessment	61
	Allison D. Brenneise and Mark Congdon, Jr.	
3	Honoring Vivencias: Vivencias: A Borderlands Approach to Higher Education Pedagogy Justice	91
	Leandra H. Hernández and Sarah De Los Santos Upton	
4	Walking the Tightrope: Navigating the Tensions of Teaching and Grading Communication Content Inside and Outside the Discipline	109
	Juliane Mora	
5	Student-Activist Mentor Letters as a Form of Social Movement-Building in Communication Activism Pedagogy	133
	David L. Palmer	

vi *Contents*

6 Love Letters Gone Wrong: Complicating the Romantic
Ideal of Democratic Processes in the College Classroom   163
Londie T. Martin and Kristen A. McIntyre

7 Are We *Just* Grading or Grading *Justly*?:
Adventures with Non-Traditional Assessment   195
Kristen C. Blinne

8 "Ungrading" Communication: Awareness Pedagogy as
Activist Assessment   255
Kristen C. Blinne

9 Resisting the Detrimental Effects of Grade Inflation on
University Faculty and Students through Critical
Communication Pedagogy   297
David H. Kahl, Jr.

10 Rate My Performance, or Just Sing Along: A Critical Look
at Student Evaluations of Teaching   309
Summer R. Cunningham

11 The Seven Lesson Faculty Member: Outling Assessment's
Harm to Faculty   331
C. Kyle Rudick

Index   353

About the Contributors   359

List of Tables and Figures

TABLES

Table 6.1	Midterm Reflection: Self-Assessment Criteria	189
Table 6.2	Student's Overall Grade Assessment	192
Table 7.1	Sample Grade Plan	218
Table 7.2	Sample Assessment Plan Amendment Opportunity	244
Table 7.3	Sample Self-Assessment Chart	246
Table 7.4	Proposed Assessment Categories and Grade Range Requirements	249
Table 8.1	Awareness Self-Assessment	287
Table 8.2	Semester Self-Assessment Guide	288

FIGURES

Figure 6.1	Voting on Our Guidelines for Course Conduct	171
Figure 6.2	Quantitative Representations of Course Evaluation Results	178

Acknowledgments

First and foremost, I would like to thank Ahmet Atay and Deanna Fassett as well as the team at Lexington Books. I would also like to thank all of the contributors for sharing their teaching and learning experiences aimed at *grading justice*. I further wish to express my gratitude for all of our mentors, teachers, and students, in addition to the many educators and institutions working tirelessly to reimagine the role of grading and assessment within our teaching lives. Of these, I wish to especially thank Mariaelena Bartesaghi for her mentorship and friendship, both of which helped to make this project possible. Finally, I wish to acknowledge our colleagues, friends, and families for providing inspiration and support for our work. Thank you to my mother, Lynette Bradford Blinne, a lifelong educator, for the role she has played in shaping my teaching and learning life.

—Kristen C. Blinne

Preface

Shortly after this edited collection went into production in mid-March 2020, many institutions of higher education around the United States closed suddenly, sending students and employees off-campus to work, teach, and learn remotely, due to stay-at-home orders issued as a result of the COVID-19 global pandemic. Even now, we continue to see a rising death toll related to COVID-19, in addition to the loss of economic stability for millions of people who became unemployed as a result of businesses closing (temporarily or permanently). Many have lost (and continue to lose) loved ones, friends, neighbors, and community members even as the country begins to slowly reopen. As institutions, faculty, and students grapple with the future of higher education during these difficult and uncertain times, students across the country are filing "breach-of-contract" lawsuits, demanding tuition and room and board fee refunds as well as compensation/damages based on a perception of the reduction of educational quality, placing many financially fragile institutions at risk of closing.

At the end of the spring semester, a huge wave of racial justice protests erupted throughout the country and globe after a video showing the brutal murder of George Floyd on May 25, 2020, by a Minneapolis police officer was widely circulated. His tragic death is just one of many Black lives that has been cut short due to police brutality, systemic racism, and the continued perpetuation of White supremacist systems that perpetuate this hate. As a result, institutions of higher education are issuing statements about diversity, equity, and inclusion while also exploring how to better teach and embody anti-racist pedagogies and practices. Students have petitioned their institutions to require coursework and policy changes focused on racial justice, in addition to demands to shift campus police procedures, acknowledge racist practices or histories, or to remove students or employees, clubs or organizations, or other groups that engage in racist acts from the campus communities.

The demand for racial justice in higher education and beyond, as related to this collection is of utmost importance to conversations about *grading justice.* Throughout these discussions on grades and grading during a pandemic, I regularly encountered a meme quoting Sim Kern, which states, "If teachers are assigning grades right now, what they are grading is PRIVILEGE. Without the equalizing force of the school building and its services, limited as they are, teachers are grading on access to technology, Wi-Fi, food, housing security, and ableism." While this view does not fully account for the material disadvantages still present in a brick and mortar institutions and their services, it does speak to the heart of this edited collection—the importance of interrogating the purpose and role of grades and grading within teaching and learning, including the ways in which grading systems can increase injustices *or* work towards equity and justice. Further, as a result of these grading system changes, many institutions decided to abandon student evaluations of instruction for the semester, others created modified versions, and some are offering faculty the option of not including their semester evaluations in hiring, contract renewal, or in their tenure/promotion dossiers.

The COVID-19 global pandemic created an opening for institutions to suddenly embrace new assessment approaches, amending their grading policies to adopt models outside of the traditional A–F grading system during the spring semester. Students at various colleges and universities petitioned their institutions for pass/fail or other alternative grading systems during the spring term. To this end, for example, after exploring the Facebook Group, *Pandemic Pedagogy,* which has over thirty thousand members, I encountered over ten different grading approaches institutions adopted to help balance the grading power dynamic, including:

- Pass/Incomplete, Pass/Fail, Pass/No Pass, or Pass/No Record
- Credit/No Credit (CR/NC) or Graded/No Credit
- Satisfactory/Unsatisfactory or Satisfactory/No Credit
- Satisfactory/D/F (the F not impacting one's GPA)
- S (A–C), S- (D), or U (the F not impacting one's GPA)
- ABCPF (D is considered a "pass")
- ABCDU (U meaning "unsatisfactory)
- ABCNP (ABC is a pass, and NP is equivalent to a D or F)

In some cases, students were automatically placed into these updated grading systems, in other cases, they had to opt in or out of them, and there were also

Preface xiii

some instances where students could retroactively apply them after seeing their letter grades. How these grades impacted the students' grade point averages, if they would count towards prerequisites into advanced courses, or if they were allowed for major or general education courses, greatly depended on the institution. For some institutions, to "pass," students needed a C grade or above; for others, a C-, D, or even a D- grade. Moreover, whether failing grades impacted a student's GPA or if they were reported or recorded was also widely considered. As an example, one institution utilized the students' in-person grades prior to remote learning as the baseline for the remainder of the semester. Per their approach, students with A or B grades could only move down one letter grade during the remote portion of the term, and students with C or D grades could move up but not down. Beyond institutional policies, faculty, too, created a wide range of creative options for grading (e.g., an A grade for everyone, along with many other approaches) as discussed in numerous online faculty discussion groups.

One of the clear takeaways about these grading system transitions during the spring 2020 term was the need to create more equitable and flexible options for students and faculty, resulting from the increased anxiety and stress and learning inequities related to these disruptions to students' learning experiences, along with a variety of other highly consequential factors. Based on my own observations of faculty conversations about grades and grading, people drew fairly clear lines in the sand about their views on grade inflation (i.e., advocating against it or for it, depending); modifying grading standards/systems (i.e., whether one should or not); shifting workloads (some increased, others decreased); setting deadlines for assignments or accepting late or incomplete work (i.e., flexible or inflexible approaches abounded); offering extra credit or other incentives (or punishments); balancing grade distribution (i.e., higher than a "regular" semester or similar to one's norm); and utilizing less or more authoritarian approaches (e.g., LockDown/remote proctored exams), among other conversations.

Per my view, the Black Lives Matter and associated equity and justice movements are fighting to resist the ongoing injustices many face have and are paving a new path forward for higher education. Based on this, it seems clear that there is no better time for teachers and students to act as change agents to create the teaching and learning environments where learners do more than just survive (and tragically, not all will due to these injustices) but also thrive. While focusing on the role of grading justice is only one small step on the longer journey towards equity and justice more broadly, we hope that this edited collection will inspire you to reflect on and question your own ideas about grades and grading, so we can begin to create a more just educational world together. May we all listen and learn from those suffering,

xiv   *Preface*

while also actively working to create a more humane and just world together. We, the contributors in this volume, hope to continue this conversation beyond this collection, so please share your ideas about *grading justice* and any justice-related teaching resources at: www.gradingjustice.com.

Introduction

Grieving (Un)Grading (In)Justices

Kristen C. Blinne

Picture this: It is 10:00 p.m. and you have just finished submitting your final course grades. The break is so close you . . . *bing, bing, bing, bing, bing, bing* . . . the sound of email notifications landing in your inbox. It is 10:08 p.m. Never mind that you told the group at least ten times *grades will not and cannot be discussed by email.* You strongly consider *not* opening the messages *ever,* but then with a deep sigh, you decide to wade through what you imagine will likely be the murky grade appeal and/or grievance waters. As you dive in, you are reminded of Harrison's (2003) taxonomy of dispute orientations, and these emails certainly do not disappoint as exemplars of this model. First, you encounter an *information seeker*, a student that is just curious and hoping to better understand how and why they received the grade they did. Next, you encounter the *exception seeker*, who is not just seeking information and understanding about their grade, but instead hoping you will treat them as an exception, letting go of this and that policy because [insert reason here].

You are only two messages in and you are already feeling tired, but then you open the next message, which has some all caps wording and excessive punctuation! This student, let's call them the *victim*, feels like you are punishing them for [insert reason here]. Now things are really getting interesting. You sit with this message, reflecting on similar examples of messages your colleagues shared with you in the last few days. The "fun" continues as you open the next message, wherein you encounter an *enforcer*. This person is blaming you for their grade, stating that you treated them unfairly given their [insert reason here]. They are seeking justice, expecting you to treat them *more* fairly because you [insert reason here]. At this stage, you are trying to decide if you have the strength to open the last two emails.

After a short break, you head back and open a similar message as the previous one except this time the person is attempting to be a *protector*, insomuch that they do not want you to harm other people in the way they feel harmed by their grade because of [insert reason here]. Happily, the last message is not from one of your students. Instead, it is from members of the departmental grievance committee of which you are also a member. In this instance, the group is discussing a case of a *destroyer*—a student that is seeking vindication from and punishment of the professor who awarded them their grade. In fact, they want the professor, one of your colleagues, to be fired and they and their parents have already been in communication with the chair, dean, and president of the college. In this moment, even though your break has not yet started, you already feel it slipping away.

***

How do you assess your own approach to grading in your teaching? In *Grading Justice: Teacher-Activist Approaches to Assessment*, new and seasoned teachers are invited to explore socially-just approaches of assessment, including practices aimed at resisting and undoing grading and assessment altogether, to create more democratic grading policies and practices, foregrounding the transformative potential of communication within college courses. The contributions in this collection invite readers to consider not only how educators might assess social justice work in and beyond the classroom, but also to imagine what a social justice approach to grading and assessment would mean for intervening into potentially unjust modes of teaching and learning by creating more just practices and policies. In many ways, this collection also serves as its own kind of grade appeal or grievance.

Within the realm of critical communication pedagogy (CCP), there is a movement towards crafting meaningful grading and assessment approaches and practices which fit with the commitment of CCP to transform unequal power relationships within educational settings, among other goals. As teachers face increasing pressure to "assess" and "measure" learning as part of a growing "assessment culture" within higher education, it is imperative that those employing CCP develop grading and assessment strategies that reflect their teaching and learning values.

Assessment, in many institutions, which is particularly focused on learning outcomes, is often mandated at the course, department, initiative, and institutional level. As such, teachers are routinely required to develop new language around teaching and learning goals and objectives, in addition to gathering grading and assessment data to evaluate instructors, courses, programs, and institutions via both internal and external review mechanisms. Unfortunately, many of these assessment efforts not only perpetuate learning inequalities, but they also tend toward standardization, or rather a kind of pedagogy of homogenization that serves what some have termed the "assessment industrial

Introduction 3

complex." The link between governing bodies and accrediting agencies further casts a shadow on student-centered, faculty-driven efforts aimed at best teaching practices, especially those that critical communication pedagogues seek to enact in their teaching and learning lives.

In this spirit, this collection will examine the relationship between grading student learning and assessing or improving student learning, considering the ways grading and assessment policies and practices impact students' understanding and experience of learning as a liberatory practice and process. By doing so, the goal of this collection is to explore the ways in which grading and assessment practices are personal, social, and political—never neutral or objective—offering a range of ways that critical communication pedagogues can reflect on, resist, expand, experiment with, and/or reimagine how these "measures" can better serve teacher-activists who wish to challenge and create new approaches that reflect their critical, creative, contemplative, and/or collaborative commitments.

This edited collection will contribute to the growing number of books dedicated to critically exploring communication pedagogies, including: Fassett and Warren's (2007) *Critical Communication Pedagogy*; Frey and Palmer's (2014) *Teaching Communication Activism*; Atay and Toyosaki's (2017) *Critical Intercultural Pedagogy*; and Rudick, Golsan, and Cheesewright's (2017) *Teaching from the Heart: Critical Communication Pedagogy in the Communication Classroom*; Atmay and Pensoneau-Conways' (2019) *Queer Communication Pedagogy*; Atmay and Fassett's (2019) *Mediated Critical Communication Pedagogy*, among others.

Beyond the communication discipline, this edition collection seeks to also contribute to interdisciplinary conversations centered on grading and assessment as advanced in projects such as Bower and Thomas' (2013) *De-Testing + De-Grading Schools: Authentic Alternatives to Accountability and Standardization*; Haugnes, Holmgren, and Springborg's (2018) *Meaningful Grading: A Guide for Faculty in the Arts,* in addition to the following works that are geared more towards K–12 educational systems such as Guskey's (2015) *On Your Mark: Challenging the Conventions of Grading and Reporting*; Sackstein's (2015) *Hacking Assessment: 10 Ways to Go Gradeless in a Traditional Grades School*; Greenstein's (2018) *Restorative Assessment: Strengths-Based Practices that Support all Learners*; and, Feldman's (2019) *Grading for Equity: What It Is, Why It Matters, and How It Can Transform Schools and Classrooms.*

More specifically, this collection will offer a much needed exploration of the role of grading and assessment within critical communication pedagogy, offering alternative approaches to traditional assessment ideologies and practices that tend towards perpetuating neoliberal educational agendas.

Kristen C. Blinne

Interdisciplinary teachers in higher education, particularly in the discipline of communication, committed to or interested in social justice teaching and scholarship, grounded in critical communication pedagogy, are the primary audience for this text as well as those educators wishing to explore innovative, critical modes of grading and assessment within their teaching. This project also aims to be a relevant pedagogical tool for teacher training within graduate programs.

GRADING (IN)JUSTICES

> Grades have been given the impossible task of neatly quantifying the abilities of all students. But in attempting to reduce all students to quantifiable units on a five-point scale, we fail to evaluate students in their nearly infinite qualitative variations. Grades are a symptom of an educational philosophy that treats intellectual and artistic diversity as inconveniences to be classified rather than as virtues to be cultivated (Tomar n.d.).

While there are a growing range of colleges that either do not issue grades such as Goddard College, Antioch College, Bennington College, Evergreen College, New College of Florida, and Hampshire college, as examples, *or* those that limit or shift the power of impact of grading (e.g., Brown University, Sarah Lawrence College), the majority of institutions of higher education in the United States have adopted an almost "religious acceptance" of the five-letter A–F grading system, as Tomar (n.d.) contends. In fact, as Schneider and Hutt (2013) also argue, "Grading is one of the most fundamental facets of American education," (1). Like credit scores and other social rankings, which situate a person's numeric worth or value, grades, including one's grade point average, are highly consequential, insomuch that not only do they judge an individual's academic achievement, but also for some "serve as a key determinant of future success" (Schneider and Hutt 2013, 1). Even so, educators increasingly argue that our five-letter grading system is not that informative, effective, or educational (Tomar n.d.; Blum 2017), nor can it be considered "valid," "reliable," or "objective," and, as Kohn (1999) asserts, ultimately operating as "a subjective rating masquerading as an objective evaluation." Put differently, "Bad grades can stigmatize and discourage those who need help. Good grades tend to reward and elevate those who have all the intellectual and cognitive advantages" (Tomar n.d.). In both cases, many agree that grades represent an oversimplification of a student's learning ability and process.

As Paul Dressel wrote in 1976, "A mark or grade is an inadequate report of an inaccurate judgment by a biased and variable judge of the extent to which a

Introduction 5

student has attained an indefinite amount of material" (cited in Bower 2010a). Before we explore this idea in more depth, it is important to first situate how this system of grading has become such a structuring part of our educational system. Schneider and Hutt (2013) contend that grading is a "crucial expression of the modernist impulse," which has not always been part of education in the United States, nor have grading systems looked the same, served the same purpose, or had the same impact (2). Per their research on the history of American grading systems, they ultimately situate the various grading schemes as "a key technology of educational bureaucratization, a primary means of quantification, and the principal mechanism for sorting students," influenced by European models focused on competition, reward, and rank ordering, in addition to operating as a form of communication developed alongside the movement towards mass compulsory schooling (Schneider and Hutt 2013, 2).

A quick history of the A-F grading system suggests that the earliest official record of a grading system was utilized by Yale in 1785, wherein they sorted seniors into four categories—*Optimi*, second *Optimi, Inferiores*, and *Pejores* (Schneider and Hutt 2013; Schinske and Tanner 2014). Prior to this, earlier forms of grading consisted of narrative evaluations or exit exams before awarding a degree. These grades were often kept secret from students. Beyond Yale, William and Mary, too, experimented with ranking and grading systems, distinguishing students based on conduct as well as achievement, including measures that took into account non-academic criteria. Competition was a key feature of early grading systems, involving a great deal of comparison and direct public ranking against one's classmates (Schneider and Hutt 2013). It was thought that ranking one's class standing would motivate students towards achievement, even as the "constant ranking and re-ranking placed emphasis on the immediacy of competition rather than on intellectual and moral development" (Schneider and Hutt 2013, 4). Later, report cards, which were likened to merchant ledgers, entered into the process as tools to craft an on-going account of a student's success.

By 1837, some professors at Harvard were also utilizing a 100-point system (Schinske and Tanner 2014, 60). During this time and beyond, grading systems were constructed in various ways shifting regularly at a range of institutions, including lettered systems, percentage systems, and other numerical systems (Schneider and Hutt 2013). In keeping with their communicative function, grades (regardless of the form they took) began acting as a mechanism aimed at standardization. Schneider and Hutt contend that by the 1870s, schools were engaging in more aggressive actions to standardize grades, suggesting that grades could not only communicate something about a student's performance and standing while also operating as a motivational tool, but also they could communicate information outside of the learning institution (9). However, in order to accomplish this, grades needed to "mean" something that could be easily understood in a range of contexts. In the pursuit of this grading standardization, grading was constructed alongside the development of honors distinctions, as well as in alignment with the growing "mental testing movement" and the later standardized testing movements, which further sorted learners along hierarchical categories of intellect and ability (Schneider and Hutt 2013).

By the 1940s, nearly 100 years later, the A–F system was not yet the standard grading scheme; however, it had definitely emerged as one of the dominant systems. While grading on a 100-point scale was quite common by the early 1900s, it was also considered highly unreliable, which paved the way for creating a five-category scheme, utilizing letter grades (Schinske and Tanner 2014, 160). During this period, schools experimented with 3-point (e.g., Excellent, Average, and Poor) and 5-point (e.g., Excellent, Above Average, Average, Below Average, and Failing—each corresponding with a letter grade) systems as well (Percell 2014, 21). As part of the A–F system, now the most dominant grading system in contemporary educational practice, letter grade categories correspond to a range of percentage scores. As Schinske and Tanner (2014) suggest, "E" grades seemed to have disappeared by the 1930s, potentially to avoid the equation of "E" with "excellence" instead prioritizing A, B, C, D, and F (meaning "fail") (160). As Schneider and Hutt state, by the mid-twentieth century, the A–F grading system had become largely standardized, with letter grades aligning with numerical values, in use by over 80 percent of schools by 1971 (15). Per their view, a series of unintended consequences have arisen from this standardization. First, grading systems have greatly stripped teachers of their autonomy, forcing them into a system of expectations centered on grade distributions (e.g., norm-referenced grading and the "bell curve").

When considering how grades are employed as an instrument of comparison, we see that "grading on a curve arose from studies in the early twentieth century suggesting that levels of aptitude, for example, as measured by IQ, were distributed in the population according to a normal curve" (Schinske and Tanner 2014, 162). This kind of "norm-referenced grading" places students into a tiered model that creates the "illusion of legitimacy in the grading system without any direct connection between grades and achievement of learning goals" (Schinske and Tanner 2014, 162). Finally, as an objective evaluation of student knowledge, it is quite clear that grades are inconsistently, and dare I say, often unjustly applied, rendering the A–F grading system as a highly problematic indicator of a student's learning ability or knowledge. We see this play out in a range of ways, including the variations among how teachers integrate "non-academic" factors into the grading process, along

Introduction 7

with the lack of consistency among teacher grading practices and policies, in addition to the very real manner in which teachers may grade students based on their feelings about them (unconscious and intentional or not).

Building on these ideas, in considering why colleges exist as well as what students should value and aim for when attending college, Tagg (2004) examines the communicative content that colleges actually preserve about the learners that attend them stating, "Kellogg makes cereal; colleges make transcripts" (3), and at most institutions, these transcripts focus on one thing—a student's grades. Because of this, he also queries, "Are we teaching students to grub for grades or how to learn in deep and lasting ways?" (2). Considering this further, he discusses the implications of students adopting a "performance goal" approach to learning, which centers on receiving positive judgment of one's competence, attempting to avoid negative feedback, as opposed to a "learning goal" approach that focuses on increasing understanding. As such, in higher education settings, it is not uncommon for students to report that they received a "high" grade in a course in which they feel they have learned very little; at the same time, teachers often encounter students who have received what many might deem a "low" or even "failing" grade, yet these students may attest that they learned a great deal from the course.

Tagg provides an example of a student "Jack" who got an "A" grade in his course but does not remember anything related to the content, in comparison with another student "Jill" who failed the course but continued to engage the learning well after the conclusion of the course. He queries, "Which of the two students would you consider more successful?" (3). As he explains, for him, Jill is the more successful learner because the learning became part of her, continuing beyond the course, changing her understanding, and impacting her ideas nearly a year after having failed, whereas Jack, conversely, left the learning behind him. If we go by the grade alone, it would appear that Jack is the more successful learner because he supposedly "excelled," earning an "A," when Jill failed. As Tagg states, per the view of the institution, Jack is the better student, even though it is quite clear that now a year later, in both cases, the "grade" has ceased to be valid evidence of either of their learning (3). If both students were graded again a year later, it is quite likely that the results might be completely different, even opposite.

As Tagg's student examples illustrate, Jack represents the student who is embracing a "performance goal," whereby he received enough points to merit an "A" grade, thereby chasing the grade versus embracing the possibilities for deep learning. Jill, on the other hand, did not "succeed" in the traditional grading sense, but regardless, she was able to embody the "learning goal" approach, which changed her as a person. Another way of saying this, per Tagg's view, is that Jack focused on producing a satisfying performance, and

Jill worked on personal development and growth. Within this framework, if we carefully consider the role of institutions of higher learning, beyond exploring the purpose of for what and for whom they serve, in addition to what students value about their own learning, we tend to see students struggle with the relationship between grading and learning, especially when many institutions consider a student's future employment as the primary evidence of successful learning.

Blum (2017) describes this idea in a similar manner by suggesting that students are taught to focus on schooling in the realm of achievement rather than on learning. Thus, it is unsurprising, in her view, that students often treat college as a game that involves amassing points, winning at any price, and playing the game simply for the game's sake *only*. As Blum contends, part of the reason it is so easy for students to play this "game of school" is because they see grading as both arbitrary and inconsistent, particularly the great variance between teacher's policies related to grading (e.g., late work, partial credit, use of zeros, attendance, policing of non-academic behaviors, participation policies, and so on). To play the game, students only need to "learn" what each professor wants and then attempt to perform that goal, regardless of whether they actually "learn" something related to the course content in addition or not.

Moreover, within standardized grading systems, students could easily learn how to simply partake in "performance goals" in Tagg's (2004) view or game the system as Blum (2017) contends. In other words, students could drop courses deemed "too difficult," seek out particular teachers with more lenient grading, or take courses described as "easy As" (Schneider and Hutt 2013, 16). One need only to quickly peruse the website "Rate My Professors" to see evidence of this in action, many students commenting on teachers that one should embrace or avoid, based on how they "do" grading in their courses. Other online resources allow students to shop for courses based on the number of exams, quizzes, and projects—each of which are ranked by the frequency given and the perceived level of difficulty. Additionally, in some cases, students can also access professors' grade distribution data, allowing them to search for what might be "easy A" courses.

Because grades historically were first designed to communicate information internally among teachers, students, and families, and then later became forms of external communication and organization between and among institutions, grades are tools for "systems-building rather than pedagogical devices—a common language for communication about learning outcomes" (Schneider and Hutt 2013, 3). In keeping with the aims of neoliberalism, we too can see how the standardization of grades has further commodified the learning experience, constructing it in capitalistic terms aimed at "customer satisfaction" models, whereby consumers (students) rate their learning experience by evaluating teachers' performances, which Schneider and Hutt link to the notion of "grade inflation" and its associated implications (e.g., teachers give higher grades to receive more positive evaluations *and* the notion that students are receiving grades not indicative of their ability or learning see Hunt, 2008). This consumer model becomes even more complex when one starts to analyze the wide range of grading policies at various institutions. For instance, one institution may use a plus/minus A–F scale, and another may simply use an A–F model (or even an A–E model). As an example of this in practice, I once worked at an institution that allowed instructors to select the plus/minus scale (or not). Thus, within that context, students had some courses that operated with a plus/minus structure and some that did not. Institutions may offer an A+ grade (factored into a student's grade point average or not), whereas others may include numerous pass/fail options. Further, many institutions have policies requiring a specific grade point average for admission to and retention in a major program, in addition to having cumulative GPA requirements for graduation, among other opportunities like access to independent studies, teaching or assistantships, or credit-overloading.

Additional consequences that Schneider and Hutt raise include the growing concern, as early as the 1960s and 1970s, that grades were not promoting learning and instead were creating unhealthy levels of anxiety and competition along with encouraging cheating (17). As teachers already know, grades and grading communicate but also are a powerful form of communication, containing the authority of evaluation and judgment which labels learners in extremely consequential ways, producing hierarchal categories of value that contribute to production, reinforcement, and maintenance of social inequalities. Even so, by this stage, standardized grades were entrenched enough with the educational system(s) as a tool said to motivate students, determine placement, and communicate *something* about student learning.

In summary, even though early grading schemes focused on the communication of class ranking for outside audiences, they were still primarily designed to operate internally within the institution. Later, after years of experimentation with numerous grading systems, we see institutions attempt to communicate information about student achievement externally. As Schneider and Hutt contend, grades and their accompanying grading systems became a product of standardization as school enrollments grew, becoming constructed as "objective assessments of student achievement" as opposed to the previous "subjective" teacher-based assessments previously employed (18). As grades were utilized as a tracking device for student learning, they started to become an end in themselves—even when "arrived at arbitrarily or unfairly" (Schneider and Hutt 2013, 18). It is unsurprising, given this, that alongside the developments of standardized grading systems, an anti-grading movement has also been underway. As Percell (2014) argues, "It is paradoxical at best, at worst oxymoronic, for educational leaders to expect schools that operate on standardized patterns of minimized achievement levels to generate students who exhibit innovative, dynamic thinking skills and possess exemplary creative abilities" (5).

Percell further examines the relationship between "traditional grading systems," which are born of the movement towards standardization and those approaches that are deemed "alternative" or "non-traditional." For clarity, "traditional grading systems" are those that utilize points, which are averages to arrive at a final percentage that is then translated to a particular letter grade category," whereas "alternative" or "non-traditional" grading systems can simply be conceptualized as any approach that differs from traditional grading (6–7). Within the realm of "alternative" or "non-traditional" grading systems, we see a wide range of options such as narrative evaluation, pass/fail, and assessment that involves no letter grades, points, or percentages along with innovative methods that still arrive at letter grades. Regardless of which grading system one employs, it is clear that within all grading systems, there are huge discrepancies between the grades different teachers would award to the same assignment. Because of this, many still argue that grades hold very little meaning (e.g., Kohn 1999, 2011; Bower 2010a, 2010b; Percell 2014; Blum 2017). Even so, the rise of "assessment culture" continues to permeate the educational landscape.

ASSESSMENT (IN)JUSTICES

The academic embrace of the "assessment industrial complex" is just another example of what Muller (2018) speaks about in his book, *The Tyranny of Metrics*. In considering the purported relationship between measurement and improvement, Muller comments that almost anything that can be measured can be approved, further suggesting that many industries have developed a "metric fixation," which he describes as follows:

> the belief that it is possible and desirable to replace judgment, acquired by personal experience and talent with numerical indicators of comparative performance based on standardized data (metrics); the belief that making such metrics public (transparent) assures that institutions are actually carrying out their purposes (accountability); the belief that the best way to motivate people within these organizations is by attaching rewards and penalties to their measured performance, rewards that are either monetary (pay-for-performance) or reputational (rankings) (18).

Introduction 11

As part of this process, Muller argues that ultimately a "metric fixation" centers on the persistence of the above beliefs even when faced with unintended negative consequences once these metrics are put into practice. Moreover, Muller discusses how a "metric fixation" can easily create a "measurability bias," whence organizations start moving towards assessment options simply because they are more easily measured. Per his view, not only do problems arise when these measures form a system of reward and punishment, but also they significantly shape how assessors talk about the world, understand it, and act within it as a result. Some of the ongoing and reoccurring flaws that Muller has identified regarding metrics include practices aimed at measuring the most easily measurable items; measuring the simple when the desired outcome is complex; measuring imputes rather than outcomes; and, degrading information quality through standardization (23–24).

As he contends, another major issue with a "metric fixation" "occurs because not everything that is important is measurable, and much that is measurable is unimportant" (18). Muller's work makes an important contribution to the "unexamined faith that amassing metric data and sharing it solely within an organization will result in improvements of some sort" (xxiii). His work offers much for further discussion, particularly in relationship to the Learning Outcomes Assessment (LOA) movement, but also the continued metric-race towards further educational standardization, in addition to the ever-growing "assessment industrial complex."

There is no doubt the LOA movement in higher education has taken hold. As part of this "movement," as Bennett and Brady (2014) state, "teachers and administrators are asked to articulate the goals, objectives, measures, and outcomes of the educational process at every level: from the classroom to the department to the institution as a whole" (147). Per this process, the gathered information or collected data is then utilized to evaluate instructors, in addition to curricula, programs, and institutions more broadly both through internal and external review mechanisms. This movement, which Bennett and Brady state can be traced to Taylorism and theories of scientific management, is really just a further manifestation of the "standards movement," emerging at the turn of the twentieth century (147). They caution that educators must distinguish between the LOA movement and faculty driven efforts aimed at curriculum development, best assessment practices, and course evaluation, especially the further away learning outcomes travel from the teacher and the course to broader uses within the institution.

In challenging the LOA movement, Bennett and Brady argue that learning outcomes become a "device for monitoring and auditing educators" rather than a tool that aids teaching and learning, further suggesting that this movement has more to do with "administrative and regulatory necessity rather than education" (147). They make clear connections between the growing interest in learning outcomes as related to accreditation, staring in the 1980s, suggesting a strong link among LOA discourses and the corporate world, think tanks, and non-governmental agencies. They go so far as to state within this movement "the business of higher education is business; teachers and students should be subject to the same disciplinary measures as any other workers and their products" (148). It is not surprising then that within this discourse, we encounter a wide range of neoliberal buzzwords, such as "consumers," "target market," "competitiveness," "value," "efficiency," "productivity," "stakeholder demands," "return on investment," or "value-added education," among a whole host of other terms and phrases (148). They argue that the effects of the LOA movement can be seen most powerfully in K–12 educational contexts, wherein high stakes testing forms part of a "bipartisan campaign to privatize the system of education" (150). When low scores are the result, it offers a perfect excuse to reallocate public educational funding to private companies to create more charter schools, in addition to helping to fuel the booming testing industry.

It is well-established that high stakes testing creates more inequality rather than closing achievement gaps as a test like the SAT (Scholastic Apptitude Test) illustrates with positive testing outcomes being strongly attributed to family income (150). To this end, Bennett and Brady also argue that what the LOA movement is really "measuring and maintaining is inequality," particularly since in their view, the "actual reasons that students drop out of school, fail classes, or are unable to secure a 'good job' have nothing to do with factors that can be measured by LOA" (150). Because LOA typically ignores contextual situations that highlight learning or educational differences, it is not that surprising as an outcrop of movement towards standardization that it has a strong role in the production, reinforcement, and maintenance of structural inequalities. As a result, Bennett and Brady believe that LOA is a danger to students on the grounds that it pretends that their learning problems are related to easily quantifiable outcomes rather than creating learning environments which prioritize engaged learning through faculty-driven efforts (151) (see Brenneise and Congdon; Hernández and De Los Upton Santos; Mora; Palmer; Martin and McIntyre, within this volume for examples of faculty-driven efforts in practice). As they state,

> The kind of policies that would truly help students with whom we work are not more hearings, campus visits, and testing, but adequate funding for secondary education; child care; a living wage; debt relief or, better yet, free universal post-secondary education; an adequately compensated academic workforce exercising free inquiry and building an educational community; and universal healthcare (150).

Introduction   13

They also argue that LOA is a danger to teachers as it places them (particularly those not tenured or on tenure tracks) in service to disciplinary mechanisms that impact academic freedom, creating the risk of unfair surveillance, in addition to requiring faculty to engage in "uncompensated or poorly compensated labor for dubious purposes" (151) (see Cunningham; Rudick, this volume). As they contend, at a time when the tenure system, faculty self-governance, and open inquiry are all under assault, it is imperative for educators to resist the continued institutionalization of the LOA movement (151). They challenge educators to advocate for what students need most in order to be successful, particularly "at-risk" students.

When considering grading, we must also take assessment into account as both operate as different sides of the same coin. To this end, Percell (2014) states "while assessment informs grading practices" often "grading policies will influence how assessment is carried out" (18). While each practice is different in and of itself, they are tied together as the LOA movement illustrates, starting first with the teacher and then course and then extending outward to the department-level and to the institution as a whole, especially when program review and accreditation are at stake. Beyond LOA, it is important to also reflect on the ways in which hiring, contract renewal, and tenure and promotion practices are impacted by both grading and assessment. First and foremost, a clear connection can be made between teachers grading practices, student evaluations of their teaching, and peer and administrator evaluation of instruction (see Cunningham, this volume). These evaluations or assessments of instruction are highly consequential for faculty, depending on the weight an institution places on their value.

Additionally, it is not uncommon for teachers to have to submit grade distribution data as part of annual reviews or renewal and promotion processes. Grade distribution data institutionally tracks teachers' grading practices alongside their colleagues (within the same department and/or discipline) as well as across the institution. These comparisons offer nothing that speak to the grading variables in play, particularly differences in pedagogies, expectations, or ideologies across disciplines, between and among teachers, within an institution itself, or in comparison to multiple institutions. Regardless, this "data" is said to help institutions monitor grade inflation, identifying teachers that might be too generous (or not generous enough) with "A" or "B" grades, in addition to creating hierarchies around disciplinary (or institutional) rigor, among other consequences.

I now turn my attention to discussions regarding the "purpose" of grading to help better illuminate the relationship to assessment and its connection to standardized grading systems, both cases involving systems that prioritize and are built on the value of competition rather than on collaboration.

Because the "grading system is the skeletal framework that provides a class its structure and informs its procedures and processes" (Cox 2011) with many institutions having mandated grading practices, it is vital that teachers continue to ask the following questions: "Does grading provide feedback for students that can promote learning?" "How might grades motivate struggling students?" "To what extent does grading provide reliable information about student learning?" (Schinske and Tanner 2014, 159). If for no other reason, teachers on average spend a considerable amount of time grading, which has the potential, as Schinske and Tanner argue, to distract them from "other, more meaningful aspects of teaching and learning" (159). Put differently, per their perspective, teachers need to become skeptical of what grades mean and what they really measure. This becomes increasingly important when one reflects on the ways in which grades come to shape student's identities, including all of the expectations and stereotypes associated with the "A-student" or the "D-student" as examples. As students continue to compete for grades, teachers continue to engage in the often tedious and time-consuming task of recording students' "achievement" so that they can be sorted into piles based on categories and rankings, worthiness of admission into additional learning opportunities, funding and/or scholarships, among other socially-sanctioned distinctions—all of which give rise to a wide range of educational inequalities—while at the same time teaching students to embody the notion "you are what your grade is" (Percell 2014).

As such, traditional grading systems, which actively compare students, based on their relative rankings under the guise of analyzing achievement and recognizing excellence through the quantifying and reduction of a student's learning into neatly packaged categories, continue to be a cause of critique and alarm for many educators. It is no wonder students become grade-grubbers in a system that values the pursuit of points as the primary point of learning. Sure, it can be argued that the function of grades is to inform teachers of student performance, serve as indicators to students regarding their performance, and also provide a platform for communicating about student's progress with parents, other teachers, administrators, or other institutions (Percell 2014, 25).

Others suggest that the purpose of grades—both past and present— involves the use of grades as feedback on performance, as just stated, but also as a motivator of student effort, as a tool for comparing students, *and* as an "objective evaluation of student knowledge" (Schinske and Tanner 2014). As a form of feedback, grades operate *evaluatively* (i.e., judge the quality, value, or worth); however, they offer very little information to help inform student's future learning efforts in that they do not readily provide *descriptive* information on how to improve, nor do they accurately illustrate *evaluative*

Introduction 15

information that explains how or why the work was judged. Another way of saying this is that a "B" grade means something quite different to instructors, within disciplines, and as part of an institution's cultural context. Within the realm of motivation, it could easily be argued that instead of motivating students to learn, what grades actually motivate students to do is to attempt to avoid receiving bad grades, playing on the fears of punishment (Schinske and Tanner 2014). Similarly, it could be said, in the case of "high-achieving" students, the quest for grade reward seems to primarily motivate students towards striving for high grades.

In my view, while there are more "pros" than "cons" for why the current and dominant A–F grading system and its associated standardized assessment practices should be eliminated in colleges (and K–12, for that matter), Tomar (n.d.) offers a look into this debate suggesting some reasons for elimination would include a movement towards learning for learning's sake, wherein students could "find motivation in something beyond a readily quantifiable score" and still gain practical skills without employing a "simple ranking imperative of a grading scale" as an "outdated holdover from America's industrial era." He further contends that by eliminating the grading system, educators could move away from attempting to quantify knowledge, reducing students into units on a five-point scale, entirely missing "their nearly infinite qualitative variations." Another "pro" Tomar offers is the "inevitably subjective" nature of grading, including all of its associated ideological prejudices as well as internal biases—all of which shape grading practices including grade inflation.

Counter to these points, Tomar also addresses the "cons" of eliminating grading altogether stating that because students are so conditioned by the system as it currently operates, many may not know how to learn without grades. To this end and per his view, grades also carry considerable weight in the "outside world," making the movement towards abolishing grades and grading even more challenging, especially when grades are treated as "short-hand for a sense of qualification and potential." Beyond this, Tomar suggests that removing grades would actually remove teacher authority because, as he also argues, grades are designed to control students. In other words, he contends, "The grading system's capacity to dole out punishment is among its strongest features." Ultimately, he claims that educators can make improvements to the system without throwing grades away completely, even though they are "deeply imperfect." Thus, he argues for grades to be "de-emphasized without being dumped." Tomar's discussion of the "pros" and "cons" of eliminating the grading system is a great jumping off place to our next section, which focuses on the ever-growing "ungrading" and "no-grading" movements, designed to disrupt unjust traditional grading systems through a wide range of alternative and non-traditional assessment practices.

16   *Kristen C. Blinne*

(UN)GRADING JUSTICE

Percell (2014), in discussing some of the drawbacks related to traditional grading, offers four principle shortcomings worth further reflection, including grade inflation, the use of zeros in grading, a loss of the love of learning, and finally, the ways in which grading functions as a system of reward and punishment (31–35) (for deeper discussions of grade inflation see, Deifell; Kahl; Cunningham; this volume). To start, Percell contends that the use of zeros creates a "statistical imbalance" in students' final grades as a result of giving zeros on assignments, especially when teachers utilize a 100-point grading scale (32). Citing both Guskey (2004) and Reeves (2004, 2008), leading voices against the use of zeros in grading practice, Percell considers how this seemingly simple practice can have profound impacts on a student's learning as well as their overall grade. He suggests alternatives such as offering "incompletes" or engaging in "minimum grading" (to be discussed shortly) to allow for grading not to bind students to momentary struggles they may be experiencing, causing them to miss work, thereby punishing them for these struggles with a zero (31).

Moreover, as another shortcoming, Percell states that traditional grading systems create and implement a "token economy," normative conduct encouraged through a system of reward and punishment (34). Per this viewpoint, grades become a type of currency that requires students to build as much capital as possible to "buy the grade," investing in points (now devoid of relative worth or importance) rather than learning (35). Percell, too, considers a wide range of grading system options that attempt to disrupt these system shortcomings, presenting variations such as Marchionda's (2010) "Point by Point" grading, which tries to break projects into formatively assessed tasks worth 2, 5, or 10-points, and Cherepinsky's (2011) "Self-Reflective Grading," which focuses on utilizing "correctives" for exams, wherein students receive returned exams offering no feedback but instead markers that state if the answers are "right" or "wrong." Students are then able to investigate the questions further during a specified period of time to attempt to recover lost points (37). Going back to Guskey (2004) and Reeves (2004, 2008), Percell explores "Minimum Grading" as a practice that attempts to remove the "statistical deficits" of assigning zero grades by instead setting a "minimum grade" students can receive on a 50 or 100-point scale. This system is designed to keep students from receiving a zero for missing work or absence as a tool to not disproportionately impact their overall grade (38).

Each of these options is designed to add nuance to the traditional A–F grading system, offering small shifts to attempt to be more fair in the grading

Introduction 17

process. Beyond these, Percell also describes the possibilities associated with "criterion-referenced" grading systems as moving further away from traditional "norm-referenced" grading systems, including: pass/fail systems (e.g., students receive passing scores for documentation of meeting requirements); narrative evaluation systems (e.g., offering constructive feedback only); and also what he refers to as blanket systems (e.g., where students start with a specific grade and then they work to maintain or change that grade) (40). Also under the umbrella of criterion-referenced grading is "standards-based grading" and "mastery grading" (discussed in more depth in Blinne, this volume). In both of these approaches, the focus is on meeting a standard or mastering a concept or skill, using predetermined learning outcomes as a guide for achieving competence (41). In both instances, students work in a tiered manner, and "retakes" are allowed so students can demonstrate their competence in relationship to the prescribed standard. Each approach attempts to break away from letter and points-based grading, offering different evaluative and numerical formulas to achieve this aim.

Another alternative Percell offers as an example comes from Peha (2005), who employs an approach called "3-P's" grading, which focuses on three primary assessment categories: participation, progress, and performance, each weighted with a final percentage (44). Within this system, students receive the following marks: √ (sufficient), √+ (outstanding), and √- (unsatisfactory). As part of this process, students are able to revise minuses until they reach a new level of proficiency. Building on "mastery grading," Percell has created his own "No Points Grading System," which entirely removes points from the process, instead employing a checklist of minimum requirements and tiered levels of mastery to determine final course grades (see Blinne, this volume). His goal in creating this alternative grading option is to increase students' intrinsic motivation while also fostering authentic mastery learning (2013, 1). As a final category of alternatives to traditional grading systems, Percell (2014) considers the "no grading" or "ungrading" movement, which seeks to abolish the grading system altogether, the focus of the remainder of this section.

Even though a range of assessment options exist, as Percell (2019) contends, "Traditional grades continue to be the ruling order of the day" (181) so much so, in his view, that traditional grades are "so deeply entrenched in our societal status quo that it is difficult for the lay population to conceive of school without them, and many people attribute their understanding and progress within school to the traditional grading measures" (181). As he further argues, in regard to the documentation of learning, "educators appear to be stuck with the process of grading, and traditional grading, specifically, contains inherent flaws that have been empirically proven by assessment experts" (183). In considering the role of democracy in grading, Percell queries: "How can teachers grade students in ways that foster democratic ideals and communities?" In answering this question, he contends that educators must "carry our pedagogical practices all the way to our gradebooks" (188). Guskey (2013) similarly contends, "assessment and grading have become a major focus in education reform," (68) further stating that "assigning fair and meaningful grades to students will continue to challenge educators at every level" (72).

Kohn (2011), in making a case against grades, clearly states that educators must continue to collect information about how students are doing so they can communicate that information with students (28). However, in recognizing this need, Kohn also argues that *"Collecting information doesn't require tests, and sharing that information doesn't require grades"* (28). Considering this in more depth, Kohn (2011) makes a compelling case for the ways in which the use of letters and numbers to report how students are doing tends to do the following: diminishing student interest in learning, particularly when they adopt a "grade" orientation over a "learning" one; creating a preference for the easiest possible task, meaning they only engage with content that is required for the accumulation of points and progress towards them; in addition to, reducing the quality of students' thinking, forcing them to focus on what is being graded as the primary motivation (29–30). For these reasons, Kohn (2011) states that "grading for learning" is like "bombing for peace," (31) particularly since research on grading has illustrated that grades impact motivation significantly and undermine achievement as they attempt to quantify learning (30).

Kohn calls for educators to have the courage to change the system, stating that first and foremost it is not "enough to replace letters or numbers with other labels (e.g., exceeds, meets expectations, and so on) as the end result is still focused on sorting students into reductionist categories (31). He also argues that it is not enough to give them more information of what is expected of them in advance, nor is it enough to share grades more efficiently with them or to just add narrative reports to the grading process. In advocating for replacing letter and number grades with narrative assessment and teacher conferences with students, Kohn illustrates the ways in which schools have successfully abandoned grading through these practices.

Additionally, Kohn (1999) suggests that grades distort the curriculum, waste a lot of time that could be spent on learning, encourage cheating, spoil teacher-student relationships as well as student to student relationships, among other disturbing consequences. While Kohn clearly recognizes that the difficulties with abolishing traditional grading systems are quite real, he queries "the key question is whether those difficulties are seen as problems to be solved or excuses for perpetuating the status quo." Because grades operate as instruments of control in Kohn's view, he encourages educators to "reflect on whether mindless compliance is really our goal." Kohn, in countering claims that grades assist educators in getting students to show up to class, hand in work, and do what they are told, argues that to maintain the notion that without grade bribes (As) and threats (Fs), students would not participate in the learning process, placing issues on the learners, instead of examining the problems with grading systems or one's own teaching practices. Kohn invites educators to abolish grades, starting with eliminating curve grading and practices designed to sort students to begin to disrupt the "demonstrated harm of traditional grading on the quality of students' learning and their interest in exploring ideas" as one means to challenge "these archaic remnants of a factory-oriented approach to instruction." He ultimately contends that "grades are not a necessary part of schooling" and that educators must move away from the "desire to assess more often, or to produce more data, or to improve the consistency of our grading" (32) and instead ask "not how to improve grades, but how to jettison them once and for all" (33).

Kohn's call to abolish grades, along with other educators who advocate for going "gradeless," "ungrading," or "no-grading" such as Hunt (2008), Bower (2010c), Sackstein (2014), and Blum (2017), among a whole host of other teachers, illustrates an educational movement to resist traditional grading systems. For instance, the Facebook group, "Teachers Throwing Out Grades," has over 10,000 members. Within this discussion group, educators share ideas and resources for going gradeless. Moreover, the educational network, "Teachers Going Gradeless," features a wealth of information regarding the "gradeless movement." On top of these networks, "The Human Restoration Project," an advocate for progressive education, offers a wide range of support for educators who wish to embrace "gradeless" teaching and learning practices, including help sheets and guides for best practices in this realm. Numerous educators, too, have created their own guides to share their experiences with others, as well as blogs that detail instructor approaches. Interestingly, recently even *Teen Vogue* featured an article titled, "Why are Grades Important? Some Teachers Say They Do More Harm Than Good," by Zach Schermele, a first year student at Columbia University. Beyond these examples, the hashtags #nogrades, #ungrading, and #gradeless are gaining cultural currency as this movement gains additional momentum.

Blum, in discussing her own teaching journey to going "gradeless," states that she came to the conclusion that grades are "meaningless" and even "harmful," creating a barrier between professor and student *and* between students and their learning (cited in Supiano 2019). Blum began "ungrading," which she describes as a practice designed to redirect time and energy away from grading towards a process, allowing students to determine their own grades (though she has the right to change them, in conversation with them), requiring self-assessments for all projects. In Blum's case, she no longer even mentions grades on her syllabus, a practice that many instructors would not be able to emulate, unfortunately. Per her view, she argues that if the purpose of grades is to convey information about students' "accomplishment, adequacy, excellence, compliance, effort or gain in learning—they fail to do so" (Blum 2017). Because of this, Blum attempts to help students reframe their experience away from a "what did you get" perspective to one that embraces a "what did you learn" orientation. She offers the following scenario, which serves as an excellent example, in my view of why Blum does not grade anymore:

> Is a student who enters already knowing a lot and continues to demonstrate knowledge at a high level, but then misses an assignment because of a roommate's attempted suicide and ends up with a B-plus, the same as someone who begins knowing nothing, works really hard, follows all the rules, does quite well and ends up with a B-plus? What information is conveyed? What about someone who loves biology and excels in those classes, but who loathes history, bombs in history classes and ends up with a 3.0 GPA, compared to someone who muddles through every class with a similar GPA, yet with no passion, excellence or highs or lows? What do we learn from the GPA? What does a course grade mean? (2017)

Building on this example, Blum (2017) states that going "gradeless" can be done with any course size and that it provides opportunities for students to build intrinsic motivation (learning for learning's sake) versus extrinsic motivation (for external benefit) while placing self-evaluation at the heart of her going "gradeless" endeavor. Bower (2010a, 2010b), who describes assessment as a conversation, not a spreadsheet on his blog, describes his own experiences with "ungrading," comparing students' relationship with grades as akin to a kind of addiction, suggesting they often have to go through "grade detox" and "withdrawal" to be able to embark upon a "gradeless" learning experience.

In the "Grading/Assessment Guide," created by the Human Restoration Project, it discusses the role rubrics play within grading systems, particularly serving as an "pinnacle of assessment" that instructors continue to attempt to build new, improved, and more streamlined versions (3). For them, rubrics offer an excellent example of the subjectivity of grading, especially since it is most likely that varying instructors would understand and score the same rubric in quite different ways, depending on their experiences, interests, and

Introduction 21

unique interpretations. Because of this, they query, "What if the entire system was flawed from the beginning" In addition to asking, "Why not throw out the entire system?" They argue that giving feedback is the most important mechanism teachers can employ to communicate with students about their learning. Citing a study by Ruth Butler in 1987, the guide argues that Butler's work makes a strong case that students learn the most when offered feedback without a grade, as opposed to a grade and feedback, or just a grade (3). As part of the Human Restoration Project's approach to "ungrading,' they advocate for students to track their own learning progress, engaging in assessing themselves as a first step towards enacting *(un)grading justice.* Justice, in these examples of educators employing "ungrading," is designed around undoing the unjust practices reinforced by traditional grading and assessment systems.

(CRITICAL) COMMUNICATION (PEDAGOGY) AND GRADING JUSTICE

Kohn (1999) contends one can tell a lot about a teacher's values just by asking them how they feel about giving grades, some defending the practice as necessary, others enjoying grading, and many despising the process of giving grades altogether. To this end, there are no shortages of humorous grade-focused memes. Some of my favorites include: "Students may come and go but grading is forever"; "A day may come when I finish grading papers but it is not this day"; "If you didn't get the grade you wanted, it is highly possible I didn't get the work I wanted"; "When I am grading papers and I write more than they did"; "Oh, so your teacher gave you a bad grade? Tell me about how it is their fault"; "I enjoy grading essays said no teacher ever"; and "So you are saying I should have cared about my grade all semester?"

Memes aside, Walvoord and Anderson (1998), in describing grading as the *process* by which teachers assess learning, the *context* in which teacher establish this process, and the *dialogue* that surrounds what grades mean for various audiences, suggests four primary roles of grading serves, including: *evaluating* student work, *communicating* with the students and others such as administrators and/or employers, *motivating* how students study and involve themselves with the course, as well as *organizing* and marking transitions, bringing closure, and focusing efforts (2). As a result, they suggest that due to these many processes in play, grades operate as "isolated artifacts," which are "neither useful nor appropriate for institutional assessment needs" (2). They further argue that for grading to be valuable, teachers must abandon three false hopes: first, that grading is objective; second, that grading involves total agreement, and third, the hope for a "one-dimensional student motivation for learning."

Because grading is a powerful tool that communicates a range of meanings, they urge educators to recognize that grading is a "socially constructed and context dependent process." As a result, no grading system is more "right" than others and further, the role of grades changes over time, depending on the historical moment, educational context, and in relation to the people doing the grading. Based on this, Walvoord and Anderson suggest that educators make sure that their policies reflect their values and beliefs about learning, creating assignments that reflect these (and those worth grading), while also recognizing the value in separating feedback from grading, in addition to helping students truly understand what each grade represents and means.

If we, as educators, truly wish to help our students become active, informed citizens, we, too, must be active and informed about the consequences of our grading systems and practices. As Ward (2009) argues, the power to evaluate, judge, and grade needs to be balanced with modes of action, which resist the colonization of ideas the educational system imposes via these dominant grading discourses. As he further contends, grading and assessment systems that strive for standardization, ignoring cultural differences, "turn out to be a significant contributor to the process of social, cultural and economic reproduction and a major hindrance to social transformation."

Ward suggests that the main goal of this type of evaluation is to establish a cultural norm (e.g., as evidenced by curve grading). Not only does this maintain and reproduce a "Eurocentric" approach to evaluation, which prioritizes teacher authority, a judgmental learning environment, individualized, competitive learning, extrinsic rewards and punishments, external evaluation, culturally neutral content, large class sizes, bored students, abstract and/or partial projects, plagiarism, and school-centered curriculums. Ward advocates for educators to instead engage in a culture of resistance which embraces the opposite: teacher/student authority partnerships, non-judgmental learning environments, collectivized, cooperative approaches to learning, shared evaluation, real-world projects, learning by doing, shared pedagogy, culturally meaningful content, small classes, and excited students.

Some of the difficulties with enacting the approach Ward advocates includes traditional educational taboos against consensus authority versus teacher authority; group work rather than individual work; consensus grading rather than top-down, imposed teacher grading; real world projects versus abstract exercises; and culturally meaningful content as opposed to the pursuit of "objective" or neutral content. In arguing for consensus grading, Ward ultimately argues that "The ability to assess one's own perceptions and performances against the background of an agreed and collective norm is a fundamental aspect of the learning experience, as also is the ability to witness how one is perceived by a community of individuals with whom one works" (For a more detailed discussion of educators embracing consensus models, often based in contract grading approaches, see Blinne, this volume).

I believe it is time for communication teachers, particularly those invested in critical communication, communication activism, and social justice pedagogies to commit to embodying grading justice within their teaching practices, if they are not doing so already. The time for a grading justice revolution is now. To this end, the communication discipline is perfectly situated to address this call as first and foremost grading, as already discussed, is a powerful form of communication insomuch that it constitutes student identities as well as teacher identities (based on how and why they grade as they do), while also serving as a primary practice associated with teaching and learning. To better understand the possibilities of enacting grading justice, teachers and students (along with administrators) must begin to address the educational inequalities, produced, reinforced, and maintained through various grading systems, engaging in collective inquiry to practice and promote social justice within both grading and assessment processes.

Social justice, per this process, involves employing communication resources (i.e., theories, methods, pedagogies, and other practices) in collaboration with individuals and groups whose lives are affected by prejudice, discrimination, oppression, domination, and other sociopolitical struggles to intervene into and reconstruct unjust discourses in more just ways (Frey and Blinne 2017). In doing so, grading justice approaches should be designed to raise questions about educational and structural inequalities (through a variety of standpoints), fostering transdisciplinary dialogues aimed at imagining and creating learning opportunities that strive for equity, engagement, and transformation, while also working to create a more just world both within the classroom but also outside the walls of the academy.

Applying this to the educational contexts in which we operate, I turn to Frey and Palmer (2014), who in discussing communication activism pedagogy suggest that education "offers one of the best opportunities for challenging and changing unjust systemic structures and practices" (1). To situate education in this manner, however, requires that "people first become aware of the practices that create and sustain those problems, and collaborate together to intervene to make those structures and practices more just" (1). Thus, communication activism pedagogy works to help students studying communication "use their communication knowledge and capabilities to promote social justice, showing exemplars of how communication educators have accomplished that goal in practice" (2). Both critical communication pedagogy and communication activism pedagogy, in my view, engage in processes aimed at "educating for action" so that students can confront "painful injustices that might overwhelm some and be denied by others" (Del Gandio and Nocella 2014, xi).

As Fassett and Warren (2008) state, in reference to critical communication pedagogy (CCP), in its most fundamental form, this approach is a "dialogue or engagement among constituencies," in addition to being "dialogue that builds spaces for transforming the world as it is in favor of a collaborative vision of what could be" (6). Guided by a series of commitments, critical communication pedagogues understand that identity is constituted in communication (as are our social realities); that power is fluid, complex, and dynamic, involving a process with which we engage and one that engages us; that culture is a central component of teaching and learning, including the micro and macro communication practices that shape how we each "do" culture; that the study of language, including how language constitutes self, other, and culture are vital aspects of understanding communication practices, including how power and oppression operate within them; that reflexivity is an important component of inquiry, as is the interplay between research and pedagogy, centering praxis as central to disrupting dominant norms; that our communicative choices are nuanced, complex, and limited by our unique positionalities and group memberships; and that dialogue is needed to re-enforce our shared humanity across our differences. These commitments combined offer communication teachers a variety of means for confronting injustices broadly, while at the same time striving towards a more just and humane world.

To this end, as previously introduced, the purpose of this collection is to invite readers to consider not only how educators might assess social justice work in and beyond the classroom, but also to imagine what a social justice approach to grading would mean for intervening into potentially unjust modes of teaching and learning by creating more just practices and policies. Each of the contributions offers a different view into the concept of grading justice, offering unique insights regarding philosophies and practices with this aim. This project started with an open call on the CRTNET (Communication Research and Theory Network) listserv and at the National Communication Association annual convention in Salt Lake City, Utah, seeking contributions from communication teacher-activists regarding the ways in which they make sense of the relationship within grading, assessment, and social justice. Like any collection, this one, too, is only a small window into a much larger and necessary conversation within the discipline. In reflecting on the collection overall, I note that topics as large as grading and assessment, particularly practices aimed at grading justice, need far more voices than are currently present within this volume. As a result, it is imperative these conversations continue to happen far beyond the boundaries of these pages with a much wider network of teacher-activists. It is my greatest hope that this collection can inspire robust conversations among communication scholars regarding the possibilities of infusing social justice into grading and assessment practices, while also disrupting traditional or norm-referenced grading in communication courses and beyond.

It is worth repeating that the time for a grading justice revolution is now. We are at a pivotal moment socially with ever mounting injustices permeating people's everyday lives. Institutions of higher education are under assault both from internal and external sources, rendering educational systems ever more precarious for all those employed by them. The communication discipline, too, is undergoing important shifts, as evidenced by the National Communication Association's (NCA) recent "Distinguished Scholar" controversy, which has resulted in a wide range of discussions regarding merit, diversity, inclusion, bias, and a whole host of other conversations and fierce debates. For more information on this controversy, see the Departures in Critical Qualitative Research special issue on "Merit, Whiteness, and Privilege" (see Rodriguez, Dutta, & Desnoyers-Colas 2019). Within this special issue, not only do the essays evaluate the concept of merit, but also critique and interrogate disciplinary structures that circulate these notions; thus, is argued, "the critical interrogation of whiteness and articulations of merit offer a basis for articulation of strategies of resistance and transformation" (Rodriguez, Dutta, & Desnoyers-Colas 2019, 7).

As part of this "critical moment," the Communication Scholars for Transformation Facebook page emerged, now with over 3,000 members, creating a space for communication scholars and practitioners to engage in the following goals articulated by the group: Develop and implement diversity and inclusion strategies in the communication field writ large; Initiate collaborative initiatives on diversity and inclusion outside the field's professional organizations; and provide support for colleagues on the margins. NCA, as an organization, continues to be critiqued and challenged for its White-centered infrastructure, which perpetuates and maintains structural and institutional racism, impacting the "perceived" merit, publication, and promotion of scholars of color within the field (Smith, 2019). The hashtags #NCASoWhite, #CommSoWhite, and #CommunicationSoWhite illustrate the ongoing disgust with and distrust of the direction both the organization and the discipline as a whole are heading. As part of this disciplinary conversation, the NCA Activism and Social Justice Division officers (of which I was one at the time along with Patricia Parker, Jason DelGandio, David Palmer, and Jennifer Guthrie) issued the following statement—one of many statements drafted by NCA Divisions, Caucuses, or related organizations:

> The Activism and Social Justice Division is dedicated to supporting and collaborating with community members whose lives are affected by oppression, domination, discrimination, and other sociopolitical struggles due to differences

in race, gender, class, sexual orientation, age, ability, religion, and other identity markers. Within our professional work and everyday lives, we seek to intervene into and reconstruct unjust discourses in more just ways. As such, ASJD's elected officers unapologetically condemn the exclusionary nature of the Distinguished Scholars award and the statements supporting its exclusionary history. Thus, not only do we seek to disrupt and dismantle the colonization of the communication discipline, but also we aim to actively fight against racist, cis-heterosexist, classist, transphobic, ageist, ableist, and other "power-over" systems that enable, produce, and sustain "imperialist, white-supremacist, capitalist, patriarchy" both within and outside of NCA.

It is obvious that the current situation has created—or perhaps more accurately, revealed—a fissure within the NCA community. The contention is unfortunate but not unproductive. Positive, constructive change often emerges from genuine, arduous, and painful conflict. If approached wisely and equitably, such conflict can produce auspicious opportunities replete with transformative potential. It is our hope that the current controversy leads to a more conscionable and socially just NCA that willfully and proudly moves beyond rather than reinforces various inequities and stratifications. With this in mind, ASJD's elected officials unequivocally applaud, support, and act with any and all NCA members who are taking efforts to create a more inclusive, just, and righteous National Communication Association in all forms and at all levels—be it the Distinguished Scholars award or otherwise. (Statement from the NCA Activism and Social Justice Division Leadership, June 19, 2019.)

I share this example because this conversation has implications for our understanding of grading justice for a variety of reasons. First, I turn to Smith (2019), who in discussing communication pedagogy as a microcosm of communication studies, reflects on the consequences of continuing to place Whiteness at the center of communication pedagogy, which reinforces the inequities many people face within the discipline. As Smith contends, "Communication faculty must be willing to discuss and deal with the conflicts of racial and cultural differences in their classes to promote cultural dexterity"; he continues to state, "Communication studies should be a discipline in which all languages, literacies, histories, and cultural ways are affirmed" (39). Just as the "Distinguished Scholar" Award functions to sort scholars into a category of distinction, aimed at "celebrating" their contribution to the discipline, it also clearly serves a normalizing and hierarchal function, insomuch as it illustrates what types of work are valued most as well as who gets valued in the process.

Similarly, within our classrooms, grades serve a related function, awarding some as meriting the highest marks, while also denying others access to particular categories of merit. As Feldman (2015) states,

Inequity is woven into our current grading practices in an even more obvious way: categories included in grades such as "effort," "growth," and "participation" are based entirely on a teacher's subjective judgments. We know that teachers interpret student behaviors differently based on the student's race, gender or socioeconomic status.

As critical communication pedagogues, we know that prejudice, discrimination, and oppression are all too common within educational systems (and beyond), as evidenced by employee hiring practices and student admissions; the recruitment and retention of students and employees; the daily microaggressions experienced by students and employees; as well as the biases built into educational practices such as norm-referenced grading or high stakes testing, which has clearly shown to be a poor indicator of future success. Within this landscape, the quest for "data," reducing individuals to small quantifiable units, particularly through traditional modes of grading (especially curve grading), utilizing evaluations of teaching and grade distribution data as indicators of teaching effectiveness, or situating employees as "diversity hires" aimed at box checking, only serves to further educational injustices and inequities.

Smith (2019), in discussing the way standardized grading and assessment systems produce, uphold, and reinforce White supremacy and privilege states, "White supremacy is a product or effect of systems and structures, our SOPs (standard operating procedures), despite anyone's intentions, that produce political, cultural, linguistic, and economic dominance for White people" (8). For Inoue, "grading is almost always employed in order to control students (and sometimes their teachers), force students to be accountable (and sometimes their teachers), and measure or rank students (and sometimes their teachers), either against each other or against a single standard" (5). Inoue invites educators to confront and undo institutional racism by discontinuing assessment practices that embody a "White standard" to grade students. Employing a singular or dominant standard to judge students, in Inoue's view, simply maintains dominant racist and White supremacist ideologies when utilized uniformly within one's teaching (3). As Inoue comments, White standards are so structurally ingrained that they seem natural and are thus normalized, so much so that "many of us cannot see it as such in our classrooms, our disciplines, in our ways of reading and valuing students" (8).

Without a doubt, many people perceive higher education as playing an important role in social mobility, insomuch that generally speaking, higher occupational earnings are often associated with higher levels of education. Additionally, many argue that obtaining a college degree is vital to improving one's occupational opportunities, as well as one's quality of life. Even so, studies also show a range of disparities in undergraduate grade point averages, a measure often linked to "academic success," especially for first-generation students as well as among students of color. Data from the US Department of Education (2012) highlights that 75 percent of White students receiving a bachelor's degree have a grade point average of 3.0 or higher, whereas only 55 percent of students of color have a similar GPA range. Moreover, the data illustrates that White students are twice as likely to graduate with GPAs higher than 3.5. The report also suggests that students of color were three times more likely to graduate with a GPA of less than 2.5. The data also suggests that fewer than one in five students of color have achieved a GPA greater than 3.5.

When other intersectional identity factors are taken into account, studies also indicate that GPAs vary significantly among first generation students and those that are not, particularly when gender, race, and ethnicity are analyzed as variables. For instance, based on their research, Holmes and Slate (2017) contend that college students whose parents have higher levels of education are more likely to have higher GPAs than first generation students. Further, they suggest that students with the highest income levels are more likely than those at the lowest income levels to have GPAs of at least 3.0.

Stuber (2011), in considering first generation students, estimates that of the 34 percent of first generation students enrolled in colleges and universities, 73 percent do not return to school for their second year. Atherton (2014), in studying the academic preparedness of first generation students, has found that non-first generation students whose parents both attended colleges have standardized test scores that are 48 percent higher than first-generation college students. Defritas and Rinn (2013) have explored the relationship between self-concept and GPAs among ethnically diverse students at a four-year undergraduate institution, determining that students with lower self-concepts also often had lower GPAs. With this in mind, Massey and Fischer (2005) have found that college climate is related to academic performance, reporting that students, who experience racial stereotyping, often earn lower grades than students who do not experience similar stereotyping.

Research also suggests that both racial and gender-based achievement gaps begin at a young age and widen as students move through various educational systems (Fryer and Levitt 2004; Perna and Swail 2002; Schieder, et al. 2006; Kao and Thompson 2003). As such, achievement differentials based on multiple datasets show cumulative grade point averages of White and Asian students to be a full point higher than the average for Black and Latinx students (Lewis and Diamond, 2015). Returning to first generation students, Holmes and Slate (2017) state, "Disparities in GPA may contribute to perpetuating inequity for low-income and first generation students."

As Rodriguez (2014) aptly states, "Numbers are the foundation of quantitative research, which guides most of the research in communication studies." He continues, "The primary assumption in quantitative research is that human behavior is quantifiable, measurable, and observable" (105). Because

Introduction 29

quantitative research values objectivity, while also distancing itself from differences that might impact variables, Rodriguez contends (and I agree) that this "diminishes human diversity" while also perpetuating dominant definitions of communication that also downplay the complexity of both communication and humanity (116–119). Within the realm of grading and assessment, traditional grading and assessment systems embrace quantitative measures, applying labels and categories on learning, in an attempt to sort learners into limiting boxes. As Rodriguez also argues, not only do these "boxes diminish our complexity, diversity, mystery, and ultimately our humanity by reducing us to units," but also they promote stereotyping, conformity by attaching certain expectations to different boxes (e.g., they are a "C student"), and alienation in the ways that these boxes keep us bound to the expectations associated with them (122–124). As a result, per his view, communication studies

> reflects a lack of epistemological imagination—lacking the ability to reimagine what communication can be. Nothing is inherently wrong with using a certain epistemology, or a certain set of theories and methodologies, to understand communication. The problem is when a certain epistemology is so dominant that it displaces other epistemologies, blocks the rise of new epistemologies, and is even openly hostile to different epistemologies. The problem is particularly debilitating when this dominant epistemology forwards a narrow view of communication that impoverishes our sense of wonder and imagination (229).

Building on these ideas, this edited collection also aims to embrace Rodriguez's call for both epistemological generosity, a way of understanding the world by considering a range of different worldviews by removing the hegemony of our theories, pedagogies, and methodologies, and epistemological imagination within the communication discipline (229). While there are many paths one could take to embark on this journey, within the contributions contained herein, the authors attempt to regain a sense of imagination towards the construction of grading justice. In doing so, we invite readers to join us in this process, sharing ideas and resources to support not only this *Grading Justice Project*, but also to help us create a grading justice revolution within the discipline and beyond.

OVERVIEW OF THE BOOK

In chapter 1, "The Rhetoric of Grades: Evaluating Student Work and its Consequences," David Deifell, PhD, examines the entrenched structure of grading as a condition instructors often take for granted as a "natural" part of teaching and educating. In his words, "to use more 'scientistic' terminology, as Kenneth Burke might call it, grades represent measurements of students' academic learning. Such a framing, though, belies the rhetoric of those representations as having public consequences." Within this chapter, Deifell further queries: "What do grades communicate and to what audiences? What is the symbolic influence of grading, privately and publicly?" In doing so, he argues that a rhetorical tension lies between a private, interpersonal teacher-student exchange about individual learning and the public, ideological expectations and consequences of teachers' value judgments reduced to a letter and its corresponding number. As part of this argument, Deifell invites teacher-activists to reflexivity struggle with the rhetorical consequences of grades and grading as an opportunity to interrogate the grade system and their position and participation within these systems.

Moving into chapter 2, "Mobilizing a Critical Universal Design for Learning Framework for Justice Minded Course Design and Assessment," Allison D. Brenneise, PhD, and Mark Congdon, Jr., PhD, offer educators/scholars strategies to consider when thinking about becoming more socially just in their assessment of students in higher education. They contend that combining universal design for learning (UDL) and critical communication pedagogy (CCP) allows for the needs of more students to be met, further arguing that engaging all of our students in our classrooms changes us as educators and makes our pedagogies more socially just. As pedagogues concerned with how students learn and progress in life, they combine specialized disability knowledge with CCP and UDL to course design and assessment/grading to improve student learning in two ways. First, they see students' differences as strengths and move toward a strengths-based assessment approach. Second, they suggest that students leave their classrooms knowing what they need to be successful in future learning and have a concrete experience from which to talk and advocate.

In chapter 3, "Honoring Viviencias: A Borderlands Approach to Higher Education Pedagogy Justice," Leandra H. Hernández, PhD, and Sarah De Los Santos Upton, PhD, describe their experiences as Chicana feminist profesoras at a borderlands Hispanic Serving Institution and at an institution that primarily works with military student populations. In doing so, they draw from the conocimiento of their borderland subjectivities, seeking to challenge objectivist, Western systems of knowledge in favor of border/transformative pedagogies (Elenes 2010), theorizing a nepantla approach to assessment. In their words, "Nepantla is a liminal, in-between space offered by Gloria Anzaldúa (1987) where fronterizas draw from the physical, psychological, and spiritual borderlands to contest, challenge, and construct identities in ways that privilege transformation." As part of this discussion, Hernández and De Los Santos Upton describe developing their syllabi, class discussions

Introduction

and activities, and grading rubrics in ways that further facilitate this process of transformation. They contend that by "utilizing this nepantla approach to assessment, we hope to reach our "non-traditional" student body populations in more effective ways that do justice to their lived experiences and equip them with tools to help them move through the world and through academia more effectively."

For chapter 4, "Walking the Tightrope: Navigating the Tensions of Teaching and Grading Communication Content Inside and Outside the Discipline," Juliane Mora, PhD, shares her experiences teaching communication content primarily to students outside of communication departments, most often in business and engineering. Mora describes the fragmentation and contradiction that can result from teaching in these contexts, asking: How can I be a social justice educator in both of these spaces and how can my approach to teaching and assessment reflect that mission? What does grading justice look like in these contexts? How might a teacher-activist in these contexts "level the playing field" or "balance the scales" particularly for underrepresented students in STEM fields? What strategies are there to employ when working with engineering faculty who may or may not feel competent evaluating communication activities, or be able to recognize implicit bias in their evaluation behaviors when it comes to traditionally marginalized students? How does this impact teaching the content when there is a feeling that it is being shoehorned into their "real" discipline? Within this chapter, Mora explores how communication material might be reframed as a practice of lifelong learning, grappling with the complexities of teaching communication within a range of educational environments.

In chapter 5, "Student-Activist Mentor Letters as a Form of Social Movement-Building in Communication Activism Pedagogy," David L. Palmer, PhD, examines assessment tactics he employs in his activism course, including a student-activist mentor letter to future course students, outlining his approach to managing and assessing those assignments in relation to the course design and student activity. As he contends, "where orthodox assessment models frame students as competitive, self-interested, and apolitical market personnel, activism assessment connects students as stakeholders in social movements who are cooperative, justice-oriented and socio-politically change-driven." For Palmer, assessment serves both evaluative and movement-building functions as it invites students to mentor and support each other's activist work. As he states, "unlike orthodox assessment models, which evaluate rote, static information and produce isolated, perishable outcomes, activism education assessment promotes vibrant civic action and support and produces lasting outcomes as it bonds socio-political change agents in their collective efforts to forge a more just world."

In chapter 6, "Love Letters Gone Wrong: Complicating the Romantic Ideal of Democratic Processes in the College Classroom," Londie T. Martin, PhD, and Kristen A. McIntyre, PhD, present a co-teaching experience in an honors-level Written and Oral Communication course, sharing their processes of working together to move toward a more democratic classroom, which includes a scaffolded curriculum to engage students deeply in the processes of reflection and revision of their own and each other's work, situating these experiences within a larger and ongoing class conversation about the problematic role of grading in liberatory learning environments (Strommel 2017) and the constraints of prescriptive rubrics for assessment (Kohn 2006). They then explore the complications that can arise when these democratic processes are romanticized, finding that the more just their attempted practices, the greater the toll it took on them as invested practitioners, arguing that sometimes classrooms which have focused significantly on recognizing and negotiating power dynamics through just teaching practices can result in not only greater pedagogical labor, but also greater affective labor as well.

In chapter 7, "Are We *Just* Grading or Grading *Justly?*: Adventures with Non-Traditional Assessment," I, Kristen C. Blinne, offer five different social justice-inspired approaches to grading and assessment, which I have developed and utilized in my communication courses over the last decade, in an attempt to embody the spirit of grading justice as outlined in this edited collection. Throughout this chapter, I hope to model the process-based pedagogy I enact in both my teaching and learning practices. By doing so, I invite readers into my experience, experimenting with various grading systems, illustrating a range of assessment methods designed to reframe student success—not against student failure as articulated in traditional modes of grading and assessment—but instead as practices aimed at grading justice. As part of this discussion, I provide some background regarding my teaching-learning journey to set the stage for what follows. Next, I explore conversations surrounding alternative or "non-traditional" approaches to grading and assessment. Finally, I round out this chapter with a detailed discussion of a range of grading and assessment methods I have experimented with in my communication courses, offering resources for further reflection and implementation.

In chapter 8, "'Ungrading' Communication: Awareness Pedagogy as Activist Assessment," I, Kristen C. Blinne, build on my experimentation with grading and assessment discussed in chapter 7, "Am I *Just* Grading or Grading *Justly?*: Adventures with Non-Traditional Assessment." In doing so, I introduce *awareness pedagogy* as an approach that aims to cultivate grading justice through its associated philosophies and processes, having the capacity to serve as a kind of activist assessment, which could be utilized and adapted

Introduction 33

both within communication and broader interdisciplinary courses. Moving through this chapter, I situate awareness broadly before delving into its more specific application as related to awareness pedagogy and grading justice. Thereafter, I offer a sample course map to illustrate these ideas in-action, rounding out this conversation with some concluding reflections on how one might embody and enact these principles within their own teaching and learning journeys.

For chapter 9, "Resisting the Detrimental Effects of Grade Inflation on University Faculty and Students through Critical Communication Pedagogy," David H. Kahl, Jr., PhD, examines issues surrounding grade inflation through the lens of critical communication pedagogy (CCP), offering ways in which faculty can resist the neoliberal pressure to engage in grade inflation by teaching students about the neoliberal system which has inculcated them to believe that profit, success, and individualism are the only measures of a meaningful life. Kahl discusses how instructors can challenge students to resist neoliberal hegemony, holding high academic standards for themselves, and tying learning to outcomes that affect their futures—power and their response to it. Kahl also contends that in order for tenure-track and contingent faculty to be able to resist the pressure to inflate grades, they must work to teach students to resist neoliberal ideology that instills the thought processes that lead to grade inflation. In so doing, students may begin to learn to engage in resistance behaviors to neoliberal power structures that marginalize them.

In chapter 10, "Rate My Performance, or Just Sing Along: A Critical Look at Student Evaluations of Teaching," Summer R. Cunningham, PhD, focuses on the way that student evaluations of classroom teaching—essentially student grading and assessment of faculty—can further marginalize faculty as well as the student-teacher relationship. More specifically, Cunningham explores the following aspects and implications of student evaluations of teaching: impacts on the quality of student-teacher relationships and student learning; the constraints, binds, and limits these processes create for non-tenured faculty (e.g., tenure-track or contract faculty); the virtues and downfalls of anonymity in the evaluation process (particularly when student feedback is derogatory, racist, sexist, or otherwise harmful to instructors); the ways in which student and teacher evaluations might work in tandem to reinforce a system that devalues learning, thinking, and connecting in favor of productivity and compliance; the possibility for creating more just processes for student assessment of teaching; and, finally, the creative ways we might invite students, faculty, and administration into critical and reflexive conversations about these processes.

For chapter 11, "The Seven Lesson Faculty Member: Outlining Assessment's Harm to Faculty," C. Kyle Rudick, PhD, describes the effect assessment has on faculty, addressing the kind of instructor one becomes through the process of assessment. As part of this analysis, Rudick is interested in understanding how assessment as a practice is performed and perfected within an institutional culture, and how the normalization of this ritual constitutes a form of organizational socialization. Rudick claims that there is "no practice of assessment—no buzzword, philosophy, or ethic—that can undo the violence inherent in its practice." Within this conversation, Rudick interrogates the notion that assessment is an important educational tool, offering seven lessons to disrupt assessment's hold on faculty, further inviting educators to reflect on the following questions: For whom is assessment important? Legislators? Administrators? Students?

Before moving into each of the contributor's views on grading justice as applied to grading and assessment within communication and beyond, I invite you engage in another brief visualization.

***

Imagine:

It is 10:00 a.m. and you have just arrived in an office suite during final exam week. As you stand in the main office, you see a corridor with numerous office doors all open, professors in each, busily grading exams, student papers, meeting with groups, and reviewing visual work and presentations. Reflecting on their approaches to grading, you realize that each professor appears to represent a different kind of grader. For fun, you imagine each as grading superhero or villain, depending on their approach. Of course, you also recognize that the lines between good and evil and right and wrong can easily become blurred in the realm of teaching so you do not intend to cast judgment towards any of their approaches.

Behind door number one, you encounter the *pretender*: this professor is one that goes through the grading and assessment motions, only out of obligation as a requirement of the job. In fact, the *pretender* despises grading through and through, avoiding it for as long as possible, doing whatever it takes to streamline the process, most often using scantron exams to do the least amount of grading they can possibly do. You pass by their door, noticing they are reading an article on their computer with a stack of scantron sheets nearby—likely needing to be entered into the grade book. In the office next door to the *pretender,* you encounter the *defender,* a similar but different kind of grader. The *defender* staunchly believes that grades objectively capture and represent students' learning commitments and abilities, and the *defender* is unafraid to engage in heated debates about grade inflation, the loss of rigor, their love of the bell curve, or they may instead offer a longwinded treatise on how students are not given grades—no, they earn them. As you pass by

Introduction 35

the *defender's* office, you hear them engaged in exactly these conversations with a student.

Across the hall, you encounter what you like to call the *punisher.* In the realm of grading and assessment, the *punisher* delights in the grading process, keeping copious records of students' shortcomings, waiting for them to slip up so they can better balance their grade book. Like the *defender,* the *punisher* also believes students "earn" their grades and that the grades they earn properly punish them, or rather reflect the student's "true" effort. Walking by the *punisher's* office, you notice they are deeply engaged in reviewing scoring checklists focused on non-academic behaviors such as attendance, participation, and other conduct-related offenses. Interestingly, in the office directly next to the *punisher,* you find the *rewarder.* Unsurprisingly, the *punisher* and the *rewarder* can often be found engaging in philosophical conversations about grading and assessment; whereas the *punisher* sees grading practices as part of their sworn duty to serve as a rigid gatekeeper, much as the *defender* does, the *rewarder* sees their role as being more like a *protector* of academic integrity. Thus, the *rewarder* is less motivated by punitive measures or grade threats, but instead focuses on grading as a kind of survival game, such that whoever comes out on top is most worthy of their praise. The *rewarder* does not shy away from extra credit opportunities because they value the competition that can ensue from seeing who can arrive at the top point, percentage, or letter grade mountain first—a feat worth awarding indeed. As you peek into the *rewarder's* office, you notice them counting extra credit points with a smile.

Venturing further into the office suite corridor, you happen upon another door, finding the *restorer* hard at work grading papers. The *restorer* appears to be partially buried behind stacks of essays so high that you wonder how they will ever manage grading them all. On top of this, from the look of it, the *restorer* may have pulled an all-nighter, given their haggard appearance. The *restorer* takes the grading process very seriously, committing hours on end, offering constructive feedback for students in an attempt to restore their love of learning, while also trying to create some restorative justice opportunities in the realm of grading and assessment. Though they are not afraid of giving letter grades, using points and percentages, or utilizing more traditional modes of grading, they are also open to new approaches, which challenge dominant modes of assessment to restore their own faith in the process.

In the office across the hall from the *restorer,* you encounter the *negotiator.* Like the *restorer,* the *negotiator* is willing to embrace new grading and assessment approaches, employing both traditional and non-traditional grading systems; however, what is most important to them is involving students in the assessment process, typically through forms of peer feedback, self-evaluation, or by other means such as consensus models aimed at collaborative assessment. In their attempt to share grading and assessment power with students, the *negotiator* is willing to allow students to argue for different grades, engaging in negotiation processes aimed at involving students in evaluation. In like fashion, you find the *negotiator* involved in a lively conversation with a student, hearing them ask, "So, what you are telling me is you think you should receive an 'A' grade even though you missed how many classes?"

Though you consider pausing to listen to the conversation a bit more, you decide to proceed to the last offices in the suite. Of these, you notice one of the doors is open but the lights are dimmed. As you approach, you see that the *disrupter* is not there—a sign on the door says, "be right back" with a time stamp from an hour ago. Pausing, you laugh at this because you realize that it makes sense for them to be out of the office and not grading because their whole approach to grading and assessment is focused on abolishing the grade system altogether, actively attempting to challenge, disrupt, or undo traditional approaches to grading. Even though their job requires that they enter a letter grade for each student at the end of the term, they only do so with extreme disgust, giving the students every opportunity to grade themselves. Nearby the *disrupter* are three more offices: one is occupied by the *pleaser* and the other by the *creator.*

The *pleaser* loves helping students, so much so they often accept whatever excuse, reason, or story given as to why a student failed to turn something in, was not present in class, or why they missed the majority of the semester. The *pleaser* just wants everyone to be happy, so they give A grades like candy, offering extra credit, do-overs, and a sliding scale of empathy depending on what is needed. As you pass by the *pleaser's* office, you hear them counseling a student, who is pleading for a change of grade, which the *pleaser* is in the process of obliging.

The *creator,* conversely, has little time for such nonsense as, like the *pretender,* they see the entire grading endeavor as a complete waste of time. Thus, it is not uncommon for the *creator* to basically just pull grades out of thin air. Like a clever oracle, the *creator* has a keen sense of when projects "feel like a B+" versus an "A" grade, and their entire grading practice operates much like a game of chance or a psychic reading, depending on the day. Today, you find the *creator* randomly entering what looks like grades into a grade book with no supporting work anywhere in sight. Heading to the last office, you unlock the door, wondering which of these grading and assessment super heroes or villains you might be, or whether your approach represents another kind of character in this grading and assessment saga altogether. In the end, all you know is you believe in grading justice and you hope you enact it in your teaching and learning life.

REFERENCES

American Association of Colleges and Universities. 2010. "How Grade Point Average Correlates to Various Personal Characteristics." *Diversity and Democracy* 13 (3). Accessed January 10, 2020. https://www.aacu.org/publications-research/periodicals/how-grade-point-average-correlates-various-personal.

Anzaldúa, Gloria. 1987. *Borderlands/La Frontera: The New Mestiza.* (Vol. 3). San Francisco: Aunt Lute.

Atay, Ahmet, and Deanna L. Fassett, eds. 2019. *Meditated Critical Communication Pedagogy.* Lanham, MD: Lexington Books.

Atay, Ahmet, and Sandra L. Pensoneau-Conway, eds. 2019. *Queer Communication Pedagogy.* New York: Routledge.

Atay, Ahmet, and Satoshi Toyosaki, eds. 2017. *Critical Intercultural Pedagogy.* Lanham, MD: Lexington Books.

Atherton, Matthew C. 2014. "Academic Preparedness of First-Generation College Students: Different Perspectives." *Journal of College Student Development* 55 (8): 824–829. https://eric.ed.gov/?id=EJ1046416.

Bennett, Michael, and Jacqueline Brady. 2014. "A Radical Critique of the Learning Outcomes Assessment Movement." *Radical Teacher* 100 (Fall 2014): 146–152. https://doi.org/10.5195/rt.2014.171.

Blum, Susan D. 2017. "Ungrading." *Inside Higher Ed.* Accessed December 12, 2019. https://www.insidehighered.com/advice/2017/11/14/significant-learning-benefits -getting-rid-grades-essay.

Bower, Joe. 2010a. "Replacing Grading." Accessed December 15, 2019. http://www .joebower.org/2010/02/replacing-grading.html.

Bower, Joe. 2010b. "Detoxing Students from Grade-Use." Accessed December 15, 2019. http://www.joebower.org/2010/03/detoxing-students-from-grade-use.html.

Bower, Joe. 2010c. "The Day I Abolished Grading," Accessed December 20, 2019. https://joe-bower.blogspot.com/2010/08/day-i-abolished-grading.html.

Bower, Joe, and Paul L. Thomas, eds. 2013. *De-Testing + De-Grading Schools: Authentic Alternatives to Accountability and Standardization.* New York: Peter Lang.

Burke, Kenneth. 1966. "Terministic Screens." In *Language as Symbolic Action: Essays on Life, Literature, and Method*, edited by Kenneth Burke, 44–62. Berkeley: University of California Press. (Original work published August 1965).

Cherepinsky, Vera. 2011. "Self-Reflective Grading: Getting Students to Learn from their Mistakes." *Primus* 21 (3): 294–298; 301. https://doi.org/10.1080/10511970903147861.

Communication Scholars for Transformation. Facebook Group. Accessed December 15, 2019. https://www.facebook.com/groups/457629181722810/.

Cox, Keni B. 2011. "Putting Classroom Grading on the Table: A Reform in Progress." *American Secondary Education* 40 (1): 67–87. https://www.jstor.org/stable/23100415.

DeFreitas, Stacie C., and Anne Rinn. 2013. "Academic Achievement in First Generation College Students: The Role of Academic Self-Concept." *Journal of the Schol-*

arship of Teaching and Learning 13 (1): 57–67. https://files.eric.ed.gov/fulltext/EJ1011678.pdf.

Del Gandio, Jason and Anthony J. Nocella. 2014. *Educating for Action: Strategies to Ignite Social Justice.* Gabriola Island, BC, Canada: New Society Publishers.

Elenes, C. Alejandra. 2010. *Transforming Borders: Chicana/o Popular Culture and Pedagogy.* Lanham, MD: Lexington Books.

Fassett, Deanna L., and John T. Warren. 2007. *Critical Communication Pedagogy.* Thousand Oaks, CA: Sage.

Fassett, Deanna L., and John T. Warren. 2008. "Pedagogy of Relevance: A Critical Communication Pedagogy Agenda for the 'Basic' Course." *Basic Communication Course Annual* 20 (6): 1–34. https://ecommons.udayton.edu/bcca/vol20/iss1/6.

Feldman, Joe. C. 2018. *Grading for Equity: What It Is, Why It Matters, and How It can Transform Schools and Classrooms.* Thousand Oaks, CA: Sage.

Frey, Lawrence, and David Palmer, eds. 2014. *Teaching Communication Activism: Communication Education for Social Justice.* New York: Hampton Press.

Frey, Lawrence R., and Kristen C. Blinne. 2017. "Activism and Social Justice." In *Encyclopedia of Communication Research Methods,* edited by Mike Allen. Thousand Oaks, CA: Sage. https://dx.doi.org/10.4135/9781483381411.n6.

Fryer, Ronald G., and Steven D. Levitt. 2004. "Understanding the Black-White Test Score Gap in the First Two Years of School." *Review of Economics and Statistics* 86, 447–464. http://pricetheory.uchicago.edu/levitt/Papers/FryerLevittUnderstandingTheBlack2004.pdf.

Greenstein, Laura M. 2018. *Restorative Assessment: Strength-Based Practices that Support All Learners.* Thousand Oaks, CA: Corwin.

Guskey, Thomas R. 2004. "0 Alternatives." *Principal Leadership* 5 (2): 49–53. https://tguskey.com/wp-content/uploads/Grading-5-0-Alternatives.pdf.

Guskey, Thomas R. 2013. "The Case Against Percentage Grades." *Educational Leadership* 71 (1): 68–72. http://www.ascd.org/publications/educational-leadership/sept13/vol71/num01/The-Case-Against-Percentage-Grades.aspx.

Guskey, Thomas R. 2015. *On Your Mark: Challenging the Conventions of Grading and Reporting.* Bloomington, IN: Solution Tree Press.

Harrison, Tyler R. 2003. "Victims, Targets, Protectors, and Destroyers: Using Disputant Accounts to Develop a Grounded Taxonomy of Disputant Orientations." *Conflict Resolution Quarterly* 20, 307–329. https://doi.org/10.1002/crq.27.

Haugnes, Natasha, Holmgren, Hoag, and Martin Springborg. 2018. *Meaningful Grading: A Guide for Faculty in the Arts.* Morgantown, WV: West Virginia Press.

Holmes, Deshonda L., and John R. Slate. 2017. "Differences in GPA by Gender and Ethnicity/Race as a Function of First-Generation Status for Community College Students." *Global Journal of Human Social Science: Arts & Humanities—Psychology* 17 (3). https://static1.squarespace.com/static/5cdeb2955021740001d51782/t/5d822476d4a414168dcf1870/1568810103494/Differences+in+GPA+by+Gender.pdf.

Human Restoration Project. "Ungrading Resources." Accessed January 16, 2020. https://www.humanrestorationproject.org/ungrading-resources.

Human Restoration Project. "Grading/Assessment Guide." Accessed January 18, 2020. https://static1.squarespace.com/static/5ad8fe065b409b07609cb7ae/t/5cd87

5f0ae45060001e9cdaa/1557689842228/Grading+is+Not+Equal+to+Assessmentv
.pdf.

Hunt, Lester H., ed. 2008. *Grade Inflation: Academic Standards in Higher Education.*
New York: SUNY Press.

Inoue, Asao B. 2019. *Labor-Based Grading Contracts: Building Equity and Inclusion in the Compassionate Writing Classroom.* Fort Collins, CO: The WAC Clearing-house.

Kao, Grace, and Jennifer S. Thompson. 2003. "Racial and Ethnic Stratification in Ed-ucational Achievement and Attitudes." *Annual Review of Sociology* 29: 417–442. https://doi.org/10.1146/annurev.soc.29.010202.100019.

Kohn, Alfie. 2011. "The Case Against Grades: When Schools Cling to Letter and Number Ratings, Students Get Stuck in a System that Undermines Learning." *Educational Leadership* 69 (3): 28–33. https://www.alfiekohn.org/article/case -grades/.

Kohn, Alfie. 1999. "From Degrading to De-Grading." High School Magazine. https:// www.alfiekohn.org/article/degrading-de-grading/?print=pdf.

Kohn, Alfie. 2006. "The Trouble with Rubrics." *English Journal* 95 (4): 12–15. https://www.alfiekohn.org/teaching/rubrics.pdf.

Lewis, Amanda E., and John B. Diamond. 2015. *Despite the Best Intentions: How Racial Inequality Thrives in Good Schools.* Oxford: Oxford University Press.

Marchionda, Denise. 2010. "Point by Point: Adding up Motivation." Teaching Eng-lish in the Two-Year College 37 (4): 408–413. https://library.ncte.org/journals/ tetyc/issues/v37-4.

Massey, Douglas S., and Mary J. Fischer. 2005. "Stereotype Threat and Academic Performance: New Findings from a Racially Diverse Sample of College Fresh-men." *Du Bois Review: Social Science Research on Race* 2, 45–67. https://doi .org/10.1017/S1742058X05050058.

Muller, Jerry Z. 2018. *The Tyranny of Metrics.* Princeton, NJ: Princeton University Press.

Peha, Steve. 1995. "The 3ps Grading System: A Faster, Easier, Better Way to Grade." *Teaching That Makes Sense.* Accessed December 28, 2019. www.ttms.org.

Percell, Jay. 2019. "Democracy in Grading: Practicing What We Preach." *Critical Questions in Education* 10 (3): 180–190. https://academyedstudies.files.wordpress .com/2019/06/percellfinal.pdf.

Percell, Jay. 2017. "Lessons from Alternative Grading: Essential Qualities of Teacher Feedback." *The Clearing House: A Journal of Educational Strategies, Issues and Ideas* 0 (0): 1–5. https://doi.org/10.1080/00098655.2017.1304067.

Percell, Jay. 2014. "Essentially Point-Less: The Influence of Alternative, Non Points-Based Grading on Teachers' Instructional Practices" PhD diss., Illinois State Uni-versity, 2014. https://ir.library.illinoisstate.edu/etd/196/.

Percell, Jay. 2013. "The Value of a Pointless Education." *Educational Leadership* 71 (4): 1–5. http://www.ascd.org/publications/educational-leadership/dec13/vol71/ num04/The-Value-of-a-Pointless-Education.aspx.

Perna, Laura W., and W. Scott Swail. (2002). "Pre-College Outreach and Early Intervention Programs." In H. Donald (Ed.), *Condition of access: Higher educa-*

tion for lower income students (pp. 97–112). Westport, CT: American Council on Education/Praeger.

Reeves, Douglas B. 2004. "The Case Against the Zero." *Phi Delta Kappan* 86 (4): 324–325. https://www.ccresa.org/Files/Uploads/252/The_Case_Against_Zero.pdf.

Reeves, Douglas B. 2008. "Leading to Change / Effective Grading Practices." *Educational Leadership* 65 (5): 85–87. http://www.ascd.org/publications/educational-leadership/feb08/vol65/num05/Effective-Grading-Practices.aspx.

Rodriguez, Amardo. 2014. *Communication: Colonization and the Making of a Discipline.* Fayetteville, NY: Public Square Press.

Rodriguez, Amardo O., Dutta, Mohan J., and Elizabeth F. Desnoyers-Colas. 2019. "Introduction to the Special Issue on Merit, Whiteness, and Privilege." *Departures in Critical Qualitative Research* 8 (4): 3–9. http://dx.doi.org/10.1525/dcqr.2019.8.4.3.

Rudick, C. Kyle, Golsan, Kathyrn B., and Kyle Cheesewright, K. 2017. *Teaching From the Heart: Critical Communication Pedagogy in the Communication Classroom.* San Diego, CA: Cognella Academic Publishing.

Sackstein, Starr. 2015. *Hacking Assessment: 10 Ways to Go Gradeless in a Traditional Grades School.* Cleveland, OH: Times 10 Publications.

Schermele, Zach. 2020. "Why Are Grades Important? Some Teachers Say They Do More Harm Than Good." *Teen Vogue.* Assessed January 15, 2020. https://www.teenvogue.com/story/why-teachers-getting-rid-grades.

Schinske, Jeffrey, and Kimberly Tanner. 2014. "Teaching More by Grading Less (or Differently)." *Life Sciences Education* 13 (Summer 2014): 159–166. https://www.ncbi.nlm.nih.gov/pmc/articles/PMC4041495/.

Schneider, Jack, and Ethan Hutt, E. 2013. "Making the Grade: A History of the A–F Marking Scheme." *Journal of Curriculum Studies.* http://dx.doi.org/10.1080/00220272.2013.790480.

Smith, Lionnell. 2019. "Can We Share the Light? De-Centering Communication Whiteness with Communication Pedagogy." *Departures in Critical Qualitative Research* 8 (4): 35–40. http://dx.doi.org/10.1525/dcqr.2019.8.4.35.

Strommel, Jesse. 2017. "Why I Don't Grade." Accessed January 16, 2020. https://www.jessestommel.com/why-i-dont-grade/.

Stuber, Jenny Marie. 2011. "Integrated, Marginal, and Resilient: Race, Class, and the Diverse Experiences of White First-Generation College Students." *International Journal of Qualitative Studies in Education* 24 (1): 117–136. https://doi.org/10.1080/09518391003641916.

Supiano, Beckie. 2019. "Grades Can Hinder Learning. What Should Professors Use Instead?" *The Chronicle of Higher Education.* Accessed January 12, 2020. https://www.chronicle.com/interactives/20190719_ungrading.

Tagg, John. 2004. "Why Learn? What We May *Really* be Teaching Students." *About Campus* March/April, 2–10. https://eric.ed.gov/?id=EJ791236.

Teachers Going Gradeless. Accessed January 5, 2020. https://www.teachersgoinggradeless.com/.

Teacher Throwing Out Grades. Facebook Group. Accessed January 5, 2020. https://www.facebook.com/groups/teachersthrowingoutgrades/.

Tomar, Dave. n.d. "Eliminating the Grading System in College: The Pros and Cons." *The Quad.* Accessed January 9, 2020. https://thebestschools.org/magazine/eliminating-grading-system-college-pros-cons/.

US Department of Education. 2012. "Profile of 2007-2008 First-Time Bachelor's Degree Recipients." Accessed January 10, 2020. https://nces.ed.gov/pubs2013/2013150.pdf.

Walvoord, Barbara E., and Virginia Johnson Anderson. 1998. *Effective Grading: A Tool for Learning and Assessment.* San Francisco: Jossey-Bass.

Ward, Tony. 2009. "Evaluation and Grading: The Introduction of Intrinsic Reward Systems." Accessed January 9, 2020. https://www.academia.edu/6689478/Critical_Evaluation_and_Grading.

Chapter One

Rhetoric of Grades

Evaluating Student Work and Its Consequences

David Deifell

Grades in higher education have been a concern of activists for decades in the United States. In 1966, Carl Davidson called upon the Students for a Democratic Society to refocus its critique of the dehumanized and oppressive system of corporate liberalism by advocating for a student syndicalist movement to "adopt as its primary and central issue the abolition of the grade system." The idea of abolishing grades altogether may seem like extreme thinking by 1960s radicals until we consider Scott Jaschik's report in *Inside Higher Ed* about the annual meeting of the Association of American Colleges and Universities. According to Jaschik (2009), nearly all the participants attended the meeting with an interest "to move beyond grades" because "the system isn't working." In their more recent review of the history and research of grades and grading, Schinske and Tanner (2014) not only reveal the problematic history of the construction of the grade system but also demonstrate the troubling research on the ineffectiveness and harm that grades and grading have on education and learning.

Despite writing as a mid-1960s student radical, Davidson (1966) summed up many of the arguments at the heart of these twenty-first-century concerns:

> Grading is the common condition of the total student and faculty community. It is the direct cause of most student anxieties and frustrations. Also, it is the cause of the alienation of most faculty members from their work. Among our better educators and almost all faculty, there is a consensus that grades are, at best, meaningless, and more likely, harmful to real education.

If we, as teacher-activists, take Davidson's perspective seriously, then we face the real possibility that the only social justice approach to grading is not to grade.

In our age, however, instructors cannot avoid grading. In their seminal book on critical communication pedagogy (CCP), Fassett and Warren (2007) have little to say about how fellow teacher-activists should approach grades, grading, or the grade system.[1] The only approach they provide is one for a graduate-level communication pedagogy class, for which students designed a syllabus "agreeing students could create their own, individual assessment criteria," but one student still worried about the lack of a grade on his returned assignments (128). Fassett and Warren's response to his query was an explanation of their desire "to focus on his work and ideas in process, instead of an end product" (128). Regardless of this wish to sidestep it, the grade cannot be avoided. If we are to remain college instructors, we have little choice but to grade, as most of us are required to submit grades by the educational apparatuses that employ us. This requirement, though, does not relinquish teacher-activists from confronting questions about why we have a grade system and the potential of its inherently unjust consequences.

The entrenched structure of grading is a condition that we often take for granted as a natural part of teaching and educating. Grades represent individual instructors' evaluations of individual students' performances on specific assignments and for particular classes. To use more scientistic terminology, as Kenneth Burke (1966b) might call it, grades are measurements of students' academic learning. Such a framing, though, belies the rhetoric of those representations as having public consequences. What do grades communicate and to what audiences? What is the symbolic influence of grading for those audiences, personally and publicly? A rhetorical tension lies between a private, interpersonal teacher-student exchange about individual learning and the public, ideological expectations and consequences of teachers' value judgements reduced to a letter and/or its corresponding number. Though each have their own specific situations, teachers grade with rhetorical force and because of rhetorical force. By recognizing and wrestling with socially constructed symbolic pressures of grades, this chapter argues for treating grades and grading through a rhetorical lens. Moreover, I argue that reflexively struggling with the rhetorical consequences of grades and grading offers teacher-activists the opportunity to interrogate the grade system and their position and participation within it.

In the following pages, I describe the rhetoricity of grades; that is, the qualities with which grades operate rhetorically. I begin with some of the features that rhetoric and grades share, particularly that both are situated, subjective, and persuasive. After interrogating how and why those shared characteristics matter, I turn to an analysis of grades' rhetorical form, specifically that of value argumentation and its stock issues of value, criteria, and application. Finally, I conclude reflexively, as I struggle between my desire for grade system abolition and my obligation to assign grades.

SITUATED

In their expansive, well-cited survey study of employers, faculty, students, and parents, *Making Sense of College Grades*, Milton, Pollio, and Eison (1986) found it "encouraging that all four groups surveyed want the chief purposes of grades to be that of communicating to students [by teachers] and of serving the cause of teaching and learning" (225). This consensus puts grades in predominantly interpersonal terms and reveals a broad desire for grades to serve interests of a private educational sphere. In her Forward to the book, Laura Bornholdt (1986) strengthens the exclusivity of this attitude in her reading of the book:

> Grades are relative to contexts, never independent of them. To reify grades and assume a cross-situational stability is to abuse both the student and the evaluative meaning of the procedure. Grades ought to refer more to the educational process and less to evaluative use by society (x).

Bornholdt is right to remind us that grades are situated, like all rhetoric. The grades that we, as instructors, generate do come from specific circumstances between particular people. Such thinking individualizes and privatizes the grading that happens between teachers and their students. However, those limitations are enforceable by law after all (e.g., FERPA—Family Educational Rights and Privacy Act), so grade privacy is a public concern.

Limiting the situation of grading to such teacher-student relationships, perhaps accounting for institutional reporting to the Registrar, does not consider the layers of context that always already influence the cause and impact of grades. Plus, the desire to limit the purpose of grades to private situations is a myth. Students are not the only audiences of our grades, which students routinely share with their peers and others. FERPA allows different constituencies within the university to be privy to students' grades beyond the student receiving them and instructor submitting them, so as to further punish (e.g., probation), to offer additional help (e.g., support service staff), or to celebrate (e.g., graduation honors). Where I have worked, students are regularly asked to sign away their FERPA rights with a waiver so that the institution can share their grades with their parents. Other audiences include, but are not limited to, scholarship committees, admissions committees, employers, loan officers, legislatures and even insurance companies (e.g., "good student discounts" are

46 *David Deifell*

based on grades). Just as a speech may be situated for a particular audience but speak to historical publics, so too will a grade's rhetoricity transcend the interpersonal for evaluative use by wider audiences.

SUBJECTIVE

Limitations of context are not the only restraints placed upon conventional notions of grades and grading. In their 2002 study, Rosovsky and Hartley define what they believe to be the consensus view of grades within the academy:

> Grades are intended to be an objective—though not perfect—index of the degree of academic mastery of a subject. As such grades serve multiple purposes. They *inform* students about how well or how poorly they understand the content of their courses. They *inform* students of their strengths, weaknesses, and areas of talent. . . . They also *provide information* to external audiences [such as institutional colleagues, other institutions, and employers] (3, emphasis added).

While Rosovsky and Hartley (2002) recognize the larger set of contexts for which grades are used and useful, they characterize grades as mere information. For them, grades are an indexical sign. Their repetition of "inform" insists that we believe that grades empirically report an existing reality, oxymoronically suggesting that grades re-present the truth of a value. Grades do provide information for interpretation, but they also assert a judgement and evaluation. No grades are ever objective, except for the fact that they exist, as a socially constructed reality.

Grades assign value. Assigning student performances a value is why grading is always already subjective. This condition may be more obvious for assessments common in critical communication pedagogy (i.e., written and spoken work), but even so-called objective, multiple-choice tests are subjective insofar as choices are made: knowledge deemed worthy enough of to be tested, what ends up appearing on a given test, how many questions in what timeframes, the language that frames questions and potential answers, the length of questions and answers, the order in which questions appear, what options are available and how many. Using publisher test banks merely delegate some choices to people working in corporations, and automatic grading assigns other choices to technology. With each choice, bias can rear its ugly head. For example, those proxies of subjectivity (e.g., test banks, auto-grading) expose other biases in any attempt to index academic mastery objectively, since most instructor-only resources are available online and are purchased by students to use to get a desired grade without having to learn much (Cheng and Crumbley 2018). Regardless, denying subjectivity is inherent to grading and assessment does not do the learning work of instructors and students justice.

Grades, instead, obscure the full realities of learning. From a Burkean perspective (1966b), the grade system is a terministic screen through which students, teachers, administrators, employers, parents, and the public talk about the value of students' education. The question is presented as if the value of a student's learning *is* or *is not* excellent, proficient, satisfactory, mediocre or failing (a scientistic perspective of grades). From Burke's dramatistic perspective, grades consequentially exhort their audiences to believe how students and their learning *should be* or *should not be* seen as excellent, proficient, satisfactory, mediocre or failing. Consider this revision of Burke's famous quote[2] about terministic screens: even if any given grade is a reflection of a student's learning, by its very nature as a grade it must be a selection of a student's learning; and to this extent must function also as a deflection of a student's learning. Indeed, students learn more and differently than any grade could ever reflect or measure.

PERSUASION

Grades are attempts at persuasion, the heart of traditional notions of rhetoric. Students are convinced by teachers' evaluations, or they are doubtful. After all, students sometimes appeal their grades. If grades were not persuasive symbolic acts, then grade appeals could not exist because people cannot disagree if they have not been asked to accept. In additional to asserting rational arguments (logos), grades also convey credibility (ethos), shape culture (mythos), and trigger emotional responses (pathos). Let me address each of these below.

Grades appeals commonly happen when a student arrives at a faculty member's office to question a grade that they received. Appeals can also transcend the educational process of the teacher-student relationship when other faculty and university administrations become involved in the bureaucratic processes of the grade system. Grades and grading can even transcend the college and go to court, a classic arena for rational rhetoric. In one well-known case (*Parate v. Isibor* 1989), the Sixth Circuit Court took grades well outside of the intimacy of the teacher-student relation by ruling that "the assignment of a letter grade is symbolic communication intended to send a specific message to the student, the individual professor's communicative act is entitled to some measure of First Amendment protection." In addition to reading Natthu Parate's assignments of grades as protected speech (and therefore operating in a civic context), the judges' decision also took the ultimate authority for the grades out of his hands since the judges also ruled that Tennessee State University's administration could simply change the grade in a student's record without having to force the professor to do it.

While the institutional apparatus provides instructors with the power and legitimacy for their grading to have persuasive force, so too does faculty grading provide institutions with the academic credibility for their degrees to have worth in society. Unfortunately, that credibility is eroding. Students, parents, employers, activists, and the public are increasingly questioning whether a degree is worth it. Cost is one factor, too complex to address here. Grading is another (Milton et al. 1986; Abbott 2008; Arum and Roksa 2014). Are we giving honest assessments when we grade, and do students believe those evaluations when they receive them? Do other audiences believe them? Too often have I heard a faculty colleague complain about the inadequacy of a student's work while proceeding to give them a good grade. If instructors lie to their students about the quality of their academic performances, then why should faculty be trusted to speak the truth about the knowledge and insight they impart? Students will only learn from grades they perceive as credible. When students are constituted to believe the As they regularly receive, then are they less likely to trust a teacher who honestly gives them less? Furthermore, as grading practices lose credibility in the eyes of the public, so does education. Grading practices already lack credibility, exemplified by two late twentieth-century employer surveys (Curtis et al. 1998; Winsor et al. 1997), which reveal that GPA is at the bottom of a list of factors for hiring or predicting employment success. To what degree should any student trust teachers that suggest their work is excellent or distinguished by awarding them each an A? The public is already suspicious.

Subject *to* both faculty and institution but also subject *of* them both, students make their way through educational processing by learning what they have been persuaded to learn to the degree that they have been persuaded that they have learned it. Grading shapes students culturally. For example, John Tagg (2004) worries that what we, as faculty, are *"really* teaching students" is to be concerned with grades rather than discovery and transformation. Students often seek and find classes (and instructors) in which they can get good grades and actively avoid ones that are more challenging. All too often, becoming learned is a fringe benefit rather than the main point of being in college. Moreover, grades are a significant part of traditional aged students' being in a world in which they have never not been a student, as far as they can remember. Grades become such a significant part of some students' being that they often defined themselves by their grades, such as self-purported A-students. Furthermore, as David Bleich (1997) puts it, grading "educates the students as to their place in society: as individuals in competition with every other individual for jobs and other valuable items" (19). In other words, grades subjugate.

Compound these subjugating qualities, grades convey emotional appeals. In this respect, it is useful to remember Davidson's (1966) concern about grades as source of "student anxieties and frustrations." In their study about the meaning of grades through metaphor, Goulden and Griffin (1995) found that nearly a quarter of the students they surveyed used "emotional trigger" metaphors to describe grades, second to only metaphors related to "information about achievement," which comprised half. While a "bad" grade can be disheartening, a "good" grade can be encouraging, even make students feel empowered. In these cases, however, the emotion of the grade may be the only feedback to which a student pays attention, regardless of whether or not elaboration is provided. Limited to the feelings from grades (esteem building or discouraging) may not actually empower or disempower students. Not until grades prompt student reflection about their academic actions do we see empowerment through praxis that Paulo Freire (2000) preaches. Imperfect grades exhort students to engage feedback, reflect, and act differently (i.e., to transform). Without that nudge, students may not consider strengthening their critical thinking, developing more ethical and effective communication, honing language skills, and deepening knowledge and understanding. Furthermore, grading can empower students by motivating them to reflect on the differing qualities of their own work. In a letter to students about a change in institutional grading policy, Dean of the College at Princeton, Nancy Weiss Malkiel, explained it well: "high and homogeneous grades do not help you to distinguish your best work from your ordinary work, and they do not motivate you to stretch to do the most imaginative work of which you are capable" (B.T. 2004). Finally, students' reconciliation of disappointing grades as "personal growth" and "genuine learning" can enable feelings of personal success (Sanders and Anderson 2010). In this sense, grading can urge reflexivity, which leads to learning, which leads to becoming empowered agents in society. Anything that we consider to be grading justice should stimulate this transformative chain reaction.

However docile they may seem, students are not powerless in the face of their grades. They are persuaded. The subjugation of grading is not total or complete. In our classrooms, students not only learn "the material" (whatever that is), but they should also learn bits and pieces of what it takes (or what they think it takes) to be more successful as workers, citizens, artists, and scientists than they might otherwise be. In the spirit of Michel de Certeau's (1988) walk through the city, students learn to perform within the strategic frameworks of institutional scripts and only then can develop resistant tactical responses. The grade system is part of the ideological infrastructure of education in America.

As Fassett and Warren (2004) suggest, "awarding an A or a B is ideological, is a question of power" (31). The question is, how is that power to be wielded and for whom? Even if we do not like grades or even believe them harmful to learning, grades remain a significant way in which students make sense of their learning process, and therefore we do them a disservice by rejecting grades' possible use as a means for intellectual empowerment.

VALUE ARGUMENTATION

As a sign of value, a grade is recognizable as a rational rhetorical form. At its simplest, grading follows the basic algebraic script of a value proposition: X is Y (e.g., the essay deserves an A, the exam score is an F). Argumentation textbooks often devote a chapter to discussing value arguments. Inch and Warnick (2002) provide a useful framework for the stock issues of value argument: Value, Criteria, and Application. "X" is a value object. In an educational context, that artifact, for example, might refer to a presentation, a performance on a test, or a research essay, but the object may also refer to a student's performance in a course, an aggregated, sometimes fragmented, accumulation of grades across assignments.

Value

The value attributed to any artifact is derived from a hierarchy, which determines the relative worth of the object. As instructors operating within the US grade system, we usually must rely on the A-B-C-D-F hierarchy to report grades. Hierarchies are inherent to value judgements, and so value judgements are necessarily embedded with inequality, no matter how much activist-teachers want to avoid it, even if all students get As. This necessary condition of labeling judgements with a letter may be one of the central means by which the grading system perpetuates social injustice. "The grading system has been," Bleich (1997) observes "an instrument meant to preserve the traditional hierarchical arrangements in society" (31). The idea that I might be supporting traditional hegemonies is troubling, another reason I would rather there were no grades. Bleich makes a compelling case that the grading system reproduces corporate, bureaucratic hierarchies that reward compliant students and punish "imaginative, creative, and resourceful students" (31). Should we not be critical of the ways in which grades produce this "bureaucratic mentality," as Bleich calls it, excluding students who think differently? Is it possible that the going-through-the-motions requirements in my assignments (e.g., topic and length parameters, citation minimums, spelling and grammar) reward the conformists and punish the imaginative and resourceful? Yes, it happens, which is why I often give grace. However, parameters are not always suppressive. Creativity can flourish under such constraints (Stokes and Fisher 2005). A more probable injustice happens to those students who grew up outside of privileged educational environments, punished for not conforming to requirements because they did not have access to the means for developed the aptitudes or understanding for how or why to conform.

Given these conditions, I sympathize with Bleich's radical claim, "grade inflation is a subversive response to runaway corporate power, greed, and ruthlessness" (1997, 31). Subverting such societal evils is appealing. Critical communication pedagogues may agree with Bleich's reasoning: "Because of excessive pressure to building up for an ever-more compliant bureaucratic managerial class of employees, more and more 'good students' are needed; that is, those that will 'ace' the grading system" (1997, 31). Although, we should also wrestle with how grade inflation also perpetuates corporatization and greed within higher education and privileges hegemonic neoliberal arrangements that already exist in society (Kahl, this volume). Within the capitalist economy inside institutions of higher education, competition for students between colleges and among departments and programs determine the availability of resources, faculty lines, tenure decisions, not just to thrive but to survive. Grades become currency, and the grading system becomes a market for attracting students, majors, minors, or simply enrollees. In fact, research demonstrates instructors' incentive to "buy" student evaluation scores by inflating grades (Ewing 2012). Regardless of intent, grade inflation feeds the beast of neoliberal corporatization within higher education.

Furthermore, already-privileged students benefit most from a compressed (aka inflated) grade distribution. They have less need of a means to distinguish themselves because they already have the resources, networks, and capital to maintain their hegemonic status, regardless of whether they get As or Bs, and even Cs. President George W. Bush (2015) provides a quintessential example when he famously joked with his Southern Methodist University audience during his Commencement address: "As I like to tell the 'C' students: You, too, can be president." Students with his privilege would find that more possible than those without it. They can simply be "grade-oriented" (Milton et al. 1986) and fulfill just enough of the "performance goals" (Tagg 2004) to maintain their status quo. They need not be "learning-oriented" (Milton et al. 1986) and need no "learning goals" (Tagg 2004); they only need a degree to transition neatly into existing structures of power. Grade inflation means that the privileged can do less for the same outcome: hegemony.

Moreover, compressed high grades provide less space for marginalized students to stand out. Higher education was widely perceived in America as a ladder of social mobility for marginalized and underprivileged students, but those beliefs have eroded and attitudes have become "cynical" about mobility assertions (Berg 2010). This erosion is bound up with deleterious effects of the grading system. The ability of women, Latinx, and Black students to perform their best is diminished within the context of "stereotype threat" (Steele and Aronson 1995; Walton and Spencer 2009), and the college grading system disproportionately "disadvantages those who have the most ground to make up—the lower classes" (Berg 2010, 163). All the more reason, however, good grades from the underprivileged should carry distinguished meaning. "The echo of the accomplishment of a single low-income college graduate can reverberate through subsequent generations and have a very large impact, greater than that of one more high-achieving child from an advantaged family," observes Berg (2010, 163). Especially when perceived under the conditions of grade compression, such accomplishments are diminished and/or more easily dismissed. One pernicious example is Mansfield's (2001) suggestion that White professors artificially gave higher grades to Black students as a form of affirmative action and covered their tracks by elevating White students' grades, too. The circulation of such disparaging sentiments reproduces injustice by discounting what might be truly deserved. However, it does point to the possibility that grade inflation narrows an avenue for underprivileged students to distinguish themselves with grades as signs of overcoming obstacles of marginalization.

Be inflated or not, the grading system overall preserves hegemonic hierarchies. Instructors should wrestle with these implications, but not shirk from making judgements and therefore hierarchies. If people are "goaded by the spirit of hierarchy (or moved by the sense of order)," as Kenneth Burke (1966a) would have us believe, then teacher-activists have a responsibility to shape those hierarchies with our judgements. After all, activists do on the public stage.

Value judgements and hierarchies of value (i.e., grading) are as necessary for activism as they are for teaching. To call out injustice is to place something low on a hierarchy of justice. Keeping in mind the attribution of an "A" or a "C" does not solely exist (or solely have meaning) in the classroom bubble or for educational institutions, we might consider how meanings about and associations with specific letter grades circulate in public. Activist organizations from Greenpeace to the National Rifle Association use the A to F system to communicate their evaluations of political candidates' positions. However imperfect, the heuristic of a letter grade asserts a judgement, which the public can decipher easily and by which they can be persuaded (or not). Presumably, this activist grading is designed to challenge candidates to improve their rhetoric and policy positions.[3] Activists make judgements in public; as activist-teachers, we should not shirk from making judgements in our classes. Similarly, grades need not always be final, at least before a semester/quarter ends. As instructors, we can provide time and space for students to revise and resubmit to improve their learning, incentivized by a desire to improve their grade.

Criteria

Any hierarchy of value argumentation is based on some criteria, be they implicit or explicit. Inch and Warnick (2002) define criteria as field- or sphere-dependent measures, norms, or rules used to determine whether a value object fulfills certain values of an audience. Criteria are the standards we use to make judgements, sometimes explicitly in the form of rubrics for speech or writing performances but also implicitly when deciding how to phrase a question or which question to ask for a test.

Rhetorically, grading criteria do more. Drawing on Michel Foucault's work, Tim Peeples and Bill Hart-Davidson (1997) refer to these criteria as the "technical code of grading," which is more than just an evaluation tool but "the network of cultural, institutional, and personal values, rules and decisions" undergirding and shaping the elements in those tools (97). Such criteria vary depending on the assignment, the test, the class, the institution, the subject matter, the academic discipline, and, of course, the instructor, but all of them communicate to the student what audiences may deem as more or less important to know and to learn. Also, though, the values, rules, and decisions embedded in the technical codes of education (and therefore evaluation) are also shaped by the values of legislatures, workplaces, communities, and other publics.

Criteria do more than help college instructors determine the grades that result from discrete student performances, as if the classroom or the institution were hermetically sealed from the rest of society. The choice of some values over others and opposed to others is at the crux of the struggle over grading for critical pedagogues. The ideological power and judgement inherent to awarding a grade, as Fassett and Warren (2007) suggest, is a "reproduction of certain values and not others" (37). Whether all students get an A or grade distributions look like a bell curve, instructors cannot avoid the fact that they are caught up in a grading system that is always already ideological. So, as critical communication pedagogues, we should ask, what are the values we will enforce and reinforce? To what degree do those values do justice to the students, to the institutions as spaces for a "higher" education, to our academic communities (e.g., disciplines), or to the public sphere?

Whether we like it or not, our standards teach students what is important and what is not, and therefore advise them how to act, what to say, and what

54   *David Deifell*

not to say; that is, they tell students how to become who they *should* become. Peeples and Hart-Davidson (1997) point out that the assignments/tests in combination with this technical code "are *designed* to produce some cultural condition" not merely assessment results and educational artifacts (97). Instructors may identify criteria or create rubrics with only the assignment and class in mind, or they may adopt rubrics from a colleague, the institution, a publisher, or some disciplinary association. In any case, they also create the conditions for reproducing subjectivities in the service of the ideological apparatuses that constitute our culture, society, and polity. All the more reason we should be careful about what those criteria are and what they mean.

Application

A third component of the value argument that we make while grading is application, which is the use of evidence from artifact(s) to say whether it meets (or does not meet) the criteria in order to be deemed excellent or something less valuable. Jasinski (2002) describes application as "engaging in the process of evaluation" (596). Application is where the rubber hits the road, specifically focusing attention on how the criteria applies to some *thing*, the value object (e.g., the essay, the speech, the test). Application is the most contingent, most situated, and arguably, the most rhetorical part of the grading process.

Application should not be confused with the value claim, but the letter grade is sometimes used synecdochally, substituting the grade-argument with the grade-claim. Exacerbating this reductionism, students, institutions, employers, graduate schools, and the public use the average of grade-claims (GPA) to distill the many individual grading processes over lengths of time or to convey the overall worth of their education or even of themselves. This GPA distillation is the perpetuation of the "bureaucratic mentality" that disturbs Bleich (1997) so much, which is why he proposes to elevate "narrative evaluation" from its secondary role to replace grades, which he suggests doing through grade inflation (see above). In this respect, Bleich is right that narratives resist quantification, making it difficult for bureaucracies to use and abuse. For instructors, such feedback already serves the purposes of justifying, explaining, or guiding the interpretation of a grade by making student errors, strengths, weaknesses, and insights explicit. Bleich (1997) considers these narrative evaluations transformative because it substitutes "judgement for discussion" among other conversational frameworks. However, even if no letter grade-claim or no criteria are explicitly identified, the elaboration of considerations or encouragements for improvement is still application, which necessarily implies the existence of value and criteria. This rhetorical structuring of value judgement is baked into any evaluation of student work, whether or not "the grade" is empirically present. Supporting narrative evaluation *and* grade inflation, consequently, Bleich creates a rhetorical contradiction that undermines the meaningfulness of both the grade and the evaluation.

With somewhat different concerns, grade inflation detractors decry the weakening of standards (i.e., criteria), but they really seem concerned with application. In his influential review about grade inflation in *The Chronicle of Higher Education* that continues to spark debate, Harvey C. Mansfield (2001) argues that teachers should "rate students accurately" or give students an assessment of "where they stand in relation to others." However, these concerns are less about standards and more about application or, as Mansfield might say, misapplication: that students do not deserve the grades that they are receiving for the work that they do. The perceived misalignment of the value and the criteria seemingly make each school a Lake Wobegon, where "all the children are above average." In his 2004 *New York Times* essay, Michael Bérubé flippantly suggests that some elite schools have become places "where everyone is so far above average that the rule of the Caucus Race in 'Alice in Wonderland' apply: everybody has won, and all must have prizes." A similar trophies-for-participation, regardless of any particular performance, is purported to be pervasive in colleges throughout the country.

Because of its situatedness and radical particularity, however, application is an aspect of grading in which these worries of "grade inflation" get complicated. It's one thing to complain about the general rise of GPAs documented by sites like gradeinflation.com, maintained and updated about every five years by Stuart Rojstaczer. It's quite different to say that an individual student did not deserve a certain grade for a particular performance on a specific assignment. Application cannot be aggregated or averaged, which is Bleich's point. The problem with such grade inflation critiques is that they obscure the process of evaluation and treat grades as assessments of people rather than their performances. Grade-oriented students self-identifying as an A-student or placing their 4.0 GPAs on their résumés are doing the same thing; that is, detaching the human practice of value argumentation with statistical abstractions for comparison. Such dehumanization is at the heart of what is unjust in the grade system.

A recognition of application as both particular and principled embraces the difficult web of tensions of the grading system in which teachers and students are caught. Students can and often do perform well in one instance and poorly in another, and grades can challenge students to reflect on those differences. The attempt to avoid judgement is patronizing to college students, as if they are children too immature to take grades as an inextricable part of the value argumentation feedback from which to learn.

FINAL REFLECTIONS

However much many of us may like them to disappear, grades are a part of the ideological infrastructure for learning in American institutions of higher education. That status is unlikely to change anytime soon, though many colleges and universities responded to COVID-19 by providing students with the option of taking their suddenly-online classes as pass/fail instead of a letter grade. Clearly, no-grades is not impossible. Perhaps, we can advocate for the abolition of the grade system. The pandemic revealed receptiveness. Institutions showed flexibility. Faculty altered expectations, and some critically reflected on their grading. Being forced online because of the pandemic is "making me think more deeply about what grades are for and why we assign them and why we have the system that we have in place for them," Patrick Iber, associate professor of history at the University of Wisconsin-Madison, told Simonetti of *Vox* in June 2020; "It may be that I never go back to the grading systems that I have used up to now." All faculty could use similar soul searching, even if we have to do still have to engage in some kind of grading in order to keep our teaching jobs. Sometimes, I feel like abandoning the whole profession, but that would signify a loss of hope; that is not grading justice. At times, I feel like giving up by just giving every student an A, regardless of the quantity or quality of their work, but that would be dishonest; that is not grading justice. Other times, I feel like upholding the integrity of higher education against the lies, laziness, and/or negligence enabled by permissive grading, but that can unfairly punish students seeking to learn or simply to survive; that is not grading justice. Mostly, I worry about what grading is doing to us, all of us in higher education.

Grades shape us because they are rhetorical. They are a form of symbolic action and a discourse. Fassett and Warren (2007) remind us that "we are, as scholars, constituted in our discourse, constituted in our moments of praise and confusion and candor" (91). Throughout this chapter, I discuss some of my concerns with grades, grading, and the grade system in terms of rhetoric. The rhetorical tensions operating within the value propositions we call grades should require critical communication pedagogues to reflect. For me, I ask questions.

How should I balance 1) the grade as interpersonal communication to a student situated within a specific course in which I communicate an assessment of a student's work on a particular assignment with 2) the grade as speaking to a larger array of audiences with whom a student shares the grade (and ones with whom they do not)?

How should I embrace the subjectivity human activity that is inherent to making evaluations of a student's performances while keeping my own biases in check and without undervaluing what the students learn that may not being assessed?

How should I negotiate intellectual honesty about the correspondence between the grade and my evaluation with the persuasive impact that grades will have on its audiences? For a student, to what extent should I be concerned with the degree to which my grade will be taken seriously by the student, whether a grade will reinforce a student's self-image or transform it, and/or the ways in which a grade will discourage or motivate further learning?

How is my grade doing constitutive work? That is, how does my grade teach a student to become grade-oriented and focused on performance goals not just as student but after graduation, and how does my grade teach a student what to expect of themselves as excellent, proficient, average, or mediocre and what to expect from others?

How do I act justly with the obligation of making value judgements? What is it that I am valuing and what am I not? Whose interests are being served when I am too lenient or too harsh with my value judgements? How should I handle being goaded by the spirit of hierarchy when grading hierarchies have historically been designed to preserve hegemony? Which values do I reproduce with my expectations for one grade or another, and which values do I resist? What are the cultural conditions that I am helping to constitute with my grading expectations? To what degree is my grade justly and humanely applied while accounting for the constitutive features of value argumentation?

As teacher-activists, we are committed to creating a better world through education. Although I do not have answers to all of these questions all the time, we would be wise to recognize our grades' rhetorical tensions between the reproduction of hegemony and the empowerment of students to be more discerning and more able to act with impactful agency in society. The point is not to resolve but to highlight the places within which teacher-activists can reflexively struggle for more just evaluation and pedagogy for students, ourselves, and society.

NOTES

1. Fassett and Warren make brief references, but they are not significant enough to warrant a mention in their index.

2. "Even if any given terminology is a reflection *of reality, by its very nature it must be a* selection *of reality; and to this extent it must function as a* deflection *of reality"* (Burke 1966b, 45).

3. Though reluctant to make a causal claim, I find it interesting that initial reports of Greenpeace's June 2019 grades indicated that no candidate for president received an "A" (Teirstein 2019), but that changed by August. Many candidates changed positions, and their grades from Greenpeace improved. For example, Joe Biden moved from a "D-" in June to a "B+" by August.

REFERENCES

Abbott, William M. 2008. "The Politics of Grade Inflation: A Case Study." *Change: The Magazine of Higher Learning* 40 (1): 32–37. https://doi.org/10.3200/CHNG.40.1.32-37.

Arum, Richard, and Josipa Roksa, J. 2011. *Academically Adrift: Limited Learning on College Campuses.* Chicago, IL: University of Chicago Press.

Berg, Gary. 2010. *Low-Income Students and the Perpetuation of Inequality: Higher Education in America.* New York: Routledge.

Bérubé, Michael. 2004. "The Way We Live Now: 5-3-04: Essay; How to End Grade Inflation." *The New York Times*, May 2, 2004. https://www.nytimes.com/2004/05/02/magazine/the-way-we-live-now-5-2-04-essay-how-to-end-grade-inflation.html.

Bleich, David. 1997. "What Can be Done about Grading?" In *Grading in the Post-Process Classroom: From Theory to Practice,* edited by Elizabet Allison, Lizbeth Bryant, and Maureen Hourigan, 15–35. Portsmouth, NH: Boynton/Cook Publishers.

Burke, Kenneth. 1966a. "Definition of Man." In *Language as Symbolic Action: Essays on Life, Literature, and Method*, edited by Kenneth Burke, 3–24. Berkeley: University of California Press. (Original work published August 1963).

Burke, Kenneth. 1966b. "Terministic Screens." In *Language as Symbolic Action: Essays on Life, Literature, and Method*, edited by Kenneth Burke, 44–62. Berkeley: University of California Press. (Original work published August 1965).

Bush, George W. 2015. Remarks by President George W. Bush at SMU's 100th Spring Commencement Convocation. Accessed January 16, 2020. https://www.smu.edu/News/2015/commencement-may-bush-address.

Bornholdt, Laura. 1986. Foreward. In *Making Sense of College Grades*: *Why the Grading System Does Not Work and What Can Be Done About It,* edited by Ohmer Milton, Howard R. Pollio, and James A. Eison, ix–xii. San Francisco: Jossey-Bass, Inc.

B.T. 2004, May 14. "Too Many A's? University Offers Proposals to Address Grade Inflation." *Princeton Alumni Weekly.* Accessed December 12, 2019. https://www.princeton.edu/~paw/archive_new/PAW03-04/14-0512/notebook.html.

Cheng, Christine, and D. Larry Crumbley. 2018. "Student and Professor Use of Publisher Test Banks and Implications for Fair Play." *Journal of Accounting Education* 42, 1–16. https://doi.org/10.1016/j.jaccedu.2017.12.001.

Curtis, Dan, Winsor, Jerry L., and Ronald D. Stephens. 1989. "National Preferences in Business and Communication Education." *Communication Education* 38 (1): 6–14.

Davidson, Carl. 1966, August. "Toward a Student Syndicalist Movement, or University Reform Revisited." 1966 Students for a Democratic Society Convention. Accessed December 28, 2020. http://www.forstudentpower.org/docs/student syndicalism.pdf.

De Certeau, Michel. 1988. *The Practice of Everyday Life.* (S. Rendall, Trans.). University of California Press: Berkeley (Original work published 1984).

Ewing, Andrew M. 2012. "Estimating the Impact of Relative Expected Grade on Student Evaluations of Teachers." *Economics of Education Review* 31 (1): 141–154. https://doi.org/10.1016/j.econedurev.2011.10.002.

Fassett, Deanna L., and John T. Warren. 2007. *Critical Communication Pedagogy.* Thousand Oaks, CA: Sage Publications, Inc.

Freire, Paulo. 2000. *Pedagogy of the Oppressed* (M. B. Ramos, Trans.). New York: Continuum. (Original work published in English in 1970).

Goulden, Nancy Rost, and Charles J. G. Griffin. 1995. "The Meaning of Grades Based on Faculty and Student Metaphors." *Communication Education* 44 (2): 110–125. https://doi.org/10.1080/03634529509379003.

Greenpeace USA. 2019. "Where's Your 2020 Candidate on Climate?" Available https://www.greenpeace.org/usa/climate2020/.

Inch, Edward, and Barbara Warnick. 2002. *Critical Thinking and Communication: The Use of Reason in Argument.* (4th ed.). Boston, MA: Allyn and Bacon.

Jaschik. Scott. 2009, Jan 22. "Imagining College Without Grades." *Inside Higher Ed.* Accessed December 28, 2019. https://www.insidehighered.com/news/2009/01/22/imagining-college-without-grades.

Jasinski, James L. 2001. *Sourcebook on Rhetoric: Key Concepts in Contemporary Rhetorical Studies.* Thousand Oaks, CA: Sage Publications.

Mansfield, Harvey C. 2001. "Grade Inflation: It's Time to Face the Facts." *The Chronicle of Higher Education.* April 6, 2001. https://www.chronicle.com/article/grade-inflation-its-time-to-face-the-facts/.

Milton, Ohmer, Pollio, Howard R., and James A. Eison. 1986. *Making Sense of College Grades: Why the Grading System Does Not Work and What Can Be Done About It.* San Francisco: Jossey-Bass, Inc.

Parate v. Isibor, 868 F.2d 821. United States Court of Appeals, Sixth 6th Circuit. 1989.

Peeples, Tim, and Bill Hart-Davidson. 1997. "Grading the "Subject": Questions of Expertise and Evaluation." In *Grading in the Post-Process Classroom: From Theory to Practice,* edited by Elizabet Allison, Lizbeth Bryant, and Maureen Hourigan, 94–113. Portsmonth, NH: Boynton/Cook Publishers.

Rosovsky Henry, and Matthew Hartley. 2002. *Evaluation and the Academy: Are We Doing the Right Thing?* Cambridge, MA: American Academy of Arts and Sciences.

Sanders, Matthew L., and Sky Anderson. 2010. "The Dilemma of Grades: Reconciling Disappointing Grades with Feelings of Personal Success." *Qualitative Research Reports in Communication* 11 (1): 51–56. https://doi.org/10.1080/17459430903515228.

Schinske, Jeffrey, and Kimberly Tanner. 2014. "Teaching More by Grading Less (or Differently)." *Life Sciences Education* 13 (Summer 2014): 159–166. https://www.ncbi.nlm.nih.gov/pmc/articles/PMC4041495/.

Simonetti, Isabella. 2020, June 12. "How will teachers grade their students during a pandemic?" *Vox.* Accessed 15 June 2020. https://www.vox.com/first-person/2020/6/12/21288116/coronavirus-covid-19-schools-teachers-grading.

Steele, Claude M., and Joshua Aronson. 1995. "Stereotype Threat and the Intellectual Test Performance of African Americans." *Journal of Personality and Social Psychology* 69 (5): 797–811. https://doi.org/10.1037//0022-3514.69.5.797.

Stokes, Patricia, and Danielle Fisher. 2005. "Selection, Constraints, and Creativity Case Studies: Max Beckmann and Philip Guston." *Creativity Research Journal* 17 (2): 283–291. https://doi.org/10.1207/s15326934crj1702&3.

Tagg, John. 2004. "Why Learn? What We May *Really* be Teaching Students." *About Campus* March/April, 2–10. https://eric.ed.gov/?id=EJ791236.

Teirstein, Zoya. 2019, June 3. "Greenpeace Graded All the Presidential Candidates' Climate Policies. They Weren't Impressed." *Mother Jones.* Accessed January 5, 2020. https://www.motherjones.com/environment/2019/06/greenpeace-graded-all-the-presidential-candidates-climate-policies-they-werent-impressed/.

Walton, Gregory M., and Steven J. Spencer. 2009. "Latent Ability: Grades and Test Scores Systematically Underestimate Intellectual Ability of Negatively Stereotyped Students. *Psychology Science* 20 (9). Accessed January 11, 2020. https://journals.sagepub.com/doi/full/10.1111/j.1467-9280.2009.02417.x.

Winsor, Jerry L., Curtis, Dan B., and Ronald D. Stephens. 1997. "National Preferences in Business and Communication Education: A Survey Update." *Journal of the Association for Communication Administration* 3, 170–179. https://eric.ed.gov/?id=EJ553727.

Chapter Two

Mobilizing a Critical Universal Design for Learning Framework for Justice Minded Course Design and Assessment

Allison D. Brenneise and Mark Congdon, Jr.

Allison: I inherited a large lecture class (125 enrolled students) to deliver the course as it had been designed, including its midterm exam. My teaching philosophy does not prioritize exams, as I would much rather have students demonstrate what they know through activities that are meaningful to them, but I agreed to the course as designed. From my vantage point, traditional exams create unwarranted stress and tend to privilege some students. Some students with disabilities (SWD) who require testing accommodations in an alternate location are disadvantaged by taking tests in such locations. Research (Godden and Baddeley 1975; Goldstein 2011) demonstrates that students who test in the rooms where they have learned information do better on examinations taken in that room than do students who test in another location. Of the students enrolled in the course, approximately 20 students had disability accommodation letters. These letters described the types of accommodations the students required but did not identify the particular needs they address. The majority of the letters made allowances for testing in quiet or distraction-free settings.

As a result of systematic variability in the delivery of disability accommodations in public K–12 education, few students have been adequately prepared to be able to talk about the effects of their disabilities and how the accommodations they receive work to meet their learning needs (Cawthon and Cole 2010; Nichols and Quaye 2009). Additionally, many SWD are new to higher education and do not know how their disabilities may affect them in the college classroom; it is hard to know what one does not know. Similarly, many instructors lack the training (Stage and Milne 1996) and/or expertise to know what learning challenges are supported by specific accommodations (Murray, Flannery, and Wren 2008). While many are willing to accommodate (Quinlan,

Bates, and Angell 2012), fewer faculty have well developed disability literacies (Siebers 2008) or adequate training and guidance to navigate discussions of disability with students (Cornett-DeVito and Worley 2005; Greenbaum, Graham, and Scales 1995; Quinlan, Bates, and Angell 2012; Stage and Milne 1996). Increasing the level of difficulty for both faculty and students is the student's right to privacy. Prohibited from asking about a student's specific diagnosis and lacking a disability literacy to address the unknown, it can be difficult to change one's pedagogy and assessment practices to fully support students in the ways that would be most beneficial to the student (Cawthon and Cole 2010; Stage and Milne 1996). A tired menu of standard disability accommodations adds to the challenge; the same accommodation is offered for a wide variety of different needs (Janiga and Costebader 2002). Some students struggling with language-based learning challenges, problems with word retrieval, working or other memory-related issues get the same testing accommodation as students with attentional or social-emotional issues. Some SWD rate their accommodations as ineffective (Kurth and Mellard 2006) because the provided accommodation is not designed to meet the actual learning need it is intended to address.

As teacher-activists, we (Allison and Mark) have a responsibility to recognize how we think from and account for our privileged positionality with how we design our courses and assess/grade students. We draw from Critical Communication Pedagogy's (CCP) commitments of centering culture, identity, and dialogue (Fassett and Warren 2007) as the heart of our teacher-activist approaches to assessment[1] and course design. Specifically, Universal Design for Learning (UDL) is incorporated into our critical course design to account for the variation within and between learners that brain science confirms is present regardless of the learning task (Meyer, Rose, and Gordon 2014). An essential belief behind UDL is a course designed to address the needs of students who experience barriers to learning (SWD, students whose first languages and cultures are diverse, students of diverse races, classes, and ethnicities, and even students identified as gifted) result in classes that are designed better for everyone (Rose and Meyer 2002, 2005; Meyer, Rose, and Gordon 2014). The focus of this chapter is to propose a Critical Universal Design for Learning (CUDL) framework that connects UDL, CCP, and Culturally Sustaining Pedagogy (CSP) to offer educators/scholars in higher education a practical theoretical lens and some strategies to consider when thinking about becoming more socially just in their course design and assessment of students in higher education.

Complementing CCP and CSP, UDL offers us, as teacher-activists, an opportunity to better engage all students present in our classrooms whose variations in learning are continuously forgotten and marginalized by traditional modes of assessment and grading (Tobin and Behling 2018). I (Mark) have a learning disability and Tourette syndrome, am a first generation college student, and am a former special education teacher. I (Allison) have children with multiple disabilities and have been advocating for students, families, school professionals, and communities navigating the pre-K–12 education system (and beyond) across the United States for more than twenty years. As such, we enter and seek to foster the communication classroom and assessment approaches as a dialogic site for interrogating the personal as political and the political as personal (Ellis 2002). We believe that course design (including assessment) needs to be reconceptualized through a critical lens to make educational activities (e.g., grading) equitable and not just for those who tend to benefit from traditional modes of grading. By combining our specialized disability knowledge with critical pedagogy and UDL to course design, which includes assessment and grading, the focus moves toward empowering students to be motivated, prepared, and self-regulated (CAST 2018) with any learning task they may encounter. Additionally, this shift from providing supports and strategies previously known as *disability accommodations* to only those with disabilities to providing them for everyone is socially just. It removes and reduces power differences that reproduce stigmatization surrounding disability and associated accommodations in both the micro level individual learning environments as well as at the institutional level (Cawthon and Cole 2010; Nichols and Quaye 2009; Quinlan, Bates, and Angell 2012).

When students are prepared for learning in this way, we have found that student learning improves in two ways. First, because we offer choices for student autonomy and students can choose assessment options that play to their strengths (while still addressing areas of weakness), students feel less threatened by the learning tasks and are more motivated and engaged with course content. Second, students leave our classrooms equipped with skills and strategies to incorporate their prior knowledge with new content, a sense of autonomy, and growth in their ability to manage the emotions that are always present in learning. Knowing what they need to be successful in future learning and having concrete experiences from which to talk about and advocate allows them to be self-determined, confident learners throughout their lives. We, educators/scholars, have to actively work to provide this space of "becoming" (i.e., support, mentoring, pedagogical teaching, etc.) for transformational learning to become possible (Fassett and Warren 2007; Herakova and Congdon 2018).

Throughout the chapter, *italics* will mark the situation and conversation that brings us (Allison and Mark) to collaborate. In doing this, we first situate our choice to employ UDL within our commitments to critical communication

64   *Allison D. Brenneise and Mark Congdon, Jr.*

and culturally sustaining pedagogies (Fassett and Warren 2007; Gay 2010; Ladson-Billings 1995; Paris 2012). Then, we provide an introduction to UDL before proposing a framework for Critical Universal Design for Learning (CUDL). We conclude with a word of caution about intentionality.

Allison: Even though my class was large, it was important for me to get to know my students. In this class, I had a student whose profile reminded me of my son's (see Brenneise, 2019). My current student struggled to speak in fluent sentences. I saw evidence of the same in this student's writings. In individual meetings, I noticed difficulty with word retrieval and language fluency. I knew that an exam that asked the student to generate and recall course vocabulary to fit a scenario (both required on this test) would only test whatever barrier the student experienced and would not show me what course content had been acquired. Additionally, this student would be taking the exam in an alternate location. I was fairly certain that even with testing in a quiet location (my office) that the outcome would be suboptimal in part because the testing accommodation would deprive the student of muscle memory and contextual associations that are readily available to any student who tests in the room where they have learned the material.

I thought about creating a separate test for this student and including a word bank to limit word retrieval problems. I did not think using a word bank would make the test less rigorous but it would remove the language retrieval task. I was held back by my thought that creating a test just for this student would be discriminatory based on what I perceived to be the student's disability. The only way I could imagine providing this support was to offer the word bank to all of the students. Unsure of this strategy, I called Mark because we share an interest in disability and he has previous expertise as a special education teacher prior to his return to the academy. Mark and I share similar beliefs as critical communication pedagogues keenly interested in social justice. I hoped that he would be able to help me think of a socially just solution for everyone.

Mark asked what my purpose was in giving the exam. The question made me realize that I did not know my goal for the exam other than it was expected that I do it. I guessed that the test was to determine whether students could define and apply key course concepts, but I did not know what the assessment was designed to measure.

Mark: I remember in our call that I did not hear Allison explain the purpose of the exam or how the exam aligned to the course goals and learning objectives. This made me think of my own experiences with how we can get caught up in just administering an exam that is traditionally given in courses to "prove" that we assessed student learning without really digging deep into the what, why, and how of our assessments. Planning for and reflecting on these areas of course design can prevent the perpetuation of oppressive and unjust systems including ableism (and other -isms) in educational spaces.

Allison: Once I determined what the test did measure, I appreciated working with Mark to create a word bank consisting of more concepts than were necessary. This strategy (incorporating distractor words) required all students to choose the best answer from the available choices. By doing this, the test remained rigorous and had validity because it was designed to measure what was intended.

Mark: A word bank is an example of a great accommodation once reserved for students with special learning needs. It is one that I think is often overlooked by many educators in higher education, including myself. Our conversation encouraged me to reexamine my own pedagogical approaches to assessment. We have the power to transform our assessment practices to meet the diverse learning needs of our students.

CRITICAL COMMUNICATION PEDAGOGY

In response to static conceptualizations of power and linear modes of teaching and learning, Fassett and Warren (2007) called for a critical communication pedagogy (CCP) in the classroom, stating that students and teachers, as citizens, have a "responsibility of exploring power and privilege, even—and especially if—that process implicates [their] own work" (42). CCP is especially relevant when understanding and (re)envisioning education and educational assessment in which students and practitioners are seen as "agents of change" who interact with multiple stakeholders. The commitment of CCP is to develop deep reflection as part of the communication process and social responsibility of education—for students and teachers, in and outside of the classroom. As a result of the practitioner's responsibility to practice reflexivity inherent in the philosophy and practice of CCP, the framework grows. As CCP becomes more inclusive, it presumes all learners as competent (see Biklen 1990; Biklen and Burke 2006; Brenneise 2019). Presuming competence is an ontological promise to view all students as capable of learning (not just the likable ones but also the ones an educator is not so sure about, including those who need accommodations to access the curriculum) and to seriously commit to communication (Brenneise 2020). Educators should explicitly express these promises to students, so that students receive the message that they are "worthy of being heard" (Bilken 1990, 306). Additionally, a more inclusive practitioner of CCP commits to checking assumptions in meaning making and engages in on-going conversation with students, adopts UDL as a mindset and in so doing, endeavors to destigmatize the "isms" that populate the margins (Brenneise 2020).

Traditional modes of assessment and grading are undemocratic, unjust, and further perpetuate systemic inequalities for all learners, especially for learners with disabilities. A Critical Universal Design for Learning (CUDL) integrates the foci on disability, power, and culture present in UDL, CCP, and CSP to move educators toward grading justice. A CUDL approach to developing assessments of student learning, offers students/faculty opportunities to learn from and with each other. This process, coupled with acknowledging and owning each of their own histories, allows for the recognition and removal of barriers, which has the potential to create a more equitable educational opportunity for planned and unplanned, structured, and unstructured, educational experiences for all students. Unplanned or (incidental) learning is a "spontaneous form of learning that occurs as a by-product of a task" (Bland, et al. 2009, 124). Classroom interactions, activities, and assignments become opportunities to (re)create and (re)imagine, together, mundane communicative moments that may allow us to reflect on and meaningfully engage differences, while continuing to seek ethical openings for connecting and being-with others. However, missing from CCP is an explicit acknowledgement of understanding disability as a(n) (cultural) identity, and the need to confront ableism in our educational system, pedagogy, language, and mundane communicative behaviors (Brenneise 2020).

CULTURALLY SUSTAINING PEDAGOGIES (CSP)

As instructors and critical scholars that value all students, it is important to embody a democratic schooling experience for our students that give voice to their identity, culture, and life experiences (Freire 2000). Asante (1991) asserts, "One's basic identity is one's self-identity which is ultimately one's cultural identity; without a strong cultural identity, one is lost" (177). It is important to understand how faculty may affirm students' various identities within the context of the classroom. Students make connections between pedagogical practices, assignments, and content taught.

The expanded commitments of a more inclusive CCP and a belief in a truly inclusive democracy leads us to "culturally sustaining pedagogy" (Paris 2012) which evolves from Ladson-Billing's (1995) culturally relevant pedagogy and Gay's (2010) culturally responsive pedagogy. According to Paris (2012),

Ladson-Billings developed culturally relevant pedagogy as a resource for teachers to resist a pervasive belief in education that viewed the diverse languages and cultures used by African American students as deficient. Rejecting the deficit approach to learning, teachers incorporate cultural references into every aspect of instruction. Students benefit by seeing themselves in the curriculum (Ladson-Billings 1994). Gay's (2010) culturally relevant pedagogy is a practice designed to equip teachers with the tools they would need to span the cultural gaps between teachers and culturally diverse learners. Gay defined this pedagogy as "using the cultural knowledge, prior experiences, frames of reference, and performance styles of ethnically diverse students to make learning encounters more relevant to and effective for them" (2010, 31). Villegas and Lucas (2002) explain that culturally responsive instruction can equalize power relations within classrooms because teachers create instructional methods that recognize and build upon culturally different ways of learning, behaving, and using language in the classroom. The Education Alliance at Brown University studied the work of more than twenty researchers and organizations to identify and thematize seven constant principles of culturally responsive pedagogy: positive perspectives on parents and families; communication of high expectations; learning within the context of culture; student-centered instruction; culturally mediated instruction; reshaping the curriculum; and teacher as facilitator (Ralabate and Lord Nelson 2017).

Practitioners of culturally sustaining pedagogies must be vulnerable and reflexive in their investigation of the role that they play in de/colonizing knowledge (Collier and Muneri 2016) because they must commit to raising consciousness and unveiling the ways systems marginalize some and privilege others. For instance, Paris (2012) was concerned that the terms "culturally relevant" and "culturally responsive" might lead toward expectations that students learn the dominant language and culture at a cost of losing the richness their native languages and cultures carry. Therefore, he suggested that the word "sustaining" (Paris 2012, 96) be used instead, since this word is more inclusive of the various realities, cultures, and lived experiences of students and educators. The language we use shapes how we view and interact in our world, and using the word "sustaining" has the potential to create opportunities for students and educators to continue to embody all of the languages, literacies, and cultures they access to enhance and resist the homogenizing cultural push at the social level (Fassett and Warren 2007; Paris 2012). Teaching cultural awareness and learning acceptance promotes opportunities for social change in a society whose policies seem to oppose the cultural pluralism that is present in our diverse humanity (Au 2009; Gay 2010; Paris 2012, Shor and Freire 1987). However, missing from the principles of CSPs are a consideration of SWD and a corresponding attention to decentering ableism.

UNIVERSAL DESIGN FOR LEARNING

Universal Design for Learning (UDL) has several purposes. The first is to meet students who have been marginalized and underserved by the "illusory average curriculum" (National Center on Universal Design for Learning 2010) by meeting students where they are. Designing a curriculum for the learners at the margins makes education better for everyone. While SWD were the initial focus of the professionals at the Center for Applied Special Technology (CAST), UDL has moved toward including all learners, since decades of brain science research demonstrates that "the way people learn is as unique as their fingerprints" (CAST 2010). Another UDL goal is to create expert learners.

According to Rose, "expert learners" (Meyer, Rose, and Gordon 2014, 49) are students who are in charge of their learning. Expert learners come to the learning environment with background knowledge to activate; they have skills and strategies that assist them in learning and they want to learn more. Those who use UDL design learning experiences to ensure that every student learns. In this framework, educators think about who their students are (or who they could be), the barriers those students may encounter in those experiences, and create a flexible curriculum to minimize barriers and maximize learning for all (CAST 2010; Meyer, Rose, and Gordon 2014). While this planning might not eliminate having to provide additional disability accommodations to meet the individual needs of students, those accommodations are reduced significantly. By anticipating and planning for students who have unique needs in advance, students might not find barriers requiring their use of accommodations. Accessing course content that has already considered the needs of students with disabilities creates a sense of belonging for that student. Students are not "accommodated" as an afterthought because it was always expected that they would be present. Creating a sense of belonging for all students works to destigmatize disability and models a society where disability is considered to be a natural part of the human condition. This benefits students who register for accommodations and those who do not, including those who would never consider their anxiety, depression, or other mental wellness issues as a disability. At the same time, the environment supports students whose first languages and cultures vary, as well as honor students. UDL offers educators the opportunity to use a variety of options and techniques to witness the creativity and brilliance their diverse learners can create when given the autonomy and support to demonstrate their learning according to their strengths (National Center on Universal Design for Learning 2010). An understanding that all students learn differently, not just students with disabilities, is critical to UDL's tenet that it is the curriculum that is flawed, not the students.

Working with students on the margins (those with severe physical, sensory, and intellectual disabilities) provoked an initial response in the CAST professionals to change the student so that the student could learn from the curriculum. Over time, it became obvious to the CAST staff that the problem was not inherent in the student; the problem was in the curriculum. For example, some students with sensory disabilities could not see to read from books, some with physical disabilities could not turn the page or hold the books, and some with learning disabilities could not process the information in it. The diversity that the individual students brought to the class could not be changed; the students were the way they were. The curriculum and the materials themselves could be changed and thus began UDL.

Since the birth of UDL, our society has learned a great deal about the brain and how learning works. As researchers learned more, they recognized that there was a tremendous range of variability in the way humans learn. Yet, education systems perpetuate a myth that there exists a type of student known as an "average learner." Burbaud et al. (1995) studied brain function under functional magnetic resonance imaging. Participants answered the same mental math problems using different strategies (visual or verbal) and the imaging showed that despite solving the same problems, participant brains lit up in different areas (Burbaud et al. 1995). The plastic nature of the brain allows for each of us to have differently developed and dynamic regions based on unique profiles and interests. To drive this point home, Meyer, Rose, and Gordon (2014) compared the size and development of motor cortices in an example comparing a professional violinist and a non-musician peer. The motor cortex of the professional violinist is much larger than that of the non-musician because the violinist needs to make "very fine movements of the left hand that are critical in playing the violin" (42) where the non-musician does not. The professional violinist needs dexterity that most of us may not need, our brains are plastic and our brains respond by developing the areas that we need. Our individual brains are influenced by the languages we speak, the cultures we navigate, the sports we play, our unique interests and our neurologies. The professional violinist has a huge motor cortex and will likely be able to do finger dexterity tasks more efficiently and accurately than a peer without the same training, that peer's brain will develop to meet their own uniqueness. In the traditional curriculum, even though we are presenting students with presumably the same stimuli, the fixed nature of the curriculum is the polar opposite of variable. It expects the learner to be "average" and to engage the curriculum in one particular way.

The more science knows about the brain and how learning occurs, the more educators have to change the expectation that there is an average learner who will encounter curriculum and will respond in an average way. This is a paradigm shift for some educators who believe in the myth of an average learner. The fact is that students will come to the learning environment as they are. As teacher-activists, it is our responsibility to meet them in their humanity as they come. We can ensure that our curriculum is pliable and ready to flex to meet the variability that will exist within and between them (CAST 2010).

To be clear, variability is inclusive of disability, but variability does not only mean disability. Consistent with the social model of disability (Oliver and Barnes 2012), CAST believes that what makes something disabling is the context of the situation. A person with a print disability might not be disabled when watching a video but may become disabled if the video is in a language the viewer does not speak, requiring the person to read subtitles. All learners, regardless of the task, come to the learning environment with a range of strengths and weaknesses. In other environments or contexts, a learner may be more or less skilled. While the variability within and between learners may seem daunting, Meyer, Rose, and Gordon (2014) explain that brain science teaches us that there are three strategic networks involved in learning. Those three networks allow for educators to plan for most of the variability that exists within and between learners.

GUIDING PRINCIPLES OF UDL

Meyer, Rose, and Gordon (2014) argue that neuroscientific research demonstrates that learning happens in three broad areas of the brain: the area responsible for recognizing concepts or "the what of learning" (31), the area responsible for skills and strategies or the "how of learning" (31), and the area responsible for affect or "caring about and prioritizing" (CAST 2010), also known as the "why of learning" (Meyer, Rose, and Gordon 2014, 31). The recognition network refers to what information is presented for learning. The strategic learning network and the affective learning networks are somewhat similar. While the strategic network focuses on action and expression of knowledge, it also deals with the ability to plan and set goals for that expression. The affective network deals with self-regulation of emotion and motivation including, but not limited to, piquing interest and staying engaged in a learning opportunity (CAST 2010, 2018; Meyer, Rose, and Gordon 2014). In what follows next, we introduce how UDL attends to each learning network and the value it places on identifying curricular/assessment goals.

Deliver course content to students multi-modally. Providing for "multiple means of representation" helps to create students who know a lot and are "resourceful" (CAST 2018). CAST's UDL Guidelines (2018) offer suggestions that assist teachers in representing content with a variety of perceptual choices, options for learning language and symbols, and for comprehending content. Content should be represented in a variety of ways since few students will grasp the complexity of some of our content on the first pass. Since we are certain that all students learn differently, it stands to reason that they need information presented multiple times and in a variety of ways.

Provide students with license to demonstrate knowledge acquisition. CAST (2018) recommends that instructors plan for students to have a variety of options for physical response, for expression and communication, and for executive functions. Executive functioning occurs in the frontal lobe and is responsible for planning what learners want to know, tackling an assignment, determining where they are in the process of the task, and how to proceed. Expert learners need to develop the strategies, skills, and direction necessary to act on and express what they know. The traditional college student's frontal lobe has not developed fully (and will not stop developing) by the time they graduate from college (Sowell et al. 1999). This means that students need scaffolded instruction and guidance in setting goals to accomplish course assessments (CAST 2018). Students may need to hear how the instructor and their peers get through particularly dense readings or they might need strategies to set goals to get course readings or assessments done. They need agency for choosing the ways to express what they know. If allowed, students might be able to express and communicate learning and understanding of a discussion board question by recording their voice, making a video, posting a photo (with alt text for accessibility), or some other means of communication. Learning is enhanced through the use of multiple tools to create or compose their responses to assessment. Students need opportunities to become more fluent in the language of the discipline or the skills they are learning (e.g., video production or podcasting).

When thinking about action and expression, students can use or learn to use assistive technologies. In the ways curb cuts benefit a bicyclist, a mom pushing a stroller, or a person using a mobility device (for whom curb cuts were designed after the passage of the Americans with Disabilities Act in 1990), text-to-speech (TTS) is no longer an accommodation just for people with print disabilities. It is important to post accessible reading material on the class LMS and remind students of the option to listen to the course materials by downloading a TTS application on whatever device they use. This technology opens up options to listen to course content as they commute, or while they cook dinner, or whenever they can devote some time. Optimizing access to assistive technologies and tools will help SWD feel seen and if they so elect (SWD should never be put on the spot to be the disabled voice in the room), they can talk about their experiences with the technology, making the course richer for everyone.

Offer students multiple ways to engage. Expert learners have the "purpose and motivation" (CAST 2018) necessary to engage whatever learning opportunity they encounter. This means that the instructor plans for variability in students' interest, provides options for students to persist on the task, and provides choices to assist students in regulating their emotions. Whether we like it or not, we all experience emotions and have varying facility with the ways we talk about and manage those emotions. We are feeling creatures and every learning task we encounter causes us to feel something. Although the learning environment might appear neutral, student perceptions are at play as they are constantly appraising both how they feel and their level of arousal. How they perceive the course content or assessment tool makes students feel one way in the moment, evokes feelings about their previous experiences in similar situations, and how they feel about themselves through this lesson, assignment, and in their everyday lives. Students may love the assessment a teacher presents because the assignment fits the individual learner's strengths or they may hate it (public speaking courses, anyone?) because they feel threatened by the content or experience.

Whether a student feels positively or negatively about the learning opportunity either sets the student up for having many resources to persist to task completion or the opposite. Pekrun's (2006) control-value theory of achievement emotions demonstrates that those who have positive appraisals of their learning environment and are sufficiently activated in that environment can access many more resources (creativity, working memory, flexible thinking) than a student whose appraisal of the environment is negative and deactivates their level of arousal. When students feel threatened by the learning experience, their neurology engages the fight or flight response. Their ability to tap a variety of resources when under stress and strain is not the same as when the threat or barrier is removed. Given that one in three students report a mental health condition (LeViness, Bershad, and Gorman 2017) and evidence that anxiety among undergraduate students is rising (American College Health Association 2018), it becomes critically important to think about ways to assist students by supporting the development of their affective learning network.

The importance of identifying a goal in UDL. The most important aspect of a UDL approach to course design, lesson planning, and assessment development is an understanding of what the *goal* of the course, lesson, or assessment is (Meyer, Rose, and Gordon 2014). Some questions that can help uncover the goal of the experience are: what students should know (recognition network), do (strategic network), and care about (affective network) (CAST 2010)? CAST (2010) describes the next step after determining the goal of the experience (whether that assessment is designed to assess understanding in the moment, in the near future, or at the end of a learning unit), is to brainstorm all the ways that students can demonstrate that they have met that goal. As instructors plan, think of the barriers that students might encounter and work to reduce them. From there, instructors consider multiple methods and multiple materials that can be used to demonstrate learning. Instructors want to be sure that the assessment is "construct relevant" (Meyer, Rose, and Gordon 2014, 74; Rudner and Schafer 2002; UDL on Campus 2014), meaning that the assessment measures what it is designed to measure and not something else.

To identify whether the assessment has relevant constructs, the assessor needs to identify: what the assessment measures, which may require conducting a task analysis; what success on the assessment looks like; and what options are available for students to demonstrate that they have learned the material (Black and Moore 2019). Reflecting back to Allison's choice to include a word bank, the goal of the assessment was important in determining supports. If she wanted to access what students know about course vocabulary, she did need them to generate the words because that measures the construct irrelevant task of word retrieval and memory. If the goal of the assessment were to recall the vocabulary words, then a word bank may not have been the proper scaffold. In Allison's case, providing a word bank took the construct irrelevant tasks out of the assessment and did not affect its rigor. Allowing flexibility in how students demonstrate what they know provides a better sense of the efficacy of the instruction and the learner's acquisition of skill. It also allows students to appraise themselves in the moment more positively, creating a positive association with the learning task.

The next time students approach a similar task, they might appraise the environment differently. The UDL framework is not intended to "fix" learners. Students come to the learning environment the way they are and it is socially just to meet them there. When students are not learning, it is not the student's fault, it requires going back to the curriculum and making adjustments. The curriculum should not be so rigid that it cannot flex to meet the variability present in all learners.

Just as CCP and CSPs value and center students' culture, identity(ies), and experiences, UDL began by centering disability. As it evolved, Rose and Meyer (2005) recognized that the future of education is in the creation of a flexible curriculum, replete with the strategies and methods used to support SWD. Those are good teaching strategies for addressing the variability present in *every* learner. Using those strategies with everyone in the class removes the policing of disability and the ableist worry that disabled persons' accommodations puts the non-disabled person at a disadvantage. When those in power can move away from labeling others as deficient and policing accommodations, society moves toward dismantling ableism in the educational system. Until then, the current method where SWD must lower themselves (by identifying as deficient) to ask an institution of society for special dispensation to access it, reinforces ableism. It makes sense that disabled students do not want to self-identify, as those who do are often deemed as deficient, looked down upon, and viewed with suspicion (Fassett and Morella 2008; Nichols and Quaye 2009; Quinlan, Bates, and Angell 2012).

A weakness in UDL has been its move away from its focus on disability, which seems to coincide with multiple references to UDL in the seventh reauthorization of the Every Student Succeeds Act[2] (ESSA), which replaced No Child Left Behind in 2015. Principles of UDL are specifically mentioned in ESSA with regard to individual state plan assessments for all students; individual state innovative assessment systems; comprehensive literacy instruction; and state funding for technology supporting "rigorous learning experiences" (ESSA 2015). With its inclusion in ESSA, the infusion of UDL principles are mandated in the nation's K–12 public schools and has seemingly diverted the important disability focus that has historically driven UDL in favor of a focus on creating "expert learners" (CAST 2018). This positive outcome encourages all students to use their strengths to engage the world and models the notion that different learners use the tools and strategies that help them demonstrate their unique strengths. It creates a classroom that reflects the diversity of the human condition. However, the shift potentially decenters a focus on disability identity and disability cultural experiences (Dolmage 2017). Additionally, UDL does not explicitly acknowledge issues of power in its framework.

THE EXISTING NEED FOR CHANGE

In a study of students with learning disabilities in higher education, Quinlan, Bates, and Angell (2012) interviewed SWD. The participants perceived three kinds of accommodation: no accommodation, formal/legal accommodation, and accommodation for all (Quinlan, Bates, and Angell 2012). The current deficit model of accommodation does nothing to ameliorate the sense of dehumanization that students with approved disability accommodations feel when they do not receive them. Institutional departments that serve students with disabilities are growing as more SWD are seeking higher education.

Often underfunded (Nichols and Quaye 2009), the growth these departments are currently experiencing mean fewer spaces and resources to meet the needs of students seeking such supports.

Mark: I was recently involved in a professional learning community focused on online learning and pedagogy. During these sessions, a conversation occurred about a classroom policy banning all cell phones and communication devices/technologies, leaving it up to the discretion of the professor whether or not students can use these technologies. We were discussing how we could effect change because the policy as written does not account for students with emotional and learning needs or disabilities. During this discussion, the disability coordinator disclosed how a student with a sensory impairment needed to use a recording device and digital text to access a course. This student received institutional approval to use a smartphone to record lectures and to access the readings via formal disability accommodations. The student complied with requirements to share the notice of approved disability accommodation with the professor per the College's policy. The professor has a policy banning all communication devices from the classroom and used this policy as rationale to bar this student from gaining access to the class, including its materials and discussions. The student disclosed their embarrassment and started crying. I am not sure what happened to the student, but this really upset me! I do not understand how any post-secondary institution could have a policy like this and how a professor can reject a students' (disability) identity and deny them access to the course.

Allison: Sadly, I wish I was more surprised. Recently, I was approached by faculty at a university seeking help with a problem involving a student with a severe speech production issue improved by the use of a text to speech augmentative and alternative communication device. The student's major requires an oral communication class and the concern is how best to accommodate the student within the general education guidelines for oral communication. The faculty member pointed out that the student can communicate verbally (despite the magnitude of the expressive language problem) and that the assistive tech solution is not documented as a modification, even though the student used it previously throughout high school. In my reply, I indicated that this was not a big problem. The student should be allowed to use whatever support is necessary for the student to demonstrate mastery of the content. Removing the concern about the ability to be understood will instill confidence in the student and the student can focus on the other aspects of oral communication being assessed. Additionally, the audience will learn that some speakers use assistive technology. They will learn to listen in a new way. All of them will learn that disability is a part of life and will be presented with an opportunity to gain an appreciation for different ways of communicating. I wonder if the faculty are concerned that if one student uses a voice output device, everyone will want to use one. Imagine the creativity that could be generated by that situation! Picture the beauty in students attempting to communicate differently and in coming to terms with their ability privilege. I'm having a hard time recognizing the downside of that argument!

In the scenario above, the faculty that approached Allison highlights a common concern that exist when disability technologies, supports, or accommodations are viewed as threatening to the non-disabled community. Moore (2019a) encourages a change in the narrative surrounding these supports and reframes them as a "regulation tool" necessary for meeting a goal. This approach rejects viewing supports with suspicion, akin to cheating, labeling them a crutch or something else that needs policing by authorities. At the CAST fifth annual UDL symposium, to emphasize the point that supports should be *decriminalized*, Moore (2019b) asked the audience to list the supports they need to wake up in the morning. After prompting the audience to think about what they need to wake up for the day, Moore asked if anyone just woke up naturally. When a woman identified that her internal alarm was sufficient, Moore asked her if she ever set an alarm. The woman indicated that she did. Moore joked about the alarm being *a crutch* which helped the audience see how some supports and accommodations can be viewed as such. Like the student above, the woman could wake up on her own but sometimes needed a device to assist, in case something unforeseen occurred. Moore continued polling the audience for other supports necessary for waking up: quiet, time, a shower, and coffee. While many of us can wake up and function without coffee does not mean that we are at our best when we do. The same is true for the student who can speak but uses an assistive device; the amount of energy expended just to be understood is alleviated and presents opportunities for deeper engagement in the classroom, in course material, and in their learning.

Envisioning a Critical Universal Design for Learning Framework

When courses and assessments are designed with UDL at their centers, UDL has the potential to bring together an educator's commitment to CCP and CSP to be transformative for all learners. Researchers (Kieran and Anderson 2018; Ralabate and Lord Nelson 2017) argue that when principles of culturally sustaining pedagogy (high expectations for all, cultural competence, sociopolitical awareness, and classroom as a community) are overlaid on a course developed on the principles of UDL even more students benefit. Like CCP and CSP, UDL is a paradigm shift, which for some educators means having to set aside old notions of teaching and learning. For those educators striving to enact CCP and CSP, it may be an easier shift because these philosophies and practices commit to similar or parallel beliefs. We must recognize that SWD have been silenced and marginalized in the way we traditionally assess students and design our courses, and they are shouldering the burden. If we are going to have a critical inclusive education, we need to think about who has the power to grant and ultimately implement accommodations. If we equalize who gets the accommodation, all students will be able to express themselves the best way that meets their learning, identity, and cultural needs. Disability is a part of a person's culture and identity; the denial of access accommodations essentially strips agency from and dehumanizes them. We believe an integrated focus on disability, culture, and power interactions can work to decenter the "isms" that are perpetuated in a society focused on the mythical norm.

Therefore, we propose a Critical Universal Design for Learning (CUDL) framework that builds the humanity we want to see in our classrooms and world. Specifically, a CUDL framework attends to the following (neither a comprehensive nor exhaustive list of) equitable pedagogical principles:

- Acknowledge the centrality of power to the teaching-learning and assessment processes and consistently work to (re)negotiate power dynamics proactively. We need to examine how power is deployed and to what end, and how power influences the teaching and learning processes, in which assessment is a part of these processes. Specifically, we need to engage in a critical praxis of: 1) decentering authority away from the instructor; 2) empowering students as consumers and producers of knowledge; and 3) modeling a dialogic and democratic-based classroom practices (see hooks 1994; Rudick, Golsan, and Cheesewright 2018; Shor 1996).
- Re-frame supports: remove thinking about accommodations from a deficit mode and move toward providing students with what they need to be their best. Empowering and educating students means that we recognize that learning is as unique as one's fingerprints and all students have access to strategies that are good for all learners (see Dalai Lama Center for Peace and Education 2017; Moore 2019a; and Project Implicit 2011).
- Provide options for how students receive knowledge, including choices for self-expression, self-assessment, and to connect and grow emotionally. This involves understanding the goal of the assessment and brainstorming ways students can best demonstrate that goal. (See appendix and specific references for CAST 2018; Dweck 2006; Kieran and Anderson 2018;

Meyer, Rose, and Gordon 2014; Moore 2019b; Novak 2016; Ralabate and Lord Nelson 2017; Tobin and Behling 2018)

- Allow students to express knowledge and demonstrate learning in ways that support development of their individual strengths and teach them to leverage those strengths to make a positive impact (see resources immediately above).
- Continuously adapt and evolve course design and assessments to meet the various learning needs of all students (see Fassett and Warren 2007).
- Engage students in critical and mutual learning through problem posing using scaffolded activities and assessments. This requires a proactive and iterative process of vulnerability, reflection, action and revision, and openness to make change (see Shor 1996; Fassett and Warren 2007; Tobin and Behling 2018).

UDL underscores the importance of removing barriers. A CUDL takes this a step further to examine the hidden curriculum (Fassett and Warren 2007) for barriers students may encounter in the course, lesson, or assessment. Whose voices, values, and perspectives are privileged in the course/assessment and which are silenced? What skills and abilities are privileged by assessing student learning in a particular way, and in what ways are the assessments measuring disability or other construct irrelevant variables? Questions that can help uncover what barriers are present are:

- What is being said and taught which may reinforce particular cultural values or knowledge? (Paris 2012)
- What are existing dis/connections of pedagogical approaches to social change (critical praxis)? (See Fassett and Warren 2007; Tobin and Behling 2018)

After barriers are identified, a traditional UDL approach requires brainstorming all the ways that students can act to express knowledge acquisition, which also involves removal of the barriers that could exist. CUDL takes this a step further to recognize and interrogate various power dynamics and processes that exist, and how assessments may reinforce a banking method of education (Freire, 2000). In a CUDL framework, it is important to ensure that assessments are fairly constructed and measure only "construct relevant" (Meyer, Rose, and Gordon 2014, 74) variables.

For us, ensuring that we know what we are measuring allows us to create (more) socially just assessments. Ensuring students have options and multiple pathways to demonstrate that they have mastered the learning objective is one way we work toward grading justice. We believe that we must be attentive

Mobilizing a Critical Universal Design for Learning Framework   79

to the goals of our formative assessments and activities that we do in class to measure what students know, so that we can plan lessons and activities to support knowledge acquisition. Likewise, we must pay equal attention to the creation and implementation of any summative assessment which we conduct to measure student growth and performance. For social justice, it is imperative to solicit student feedback and to involve students in the process of developing assessment, as they are the people implicated in the assessments and can provide great insights into the grading practices (Black and Moore 2019; CAST 2018; Fassett and Warren 2007; Meyer, Rose, and Gordon 2014; Novak 2016; Ralabate and Lord Nelson 2017; Shor 1996; Tobin and Behling 2018).

While it is preferable to use the CUDL framework to design a course and its related assessments from the inception of the program or course, the reality is that UDL on its own can feel like "rocket science" (University of Minnesota 2015) even though it is not. We admit that implementing CUDL is not easy. It is definitely more work on the front end of course design. It is a process which requires a great deal of thinking about the goals of the activities (assessments) that are planned. Once the goal is understood, it requires brainstorming all the ways that students can show that they have mastered the skill and then thinking of (and reducing) barriers that may arise. Once most of the front end work is done, CUDL involves proactive and reflexive thinking that allows for continuous improvement based on feedback received from students, evaluation of student progress, and teacher insights. In appreciation of your commitment to take on this task, we have compiled some resources that can assist educators willing to accept this transformative teaching challenge in Appendix A.

If it is impossible or undesirable to design a course from scratch, Tobin and Behling (2018) offer instructors a way to begin implementing aspects of CUDL using an additive model. This approach to CUDL (adding one new universally designed element each time we teach a class) is a manageable way to infuse CUDL into one's (critical) pedagogy with less overwhelm. The plus-one practice aligns with the reflexivity inherent in the philosophies of CCP and CSP. In this way, CUDL is part of the continuous, iterative process that CCP and CSP calls for; it is "critical" as a stand-alone thing-to-do, but it becomes fully meaningful when integrated and interconnected in an overall philosophy that centers everything around all students.

CONCLUSION

CUDL is a pedagogy which draws upon CCP, CSP, and UDL and can offer meaningful and transformative educational practices for *all* students.

Together, the three practices reject a deficit orientation to human learners, replacing it with a strengths-based approach to education and human development. Through an iterative process, CUDL provides greater opportunities for all learners (students and educators) to critically examine and reflect on mundane moments and the identities, relationships, and structures (re)produced with/through communication in such moments.

We would be remiss if we did not trouble the notion of "universal." For us, universal means "all" and while UDL can and does meet the needs of many students, some K–12 students are glaringly absent from the conversation. Typically, this is because their disabilities are severe enough that they are identified for special education supports and services before they reach the age of compulsory schooling. UDL is implemented in many general education classrooms and students with intellectual and developmental disabilities usually never make it to general education classrooms. It is important to note that UDL can and does work well with these students in special education environments and in the general classroom, if they make it there and are included.

It is also important to point out that UDL's goal to make "expert learners" is in itself imperfect. Even though UDL can be easily adapted to include cultural diversity, a look at the CAST (2018) graphic organizer leaves it out, or at least appears to prefer individuality over collectivity. The same worksheet appears to leave out the cultural variance that students of color bring to enriched learning environments. What is expert learning for one person might not be the same kind of expertise another person needs.

Allison: Teaching requires a growth mindset (Dweck 2006). As much as it might seem that someone is naturally a good teacher (and maybe they start out that way), but all teachers get better though those moments of failure and trying again. As I have come to understand the principles of UDL, I recognize that the student I was thinking about was not the only student in the room who needed scaffolds for learning: SWD (identified and not), honors students, international students and those for whom English is not a first language were enrolled in the course. Additionally, the course is required and has a reputation for being hard. While I thought about how students might be feeling about some aspects of the course (especially the group work), and I engaged them in some of those ways, I did not pay as much attention, as I do now, to the affective learning network. Had I been further down the road in my understanding of UDL, I might have integrated more praise for students based on their effort and taught them more about growth mindset (Dweck 2006). I could have done more work to teach students to manage the emotional challenges this upper division course brings. The weekly reflections I assigned for students did not do the work I hoped they would. In the future, I can provide scaffolds to assist students who struggled with the reflections to improve in this area. While I did scaffold how-to information that might have been useful for students (how to manage difficult readings), and I created (limited) options for reflection, I could have introduced more rubrics and checklists that could support growth in the affective learning network.

Mark: When I was listening to Allison's experience in this particular class, I appreciated how thoughtful she was in thinking through her actions and thought process, and wanted to make sure that I listened with love (Calafell 2007; Kress and Frazier-Booth 2016), while encouraging her to think through how the word bank scaffold could be appropriate for all adult learners. Our conversation caused me to reflect on my own pedagogy of care. Sometimes we, as instructors, even if we are experienced pedagogues, struggle with implementing accommodations and scaffolds to meet the various learning needs of students, while also questioning whether or not rigor is lost (Wiant Cummings 2014). Additionally, our conversation highlighted the importance of having a network of mutual mentors where we listen, understand, support, and encourage each other to be reflexive in our teaching and interactions with others (Calafell 2007; Herakova and Congdon 2018; Yun, Baldi, and Sorcinelli 2016). I know that I have relied on you for support throughout the years and knew that your background and how you listened with love really helped me develop my own pedagogy, research, and relationships with students.

Throughout this chapter, our conversation represents some ways reflection and reflexivity can occur. We are human, feeling people, and we are constantly appraising how we feel about where we are and assessing our states of arousal. Although this may occur consciously or subconsciously, it is happening. In the video series embedded in Meyer, Rose, and Gordon's (2014) book, CAST research scientist Rappolt-Schlichtmann describes emotion and cognition as "coregulated" (33), meaning that thinking and learning is at once emotional and cognitive. Individually, Allison reflected on her problem. If she had felt overwhelmed by the situation, she may have felt alone and those feelings could prevent her from remembering Mark as a resource. As Mark thought through Allison's issue, thoughts and feelings caused him to reflect. Together, we were able to collaborate and plot out a course of action. We want to affirm the importance of developing a community of practice or what UDL describes as a professional learning community (PLC). A PLC is a community of professionals who are committed to sharing and using resources and information about a shared interest area to improve their own teaching and their students learning (Novak 2016; Ralabate and Lord Nelson 2017). We cannot stress the importance of having a community of practitioners who are available to listen and process the implications of pedagogical decisions enough. We offer ourselves to you, please reach out to us as part of your network.

It is important to emphasize that *intention* matters. If the *intent* to use CUDL is not focused on creating better learning opportunities for students and is merely used to ward off complaints about accessibility, the efficacy of the framework and its connection to CCP and CSP will fail because UDL, CCP, and CSP value the diversity that humans bring to the creation and sustainability of knowledge. They see culture as central to learning and not merely an accompaniment (Fassett and Warren 2007). Diversity and variation in learners and learning styles engage and "empower students intellectually, socially, emotionally, and politically by using cultural referents to impart knowledge, skills, and attitudes" (Ladson-Billings 2001, 17–18). CUDL, CCP, and CSP see variability and diversity that students bring to the world as enriching to the global community and view their voices as necessary to expand from a society whose goals privilege homogeneity to that of a pluralistic and equitable society (Paris 2012), which values the humanity of all.

NOTES

1. Throughout this chapter, the terms assignment and assessment will be used interchangeably. In our view, anything we ask students to produce is designed to assess student understanding and should be used to constantly adjust instruction in response to student responses (CAST 2010; Meyer, Rose, and Gordon 2014; National Center on Universal Design for Learning 2010).

2. The ESSA retains the annual standardized testing requirements of NCLB but shifts the law's federal accountability provisions to states. States and school districts have significantly more control in determining curriculum standards and accountability measures. Additionally, ESSA sets new mandates on expectations and requirements for students with disabilities. Most students with disabilities will be required to take the same assessments and will be held to the same standards as other students, except those with significant cognitive disabilities (Korte 2015; Lee 2019).

REFERENCES

American College Health Association. 2018. *American College Health Association— National College Health Assessment II: Reference Group Undergraduates Executive Summary Fall 2017.* Hanover, MD: American College Health Association.

Asante, Molefi Kete. 1991. "The Afrocentric Idea in Education." *Journal of Negro Education* 60 (2): 170–180. https://doi.org/10.2307/2295608.

Au, Kathryn. 2009. "Isn't Culturally Responsive Instruction Just Good Teaching?" *Social Education* 73 (4): 179–183.

Bartolomé, Lilia I. 2004. "Critical Pedagogy and Teacher Education: Radicalizing Prospective Teachers." *Teacher Education Quarterly* 31 (1): 97–122. https://www.jstor.org/stable/23478420.

Biklen, Douglas. 1990. "Communication Unbound: Autism and Praxis." *Harvard Educational Review* 60 (3): 291–314. https://doi.org/10.1080/21548331.1992.11705407.

Biklen, Douglas, and Jamie Burke. 2006. "Presuming Competence." *Equity and Excellence in Education 39*, 166-175. https://doi.org/10.1080/10665680500540376.

Black, Jodie, and Eric J. Moore. 2019. *UDL Navigators in Higher Education: A Field Guide.* Wakefield, MA: CAST Professional.

Bland, Carole J., Taylor, Anne L., Shollen, S. Lynn, Weber-Main, Anne Marie, and Patricia A. Mulcahy. 2009. *Faculty Success Through Mentoring: A Guide for Mentors, Mentees, and Leaders.* Lanham, MD: Rowman & Littlefield.

Brenneise, Allison D. 2020. "Presuming Competence: Troubling the Ideal Student." *Communication Education.* http://www.doi.org/10.1080/03634523.2020.1770307.

Brenneise, Allison D. 2019. "Expanding Mediated Communication for Inclusivity." In *Mediated Critical Communication Pedagogy*, edited by Ahmet Atay and Deanna L. Fassett. Lanham, MD: Lexington Books.

Burbaud, Pierre, Degreze, Philippe, Lafon, Philippe, Franconi, Jean-Michel, Bouligand, Bertrand, Bioulac, Bernard H., Caillé, J.M., and M. Allard. 1995. "Lateralization of Prefrontal Activation During Internal Mental Calculation: A Functional Magnetic Resonance Imaging Study." *Journal of Neurophysiology* 74 (5): 2194–2200. https://doi.org/10.1152/jn.1995.74.5.2194.

Calafell, Bernadette Marie. 2007. "Mentoring and Love: An Open Letter." *Cultural Studies ↔ Critical Methodologies* 7 (4): 425–441. https://doi.org/10.1177/1532708607305123.

CAST. (n.d.) Home. [YouTube Channel]. https://www.youtube.com/user/UDLCAST/featured.

CAST. 2010. "UDL at a Glance." YouTube Video, 4:36. January 6, 2010. https://www.youtube.com/watch?v=bDvKnY0g6e4&feature=youtu.be.

CAST. 2018. "Universal Design for Learning Guidelines Version 2.2." [Graphic Organizer]. Wakefield, MA: Author. http://udlguidelines.cast.org/.

Cawthon, Stephanie W., and Emma V. Cole. 2010. "Postsecondary Students Who Have a Learning Disability: Student Perspectives on Accommodations Access and Obstacles." *Journal of Postsecondary Education and Disability* 23 (2): 112–128.

Collier, Maryjane, and Cleophas Muneri. 2016. "A Call for Critical Reflexivity: Reflections on Research with Nongovernmental and Nonprofit Organizations in Zimbabwe and Kenya." *Western Journal of Communication* 80 (5): 638–658. https://doi.org/10.1080/10570314.2016.1187762.

Colorado State University. n.d. "From Theory to Practice: UDL "Quick Tips." https://accessproject.colostate.edu/udl/documents/udl_quick_tips.pdf.

Cornett-DeVito, Myrna M. and David W. Worley. 2005. "A Front Row Seat: A Phenomenological Investigation of Learning Disabilities." *Communication Education* 54 (4): 312–333. https://doi.org/10.1080/03634520500442178.

Dalai Lama Center for Peace and Education. 2017. "The Sweeper Van by Shelley Moore." YouTube Video, 29:25. March 13, 2017. https://youtu.be/Yjjz8iHj5hY.

Dolmage, Jay T. 2017. *Academic Ableism: Disability and Higher Education.* Ann Arbor: University of Michigan Press.

Dweck, Carol S. 2006. *Mindset: The New Psychology of Success.* New York: Random House.

Ellis, Carolyn. 2002. "Being Real: Moving Inward Toward Social Change." *International Journal of Qualitative Studies in Education* 15 (4): 399–406. https://doi .org/10.1080/09518390210145453.

ESSA. 2015. Every Student Succeeds Act of 2015, Pub. L. No. 114-95 § 114 Stat. 1177.

Fassett, Deanna L., and Dana L. Morella. 2008. "Remaking (the) Discipline: Marking the Performative Accomplishment of (Dis)Ability." *Text and Performance Quarterly* 28 (1–2): 139–156. https://doi.org/10.1080/10462930701754390.

Fassett, Deanna L., and John T. Warren. 2007. *Critical Communication Pedagogy.* Thousand Oaks, CA: Sage.

Five Moore Minutes. (n.d.) Home. [YouTube Channel]. https://www.youtube.com/ channel/UCU-GCW3-EwNxcbJEFKKaABw.

Freire, Paulo. 2000. *Pedagogy of the Oppressed, 30th Anniversary Edition.* New York: Continuum.

Gay, Geneva. 2010. *Culturally Responsive Teaching: Theory, Research, and Practice.* (2nd ed.) New York: Teachers College Press.

Godden, Duncan R., and Alan D. Baddeley. 1975. "Context-Dependent Memory in Two Natural Environments: On Land and Underwater." *British Journal of Psychology* 66 (3): 325–331. https://doi.org/10.1111/j.2044-8295.1975.tb01468.x.

Goldstein, E. Bruce. 2011. "Matching Conditions of Encoding and Retrieval. In *Cognitive Psychology: Mind, Research, and Everyday Experience* (3rd ed.), edited by E. Bruce Goldstein, 183–186. Belmont, CA: Wadsworth Cengage Learning.

Greenbaum, Beth, Graham, Steve, and William Scales. 1995. "Adults with Learning Disabilities: Educational and Social Experiences During College." *Exceptional Children* 61 (5): 460-71. https://doi.org/10.1177/001440299506100505.

Herakova, Liliana (Lily), and Mark Congdon, Jr. 2018. "Let Your Self In: Mentoring from/on the Margins of Academia in the Millennial Context." In *Millennial Culture and Communication Pedagogies: Narratives from the Classroom and Higher Education,* edited by Ahmet Atay and Mary Z. Ashlock, 21–42. Lanham, MD: Lexington Books.

hooks, bell. 1994. *Teaching to Transgress: Education as the Practice of Freedom.* New York: Routledge.

Janiga, Sandra J., and Virginia Costenbader. 2002. "The Transition from High School to Postsecondary Education for Students with Learning Disabilities: A Survey of College Coordinators." *Journal of Learning Disabilities* 35 (5): 462–468. https:// doi.org/10.1177/00222194020350050601.

Kieran, Laura, and Christine Anderson. 2018. "Connecting Universal Design for Learning with Culturally Responsive Teaching." *Education and Urban Society.* https://doi.org/10.1177/0013124518785012.

Korte, Gregory. 2015. "The Every Student Succeeds Act vs. No Child Left Behind: What's changed?" *USA Today.* December 10, 2015. https://www.usatoday.com/story/news/politics/2015/12/10/every-student-succeeds-act-vs-no-child-left-behind-whats-changed/77088780/.

Kress, Tricia M., and Kimberly J. Frazier-Booth. 2016. "Listening for the Echoes: Radical Listening as Educator-Activist Praxis." *International Journal of Critical Pedagogy* 7 (3): 99–118. http://libjournal.uncg.edu/ijcp/article/view/1321.

Kurth, Noelle, and Daryl Mellard. 2006. "Student Perceptions of the Accommodation Process in Postsecondary Education." *The Journal of Postsecondary Education and Disability* 19 (1): 71–84.

Ladson-Billings, Gloria. 1994. *The Dreamkeepers: Successful Teachers of African American Children.* San Francisco, CA: Jossey-Bass.

Ladson-Billings, Gloria. 1995. "Toward a Theory of Culturally Relevant Pedagogy." *American Educational Research Journal* 32 (3): 465–491. https://doi.org/10.3102/00028312032003465.

Ladson-Billings, Gloria. 2001. *Crossing over to Canaan: The Journey of New Teachers in Diverse Classrooms.* Hoboken, NJ: John Wiley & Sons.

Lee, Andrew. 2019. "Every Student Succeeds Act (ESSA): What You Need to Know." *Understood.* October 18. 2019. https://www.understood.org/en/school-learning/your-childs-rights/basics-about-childs-rights/every-student-succeeds-act-essa-what-you-need-to-know.

LeViness, Peter, Bershad, Carolyn, and Kim Gorman. 2017. *The Association for University and College Counseling Center Directors Annual Survey.* https://www.aucccd.org/assets/documents/Governance/2017%20aucccd%20survey-public-apr26.pdf.

Meyer, Anne, Rose, David H., and David Gordon. 2014. *Universal Design for Learning: Theory and Practice.* Wakefield, MA: National Center on Universal Design for Learning. http://udltheorypractice.cast.org.

Moore, Shelley. [FiveMooreMinutes]. 2019a. "Decriminalizing Supports: Knowing "When" We Need Support, Not "If". YouTube Video, 6:28. March 5, 2019. https://www.youtube.com/watch?v=LyqFcmUxHAw.

Moore, Shelley. 2019b. "Supporting Inclusive Education with UDL." Keynote presented at the 5th annual CAST symposium. Cambridge, MA.

Murray, Christopher, Flannery, Brigid K., and Carol Wren. 2008. "University Staff Members' Attitudes and Knowledge About Learning Disabilities and Disability Support Services." *Journal of Postsecondary Education and Disability* 21 (2): 73–90.

National Center on Accessible Materials. (n.d.). Home. [YouTube Channel]. https://www.youtube.com/channel/UC430oh5VnS3pdBJ89ux2bZQ.

National Center on Universal Design for Learning. (n.d.). Home. [YouTube Channel]. https://www.youtube.com/channel/UCk-BxeAygzqGabYBs1TPIHQ.

National Center on Universal Design for Learning at CAST. (n.d.) "UDL Center" [Blog]. https://medium.com/@udlcenter.

National Center on Universal Design for Learning. 2010. "UDL: Principles and Practice." YouTube Video, 6:35. March 17, 2010. https://www.youtube.com/watch?v=pGLTJw0GSxk.

Nichols, Andrew H., and Stephen J. Quaye. 2009. "Beyond Accommodation: Removing Barriers to Academic and Social Engagement for Students with Disabilities." In *Student Engagement in Higher Education: Theoretical Perspectives and Practical Approaches for Diverse Populations,* edited Shaun R. Harper and Stephen John Quaye, 39–60. New York: Routledge.

Novak, Katie. 2016. *UDL Now! A Teacher's Guide to Applying Universal Design for Learning in Today's Classrooms.* Wakefield, MA: CAST Professional.

Oliver, Michael, and Colin Barnes. 2012. *The New Politics of Disablement.* Basingstroke, UK: Palgrave Macmillan.

Paris, Django. 2012. "Culturally Sustaining Pedagogy: A Needed Change in Stance, Terminology, and Practice." *Educational Researcher* 41 (3): 93–97. https://doi.org/10.3102/0013189X12441244.

Pekrun, Reinhard. 2006. "Control-Value Theory of Achievement Emotions: Assumptions, Corollaries, and Implications for Educational Research and Practice." *Educational Psychology Review* 18 (4): 315–341. https://doi.org/10.1007/s10648-006-9029-9.

Project Implicit. 2011. *Take a Test.* https://implicit.harvard.edu/implicit/takeatest.html.

Quinlan, Margaret M., Bates, Benjamin R., and Maureen E. Angell. 2012. "'What Can I Do to Help?': Postsecondary Students with Learning Disabilities Perception of Instructors' Classroom Accommodations." *Journal of Research in Special Education Needs* 12 (4): 224–233. https://doi.org/10.1111/j.1471-3802.2011.01225.x.

Ralabate, Patti Kelly, and Loui Lord Nelson. 2017. *Culturally Responsive Design for English Learners: The UDL Approach.* Wakefield, MA: CAST, Inc.

Rose, David H., and Anne Meyer. 2002. *Teaching Every Student in the Digital Age: Universal Design for Learning.* Alexandria, VA: Association for Supervision and Curriculum Development.

Rose, David H., and Anne Meyer. 2005. "The Future is in the Margins: The Role of Technology and Disability in Educational Reform." In *The Universally Designed Classroom: Accessible Curriculum and Digital Tech,* edited by David H. Rose, Anne Meyer, and Chuck Hitchcock, 13–36. Cambridge, MA: Harvard Education Press.

Rudick, C. Kyle, Golsan, Kathryn B., and Kyle Cheesewright. 2018. *Teaching from the Heart: Critical Communication Pedagogy in the Communication Classroom.* San Diego, CA: Cognella.

Rudner, Lawrence, and William D. Shafer, eds. 2002. *What Teachers Need to Know About Assessment.* Washington, DC: National Education Association.

Shor, Ira. 1996. *When Students Have Power: Negotiating Authority in a Critical Pedagogy.* Chicago, IL: University of Chicago Press.

Shor, Ira, and Paulo Freire. 1987. *A Pedagogy for Liberation: Dialogues on Transforming Education.* Westport, CT: Bergin & Garvey Publishers, Inc.

Siebers, Tobin Anthony. 2008. *Disability Theory.* Ann Arbor, MI: University of Michigan Press.

Sowell, Elizabeth R., Thompson, Paul M., Holmes, Colin J., Jernigan, Terry L., and Arthur W. Toga. 1999. "In Vivo Evidence for Post-Adolescent Brain Maturation in Frontal and Striatal Regions." *Nature Neuroscience* 2 (10): 859–861.

Stage, Frances K., and Nancy V. Milne. 1996. "Invisible Scholars: Students with Learning Disabilities." *Journal of Higher Education* 67 (4): 426–445. https://doi .org/10.1080/00221546.1996.11780268.

Tobin, Thomas J., and Kirsten T. Behling. 2018. *Reach Everyone, Teach Everyone: Universal Design for Learning in Higher Education*. Morgantown: West Virginia University Press.

UDL on Campus. (n.d.). Home. [YouTube Channel]. https://www.youtube.com/ channel/UCJxjhBZnKoSuTHn7wGowezQ/videos.

UDL on Campus. 2014. "UDL and Assessment: An Introduction to UDL and Assessment." YouTube Video, 3:09. June 25, 2014. https://www.youtube.com/ watch?v=AzRsqPqGlPw.

UDL-IRN. 2011. "UDL in the Instructional Process. Version 1.0." Lawrence, KS: UDL-IRN. https://udl-irn.org/wp-content/uploads/2018/01/Instructional-Process .pdf.

University of Minnesota [Learning4All]. 2015. "What is Universal Design for Learning?" Tim Kamenar. YouTube Video, 9:14. February 10, 2015. https://www.you tube.com/watch?v=RDn0VEii7s0.

Wiant Cummins, Molly. 2014. "Communicating Care: A Critical Communication Pedagogy of Care in the University Classroom." PhD diss., Southern Illinois University Carbondale.

Villegas, Ana Maria, and Tamara Lucas. 2002. *Educating Culturally Responsive Teachers: A Coherent Approach*. New York, NY: State Univ. of New York.

Yun, Jung H., Baldi, Brian, and Mary Deane Sorcinelli. 2016. "Mutual Mentoring for Early-Career and Underrepresented Faculty: Model, Research, and Practice." *Innovative Higher Education* 41 (5): 441-451. https://doi.org/10.1007/s10755-016 -9359-6.

APPENDIX A: UDL RESOURCES

UDL in Higher Education

Websites

- UDL on Campus: Universal Design for Learning in Higher Education
  - http://udloncampus.cast.org/
- UDL- Universe: A Comprehensive Faculty Development Guide
  - https://enact.sonoma.edu/c.php?g=789377&p=5650604
- CAST—cast.org
- The Center for Universal Design in Education: Applications if UD in Postsecondary Education

88   *Allison D. Brenneise and Mark Congdon, Jr.*

- ○ https://www.washington.edu/doit/programs/center-universal-design -education/applications-universal-design-postsecondary-education

Books

Black, Jodie, and Eric Moore. 2019. *UDL Navigators in Higher Education: A Field Guide.* Wakefield, MA: CAST Professional.

Novak, Katie. 2016. *UDL Now! A Teacher's Guide to Applying Universal Design for Learning in Today's Classrooms.* Wakefield, MA: CAST Professional.

Ralabate, Patti Kelly, and Loui Lord Nelson. 2017. *Culturally Responsive Design for English Learners: The UDL Approach.* Wakefield, MA: CAST, Inc.

Tobin, Thomas J., and Kirsten T. Behling. 2018. *Reach Everyone, Teach Everyone: Universal Design for Learning in Higher Education.* Morgantown: West Virginia University Press.

CAST

Free Resources

E-Book and Other Learning Tools

Meyer, Rose, and Gordon (2014) Universal Design for Learning: Theory and practice (http://udltheorypractice.cast.org)

Create one account at this link and receive access to the book and five other free Learning Tools (UDL Book Builder, UDL Curriculum Self-Check, UDL Exchange, UDL Journal, UDL Studio)

Websites

- UDL Guidelines
  - ○ http://udlguidelines.cast.org/
- UDL Center
  - ○ https://medium.com/udl-center

Handouts

- UDL Quick Tips https://accessproject.colostate.edu/udl/documents/udl_quick_ tips.pdf
- UDL Instructional Planning Process
  - ○ https://udl-irn.org/wp-content/uploads/2018/01/Instructional-Process.pdf

YouTube Channels

- CAST.org
  - ○ https://www.youtube.com/channel/UCRcOOY96svErLGmrk-UfsoQ
  - ○ Highlights

Mobilizing a Critical Universal Design for Learning Framework

- UDL at a glance
- UDL Principles and Practice
- Five Moore Minutes
  - https://www.youtube.com/channel/UCU-GCW3-EwNxcbJEFKKaABw
  - Highlights
    - Decriminalizing Supports: Knowing "WHEN" we need support, not "IF"
    - Shelley Moore: Transforming Inclusive Education
- National Center on Universal Design for Learning
  - https://www.youtube.com/channel/UCk-BxeAygzqGabYBs1TPIHQ
  - Highlights
    - UDL Principles and Practice
    - Acknowledging Learner Variability
- National Center on Accessible Materials
  - https://www.youtube.com/channel/UC43Ooh5VnS3pdBJ89ux2bZQ
- UDL on Campus
  - https://www.youtube.com/channel/UCJxjhBZnKoSuTHn7wGowezQ/videos
  - Highlights
    - UDL in Higher Education
    - UDL and Assessment: An Introduction to UDL and Assessment

Chapter Three

Honoring Vivencias

A Borderlands Approach to Higher Education Pedagogy Justice

Leandra H. Hernández and
Sarah De Los Santos Upton

We honor the *vivencias* (lived realities) of our students.

As Chicana feminist profesoras at a borderlands Hispanic Serving Institution and at an open admissions institution with non-traditional students (older students, parents, full-time employees, service members, and veterans), we have had the privilege of working with students from a wide range of disadvantaged populations in terms of age, employment status, class status, race/ethnicity, and languages spoken. Through our experiences in these contexts, we recognize that our students are often facing bigger issues than what can be measured on a multiple choice exam or in a 3-page essay, for example. Our students are working full time, trying to provide for families while completing coursework; they are deployed, literally at war while working to simultaneously complete their degrees and take care of their mental, emotional, and physical health; they are separated from their families, praying that their DACA (Deferred Action for Childhood Arrivals) status will last until graduation and that their families are safe during their absence because of deployments and military missions. Our student populations are undoubtedly "non-traditional" in every sense, which necessitates an equitable, empathetic, and intersectional approach to pedagogy. We therefore approach course construction, grading, and student progress assessment by questioning how we can honor the complex vivencias, or lived realities of our students (Trinidad Galván 2015). How can our course assignments, and the ways in which we evaluate them, equip our students with tools for moving through the world, given their unique life circumstances?

Drawing from the conocimiento of our borderland subjectivities, we seek to challenge objectivist, Western systems of knowledge in favor of border/transformative pedagogies (Elenes 2010). We understand that "Assessment, in the form of tests and examinations, is a powerful activity which shapes how societies, groups, and individuals understand themselves" and that while it is often presented as objective and neutral, grading is actually influenced by culture and is heavily value-laden (Stobart 2008, 1). Cultural influences that shape the construction of assignments, the evaluation of students' competencies, and the assessment of college courses in larger contexts include the privileging of objectivist, Western systems of knowledge; rigid and formulaic assignments that often offer little room for creativity or room for faculty members to be flexible in consideration of students' everyday life struggles and circumstances; and course learning outcomes, syllabi, faculty members, and departments that privilege the English language and penalize multilingual students for minor grammatical errors or different cultural and linguistic approaches to writing. We contend with Guba and Lincoln (1989) that Western, "scientific" approaches to assessment "miss completely its fundamentally social, political, and value-oriented character" (7). In addition, we agree with Marzano (2000) that grading is problematic because "grades are so imprecise that they are almost meaningless" (1). In this chapter, we theorize a nepantla approach to assessment. Nepantla is a liminal, in-between space offered by Gloria Anzaldúa (1987) where fronterizas draw from the physical, psychological, and spiritual borderlands to contest, challenge, and construct identities in ways that privilege transformation. As teacher-activists, we seek to develop our syllabi, class discussions and activities, and grading rubrics in ways that further facilitate this process of transformation. We begin by outlining the major concepts that inform our nepantla approach, including valuing vivencia, writing identity into existence, the use of autohistoria-teoría for both ourselves and our students, and constructing assignments and rubric evaluation with mindfulness and empathy. We then offer examples of how we have used these approaches in our own classrooms. By utilizing this nepantla approach to assessment, we hope to reach our "non-traditional" student body populations in more effective ways that do justice to their lived experiences and equip them with tools to help them move through academia and through the world more effectively.

A NEPANTLA APPROACH: VALUING VIVENCIAS

As Gloria Anzaldúa described in many of her foundational works, nepantla is an in-between space, a place where individuals reside in betwixt and between and seek to make sense of divergent experiences, identities, and places in the world. Nepantla is a state of being, a vivencia, embodied by both Sarah and Leandra and later shared with students. Existing in a nepantla state can also serve as a powerful bridge between faculty members and students, as we are

Honoring Vivencias 93

able to see how our identity categories and in-betweenness provide shared choques, arrebatos, and similarities that humanize the educator-student relationship and the experiences that both faculty members and students bring to the classroom. Sarah, for example, is a mixed-race Latina from the Mexico-US border who shares many of her students' experiences pertaining to language, national identity, and regional identity. Leandra is a third-/fifth-generation pansexual Chicana feminist and military spouse who, as a contingent faculty member, worked specifically with military students and non-traditional students from 2013–2019. Her experience as a Mexican-American woman, military spouse, and contingent faculty member in a constant state of liminality provided an important lens that informed her pedagogical approaches during this time frame and continues to inform her teaching philosophy at her current institution as she works with students of diverse religious, racial/ethnic, occupational, and familial backgrounds. Building upon Trinidad Galván's (2015) work, the pedagogical strategy of valuing vivencias that we identify and develop in this chapter seeks to fundamentally radicalize the educator-student relationship in both empowering and vulnerable ways. We acknowledge that this approach might open the door to more vulnerability and emotional labor on behalf of educators and women of color, wherein research illustrates that women of color are faced disproportionately with lower student evaluations, more emotional labor, and more struggles in the classroom (Hernández 2020); however, we also believe strongly in the transformative nature of a vivencia-value approach to educational justice.

Valuing vivencias as a pedagogical approach means honoring mundane, ordinary, everyday lived experiences as important sites of teaching and learning (Trinidad Galván 2001). Trinidad Galván (2001) explains that "the kitchen table and church steps must also be analyzed as real pedagogical spaces for many underprivileged groups" (Trinidad Galván 2001, 606). Through the sharing of cultural knowledge and lived experiences that make up vivencia, individuals experience a form of togetherness that leads to convivencia, a form of gathering, sharing, and relationship building that creates meaningful and impactful co-existence (Trinidad Galván 2001, 2011, 2015). Trinidad Galván (2011) argues that convivencia allows individuals to transcend self/other divides, and in turn allows for praxis that transcends multiple borders. To experience convivencia in research means to not only move beyond the researcher/participant binary but to find yourself in "that place of discomfort that makes you agonizingly aware of each other's vivencias and our mutual humanity" (Trinidad Galván 2011, 555). In our classrooms, convivencia means that we see one another as whole beings and engage in course material and life discussions in ways that privilege our mutual humanity. The process of convivencia is healing and ultimately leads to supervivencia, or pedagogies of survival (Trinidad Galván 2015). This supervivencia is sometimes, but not always, able to move beyond simple survival to sobre-viviendo, or survivance (Trinidad Galván 2015).

Chicana and Latina education scholars have demonstrated the potential of valuing vivencias as a pedagogical strategy. In her work with campesinas participating in a small savings group in Central Mexico, Trinidad Galván (2001; 2015) reconceptualizes pedagogy as the everyday lived experiences and practices of these women, privileging a womanist perspective based in the unique socio-cultural and economic conditions affecting this rural community, as well as their practices of relationship building and identity construction. For these campesinas, convivencia means gathering to participate in small savings groups, creating space to come together, and ultimately co-existing (Trinidad Galván 2001). Delgado Bernal (2006) offers the concept of "pedagogies of the home," which privileges the language and cultural knowledge learned in the home space and in local communities. She argues that Chicana/ Mexicana students bring knowledges that are often treated as deficits, while they are in fact important cultural resources, and asserts that "a better understanding of these strategies will allow us to develop educational policy and practices that value and build on household knowledge in order to enhance Chicana academic success and college participation" (Delgado Bernal 2006, 113). Villenas (2006) demonstrates the pedagogical possibilities of vivencias and convivencias in the generational borderlands that exist in relationships between mothers and daughters. She explains:

> But somewhere in our living pedagogies, as we learn to "see" and engage the often ambiguous lessons of our mothers' bodies, words, and silences, we find the decolonial imaginary—those shades of gray, those spaces of possibilities to make new meanings, to be creative and self-fulfilled, and to love our own daughters differently (Villenas 2006, 157).

Thus, vivencias, convivencias, and pedagogies of the home are important sites of knowledge production, and thus as we work towards justice in our assessment practices, we must find ways to incorporate and honor the knowledges our students bring to class with them every day. This means rethinking how we assess classroom participation by creating opportunities for sharing lived experiences. When grading writing assignments, rather than focusing on "perfect" grammar, spelling, and punctuation in an attempt to "tame wild tongues" (Anzaldúa 1987), we should structure assignments in ways that invite students to share what they have learned at their kitchen tables, in their communities, from their experiences and relationships; furthermore, when they do share this knowledge we should honor it, celebrate it, and assess it accordingly. To demonstrate what valuing vivencias can look like as embodied praxis inside the classroom, in the following sections we explore the practices of writing identity into existence, autohistoria-teoría, and using mindfulness and empathy in course design.

WRITING IDENTITY INTO EXISTENCE

One of the fundamental pillars of a transformative vivencia-convivencia approach to educational justice centers around the notion of writing identity into existence and valuing the experiences that students bring to the classroom. Identity politics occupy a contentious and tenuous space in the current US American imaginary, particularly as it is ensconced within current debates about neoliberal higher education institutions and the "liberalization" of schools of higher education in the United States. Although some conservative schools of thought might argue that there is no room for identity politics in higher education, the theoretical, methodological, and pedagogical frameworks of writing identity into existence, testimonios, and autohistoria-teoría directly highlight the importance of and necessity of an identity politics framework in higher education. As Moya notes (2002):

> At stake in debates about identity is the legitimacy (political and intellectual) of a range of identity-based initiatives that have the potential to materially affect the lives of marginalized people in the United States. Political issues like affirmative action and bilingual ballots, educational issues such as multicultural education and textbook selection, and intellectual projects in the areas of ethnic, women's, and gay, lesbian, and bisexual studies, are all justified by a logic of identity (4).

Similarly, as we continue to discuss in this chapter, our pedagogical course development strategies are directly centered around discussing notions of difference (class, race, ethnicity, physicality, neurodiversity, age, and more) from an intersectional perspective to generate a larger social, collective consciousness about the impact of diverse institutional and power structures on our students' lived experiences.

We contend with Moya (2002) and Huber (2009), among others, that valuing students' experiences is beneficial for all parties involved. As Moya (2002) asserts, there is intrinsic value located within learning how to learn from others. Describing the myriad ideologies imbedded within US institutional systems (from elementary to higher education), Moya (2002) argues that a "truly multiperspectival, multicultural education is a necessary component of a just and democratic society" (139). Stemming from the human relations approach to multicultural education, we seek to "bring diverse groups together in order to foster understanding, respect, and more effective cross-cultural communication between them," emphasizing the continual importance of an intersectional approach to critical communication pedagogy that highlights difference in class, access, discrimination, and powerlessness (Moya 2002, 145).

As Moya (2002) describes, multicultural education seeks to "promote equal opportunity and human diversity by analyzing the links between race, language, culture, gender, handicap, and social class as institutionalized structures of inequality," (145). Our students, for example, are encouraged to highlight their daily struggles and vivencias in their assignments, a pedagogical act that we provide space for and support so that students can apply the course materials to their own experiences in powerful ways. Whether it is an assignment that links intercultural communication theories to border justice and discrimination or an assignment that links health communication and mental health approaches to post-war military PTSD, we as educators encourage students to explore their experiences in conjunction with one another to build a shared consciousness of how external institutional and power structures impact their lives. Another added benefit of this approach is it provides a space for students to destigmatize life experiences that are otherwise largely stigmatized in discursive and material contexts, such as post-traumatic stress disorder.

Valuing student perspectives and experiences, in our approach, stems directly from early Chicana feminist pedagogies and epistemologies. As Hurtado (2003) describes, germinal Chicana feminist writings and edited volumes, such as *This Bridge Called My Back*, rebelled against prevailing paradigms that "required the disassociation of their lived experiences in order to claim the label of intellectual, public or otherwise;" moreover, transgressing methodological and disciplinary boundaries, foundational Chicana feminists claimed fragmentation and hybridity as the fundamental core of their lived experience (215). By writing themselves literally into existence and exemplifying theories of the flesh, foundational Chicana feminists and feminists of color in the 1980s and beyond asserted the importance of valuing the hybridity of one's lived experience as the cornerstone of theory, method, and praxis. We extend an acknowledgement of valuing theories of the flesh by asserting that vivencias should be an additional component of the cornerstone of one's pedagogical philosophy if one seeks to disrupt heteronormative, Western, colonialist modes of education that privilege objectivity and traditional, colonist philosophies and approaches to the higher education experience. As Davis (1974) so powerfully stated, "Our weapon was the word;" we, too, believe that our students' words can function as lifesaving weapons as well (80).

Honoring Vivencias

Autohistoria-teoría is another important part of the process of writing our identities into existence. Though never explicitly defined in Anzaldua's writings, she invokes the concept of autohistoria-teoría to distinguish personal essays which theorize the personal, theoretical, and methodological value of our lived experience (Pitts 2016). As Chicana feminist profesoras, we contend with Pitts (2016) that "it is important to give theoretical attention to self-knowledge practices for women of color in particular" (355). Autohistoria-teoría allows for a collective approach to meaning-making, leads to conocimiento as a state of embodied awareness, and creates opportunities for critical self-reflection which can be both productive and painful (Pitts, 2016). As a pedagogical tool, autohistoria-teoría is important because "the act of giving meaning to oneself provides a platform for collaborative forms of meaning-making" (Pitts 2016, 357). Holling (2006) demonstrates the power of autohistoria-teoría in her experience teaching a course entitled "Chicana/ Latina Experiences." She explains that in an eight- to ten-page paper on the personal experiences and ideologies that shape their identities, her students begin to position themselves as subjects through the act of writing. This in turn leads to conocimiento because as Holling (2006) explains, "creating pedagogical assignments that have Chicanas and Latinas center and critically analyze particular lived experiences, while identifying the ideologies and beliefs that shape those experiences, heightens their sense of consciousness" (Holling 2006, 82). Assignments such as these give students the tools to liberate themselves and challenge various forms of oppression (Holling 2006), and we argue that these skills are much more important, both in life and in the assessment of our students' performance in our courses, than traditional approaches to grading are equipped to demonstrate.

Testimonios are another important way to write our identities into existence, especially as we work to heal from traumas (Castañeda 2019; Pérez 2019). As Delgado Bernal, Burciaga, and Flores Carmona (2012) illustrate, building upon Anzaldúa's (1990) works, Chicana feminists have long used testimonio as a genre that "exposes brutality, disrupts silencing, and builds solidarity among women of color" (363). Testimonios are a "voice from the margins or from the subaltern—a political approach that elicits solidarity from the reader" (Delgado Bernal, Burciaga, and Flores Carmona 2012, 364). Furthermore, testimonio incorporates the cultural, social, political, and historical histories that shape one's experience, blending these histories in efforts to elicit change through consciousness-raising (Delgado Bernal, Burciaga, and Flores Carmona 2012).

In their analysis of testimonio as a methodological and pedagogical tool, Delgado Bernal, Burciaga, and Flores Carmona (2012) note that testimonio is a valuable pedagogical framework precisely because it brings students' minds, bodies, spirits, and political urgency to the fore. Moreover, testimonio creates a new shared collective knowledge for students, affirms the value of our lived epistemologies that we bring to the classroom, and allows us to write from theories of the flesh (Delgado Bernal, Burciaga, and Flores Carmona 2012; Rendón 2009). Ultimately, part of the power in testimonio as a pedagogical tool lies in its ability to achieve new collective conocimientos for all members of the classroom space (Delgado Bernal, Burciaga, and Flores Carmona 2012). We extend their assertions by noting that it also privileges engaged learning and application more thoroughly and more deeply than objective, Westernized approaches to higher education; in other words, instead of having students apply course concepts to a current event, blending testimonio as a pedagogical tool with course concepts *and* current events allows students to see themselves in the larger narrative and to process through how the course concepts impact them directly through their prior and current lived experiences. As we will describe later in the chapter, testimonio undoubtedly has higher levels of vulnerability and emotional labor; however, we believe that the vulnerability that characterizes testimonio-style assignments leads to greater student collaboration, consciousness-raising, and empathy.

Testimonios have radically transformative potential in Chicana feminist literatures and reflections on experiences in academia; as such, we explore here the potential of testimonio in the classroom for students of color and students of diverse occupational, life, and familial backgrounds. As Castañeda (2019) explains in her exploration of testimonios as a way to untame silent tongues surrounding child sexual abuse, the open-ended nature of this approach "allows for a theoretical and political form of discourse that invites the intersectional self, the collectivist voice, and the Latinx culture of collective ways of being and knowing" (5). For our classrooms this means that we offer open-ended assignments, rather than rigidly structured rubrics, in order to allow our students space to write and speak in ways that allow for healing and transformation, and thus create greater opportunities for convivencia and supervivencia. In his work on testimonio as a queer puente for healing, Pérez (2019) highlights the power of language as resistencia. He explains that choices about when and how to use language can be just as powerful as the story itself:

> It is important for you to read my cuentos in Spanish, English, and Spanglish. As a reader, you may not understand every word that I write or you may have to look up the meaning of a phrase now and again. These stories are flor y canto resistance to growing up learning in English-first and English-only spaces (Pérez 2019, 19).

As Chicana profesoras who grew up in the linguistic borderlands of the Texas educational system and institutional systems of forced acculturation and assimilation (Hernández 2019), denied our birthright to learn Spanish as a first language because our parents were abused for speaking it in school, we understand the power of this linguistic resistencia. We therefore recognize that Spanish, English, Spanglish, and other forms of speaking and writing that are treated as "non-academic" are to be not only accepted, but respected and celebrated as we grade the work of our students. Learning from the tradition of testimonios, we ultimately privilege our students' ability to speak truth to power, and to heal from the process.

MINDFULNESS, EMPATHY, AND CONTEMPLATIVE PEDAGOGY

In addition to autohistoria-teoría and testimonio as foundational modes that construct our pedagogical approach to honoring student vivencias, mindfulness, empathy, and contemplative pedagogy complete our vivencia pedagogical arc. Contemplative pedagogy is a "quiet pedagogical revolution" that supports the identification of and development of student attention, emotional balance, empathetic connection, compassion, and altruistic behavior (Zajonc 2013). Its approach to higher education transformation manifests a blending of somatic, relational, and contextual awareness as it directly centralizes the student's lived experience within the classroom (Bai, Scott, and Donald 2009). By cultivating inner awareness through a first-person investigation (or contemplative practice), it also encourages students to consider classroom concepts as having lifelong impact on themselves and those around them; moreover, it highlights self-knowledge and ethical cultivation (Grace 2011). By transforming larger assessment strategies that focus on learning as a goal that can be quantified for academic assessment purposes, one of the tenets of contemplative pedagogy re-envisions learning as a continuous life process, not a solitary end goal.

As Blinne (2014b) illustrates, contemplative pedagogy "speaks to any teaching or learning moment that develops and expands relational awareness via self-inquiry, resulting from heightened present-moment attention and compassionate engagement with oneself and the world" (2). Furthermore, contemplative pedagogy overlaps importantly with testimonio as a pedagogical tool in that it is an "emergent process wherein we learn to acknowledge and take responsibility for our interactions with others by recognizing our shared vulnerability" (Blinne 2014a). Blinne's (2014b) writings on contemplative pedagogy highlight both the faculty member and student role;

faculty members should be "committed to transgressing teaching-learning boundaries so that [we] can respond to student/learners as unique beings, active participants in the learning process, employing a holistic approach to learning, emphasizing well-being, action, and reflection" (4). In doing so, faculty members can cultivate sustainable humanity in the classroom by showing students that their perceptions and experiences truly do matter. Ultimately, by modeling metacommunication through contemplative pedagogy, "learners can better 'see' how they communicate on multiple levels, how they communicate about communicating, and how their lives are connected to the interwoven tapestry that creates the social fabric of their interactions" (Blinne 2014b, 13).

Taken together, our vivencia approach to higher education is informed by several different pedagogical approaches that, when combined, overlap in important ways: Chicana feminisms, nepantla, autohistoria-teoría, testimonio, and contemplative pedagogy. In the next and final section, we provide a few examples that illustrate our vivencia-convivencia approach to educational justice in practice.

A NEPANTLA APPLICATION AND APPROACH TO HONORING VIVENCIAS

In our own courses, we utilize a nepantla approach to assessment through valuing the vivencias of our students in a variety of ways. For example, in Sarah's class, "Chicanx Identity Formation," three particular assignments were developed with the intention of encouraging students to share vivencias, and these assignments were ultimately graded from a position of honoring and valuing the convivencia that came from this process of sharing. First, early in the semester, students were asked to complete an "I Am From" poem, inspired by the work of Levi Romero. Students were given instructions, a handout, and a full class period to complete their poems. Many shared examples of the knowledge they learned at the kitchen table, surrounded by family. Some students shared trauma, coupled with examples of how they were working to overcome it. Most talked about the role la frontera played in creating their sense of self. Students who completed these poems were given full credit as a way to value vivencias and honor the work that it takes to share personal experiences.

These poems also laid a foundation for future assignments like an essay on identity and a group photovoice project. For the identity essay, students were asked to create autohistoria-teorías through writing a personal essay that theorized their construction of identity using a nepantla approach to identity guided by Anzaldúa's concepts of nepantla, arrebatamiento, Coyolxauhqui, nagualismo, and el árbol de la vida (De Los Santos Upton 2019). Students wrote about the experiences that made them question existing identities and forge new ways of being, the necessity of shapeshifting and crossing the physical and rhetorical borders that surround us, and the importance of culture and family for guiding their understandings of the self. Students were graded not on the formality of their academic writing, but on the depth with which they engaged in the process of autohistoria-teoría, sharing their experiences and making connections to material from our course. In a similar project, students were asked to engage in photovoice, choosing one of Anzaldúa's concepts and taking a photograph that represented that concept, then writing a short description. They worked together in small groups to create a larger photo essay by combining their individual photographs. Working with photography, as well as in a group, allowed them to explore different aspects of their vivencias that they had not previously been able to put into words. The process of working together also created greater opportunities for convivencia. Ultimately, what mattered most in these projects was not perfect grammar or citing the "right" theories. Instead, it was about drawing powerfully on lived experiences to make sense of one's identity, as well as our willingness to experience this work from a place that celebrates our mutual humanity.

Sarah has found that the nature of a "Chicanx Identity Formation" course comes with a self-selecting group of students who are genuinely interested in this elective, and this, paired with the nepantlera positionalities of the student body, has led to an overwhelming acceptance of assignments such as these. Students begin the semester embracing the course content and assignments, and over time this acceptance grows into a recognition of the value of self-inquiry. Even students who have no experience with poetry, personal essays, or photography have approached these assignments with an openness and curiosity, and many have shared that the opportunity to engage in individual self-reflection and conversations with others around race, class, gender, and sexuality has been a meaningful experience that they have not been granted in other courses. As these individual and collective assignments build over the course of the semester, students understand themselves in new ways and open up to one another with increasing depth. For example, though this is in no way built into the design of the course, several students have found this class to be such a safe space that they feel comfortable coming out in small groups, to the class as a whole, and in some cases to their partners and families as a result of the self-inquiry taking place in the readings, assignments, and class discussions. Even after the course has ended, students have continued to reach out to Sarah to share their coming out stories, and it has been a true honor to bear witness to such sacred moments. The result of these pedagogical strategies has been the creation of meaningful relationships through convivencia, and we argue that this is more valuable than any numerical score can adequately capture.

In Leandra's media studies courses and health communication courses with military-affiliated learners and adult (non-traditional) learners, many of her assignments directly and purposively involve the students' lived experiences in their assignments. In health communication courses with all military-affiliated learners, the major course project consists of the following service learning components: 1) students must select first a health topic that directly impacts them in a personal way (either a health topic they have experienced or a health topic their family members or close loved ones has experienced); 2) utilizing testimonio and autohistoria-teoría as a theoretical and methodological starting point, students must write a reflection essay that outlines the health issue, its current status in health communication contexts, and its impact on their lives; and 3) students must volunteer with a local health organization over the course of the semester that directly services clients, patients, and communities impacted by their selected health topic. As opposed to selecting a health topic and simply writing a research essay on the health topic, this semester-long project gives students a full three to four months to "sit with" the topic, process it in both personal and applied contexts, interact with practitioners and other individuals who might be impacted from this health topic as well, and later share their experiences with their classmates.

Unsurprisingly, in almost every class where this assignment is utilized, most of the military-affiliated learners select mental health topics (mostly post-traumatic stress disorder, anxiety, and depression). Their reflection essays are later circulated in the course anonymously so that students can read their classmates' reflections. During the in-class reflection essay debriefs, students come together to share their metareflections, which results in a larger shared consciousness about the severity and prevalence of mental health issues such as anxiety and post-traumatic stress disorder, the ways in which it manifests in their communities, and the ways in which (perhaps most importantly) they are not alone in their shared struggles. Students consistently disclose both in class and in student evaluations that this assignment provides an important opportunity for them to process their emotions and their experiences in a safe, collaborative space. In an occupational context such as the US military, which does not always encourage disclosure of mental health concerns without fear of repudiation or reprimand, the health communication class space informed by a vivencia-convivencia approach allows students to honor their lived experiences in solidarity and to create a freeing shared consciousness.

Additionally, in some of Leandra's media studies and health communication courses, students are assigned weekly online discussion forums where

Honoring Vivencias   103

they are provided a discussion prompt that connects the weekly topics, concepts, and theories with their personal experiences and applications. This course component is inspired by a testimonio approach wherein students are encouraged to connect the dots, so to speak, among the course concepts, their lived experiences, and their observations of practical applications (in media ethics crises, health communication campaigns, and news coverage contexts, to name a few). To encourage the testimonio and autohistoria-teoría approach, the discussion forum grading rubric emphasizes the required micro-macro connections. Throughout the semester, students use a course tool as seemingly mundane as a discussion forum to build personal connections with classmates about powerful topics such as eating disorders, gendered violence, media literacy, and identity.

For example, in one of Leandra's media ethics courses, the weekly topic focused on media ethics conundrums that journalists face through the media text lens of the film *Spotlight*, which chronicled the *Boston Globe's* Spotlight team and its investigation of the Catholic Church's sexual abuse scandals. This module's discussion forum, which was scheduled during the second month of the course, created a catalytic and cathartic moment for this particular course wherein students disclosed personal experiences at the intersections of sexuality, gender identity, violence, abuse, and religion through the lens of the course concepts and the film. While this was not the intended pedagogical outcomes of the discussion forum assignment more broadly or this specific forum more particularly, Leandra was at first shocked and then heartened to watch the conversations unfold as students addressed each other's experiences with compassion and care. Moreover, based upon conversations with students in the discussion forum, in class, and during office hours, this particular moment helped students realize that the classroom was a safe, constructive, and supportive space wherein they could *truly* talk about the course materials in a way that was meaningful for them. Thus, taken together, we both utilize a variety of pedagogical experiences to honor our students' lived experiences, and such an approach is met with both labor-associated vulnerabilities and profound rewards, which we discuss in the final section.

CONCLUDING THOUGHTS: CHALLENGES AND REWARDS ASSOCIATED WITH A VIVENCIA-CONVIVENCIA PEDAGOGICAL PHILOSOPHY

In sum, our vivencia-convivencia pedagogical philosophy is informed by Chicana feminisms, nepantla, autohistoria-teoría, testimonio, and contemplative pedagogy. Such an approach is characterized by emotional labor,

104   *Leandra H. Hernández and Sarah De Los Santos Upton*

vulnerability on behalf of both educators and students, and a mixture of challenges and rewards that highlight the impact such an approach can have in higher education classrooms. At an administrative level, neither Leandra or Sarah have faced push-back from university administrators because student emails, communication, and course evaluations have consistently highlighted the value of such a pedagogical approach. Multiple students in Leandra's courses, for example, have noted over the past several years that the applied course projects and discussion forums are two of their favorite course components. The discussion forum component, in particular, has been recognized as a course favorite because students appreciate the opportunity to tread the conversational waters online and assess the overall tone regarding the topic, which then positively impacts students' willingness to discuss the topics in more detail in the in-person classroom setting. In Sarah's course, students have expressed appreciation that they are not only given time in class for self-reflection, but also given course credit. Rather than viewing this as an "easy A," several students have shared in office hours, emails, and online course evaluations, that they learned more writing poems and essays, and analyzing their own photographs than they had from any other course assignment in their academic careers.

From a vulnerability perspective, our pedagogical approach is impossible without a certain level of vulnerability on behalf of all involved. Indeed, we do not require students to discuss personal experiences or vulnerable experiences, and not all students disclose at the same level as their peers. Students are encouraged to disclose as much as they feel comfortable doing so—some students disclose deeply personal experiences, and others disclose as they need to in order to meet the parameters of the assignments. However, students have consistently expressed that they appreciate the opportunity to learn from their classmates, which serves several important functions: this opportunity allows for the creation of a strong course community and climate, it provides a sense of solidarity amongst classmates within the larger course topics and theories, and it humanizes diverse student identities and experiences. In other words, students *see* themselves in the course materials and are directly able to see how the topics, theories, and concepts relate to them at a micro level and to larger communicative contexts and situations at a macro level. We understand that such a pedagogical approach may not be an effective tool for all educators, given the emotional labor and vulnerabilities involved; however, we detail it here because we have witnessed its transformative and humanizing potential.

When taken together, these various approaches construct a teaching philosophy and mode that honors students' lived realities, encourages shared consciousness-raising to result in an empowered and collaborative classroom, and ultimately re-envisions learning as a life process, not an end goal. Our vivencia-convivencia pedagogical philosophy is one tool of many that can be utilized to result in greater educational justice because, as we stated at the beginning of the chapter, we honor our students' lived experiences.

REFERENCES

Anzaldúa, Gloria. 1987. *Borderlands/La Frontera: The New Mestiza.* (Vol. 3). San Francisco: Aunt Lute.

Bai, Heesoon, Scott, Charles, and Beatrice Donald. 2009. "Contemplative Pedagogy and Revitalization of Teacher Education. *Alberta Journal of Educational Research* 55, 319-334.

Blinne, Kristen. 2014a. "Practicing Mettacommunication: A Guide to Contemplative Communication." Unpublished manuscript.

Blinne, Kristen. 2014b. "Awakening to Lifelong Learning: Contemplative Pedagogy as Compassionate Engagement." *Radical Pedagogy* 11 (2): 1524–6345.

Castañeda, Nivea. 2019. "Using Testimonios to Untame Our Silent Tongues: Exploring Our Experiences of Child Sexual Abuse Through an Anzaldúan Perspective." In *This Bridge We Call Communication: Anzaldúan Approaches to Theory, Method, and Praxis,* edited by Leandra H. Hernández and Robert Gutierrez-Perez, 3–16. Lanham, MD: Lexington Books.

Cervantes-Soon, Claudia G., and Juan F. Carrillo. 2016. "Toward a Pedagogy of Border Thinking: Building on Latin@ Students' Subaltern Knowledge." *The High School Journal* 99 (4): 282–301.

Davis, Angela Y. 1974. *With My Mind on Freedom: An Autobiography.* New York: Bantam.

Delgado Bernal, Dolores. 2006. "Learning and Living Pedagogies of the Home: The Mestiza Consciousness of Chicana Students." In *Chicana/Latina Education in Everyday Life: Feminista Perspectives on Pedagogy and Epistemology,* edited by Dolores Delgado Bernal, C. Alejandra Elenes, Francisca E. Godinez, and Sofia Villenas, 113–132. Albany: State University of New York Press.

Delgado Bernal, Dolores, Burciaga, Rebeca, and Judith Flores Carmona. 2012. "Chicana/Latina *Testimonios*: Mapping the Methodological, Pedagogical, and Political." *Equity & Excellence in Education* 45 (3): 363–372. https://doi.org/10.1080/1 0665684.2012.698149.

De Los Santos Upton, Sarah. 2019. "Communicating *Nepantla*: An Anzaldúan Theory of Identity." In *This Bridge We Call Communication: Anzaldúan Approaches to Theory, Method, and Praxis,* edited by Leandra H. Hernández and Robert Gutierrez-Perez, 123–142. Lanham, MD: Lexington Books.

Elenes, Alejandra C. 2010. *Transforming Borders: Chicana/o Popular Culture and Pedagogy.* Lanham, MD: Lexington Books.

106   *Leandra H. Hernández and Sarah De Los Santos Upton*

Grace, Fran. 2011. "Learning as a Path, Not a Goal: Contemplative Pedagogy—Its Principles and Practices." *Teaching Theology and Religion* 14 (2): 99–124. https://doi.org/10.1111/j.1467-9647.2011.00689.x.

Guba, Egon G., and Yvonna S. Lincoln. 1989. *Fourth Generation Evaluation.* Newbury Park: Sage Publications.

Hernández, Leandra H. 2020. "Identity Politics in the Classroom: An Application of Critical Love to Teaching Difficult Topics in the Military Classroom Battlefield." In *Working in the Margins: Domestic and International Minority Women in Higher Education,* edited by Carolyn "Carolina" Rosas Webber, 15–32. New York: Peter Lang.

Hernández, Leandra H. 2019. "'I take something from both worlds': An Anzaldúan Analysis of Mexican-American Women's Conceptualizations of Ethnic Identity." In *This Bridge We Call Communication: Anzaldúan Approaches to Theory, Method, and Praxis,* edited by Leandra H. Hernández and Robert Gutierrez-Perez, 3–16. Lanham, MD: Lexington Books.

Holling, Michelle A. 2006. "The Critical Consciousness of Chicana and Latina students: Negotiating Identity Amid Sociocultural Beliefs and Ideology." In *Chicana/Latina Education in Everyday Life: Feminista Perspectives on Pedagogy and Epistemology,* edited by Dolores Delgado Bernal, C. Alejandra Elenes, Francisca E. Godinez, and Sofia Villenas, 81–94. Albany: State University of New York Press.

Huber, Lindsay Pérez. 2009. "Disrupting Apartheid of Knowledge: *Testimonio* as Methodology in Latina/o Critical Race Research in Education." *International Journal of Qualitative Studies in Education* 22 (6): 639–654. https://doi.org/10.1080/09518390903333863.

Hurtado, Aída. 2003. "Theory in the Flesh: Toward an Endarkened Epistemology." *International Journal of Qualitative Studies in Education* 16 (2): 215–225. https://doi.org/10.1080/0951839032000060617.

Marzano, Robert J. 2000. *Transforming Classroom Grading.* Alexandria, VA: ASCD.

Moya, Paula M. L. 2002. *Learning from Experience: Minority Identities, Multicultural Struggles.* Berkeley, CA: University of California Press.

Pérez, Manuel Alejandro. 2019. "Testimonio as a Queer Puente for Healing." In *This Bridge We Call Communication: Anzaldúan Approaches to Theory, Method, and Praxis,* edited by Leandra H. Hernández and Robert Gutierrez-Perez, 17–26. Lanham, MD: Lexington Books.

Pitts, Andrea J. 2016. "Gloria E. Anzaldúa's Autohistoria-teoría as an Epistemology of Self-Knowledge/Ignorance." *Hypatia* 31: 352–369. https://dx.doi.org/10.1111/hypa.12235

Rendón, Laura I. 2009. *Sentipensante (Sensing/Thinking) Pedagogy: Educating for Wholeness, Social Justice, and Liberation.* Sterling, VA: Stylus.

Stobart, Gordon. 2008. *Testing Times: The Uses and Abuses of Assessment.* London, UK: Routledge.

Trinidad Galván, Ruth. 2001. "Portraits of Mujeres Desjuiciadas: Womanist Pedagogies of the Everyday, the Mundane and the Ordinary." *Interna-*

tional Journal of Qualitative Studies in Education 14 (5): 603–621. https://doi.org/10.1080/09518390110059856.

Trinidad Galván, Ruth. 2011. Chicana Transborder Vivencias and Autoherteorías: Reflections from the Field. *Qualitative Inquiry 17*(6): 552–557.

Trinidad Galván, Ruth. 2015. *Women Who Stay Behind: Pedagogies of Survival in Rural Transmigrant Mexico.* Tucson: University of Arizona Press.

Villenas, Sofia. 2006. "Pedagogical Moments in the Borderlands: Latina Mothers Teaching and Learning." In *Chicana/Latina Education in Everyday Life: Feminista Perspectives on Pedagogy and Epistemology,* edited by Dolores Delgado Bernal, C. Alejandra Elenes, Francisca E. Godinez, and Sofia Villenas, 147–159. Albany: State University of New York Press.

Zajonc, Arthur. 2006. "Love and Knowledge: Recovering the Heart of Learning Through Contemplation." *Teachers College Record* 108 (9): 1742–1759. http://www.arthurzajonc.org/publications/love-and-knowledge-recovering-the-heart-of-learning/.

Chapter Four

Walking the Tightrope

Navigating the Tensions of Teaching and Grading Communication Content Inside and Outside the Discipline

Juliane Mora

My life as a teacher might aptly be described as split. For nineteen years, I have been teaching communication content to students outside of communication departments, most often in business and engineering schools. The "split-ness" of mind that results from teaching in these contexts *and* traditional communication departments at the same time is what contributes to my sense of fragmentation and contradiction. Since Plato's attack on the Sophists, rhetoric has enjoyed a position fraught with tension because of vacillating emphases on the artistic versus pragmatic skill of effective communication behaviors. In the professional schools, the emphasis on skill development abounds and communication courses and content are typically framed as being a "useful skill" for practitioners in the world of work. This tension is not new and I am hardly the first person to comment on it, but the position I find myself in most often is walking the tightrope between seemingly opposite perspectives on the role and function of communication instruction, particularly as part of a core curriculum. This all occurs before getting to the issue of evaluating and grading the work students produce to show that they are learning and using their new understandings of communication material.

As bell hooks reminds us, no education is a politically neutral process, and with each discipline and setting, specific choices are made that frame and guide the material presented to students. Hence, I think there is tremendous value in exploring the types of contexts where students learn communication content, and the ways said content is presented, practiced, and evaluated. From my own experience, I have taught thousands of students at a large state school who went through "business" communication courses taught by people with a wide range of backgrounds (Masters required, but not necessarily in Communication) who emphasized "how-to" modules for giving a good PowerPoint presentation and being a persuasive salesperson. The assignments

110 *Juliane Mora*

and grading scale were fairly similar across thirty-six sections of this course every semester and students were said to have "learned" the material when they could stand and deliver smooth, well-organized sales presentations with appropriate visual aids. These are laudable goals and were met in many instances in my own classes and those of my fellow lecturers, but they hardly scratch the surface of the discipline. Nor do they consider how standardized grading practices privilege dominant identity group students, not to mention how the model of a "good (business)person speaking well" is based in White supremacist capitalist patriarchy, to use bell hooks' (1994) terms—the exact *opposite* of a social justice approach to education.

If this experience were an anomaly, I might not be so concerned, but this was only one of the five institutions I have taught for in the last nineteen years and I have found myself in much the same position at each. As a graduate student in my Master's program, I taught the required introduction to communication course for students as part of the core curriculum where we were required to include twenty-two minutes of graded public speaking as mandated by our accreditation standards. In my PhD program, I taught another required public speaking course for students from across campus who needed it to complete their undergraduate requirements. In my first tenure-track position, I was the director of our campus-wide Center for Public Speaking where I spent endless hours working with students, faculty, and staff on improving the composition, organization, and delivery of their messages to a broader public audience while also teaching a required Speech for Business class. In each of these spaces, the rationale for the course rested on the need for students to be prepared to use communication skills in civic and professional life. The emphasis was on skill development and there was a more or less standardized outline for the course with specific modes of speaking included (informative, persuasive, ceremonial, impromptu).

My current role is attempting to integrate the equivalent of the required core communication course into the existing curriculum across all four years of the engineering program. This move was made to accommodate the credit-heavy engineering curriculum without losing the liberal arts emphasis. However, as the collaboration has played out so far, there is a large gap between the "big ideas" and "core concepts" (Wiggins and McTighe 2005) being taught in the standalone sixteen-week course and what I have been able to integrate into the engineering classes where I have been invited to participate. There are also numerous misunderstandings about how oral communication content and assignments need to be integrated into the engineering courses, what to grade to assess or improve student learning of this material, and who should grade it. Many of the engineering faculty I have worked with can only conceive of oral communication as individual or group stand-up research presentations that take up a lot of class time, and that may not be a good fit for the topics and courses they are teaching. Unsurprisingly, then, they also think of evaluating student speaking based on technical correctness, use of vocabulary and terms, and whether their visual aid was helpful. These preconceptions flatten the depth and breadth of communication content to the most basic emphasis on skill development and operate in contradiction with the material presented in the full sixteen week course. And, these elements are always the first to be cut when time is an issue, or as in the spring semester 2020, when a global pandemic forced drastic changes to the curriculum and a shift to online remote instruction. Hello computer mediated classrooms relying on virtual meeting platforms for face-to-face interaction, but goodbye to instruction in effective oral communication practices and behaviors, regardless of how timely, relevant, and beneficial they might be for navigating this new situation.

Another area of concern with this faculty and student population is how the use of traditional grading policies and practices can have the effect of further marginalizing non-dominant students. For example, students of color and female students are still vastly underrepresented in STEM fields and when they do end up in the engineering classes that I have worked with, they are likely to be an *only* (only female in the class or their group, or only student of color in class or their group). Add to this environment, course content or activities that ask students to articulate engineering concepts (in speaking and writing) for part of their grade and be evaluated by their engineering instructors. Engineering faculty may or may not feel competent (or confident) evaluating speaking in the same ways as a communication faculty member and they may or may not be able to provide feedback or coaching to help students improve for the next course that has a communication component. Lastly, they may or may not know to look for, or be able to recognize, implicit bias in their own evaluation behaviors when it comes to traditionally marginalized students.

This tension in the context of the conversation in this volume is an important one as I continue to ask how I can be a social justice educator in both of these spaces and how my approach to teaching and grading might reflect that mission? What does grading justice look like in this context? What can a teacher-activist working in this context do to "level the playing field" or "balance the scales"? How does this context compare to teaching in a communication studies classroom where the students have (at least nominally) selected this content for study, rather than feeling like it is being shoehorned into their "real" discipline? How might communication material be reframed as a practice of lifelong learning? These are the questions that drove the development of this chapter and that the remainder will attempt to offer insight into. And, while I offer insights and examples from my experiences in specific disciplines, there are many ways in which the phenomena I am focusing on are relevant to individuals teaching communication from a variety of positions (graduate students and/or contingent faculty teaching predetermined courses/syllabi, teaching assistants or course graders, those teaching "service" courses for any other discipline, etc.).

CROSSING THE GAP—TEACHING COMMUNICATION CONTENT IN OTHER DISCIPLINES (BUSINESS AND ENGINEERING)

The Carnegie Foundation for the Advancement of Teaching has undertaken numerous studies of academic preparation in different professional areas, including nursing, medicine, the clergy, engineering, law, and, most recently, business. Their efforts were to survey the disciplines and understand the teaching and learning practices used to prepare students for professional employment in these areas after college. Their 2011 study, published in book form as *Rethinking Undergraduate Business Education* argues for stronger integration of the types of thinking that are the hallmark of a liberal arts education: "analytical reasoning, the ability and disposition to take multiple perspectives when confronting a complex decision or judgment, and finding and making connections of personal meaning between what one does and who one intends to become" (Shulman 2011, ix). Colby, Ehrlich, Sullivan and Dolle (2011) articulated the link between improved liberal education in business programs with oral communication in their discussion of the seminar—the setting dedicated to deliberation and exchange—where students could engage in careful argumentation, explore different ways of framing an issue, and develop understanding with others through conversation as part of the pedagogy of liberal learning.

In their previous book length study, *Educating Engineers: Designing for the Future of the Field*, published in 2009, The Carnegie Foundation for the Advancement of Teaching illustrated the types of knowledge used by engineers, as well as the skills they would need to meet the demands of the profession in the new century. Chief among them was communication, articulated therein as a means of making engineers more "accountable" to interdisciplinary teams, making sure they could explain themselves to diverse audiences and work with others to solve complex problems. Most recently, The National Academies of Sciences, Engineering, and Medicine published a consensus study report in 2018 outlining their findings to support the integration of humanities and the arts with the sciences, engineering, and medicine using the metaphor of branches from the same tree.

There seems to be no doubt that incorporating communication content into the disciplines is for the betterment of student learning in those areas (Reimer 2007), but *how* that integration happens, depends on the specific discipline, campus, school or college, administration, faculty, and to some extent, students. In my own career, I have taught communication content and skills to students in business and engineering at five different institutions across the country as a graduate student, lecturer, and, now, as an assistant professor. The nature of my collaboration has changed at each institution, but at some, I taught standalone courses (Speech for Business and the Professions; Business Presentations), while at others, I worked to integrate material into existing disciplinary courses taught by faculty in those areas. Engineering and business are interested in skill development when it comes to communication outcomes. Their emphasis is on professional and commercial success in their respective fields, for which they need effective communication skills. In these disciplines, this means clear, coherent (preferably unaccented) speech, clear organizational structure, ethical and well-supported arguments using logic, credibility, and emotion to persuade audiences. Hence, what is justice in these contexts with these expectations?

The communication content desired in these settings is typically limited to technical ability and skill at speaking, meaning there is little room for teaching rhetorical theory, social constructionism, or communication as constitutive of our social worlds, much less critiques of power and domination that occur through communication practices. In many cases, both business and engineering faculty see communication as a transactional exchange complete with inputs, throughputs, and outputs. Such a limited view of the discipline is included in this model that social justice concerns (diversity, difference, power, oppression, and marginality) do not immediately appear relevant to collaboration partners or students. If the transactional view of communication is the taken for granted norm, then there is an objective "formula" for improving communication (a checklist of dos and don'ts that students memorize and practice to become proficient). Never mind the power imbalance and injustice in the system of knowledge production, evaluation, or application outside of school in the professional realm that could be critiqued (and perhaps altered) by instruction in more of the discipline (rhetorical, discursive, critical/cultural, performative approaches).

To return to my earlier question—(what *is* grading justice in these contexts with these expectations?)—the answer, as with most things, is that it depends. Colby, Ehrlich, Sullivan, and Dolle (2011) explain how there are differing views on oral communication in the disciplines depending on whether faculty from the arts and humanities or the sciences and professions are discussing it. For those of us in the arts and humanities, we typically conceive of speaking as a *mode of learning* and sharing ideas with others through discussion, dialogue, deliberation, and debate. For faculty in the sciences and professional fields, they are more likely to conceive of speaking as *a professional skill* (similar to writing) where one shares (read: transmits) the results of their work with others to inform or persuade depending on the audience and context. From this perspective, there is no acknowledgment that language shapes reality, or that meaning is jointly constructed between the speaker and the audience. This disjuncture between the goals and purpose of using oral communication in the classroom setting can create problems for grading justly depending on which standards are used and who is doing the grading.

Undergraduate education in business is highly competitive, instructors often grade on a curve, and students view their performance as a reflection of how successful they will be after college (i.e., they have to get the "A" in their classes so it will translate into a well-paying job upon graduation). In these spaces, the language, metaphors, and maxims of business are often repeated in conjunction with performance and grades. For example, "everything is business," "survival of the fittest," "it's all about the bottom line," and "it's a dog eat dog world out there" are used to refer to the perspective of grades as a competitive exchange, something for something within a marketplace, and a zero-sum game at that, either I get it or I lose—eat or be eaten. In the business metaphor of education, the goal is always to maximize gains and minimize losses, with high grades being the gains and low grades being the losses. To accomplish this feat, students engage in any number of methods from the hard-working student who is diligent and prepares in advance to the stereotypical hustler who tries to find creative ways to get the best grade by doing the least amount of work (because less time on task for the same, or higher score, means they are being more "efficient" with the time they spend). However, none of this is about actually learning the material, or being invested in, or curious about, coming to a deeper understanding of the study of business through the use of communication. With this as a backdrop, it becomes almost impossible to enhance student learning to help them gain a deeper appreciation of the content (or how to use it) in anything other than the most mercenary ways. I once had a business student tell me he appreciated my class because he now felt like he could persuade anybody to buy anything (regardless of the ethics of the situation), and that he was glad he understood how privileged White males are in the business world because he felt like that would work in his favor and guarantee his success. Nothing that had come before, or that I have heard since, has made me feel like more of a failure as a social justice educator.

Engineering education is highly specialized and technical with the emphasis on understanding the fundamentals of math and science so they can be used to solve problems and create things in the world. The model of education followed in most programs is a linear one focused on content knowledge acquisition moving from theory to application in a lecture and lab format. The aforementioned Carnegie Foundation for the Advancement of Teaching (2009) report on the professional preparation of engineers found that this linear focus in engineering education was *not* an effective means for preparing students to enter the profession and become twenty-first-century engineers. Reimer (2007) agreed that articulating the specific communication skills were needed for the twenty-first-century engineering student and the importance of communication skills being integrated into the curriculum throughout the engineering program. Whereas a typical curriculum might emphasize memorization of formulas and calculations for different purposes (heat transfer, fluid dynamics, frequency vibrations), a networked curriculum would emphasize the contextual factors of engineering problems and when students should use theories and formulas to solve actual problems. In addition, faculty emphasized the importance of the non-technical skills of teamwork, communication, and professionalism as necessary components of an engineering education, but were hard-pressed to evaluate them because they are considered "subjective" and intangible areas for assessment. This is indicative of a knowledge gap about how to evaluate these behaviors that could be filled by individuals from other disciplines who spend all of their time evaluating (subjective) communication behavior.

There is also limited incorporation of literature from teacher education or use of it in planning course assignments and evaluation tools, and most classes are graded entirely on homework problems, quizzes, and exams—items that are nearly impossible to measure the intangibles that engineering faculty most want their students to be able to perform. This misalignment between what we want the students to learn and what they are being graded on is a fundamental component of *in*justice in grading and it does a disservice to the students because the "hidden curriculum" (Weisz and Kanpol 1990) reinforces what they need to be doing to pass the class (homework, quizzes, and exams), while the stated goals or encouragements from faculty are to become more effective team members and competent communicators for the world of work outside of school.

According to Sheppard, Macatangay, Colby, and Sullivan (2009), one of the most foundational components of engineering education is teaching students to speak mathematics, the language of engineering. As its own symbol system for making meaning, mathematics is the language that allows engineers to explore problems and express solutions. Like other types of language acquisition, this requires exposure, application in context, practice, and repetition. It is also one of the most difficult parts of the process of training

116 *Juliane Mora*

students to become engineers because they might be able to work the math on abstract concepts in class but be unable to determine when to use them in a specific applied context (i.e., in the field or on the job). As one faculty member put it, "they have to wrestle with situations where you give them a problem in plain English, and they have to translate it into a mathematics problem . . . if somebody comes to you as an engineer and asks you to solve a problem, the problem will be stated in plain English. . . . How do you get this problem that is stated in plain English translated into an abstract problem and use your way of thinking to solve it?" (Sheppard, Macatangay, Colby, and Sullivan 2009, 33).

This is most relevant to my role as an oral communication instructor integrating content into the engineering curriculum. The use of language and symbols systems to make meaning is the essence of the rhetorical tradition and already a foundational component of engineering as well, except that many engineering faculty lack that familiarity or understanding with rhetoric and communication. My job, then, is to help students (and faculty) see how their use of this new language shapes what they know and can be shared with others, how they can adapt their level of technical detail for a variety of audiences, and rely on other rhetorical forms (metaphor, simile, analogy, synecdoche, metonymy, hyperbole, etc.) to make their content understood across audiences with varying levels of technical knowledge. In much the same way that engineers need to translate a problem from "plain English" into mathematics in order to apply their form of thinking to solve it, effective communicators utilize the vast array of rhetorical forms available to transform English into a language that conveys meaning to audiences unfamiliar with engineering. Putting the unfamiliar into terms that others can understand by relying on comparisons to things that are more universal or familiar to a broader audience is the very definition of audience analysis and adaptation.

Whether they know it or not, engineering faculty rely on rhetorical forms all the time to make the material relevant to their audience or find ways to help them connect it to their existing conceptual knowledge. Analogies and comparisons to familiar objects or everyday scenarios helped students learn about stress and failure in vessels by relating them to soda cans that fail lengthwise and "pop" when frozen, or hot dogs that split when you grill them (Sheppard, Macatangay, Colby, and Sullivan 2009, 51). This semester, in our co-taught introduction to engineering course, the chair of the Electrical and Computer Engineering department used the iconic chords from the song "Another One Bites the Dust" by Queen to introduce the concept of reverberation and signal processing in his branch of engineering. Sheppard et al. (2009) further explain that engineering students need "knowing that"—knowledge of fundamental principles, theories, and concepts of engineering—so that they can engage in "knowing how"—knowing how, when, where, and why to use the theories and principles in analyzing engineering problems or situations (32–34).

While these areas of knowledge are regarded as crucial for engineering students to develop, grading practices and evaluation tools are rarely aligned with these types of knowledge creating a disjuncture between what engineering students need to know and what they are being graded on. Additionally, changes in the student body over time as a result of societal changes have meant that students entering college to major in engineering may have had no previous exposure to technical content or practices, and they might also lack any hands-on experience from other aspects of their life. In the early years when engineering was becoming an academic discipline, those studying it were more likely to have had vocational experience of some kind (farming, machining, automotive mechanics) that led them to this major. On my own campus, in the sophomore-level introduction to mechanical engineering design course, the practitioner who teaches it complains regularly that most of his students have never even been in a shop or held any of the most common tools before they are being expected to design components that will need to be assembled with those tools. This creates a significantly different environment in which to teach than many of these same faculty grew up in or were trained in themselves. How do those differences translate into their grading practices? When they want students to learn which tool to use (be it a mathematical or a physical one), are faculty providing learning opportunities or assessment opportunities that measure the students' understanding of which tool to use? Suskie (2018) reports that some faculty in these disciplines are making efforts to improve assessment practices to capture what students can actually do after instruction, but most are not, relying on the methods that they were taught. Current pedagogy in engineering emphasizes the banking model of education (Freire 1970) where knowledge and concepts are poured into students as if they are empty vessels who are expected to pour that knowledge back out on quizzes and exams. Even though some engineering faculty recognize the futility of this process, it is not yet enough of a widespread concern to change the way engineering education is fundamentally delivered.

GRADING JUSTICE IN CROSS-CURRICULAR CONTEXTS— OPPOSITE ENDS OF THE HIGH-WIRE

One of my first concerns in discussing grading justice is to operationalize the terms "grading" and "justice" that this volume advocates. The first of these, grading, calls to mind stacks of papers (or lab reports), or perhaps projects or presentations that require endless amounts of time for instructors to read/ view, evaluate, and provide copious feedback on before returning to students, then recording those scores in a gradebook or spreadsheet that gets tallied at the end of the semester to determine their overall course grade. However, grading, and its cousin assessment, are ultimately concerned with measuring student learning in some form or another, which is a complex process that cannot be completely measured by the individual snapshots of student work we typically use to assign "grades." Despite the copious amount of research and writing on grading and assessment for learning (see Suskie 2018) most academic disciplines outside of education do not spend time teaching future faculty members the nuances of both, or how to ethically and effectively grade students on whether they have been able to perform what it is we wanted them to learn. Grading individual assignments is likened to a snapshot because it freezes a specific instant in time over the course of the term when students completed something based on the course material or instruction. Freezing this moment allows us to look at it more carefully and examine it in light of the course objectives, learning outcomes, and goals for the course. Focusing on their work with this intensity provides us with insight into what they were able to *demonstrate* at this point in the term (after being instructed in the new material), but it does *not* tell us what they have *learned*.

Justice, as applied to the context of grading, requires that we behave in ways that are morally right and that we are fair and reasonable in our assessment of student work. This sounds easy in principle but is not necessarily so in practice. Research into implicit biases in the classroom indicates that we all carry implicit biases (about specific topics, content, people, methods of teaching and evaluation, etc.) and that we are not always aware of and that impact our teaching and evaluation practices (see Project Implicit, Harvard's ongoing Implicit Bias research project). However, most grading in business and engineering is traditional, relying on antiquated approaches to classroom teaching that are lecture heavy, delivered to large classes, and make use of easy-to-grade testing as their sources of evaluation. There is an assumption of objectivity in these disciplines that some might claim mitigates the need for assessing biases. Except that these areas are rife with biases in part *because* of their reliance on presumed objective measurements, cut and dried curriculum, and content matter for which there are "right" answers. This reliance on quantifiable measures exacerbates the myth of objectivity—that there is a singular truth discoverable through the application of the scientific method. Objectivity is a false hope because no measure of grading is actually objective, not even multiple-choice tests, because they rely on subjective selection of test items, phrasing of questions, level of difficulty, and cultural/ linguistic assumptions that do not resonate with all students. Each of these judgments is made by the instructor and includes that person's taken for granted assumptions and biases.

Because so much grading in engineering and business contexts is traditional rather than contemporary, it is inconsistent across instructors, sections, and programs (Suskie 2018). Learning goals are not always articulated meaningfully, outcomes or objectives make it difficult to assess them, and also likely that assignments are not tied to them as effectively as they could be, meaning grading is potentially unmoored from learning goals which increases the chances of grading *in*justice. Add to this that grading serves a gatekeeping function in US society—to allow some students to move forward and keep others in their place, and we have a recipe for further *in*justice (Walvoord and Anderson 1998). However, in a just society (a true meritocracy), the sorting function of grading should only be applied after each student has had an equitable chance to learn. Walvoord and Anderson (1998) explain that, "our entire effort, throughout the semester, should be pointed toward understanding our students, believing in them, figuring out what they need, and helping them to learn, no matter what their backgrounds" (i.e., gender, race, class, sexuality, religion, etc.) (15). For these reasons, our emphasis on justice is warranted and necessary, particularly when teaching in these contexts.

Thus justice, in these settings, is harder to come by because one must first destabilize the underlying foundational myths of these disciplines in order to begin a conversation about grading practices that are fair and reasonable. Included in all of this is the alignment between grading practices and what we wanted students to learn from the assignment in the first place. As Suskie (2018) explained, many faculty base their grading on well-defined learning goals and standards for evaluation, but just as many others base their criteria on ill-defined goals, or through the use of imprecise standards or shifting criteria (i.e., "I know an 'A' when I see one"). Walvoord and Anderson (1998) state that, "grade point averages too often represent a meaningless averaging of unclear assumptions and unstated standards" (ix). Without clear expectations, applicable standards for evaluation, and an awareness of how our own biases impact our evaluation of student work, it is nearly impossible to behave justly in our grading.

Ostensibly, the practice of grading is one method used to determine what our students have learned as a result of the curriculum presented in a classroom learning environment (i.e., lectures, readings, activities, assignments, quizzes, and exams). Our charge, as instructors, is to educate the students who come into our classrooms, thus grading is part and parcel of the process and something we should devote at least as much attention to as preparation of curricular materials. However, that is not always the case and grading can become an afterthought. Walvoord and Anderson (1998) found that there is a great deal of misalignment between the goals of instruction, the learning outcomes for courses in particular disciplines, and the methods used to grade student efforts. A typical example might be an instructor who wants her students to "think like" a member of her discipline (whatever discipline that may be), utilizing the methods and strategies that someone in the field would use to solve a problem or conduct research to answer a question. However, this instructor, met with the realities of a semester filled with teaching multiple courses, service work, research demands, advising, and a personal life, might default to using quizzes or exams to measure student learning. In this example, the learning outcome that she most wants her students to achieve is not what is being measured by what she is grading of the students' work. This scenario might sound familiar because it is all too common.

In my own teaching practice, I was advised early on to use tests and quizzes to make sure students had a common foundation of the concepts, vocabulary, and the main ideas from the content of the course, but these were paired with evaluations of student presentations and writing assignments to determine if students in my introductory communication studies courses were able to perform the desired skills at the competent or proficient level by the end of the term. Thus, there is nothing inherently "wrong" with tests, quizzes, or exams, but they are insufficient for assessing what students have (or have not) *learned* in the course because they emphasize recall and single correct answers rather than processes or patterns of thinking necessary to develop students into robust analytical thinkers for their field.

SUCCESSES AND FAILURES IN MAINTAINING BALANCE

Grading justly in interdisciplinary or cross-disciplinary teaching and partnerships relies on several factors, not the least of which is *who* is doing the grading. Since my roles have varied from co-teacher to guest lecturer and everything in between, I have had many chances to tinker with grading formats and responsibilities. Ideally, I have control over the grading rubric and am the one grading students' oral communication work. Less ideal, but still useful, is to be the one creating the categories for evaluation and the rubric even if someone else is going to actually grade student work. Least effective from a justice standpoint are the situations where I am asked to provide a guest lecture or content for a class project in business or engineering and the instructor creates the categories for evaluation and grades student work. Let me explain why: While I have no desire to limit who can be an effective evaluator of the spoken word, especially in a discipline specific setting where students are

Walking the Tightrope 121

presenting complex technical or professional information for which I am not the intended audience, I do think it important that those doing the evaluating have some knowledge and background in the form and function of oral presentations, the technical and artistic components, and how to spot them in the fleeting, ephemeral moments of an in-class presentation. An example might help illustrate my point.

A few years ago, I was working with a class of cyber-security students who were presenting on different tactics used in phishing emails and high-profile website hacks and leaks. The students presenting this material had done interesting research and were trying to explain the technical components of these events that the general public might be familiar with, but not understand how they happened. A student presenting his case study on Ashley Madison (a website for conducting illicit liaisons between married persons that guaranteed privacy—note the irony in them being hacked and their client list being made public) introduced the factual events of his case study and then proceeded to show pages of code as his visual aid (which were too small to read even from the front row). His explanation of the way that the hack was accomplished focused on vulnerabilities in specific lines of code and failures on the part of the IT team to complete basic safety protocols to avoid this kind of situation. Were his presentation meant as a training exercise for other coders or the IT team, I would have evaluated his performance differently. However, it was meant to be for a general public audience, and indeed many people from other departments and offices on campus were in the audience to add a realistic setting for these students. One of the audience members was the head of IT security for that campus and was the first to speak at the end, praising this "wonderful" presentation and saying how "excellent" he thought it was. During the break between presentations, I spoke with this man and asked specifically what he thought was so "wonderful" and what made it "excellent" from his perspective? He responded that the technical content was spot on and the student did a great job explaining how the vulnerabilities could be identified and then mitigated. I nodded in agreement. Then I asked if he thought that the majority of the audience understood it in the same way he did and if the student could have done anything differently to help them grasp those points? He responded affirmatively, explaining that it was a little too technical and that probably only "his guys" in the audience actually understood it. Then he suggested that the student could have made use of a few different examples to help the audience understand these coding flaws (he was talking about metaphors and analogies but without calling them that). "Then why did you say it was an 'excellent' presentation if there were these readily identifiable shortcomings?" I asked. He replied, "Because I liked it."

122 *Juliane Mora*

In this case, someone in a specific discipline evaluated a presentation based on hearing his preferred content presented (accurately, clearly, and comprehensively), even when the presentation of that content was *not* a key component of the assignment, or something for which the student was being evaluated. This audience member completed a feedback sheet for the student, as did everyone else in attendance, saying that the presentation was "great" while most of the others said it was hard to understand or relate to (and I know because I collected and collated them into summary comments for these students). I offer this example as a way to show how audience members may *like* a lot of things that are not necessarily aligned with the general guidelines for effective speaking practice, or that the speaker is being evaluated on. Liking something is a subjective judgment based on an individual's prior experiences, values, beliefs, and desires, but that alone is not the only, or best, measure for grading an effective presentation.

ROTATIONAL INERTIA—TO KEEP FROM FALLING

When working with faculty in other disciplines, there is a wide range of perspectives on what makes an acceptable presentation and many of them (in the sciences particularly) do not always differentiate between levels of performance in meaningful ways. While a rubric might contain gradations of performance (i.e., Good, Average, Poor; Expert, Intermediate, Novice; Exceeds Expectations, Meets Expectations, Below Expectations, etc.), I have found that faculty rarely use them in the ways they were intended—to provide qualitative feedback to help students improve their performance. Rather, I have found it common that faculty like presentations about the material of their discipline even when they are not good presentations, and they grade according to their preferences marking "Good" in every category. This is not necessarily a bad thing and it does not always mean that their grading is unjust, but in these instances, I have to do the work of explaining what I am trying to teach students to do with their presentational speaking—prepare and deliver audience-centered messages that are organized effectively for their purpose and delivered with appropriate enthusiasm for the context. Then, I have to explain why the grading my faculty partner completed is in contrast to the feedback I am providing. Most often, this has resulted in a split between what I grade versus what they grade, with the all too familiar "I'll grade the technical parts and you just grade the speaking" as if the two can ever really be separated.

Grading justice in these cross disciplinary contexts is challenging because I may not have any say in the grades assigned to student work, or I might be invited to give comments but not assign grades. In other cases, I have the autonomy to grade the "presentation portion" of the student work while their "real" instructor grades the content, and sometimes, I am solely responsible for grading their oral presentations on delivery and content. This means there is no one surefire way to grade in each instance that can be said to enhance justice in the process, and what justice means is different in each of these contexts. However, I argue that justice in grading should take into account the following factors: alignment between graded work and learning outcomes, fairness in evaluating student work, and attention to issues of power and oppression in the grading process.

Alignment. As mentioned previously, there is often a lack of alignment between what students are expected to learn in a given course and the means used to evaluate that learning. Wulff (2005) explained how alignment across multiple components of course design is necessary to create a holistic experience for the instructor and the learner and what happens if the goals at any of the stages are out of alignment. For example, if the learning outcomes for a course include students being able to "think like an engineer," but the measures used to assess that level of thinking are limited to exams, then you run the risk of misalignment between the learning goals and the methods for assessing them. Exam questions that ask for single "right answers" do not provide the space for students to demonstrate thinking or habits of mind consistent with the goals of thinking like a member of the profession. Justice in this scenario requires that the instructor spend time aligning the two areas and designing opportunities for students to show development as they learn to think like engineers. Case-based examples and scenario story problems are one way that students can be more adequately "tested" on how they are thinking within their discipline, but because they take more time to develop, and also to grade, they are not used as often (Sheppard, Macatangay, Colby, and Sullivan 2009). Projects that require students to apply their knowledge to an actual problem are much more likely in the engineering classes I have experienced, which makes alignment more achievable.

When it comes to oral communication instruction and the material that I integrate into engineering or business courses, my goal is to align the communication content with the content in the home discipline, to align the assignments with the things I want students to be able to know and do, and to align my grading with the learning goals for this collaboration. My current role is to integrate the material from the required core curriculum communication course across the entire four-year engineering program. Rather than having their students take our introduction to communication course, the engineering students are being exposed to the content and given opportunities to practice it in smaller, integrated modules across numerous courses at each grade level, with the goal of integrating this knowledge into their home discipline.

For example, in a second-year civil engineering course (Geomatics), students are learning to use mapping software to analyze various plots of land within a city to make recommendations for how to use it. The assignment from their engineering professor is to identify the best properties for development based on several factors: whether it is vacant, how flat it is, and how close it lies to existing roadways. Once they map their plot, they analyze it for possible uses and then make a recommendation for how (or if) the city should develop it. To this, we added a presentation component where the students prepare a persuasive presentation to deliver to the city planning department for how to make use of the plot. I created course content to introduce the presentation and teach communication principles relevant to the project. Content was presented via a fifty-minute lesson that overviewed audience analysis, persuasive public speaking, language choice, use of visual aids, and delivery considerations. Students record their presentations outside of class time (because there is not enough time during class) and submit them for evaluation. Once the videos have been submitted, the instructor views and grades them, and I view and grade them providing feedback and comments on the presentation. They are also assigned to other students who watch them and complete guided peer reviews, so that each student watches two other students' presentations and gives feedback.

Alignment happens in this module by mirroring the assignment description for the original project and asking students to provide an oral argument and reasons to persuade their audience to take action on their recommendation for the plot. Since the students are already tasked with the analysis and recommendation, adding the presentation component is a logical extension and provides a space to practice valuable material that could become part of their professional role. The content was aligned by identifying the specific audience (city planners), determining their level of background and technical knowledge to help students shape their messages, and providing guidance for how to translate their results and recommendations into a persuasive presentation using their data as support. The final component of alignment in this module is the feedback and grading, which includes peer, instructor, and a communication expert. Students have a structured peer review feedback form that asks them to evaluate elements of the presentation for their effectiveness, assess strengths and weaknesses, and provide feedback as an audience member. The engineering professor provides feedback on both the technical aspects of their findings and how well they used them to present a recommendation to their specific audience. I provide detailed feedback on the overarching narrative of their presentation as well as their organization, content, and delivery, and then grade their efforts based on a rubric created to align with the requirements of the assignment.

Fairness. In addition to alignment between each aspect of the course, content, and assignment, grading fairly is a necessary practice for justice. In the same way that it is not fair to test students through means that are out of alignment with the learning goals, it is not fair to grade students on a type of knowledge they have not been taught, or to grade them against a standard they have not seen. What I mean by fairness is looking at their work in the context of their major course of study, the relevance of the assignment for their professional roles, the amount of time they were exposed to the content required to perform their work, and the emphasis placed on it by their professor.

Civil engineering is the branch that creates the built environment for social life, designing, constructing, and maintaining roads, waterways, bridges, canals, and many other public works (ASCE 2019). The discipline requires that students have a depth of technical content knowledge as well as strong communication skills for interacting with and serving the public. Within the context of this definition, the assignment module for the second-year civil engineering course aligns with the field and is an example of the kind of presentation that civil engineers often give. Hence, it is fair to ask them to perform this task and to use it as a developmental learning opportunity for their future work as engineers.

However, I cannot grade student presentations in the civil engineering module described above the same way that I would students taking my introduction to communication course. At this point in their program, the engineering students have had one other module on teamwork, communication, and speaking basics in their first-year course. Given the gap in time between presentations, as well as the level and density of the engineering content they are learning, it often feels as though I am starting from scratch when I get classroom time with these students. Many of them self-report that they do not remember anything from the previous communication module, nor do they still possess the resources and handouts we used in that module to plan and practice their initial presentations. Fairness, then, requires that I evaluate their performance based on these factors and not apply the same expectations I would have for students delivering their second presentation in my continuous sixteen-week course.

The rubric contains the four criteria for which the students are being evaluated (content, organization, delivery, visual aids) with three levels of performance (Good, Average, Needs Work). The "Good" category articulates the performance expected from the student presentations at the highest level of proficiency I can reasonably expect them to attain at this point in their oral communication practice, while the "Average" and "Needs Work" categories illustrate the ways that the performance might miss the mark in common, or more unsatisfactory ways. For example, content evaluated as "Good" is carefully chosen to benefit the needs and knowledge level of the audience; includes all necessary definitions and examples for audience members to comprehend the topic; technical language and/or jargon are used sparingly and well explained; and all material is explained in relationship to general understandings for a non-technical audience. In comparison to my standalone course, this rubric is simplified and only contains three performance levels while the one I would use for students in my communication class has more gradation and detail and looks at more stylistic uses of language, movement, and imagery. Grading justly in this context depends, in part, on being fair in how I evaluate their sporadic oral communication assignments, as well as in relationship to the emphasis placed on their work from their engineering professor.

The importance of oral communication proficiency is supported by all disciplines of engineering and included in the requirements for accreditation by ABET (Accreditation Board for Engineering and Technology), the board responsible for accrediting programs in the STEM fields (science, technology, engineering and mathematics). "An ability to communicate effectively with a range of audiences" is one of the student outcomes each program wishing to attain (or maintain) accreditation must be able to assess (ABET 2019). With this emphasis, and the demand to produce assessment data showing that students have met this leaning outcome, it would be fair to assume engineering faculty would all place a similarly high degree of emphasis on integrating communication content. However, the bias towards technical content in engineering courses remains and assignments with an emphasis on learning and/or practicing communication content are not always foregrounded or assigned a significant percentage of the course grade. For example, if the entire civil engineering assignment is worth 10 percent of their grade (100 points out of 1000 for the course) and the amount allocated for the presentation is only 2 percent (20 points), then the students spend limited time and effort on their attempts because they realize that this is not as important as their "real" coursework. This practice remains a source of tension in some of my collaborative partnerships, but it is one that I foreground in all discussions about integration and assignment construction. Here, the language of justice is useful if I have to argue for the relevance of teaching communication skills for the professional realm because it is fundamentally unjust and unfair to skim over elements of their education that will be most useful in their future careers. Hence, I use the ABET criteria as well as evidence from practicing engineers and scholarship in engineering education (Reimer 2007) as leverage for balancing out the percentages assigned to the oral communication work students are assigned to produce in class.

Power and Oppression. The final aspect of grading justice in this context is attentiveness to the ways that power and oppression operate in engineering curricula. In recent years, a growing movement in engineering education has focused on social justice and engineering, arguing that "the increasing role that technology and engineering play in our lives, sometimes exacerbating injustices and inequalities and other times contributing to a more fair redistribution of resources and opportunities," making this an opportune moment for their integration (Lucena 2013, 4). This literature has, so far, emphasized models for integrating social justice concerns into engineering courses as well as understanding the unique experiences of marginalized or underrepresented students (Cech 2013). Critical pedagogy and social justice education in the humanities share an emphasis on critiquing and transforming power imbalances that have served to marginalize specific groups of students, most prominently people of color and women. These groups are still the most underrepresented in engineering programs and are strikingly out of balance with the number of their White male peers (Sheppard, Macatangay, Colby, and Sullivan 2009) even while some industry insiders claim that these gaps should be attributed to lack of interest or inability (Conger 2017). The conversation about grading justice with respect to these students in engineering can be a non-starter with some faculty who subscribe to positivist perspectives of the objectivity of the sciences (Riley 2008), the lack of students from "those groups" who are interested in engineering, or more overtly sexist beliefs that women do not make good engineers (Bright 2019). Since many professors use quizzes, homework, and exams as their methods of assessing whether the students have learned the material, and since those metrics are straightforward (from their perspective) with "right" answers, then how could their grading be anything but objective? Conversely, when we acknowledge that there is no such thing as pure objectivity and that all homework, quiz, and exam questions are written from a certain point of view and that point of view is grounded in the historical development and trajectory of the field of engineering, then it becomes easier to see how certain people's background experiences might not align with the underlying assumptions and presuppositions embedded in the questions.

The collaborative and integrated work that I pursue typically results in an oral communication assignment where students need to articulate engineering concepts or research in their own words for an audience. This kind of performance for showcasing learning is also risky for marginalized students because it places their bodies directly on display and they become the subject of scrutiny on multiple fronts. When students are speaking, they are the focus of attention, their face, body, and voice are the object of our gaze, and they are sharing information that they may or may not understand completely. In this space, they are being judged for more than their knowledge of the content as they might on a quiz or exam but on how they can explain it and how they look and sound while doing it. There is also a greater degree of subjectivity in evaluating oral presentations, even with clearly defined rubrics and categories for assessment. Rhetoric is also a historically White, male-dominated field and the standards for good oral speaking behaviors are imbued with that history favoring strong, erect posture and stature, a loud, clear speaking voice, commanding movement and gestures, and direct eye contact. Even when accounting for differences in style, these norms hold sway in the broader culture and can impact how student speakers are viewed and evaluated against these norms.

Returning, again, to the example from civil engineering, the rubric for the oral presentation delineates appropriate behaviors for delivery by student speakers with a desire to minimize historical bias. "Good" speakers are expected to use appropriate volume for the space and a confident and engaging tone of voice; explain their material competently and completely to showcase their knowledge of it; and use posture, movement and eye contact to add meaning to the material. By contrast, speakers who "Need Work" are speaking in ways that lack confidence, are unclear, or monotone; did not explain their material correctly (errors in terminology, processes, or explanations of either); and use of posture, movement and eye contact lacked purpose. These areas are not novel or unique, but the goal was to place the focus on things that the students should be doing to share their message with an audience and still have multiple options for how to do it from their embodied perspective and in their voices. In addition, the use of the rubric and comments is a space to show my engineering faculty partner how I am evaluating student presentations and which aspects I am commenting on.

Assignments and assessments like this are teaching moments to share with colleagues in another department what kind of work we (in Communication Studies) are routinely looking for in student speaking. It is also an opportunity to reinforce their understanding of how to evaluate speaking themselves. Grading justly requires understanding the historical biases associated with marginalized bodies and voices in the engineering classroom as well as the bias towards more "objective" forms of measurement to argue for a criterion-based evaluation that has a greater chance of being fair when it is completed by someone who has more expertise in evaluating this kind of work.

CONCLUSION—CARRYING A BALANCING POLE WHILE YOU WALK

Despite calls for increased interdisciplinarity and integrated curriculum models, and the apparent enthusiasm for pursuing them, there remain difficulties

Walking the Tightrope 129

in carrying out this mission while adequately representing the communication discipline. In the work that I have described here, the breadth and depth of the communication discipline has been narrowed and flattened to "fit" into the disciplinary curricula of business and engineering while still offering the singular component most prized in these spaces—effective oral presentations. Arguably, the same can be said of many other disciplinary spaces and partnerships where effective oral communication is desired and communication instructors teach this content (i.e., medical partnerships teaching health professionals improved communication skills). It could even be said to be true in many core curriculum "public speaking" courses where the desire is for every student to be able to deliver a clear, coherent presentation regardless of their discipline. In teaching three different iterations of this course at three different institutions, it was a struggle for me to maintain a firm focus on *why* this material was a required part of the core as opposed to just *how* students were supposed to perform. In the liberal arts tradition, the trivium of grammar, logic, and rhetoric were required for the good citizen to be able to perform all of the duties required of them in a democratic society. On many campuses, this foundational tenet remains the reason for requiring an oral communication course to begin with, but it is progressively buttressed with calls from industry and the professional realm for increased training in communication skills for the workforce.

Hence, we have numerous opportunities to teach our discipline in service of the tasks of other fields, but the juxtaposition between teaching in these contexts and within an actual communication studies department can be disorienting at best and divergent, or opposite facing, at worst. The inconsistency between these spaces impacts the process and product of teaching, but more importantly for this volume, the practice of grading. I have tried to elaborate on some components of grading practice that align most coherently with social justice goals when teaching communication across the curriculum. Perhaps we need to challenge the myth of objectivity prevalent in other fields followed by attention to alignment between what is being asked of students and what is being assessed (alignment between learning outcomes and what they are graded on), and, finally, criterion-based evaluations that are attentive to the histories of marginality and oppression within academic spaces that have disproportionately affected women and students of color.

In sum, these practices have been useful in my cross-disciplinary work, but they are also applicable to those teaching in a variety of other contexts and positions as well. Graduate students, lecturers, and contingent faculty are often handed a syllabus for the courses they are teaching without much influence over the design of the content or assignments, but they are the ones who perform all of the grading. In these instances, similar attention can be paid to alignment, fairness, and power and oppression by using the agency that these instructors *do* have to present the content and evaluate the student's work. By this, I mean that these instructors still have the ability to frame content from required courses and texts, emphasizing the aspects most in alignment with the required assignments and grading rubrics. They are also free to interpret those rubrics as they see fit based on how they have taught the course material, working to make them a fair assessment of the work each student produced. Attentiveness to power and oppression can become a standalone unit in the course, or a meta-discussion about the history of public address (and the teaching of it) to highlight these themes throughout. I frame the work I am engaged in as social justice pedagogy whether it is teaching a "basic" public speaking course, a segment of an engineering or business course, or an advanced communication course with a social justice title. Looking for the seams and cracks in prescribed materials for ways to make the content, assignments, and grading more justly is difficult but not impossible and provides ways to be part of the larger project of social justice even if they do not have more control over their courses or curriculum.

This work is not sexy, like other areas of social justice work (namely activism), but it is necessary to show how we can examine and change every day mundane or thoughtless grading practices for the benefit of our students learning. While overall numbers of faculty currently teaching in positions like mine across disciplines are difficult to count, it stands to reason that we may see more opportunities for this kind of work amidst calls for increasing interdisciplinarity. As other professional disciplines reach out for similar partnerships to prepare their graduates with communication skills for the professional realm, we need to be thoughtful and conscientious about the ways we engage. More so, we cannot divorce social justice content or approaches, like grading, from our practice if we ever hope to move the needle closer to a more just and equitable world.

REFERENCES

ABET. 2019. "About ABET." Accessed December 15, 2019. https://www.abet.org/about-abet/.

ASCE. 2019. "American Society of Civil Engineers." Accessed December 15, 2019. https://www.asce.org.

Bright, Peter. 2019. "Microsoft Engineer Complains that Company is Biased Against White Men." *Ars Technica.* April, 22, 2019. https://arstechnica.com/tech-policy/2019/04/now-its-microsofts-turn-for-an-anti-diversity-internal-revolt/.

Cech, Erin A. 2013. "The (Mis)Framing of Social Justice: Why Ideologies of Depoliticization and Meritocracy Hinder Engineers' Ability to Think About Social

Injustices." In *Engineering Education for Social Justice: Critical Explorations and Opportunities*, edited by Juan Lucena, 67–84. New York: Springer.

Colby, Anne, Ehrlich, Thomas, Sullivan, William M., and Jonathan R. Dolle. 2011. *Rethinking Undergraduate Business Education: Liberal Learning for the Profession*. San Francisco: Jossey-Bass.

Conger, Kate. 2017. "Exclusive: Here's the 10-page Anti-Diversity Screed Circulating Internally at Google [Updated]." Gizmodo.com. August 5, 2017. https://gizmodo .com/exclusive-heres-the-full-10-page-anti-diversity-screed-1797564320 .

Freire, Paulo. 1970. *Pedagogy of the Oppressed*. New York: Continuum.

hooks, bell. 1994. *Teaching to Transgress: Education as the Practice of Freedom*. New York: Routledge.

Lucena, Juan, ed. 2013. *Engineering Education for Social Justice: Critical Explorations and Opportunities*. New York: Springer.

The National Academies of Sciences, Engineering, and Medicine. 2018. *The Integration of the Humanities and Arts with Sciences, Engineering, and Medicine in Higher Education: Branches from the Same Tree*. Washington, DC: The National Academies Press.

Project Implicit. 1998. "Project Implicit Social Attitudes." Harvard University. Accessed December 17, 2019. https://implicit.harvard.edu/implicit/.

Reimer, Marc J. 2007. "Communication Skills for the 21st Century Engineer." *Global Journal of Engineering Education* 11 (1): 89–100.

Riley, Donna. 2008. *Engineering and Social Justice*. San Rafael, CA: Morgan and Claypool Press.

Sheppard, Sheri D., Macatangay, Kelly, Colby, Anne, and William M. Sullivan. 2009. *Educating Engineers: Designing for the Future of the Field*. San Francisco: Jossey-Bass.

Shulman, Lee S. 2011. Foreword. In *Rethinking Undergraduate Business Education: Liberal Learning for the Profession*, Anne Colby, Thomas Ehrlich, William M. Sullivan, and Jonathan R. Dolle, vii–xiii. San Francisco: Jossey-Bass.

Suskie, Linda. 2018. *Assessing Student Learning: A Common Sense Guide*. San Francisco: Jossey-Bass.

Walvoord, Barbara E., and Virginia Johnson Anderson. 1998. *Effective Grading: A Tool for Learning and Assessment*. San Francisco: Jossey-Bass.

Weisz, Eva, and Barry Kanpol. 1990. "Classrooms as Socialization Agents: The Three R's and Beyond." *Education* 111 (1): 100–104.

Wiggins, Grant, and Jay McTighe. 2005. *Understanding by Design*. (2nd Ed.) Upper Saddle River, NJ: Pearson.

Wulff, Donald. 2005. *Aligning for Learning: Strategies for Teaching Effectiveness*. Boston: Anker Publishing Company.

Chapter Five

Student-Activist Mentor Letters as a Form of Social Movement-Building in Communication Activism Pedagogy

David L. Palmer

Grading student work, as this text prudently reminds us, is an ideological act. How and why teachers assess student work reflect the worlds they envision. A survey of assessment designs in traditional education, for example, reveals a robust free market vision, one that that emphasizes market rationality, transactional individualism, and student marketability. Those values are inscribed in standard assessment forms such as exams and papers that are individuated, isolated and indexed to forecast student market value (e.g., Kahl, Jr., this volume; Palmer 2014).

Remarkably, in traditional education, justice—in particular, justice as applied advocacy—receives minor attention, at best, and largely is cast as an externality to education and the market. In a culture that touts justice as a core value, ironically, our education system clearly is much more concerned with producing market-ready personnel than it is with training our citizenry to engage in the collective work that justice demands. As a consequence, assessment is seldom connected to the living work of justice.

To grasp the nature of grading justice, scholars should study assessment designs that emphasize justice as applied advocacy. Nowhere are those alternative models more prominent than in activist education, which connects students to social causes such as gender violence (e.g., Richardson and Speedy 2019) corporate deforestation (e.g., Carey 2014), reproductive justice (e.g., Desai 2019), prison activism (e.g., Hartnett, Novek, and Wood 2013) and energy justice (e.g., Osnes and Bisping 2014). Because activism education seeks goals that acutely contrast with traditional education, activism teachers are in a unique position to re-envision and recast traditional assessment practices.

Where traditional education seeks to reproduce culture and develop market personnel, activism pedagogy seeks to impel social change and help build advocacy communities. Activism educators are motivated by the fact that moral change historically has been forged by justice movements (e.g., Choudry 2015). Forging a more just world, history tells us, takes a lot of dedicated people working together over time. It makes sense, then, that one core goal of communication activism pedagogy (CAP) is to help build social movements (e.g., Frey and Palmer 2014). Fostering social movements requires connecting students in meaningful ways to social causes about which they are passionate. In my Communication and Social Activism course, students work directly with causes that inspire them and they eagerly engineer activism projects that champion those causes.

One assignment in that course that supports movement building is a *mentor letter* that asks current students, as their final project, to share letters about their activism experience with future students who are passionate about the same cause. My environmental student-activists, for instance, draft letters that, the following year, are given to new students who pursue environmental activism. The mentor letter bridges veteran students—and, by extension, the social cause—with inbound students as veterans introduce them to the movement, describe regional initiatives, outline proven tactics, and offer words of inspiration. The mentor letter fosters justice movements as it connects student-activists to each other and to their broader advocacy fields. The study of CAP assessment reflects activism scholarship that examines knowledge production and learning within justice movements (see e.g., Choudry and Vally 2018; Kilgore 1999).

My goal in this chapter is to examine an innovative view of assessment as a means of fostering justice advocacy and movements. The chapter examines the curricular and assessment designs of the activism course; in particular, the mentor letter. I argue that grading justice in a CAP framework devalues routine assessment designs that individuate and isolate student outcomes, and instead, reimagines assessment as an opportunity for students to build knowledge and outcomes within communities responding to social problems. The chapter first outlines groundwork ideas about activism and its place within civic-justice systems and education. The second section outlines an overview of the activism course. The third section examines the mentor letter and its outcomes. The final section contrasts traditional and activism education assessment and details my approach to grading in the activism course.

ACTIVISM, JUSTICE SYSTEMS, AND EDUCATION

CAP grounds student work in the living practices of activism, and student advocacy is the focus of course instruction and assessment. Activism historically has emerged as a grassroots response to persistent injustices. Justice, simply put, is the rectification of unfair and toxic social policies and outcomes. While modern societies designate state legal and civic systems to maintain a moral society, those systems fall short of their designated goals and, in fact, often reinforce systems of injustice (e.g., Moore 2015). In response, across the last century, grassroots initiatives, often in the form of activism, emerged in unions, churches, health care, and sports to counter persistent forms of injustice, and the central role of activism in women's liberation, worker and civil rights, and environmental sustainability has greatly helped expand justice in those areas.

Those grassroots initiatives developed over time into a vibrant global network of justice-related associations, including non-governmental organizations, research and policy institutes, cause coalitions and activist communities that focus on a vast array of social causes (see e.g., Routledge and Cumbers 2009). Poverty, climate change, and human trafficking, for example, are multifaceted social crises that are now the focus of complex, organizational networks that manage problem outcomes and help engineer solutions. Amnesty International, MADRE, and Human Rights Watch, for example, reside in networks that employ various admixtures of crisis relief and solution development projects, and activism is one unique set of tactics used across those networks.

Activism is the tactical act of intervening into socio-political culture to campaign for and engineer more just conditions. Activism as intervention is both a product, such as a strike or a sit-in, and the process of organizing its production, which can be anything, from stuffing envelopes to holding meetings, that facilitates that intervention. CAP exposes students to activism as a regime of organizing and intervention tactics and it emphasizes their symbolic content.

Activism can stem from professional organization directives, such as an NAACP rally, or it can stem from less formal initiatives, such as the Greensboro Four lunch counter sit-ins (see e.g., Chafe 1980). There are notable variances between institutional and less formal forms of activism, which are distinguished with respect to range of permissible tactics. Because professional advocacy organizations covet their legal status, funding streams, and institutional hierarchies, they often limit their menu of intervention tactics. The Sierra Club, for instance, a professional environmental enterprise, limits its tactics to fundraising and recruiting, educating the public, and mobilizing legal advocacy and activism to foster pro-environmental policy. Activist networks, however, which largely are informal, horizontal, volunteer systems, are free to employ less conventional tactics to propel social change. Extinction Rebellion, for example, a loose coalition of climate change activist communities, is free to employ a wider range of tactics (e.g., civil disobedience, direct action, and nonviolent resistance) to propel change in environmental policies and practices. In many instances, these organizations work in tandem to shape environmental policy and outcomes while, at other times, they seek different levels of socio-political change.

The advancements that justice movements have made across the last century are remarkable given their scarce ties to education, and with most of those few ties transpiring only recently. Applied activism pedagogy (or, teaching designs that direct students to engage in social activism) in particular, has been remarkably undeveloped in a milieu that oddly exalts activist movements, such as civil rights, on one hand, yet frames their tactics as too political and perilous to teach on the other. Instead, liberal democratic education remains chiefly focused on student market preparation and it extols transactional individualism, corporate efficiency, and materialism, values that, in many ways, counter the spirit of justice advocacy and the possibilities of a more participatory democracy (e.g., McLaren and Kincheloe 2007). Moreover, its civic initiatives, such as traditional service learning, which grapple to appear apolitical and non-partisan, focus more on managing social problem symptoms (e.g., feeding the homeless) than on changing the structural conditions that produce those problems (e.g., Britt 2014).

Traditional education, thus, has proven largely anemic in its efforts to solve ongoing socio-political crises; in particular, its efforts to produce an informed and mobilized problem-solving citizenry. Banks (2004) reminds us that the "world's greatest problems do not result from people being unable to read and write. They result from people in the world—from different cultures, races, religions, and nations—being unable to get along and to work together to solve the world's intractable problems such as global warming, the HIV/AIDS epidemic, poverty, racism, sexism, and war" (298). Activism pedagogy that exposes students to both professional and less formal advocacy systems helps foster a mobilized citizenry that can contribute to those solutions.

THE SOCIAL ACTIVISM COURSE

I annually teach a graduate-undergraduate Communication and Social Activism course that serves twenty to twenty-five students. The course stems from my activist work, my scholarship with activist educators, and my interest in applied critical pedagogy (e.g., Frey and Palmer 2014). The core objectives of the course are to expose students to formal and activist systems and to have them examine the role of communication in the creation of and solutions to social problems. While activism educators often focus student work on a single, preset issue, my course seeks to emulate beyond-school conditions as it has students identify problems about which they are passionate and contribute every week to regional organizations that are actively working on that cause.

The course is purposefully taught online so that students can dedicate three hours a week of what otherwise would be class time to their field work. The course is split every week between the class examining activism-related content and students engaging in and reporting on civic justice work. That participatory approach is a form of *action learning* that guides students to experience and apply civic organizing and problem-solving tactics in ways that extend beyond classroom learning.

First, the course houses an intensive activism curriculum. We examine liberal versus strong democracies, theories of civic participation and social activism, consensus and community building strategies, and thematic activism tactics. Moreover, we study social movements, such as the civil rights approach, including its core organizations, their philosophies and uses of direct action and nonviolent civil disobedience, and their activism training methods. Special emphasis is placed on activism as intervention to foster change in the conditions that produce social problems, not simply the work that manages their surface symptoms.

Second, students are required to locate regional formal organizations that are connected to social causes about which they are passionate and to work with those organizations across the semester; causes that include human trafficking, homelessness, environmental advocacy, immigration issues, and reproductive rights. Justice educators emphasize community as a vital platform for advocacy work (e.g., Bettez and Hytten 2013) and, thus, routine student involvement in professional advocacy organizations is a course emphasis and subject for student reflection. Students use a variety of online databases, such as All for Good and Corporation for National and Community Service, to locate regional volunteer opportunities, and they have worked, for example, with Colorado Rising, Partners Mentoring Youth, Colorado Hands and Voices, Catholic Charities, BUENO Center for Multicultural Education, and Free Our Girls. Optimally, and often, that involvement exposes them to the structural and lived conditions of social problems and to the routinized labor found in advocacy organizations used to manage and help solve those problems.

Third, students report in every week to a discussion board to analyze and discuss the assigned activism content and to summarize their field work. The discussion board is the course's central deliberative forum where we all share and discuss our ideas and experiences. By design, students teach each other (and me) about the course content and their fieldwork experiences. Because students pursue work in a variety of social causes, their weekly posts provide a window for the rest of us into the nature of why and how people get involved in those specific causes. As each student publicly journals their journey through the social cause field, they discuss their passions and fears, the nature and causes of the problem, national and regional solution initiatives, how they gained entrée into an advocacy community, and their weekly fieldwork experience.

Fourth, each student is required to design and implement an activist event (beyond their weekly civic work) that furthers the interests of their social cause. Students review histories and menus of event ideas that they can emulate, or they can create their own original projects. Students can also blend their project with an existing organizational event. The activist event is the centerpiece and culmination of the course and we spend the entire semester—one weekly step at a time—helping students develop, organize, and implement their projects. Activism events include fundraising and resource drives, film-discussion and tabling events, cause awareness and education campaigns, engineering protests, and video activism. The activism project, like all social movement work, is an incubator for knowledge production and learning that takes place in the daily struggles for social change (see Kelley 2002).

Fifth, each student, at the end of the course, crafts the mentor letter to future students about their course-related experience. The mentor letter summarizes the student's semester-long work and provides a valuable working guide to incoming students about how they can effectively navigate the complex cultural terrain of justice work (see sample mentor letter in Appendix B).

THE MENTOR LETTER

The mentor letter came about one day as I was simply trying to think of a final assignment that my students would not find routine and uninspiring (as, let's face it, most final assignments are), but instead, one that would animate them to share their activism story. Having often been inspired myself by activist testimonies and calls to action, the idea of a personal letter from current to future students came to mind. Drafting that letter inspires veteran students to tell their story, provide cause-specific overviews, and share their experiences and wisdom, a resource that inbound students find equally inspiring and immensely useful.

The mentor letter falls within a time-honored tradition to use letter-writing as an effective form of teaching and learning. Letter writing personalizes knowledge, frames ideas in narrative formats that are easily relatable, encourages students to reflect on course content in unique ways, and is valued as much for its social connection merit as it is for its informational content (see, e.g., Burand and Ogba 2013; Fredericksen 2000). The mentor letter augments those outcomes as it provides continuity between activism course iterations and promotes for both veteran and new students a sense of connection to and solidarity with the broader movement.

The mentor letter assignment consists of two parts. The first section is a personal note to future students that welcomes them to the movement, provides advice for their fieldwork and offers words of encouragement. The second section outlines an overview of the problem, its related social cause and the student's formal and activism project work (see mentor letter assignment in Appendix A). The mentor letter's content can be grouped into five interrelated mentorship categories: (a) personal testimony and connection, (b) the social cause, (c) traversing the social cause field, (d) the activism project, and (e) general advice and encouragement. The sections below outline these categories and highlight germane student responses.

Personal testimony and connection. Social movements are not organizations; instead, they are the ongoing systems of people organizing to engineer incremental advancements along the long arc toward justice. The environmental movement, for example, since the 1800s, has been passed from one generation to the next and will continue to grow into the future.

People are drawn to social movements that embody their values and to which they have a personal connection. In fact, one chief resource of movement recruitment is the social network of existing members (e.g., Klandermans and Oegema 1987). People concerned about climate change, for example, are more prone to get and stay involved in environmental activism if they know someone who is part of that movement.

People are also drawn to social movements because they constitute publics whose combined actions can overcome barriers to justice that are beyond the purview of individual actors. When asked what drew such large numbers to the 1999 Seattle WTO protests, the environmental activist, Vandana Shiva, stated, "there was an invitation to join hands, and the joining of hands happened because . . . otherwise we are not going to make a difference. Each of us is too tiny, each of us is only addressing a tiny piece of this giant problem; and, until we join hands, we are not even going to begin to address it" (Rowley and Friedberg 2000).

The mentor letter makes a similar invitation as veteran students reach out to connect with inbound students, and to support their enlistment in a cause about which they share a deep passion. As one environmental student-activist wrote,

> Welcome and congratulations on raising your voice and joining others who seek to make this world a better place. In this upcoming semester, you will find

this course to be a beginning point for your activism journey. It does not matter what your passion is, whether it be the environment or social justice, fan the flame and don't let it go out. This is your journey, enjoy, express yourself, and be heard.

Veteran students outline how their life circumstances connected them to the problem. Sharing their story reinforces their role as a movement stakeholder and advocate for its development. An immigration reform student-activist who worked with an organization that facilitates educational opportunities for undocumented youth wrote,

> I am a Mexican-American woman who is extremely passionate about education and how it can become the avenue through which Latinx communities can thrive and create important change for the better. As a first-generation American citizen from two immigrant parents, I have witnessed the struggle that comes with trying to give future generations a better lifestyle through hard work, and unfortunately, sometimes, having to endure discrimination as well. Working with this population is instantly rewarding . . . it helps give young adults options while waiting for legislation that can legalize their status in the U.S.

For incoming students, reviewing these stories allows them to grasp what led others to get involved in the cause, reminds them of their own contribution motives, and fosters a sense of solidarity with the cause. One new student wrote,

> I really enjoyed being able to read the letters from former students. It was especially helpful for me to read [this veteran's] letter . . . because it related to my topic and encouraged me that someone else had chosen something so challenging. It was meaningful to me because I learned from what she did, and I also related to some of the struggles that she had! It made me feel like it was worth it to keep doing this work, even when I felt like I was doing nothing.

The social cause. Effective justice advocacy requires having a clear view of the problem, its underlying causes, and the history of solution initiatives. To that end, veteran students outline a concise overview of the problem, its related organizational field and core problem management and solution tactics. In addition, they outline key resources that proved especially informative to their grasp of the situation. Those overviews are valuable resources for inbound students, who are better able to strategize about how they will connect to solution initiatives and engineer the outcomes they envision. One new student wrote,

> I [found] it meaningful for a previous student to write us a letter, mainly because it gave me motivation to keep working with my organization. Knowing their

Student-Activist Mentor Letters as a Form of Social Movement-Building 141

background, and how they are people just like us helping the world, makes me want to do as they do. The advice that was given was extremely helpful in the long run because it helped me decide what areas in my cause I needed to learn more about, and what I should work on in general. For example, [this veteran's] advice was geared towards not being hesitant and being prepared. This advice was extremely helpful when it came to my activism project, where, thanks to her advice, I tried to take all the possible steps to help get the word out about my cause, and I was prepared.

Traversing the social cause field. Social causes are complex networks of national and regional organizations that have overlapping and unique connections to the problem. Even with access to the ample databases that help students connect to those networks, traversing a social cause arena can be complex and confusing. Students often struggle (as they will beyond my course) to find relevant organizations that are receptive to their inquiries and, at times, they must patchwork together participation opportunities across several organizations. They also outline their successful and ineffective tactics to connect with local organizations, a reflexive exercise from which they gain insights into their fieldwork experience. One mental health student-activist wrote,

I got involved in this social cause by reaching out to Mental Health Colorado and asking about their tactics for activism. They were very slow in getting back to me and I eventually gave up with them due to their lack of response. I found that just e-mailing people or trying to call once was not an effective strategy. I had to be very persistent in my attempts to reach out to people. I would recommend that after sending an e-mail, it is important to get someone on the phone to chat or to show up at the office of whatever place you are to get involved with. This forces someone to talk to you. I then turned to the City of Greeley and got involved with its Bike Initiative, which focuses on promoting mental and physical health for youth by providing bicycle clinics. This was really fun, but not what I was totally looking for. I finally ended up getting involved with the Student Athlete Advisory Committee on campus, which is a group of athletes, two representatives from each team, who meet to discuss athletics on the UNC campus. Through this group I got involved in mental health initiatives and got connected with the [school's] sports psychologist. This connection was very helpful, and I was able to participate in many events regarding mental health.

Inbound students benefit from the letter's first-hand overview of the organizational field, what regional organizations are and are not worth their time investment, and what involvement tactics are useful and those that should be avoided. One incoming student wrote,

I think the letters were helpful for advice when doing activism work and for maintaining passion for the work, but having the organization in common and the same cause in common helped me to connect to the student through the letter without knowing them and without them knowing me. Free Our Girls connected us and that was really helpful and cool. It made it feel more like a conversation rather than a letter to anyone and everyone.

Veteran students also describe in detail their fieldwork, including both its major activities and its routine tasks. Foley (1999) suggests that vital didactic sources in social movement activity are the mundane tasks that seem incidental, yet, upon reflection, are recognized as the essential, organizing work of activism. One member of an on-campus environmental organization wrote,

A brief summary of the events Earth Guardians and I took on this semester include: (1) Food for Thought campaign. This was our vegan cookout that was a blast! It was so great seeing students enjoying 100% plant-based options [compared] to traditional food dishes like mac and cheese. We had great feedback and students really wanted to learn about the harm the meat and dairy industry causes. We passed out a lot of viable information and were greeted with so many surprised students over the facts and delicious food. (2) Up Cycling with Organic Tie-dye. This event was so much fun! We got down and dirty in the kitchen boiling up some fruits and veggies to create our dye . . . it was super awesome to hear students joyfully say that they are going to reuse their scraps to make dye, then reuse old clothing to make it new again. We felt we did a real great job as a club promoting ourselves, our cause of wasting less and solutions to our waste! (3) Advocating for Prop 112 [an anti-fracking bill]. This was a long haul but definitely one of the events I am most proud of. For a whole month we showed our support for Prop 112 and spread the word through tabling, pamphlets and small events. Each week we were in the University Center passing out voter guides (provided to us by New Era) and stickers that we created ourselves; at events we passed out candy and other promotional items by partnering with organizations.

Incoming students benefit from internal views of an advocacy organization's operations, their social cultures, and the tactics its members employ. One theme among incoming student mentor letter responses, for example, was a sense of identification with veteran student struggles to connect to an advocacy organization's busy staff. One new student wrote,

[The letter] was meaningful because I easily connected with the cause, since it is my own, and it was helpful seeing that the communication struggles I have been having with the organization have happened to more volunteers than myself. I thought maybe I was not reaching out to the right people or sending the wrong information but seeing the validation in this letter that the very busy leaders of this organization take time to get back to volunteers made me feel much better and much more patient.

The activism project. The core course assignment, the activism project, requires students to plan, coordinate personnel and resources, and implement event logistics. Veteran students outline detailed overviews of their projects and the role communication played throughout the project, and they eagerly share their struggles and successes. One human trafficking student-activist, a graduate teaching assistant, wrote:

> I battled back and forth on what to do. Should I host a table at the University Center? Make a video of interviews? Hold a night where people can just come and talk about the issue? But then I realized, I have a huge advantage being a teaching assistant. I figured if I did the table, hosted a night of conversation, or made a video, I may not have the potential to reach as many people as I did with hosting it in class. So, originally, Free Our Girls was planning on coming in to talk, but they got too busy, so I contacted Love Made Claim and Natosha (founder) and Katie (longtime volunteer) were able to come in and speak about stats and their organization; we had questions at the end I was able to video it as well. The project was amazing! Katie talked about what sex trafficking is and the statistics, and Natasha talked about her organization and what resources they are able to provide. My students were also given a hotline to call if they or anyone they know is in danger or at-risk of sex trafficking. My students were engaged, wanted to know more, wanted to help, and there was just a lot of great dialogue.

The mentor letter provides incoming students with valuable information about successful projects, their logistical requirements, and effective and ineffective organizing tactics. Project descriptions provide insights into how to connect activism goals to useful planning and implementation tactics. As one new student wrote,

> Seeing how former students laid out a plan of action and how they planned out their events gave a realistic idea of what could get done and how it could get done.

Another new student noted,

> The [activism event] descriptions were helpful in terms of understanding different types of activism and how they can be implemented, especially because we read the letters as we learned about those different approaches. I think the specific organization and methodology of different types of activism events is a huge takeaway from this class.

General advice and words of encouragement. The hardships and complexities tied to activism are one reason people struggle with (if not avoid) justice advocacy work. The system and methods of justice work can be complex, and the labor is often demanding. The mentor letter enables veteran students to pass-along their advice for activism, including the things they did well and the things they would do differently. Moreover, they provide words of encouragement to stay committed to the exacting work of activism. One veteran student wrote,

> I've learned activism is hard work and can be incredibly draining. When you are wholeheartedly fighting for something it seems no one else cares about, it can make you feel as if you are fighting for nothing. But for every voice telling you that you can't or that you won't be able to succeed, you need to push that much harder. To be an activist, you have to have a thick hide and kind heart or else you will never succeed. The balance between these two character traits cannot be accomplished overnight, but it is a skill that will last a lifetime. You are strong, you are loving, and you can do anything if you put your mind to it.

Another veteran student wrote,

> I did not consider myself to be an activist before I took this class, [but] I got to dig into something that really made my heart shine, make a difference, spread awareness, and I learned so much about activism in general. It was truly inspiring and eye-opening! When things get tough, just remember you are doing a good thing. Tough things allow us to grow, learn about ourselves, even teach other people a thing or two about us. Take it one week at a time, give yourself some grace when things aren't going how you expected, and always communicate with your peers and professor. You really do have the power to change the world—even the smallest things can add up to be the biggest. Good luck to you!

The mentor letter has proven to be an inspiring and useful assessment tool in my activism course, and student comments reveal that they really enjoy and value this assignment. Letter outcomes reinforce peer mentorship research findings that mentoring enhances learning for both mentors and mentees (Snowden and Hardy 2012). As veteran students craft the letter, they frame its content in a mentor (not just student) voice that binds them to the task and its purpose to support future students and promote the cause. Assuming the role of activist mentor elevates students beyond their routine assessment role of isolated, reiterative learner whose knowledge gains quickly dissipate and have little (if any) civic value. Instead, their course experience and letter content are entirely unique, and students are motivated to speak as experienced, collaborative advocates who are paying their knowledge and passion forward. Moreover, the letter reinforces their identity as a stakeholder in the movement as they express pride in and hope for the social cause. One veteran student wrote,

No matter how much work you put into a cause there will typically still be an opposing force. I have had to endure being called an environmental terrorist, had things thrown at my car, and have been flipped off for trying to keep our earth safe . . . but I don't let it hinder my cause; many activists before us have endured worse (like the Civil Rights movement) and it's worth it for our voices to be recognized.

As mentioned, one chief source of movement recruiting is the social network of existing members. The mentor letter functions as a social network invitation from a peer student and fellow advocate that directly connects inbound students to the cause. The letter also provides new students with valuable insights into how to pursue their course work, and its content provides scaffolding advice and support that imbues them with the sense that they are not atypical and uninformed as they traverse their cause arena. As a result, inbound students are more equipped to connect their activism goals to practical tactics, and to avoid organizations and tactics that have proven impractical. As one new student wrote,

The letter was very helpful because around [the time I read it] I was feeling really frustrated with my event and the organization because I was totally focused on my time and my agenda rather than remembering the big picture of how much the cause needs help and how much awesome work the members of Free Our Girls were doing that was keeping them from immediately responding to me. Additionally, in the letter from [this veteran] she said, "remember all those voiceless out there who care just like you and are begging for a leader . . . think of all the changes in this you can create by taking action . . . if you give up then the world persists as usual, if you try to do something then you make an impact." This was very moving and encouraging to me and really reminded me to keep going and not be someone not trying at all. Hearing straight from another volunteer was very helpful and made me feel connected to the volunteer community.

LEARNING, ASSESSMENT, AND JUSTICE ADVOCACY

Activism pedagogy invites educators to recast the nature and goals of learning and assessment. Traditional education frames learning as the measurable gains in isolated, individual cognitive and behavioral outcomes indexed as feedback for learners and educators. CAP frames learning as a socio-political process in which citizens collaboratively produce knowledge relevant to the situated demands of advocacy work, and it employs cultural struggles for justice as its central instructional spaces. Social activism and movements are rarely formulaic; instead, they are situated responses to unfolding circumstances and challenges inherent to cultural crises (e.g., Hildyard 2016). While cognitive and behavioral learning gains remain vital in CAP, its assessment foregrounds how students build knowledge as they collaboratively contribute to problem-solving initiatives.

Because knowledge production and learning in collective action contexts have features that vary from individualized, culturally segregated knowledge forms and acquisition, clarifying those variations is vital to a grasp of activism education assessment. CAP assessment tactics are unique and informative, in part, because they neatly contrast to traditional market education assessment. In the age of neoliberal education, much of the humanities and social sciences—including communication—depict students as future market personnel and they use vocation-preparation language to frame their curriculum and teaching designs. Neoliberal education reflects the logic of the market as it prepares students to participate-in a system that is aggregated, competitive, privatized, and profit-driven. Traditional assessment tools, such as exams and papers, implicitly define students as isolated, competitive, self-interested individuals. Moreover, those tools produce perishable outcomes (e.g., isolated feedback and numerical grades) that have little civic merit or connective or teaching value to other students, current or successive.

Applied activism education, however, operates on a much different logic, one that sees students as members of social movements and that uses the language of collective moral transformative action to frame its teaching designs. CAP reflects the logic of social activism as it prepares students to participate-in systems that are cooperative, justice-oriented, and socio-political change-driven. Learning that is grounded in activism is largely experiential, inductive, and collective. As students perform both the mundane and collective organizing and intervention work of activism, they incrementally internalize knowledge and skills that support that work. CAP assessment tools, such as the activist project and the mentor letter, explicitly define students as communal, supportive, and cause focused. Moreover, those tools produce enduring outcomes that have civic merit and connective and teaching value for other students, current and successive, in ways that strengthen social movements. As one student art activist discloses in the mentor letter, "I assure you that when you tap into yourself to see how you can influence social justice, it won't just get you a grade, it will fulfill a deeper meaning to life."

Comparing traditional and activism education assessment is also informed by grasping their views about student motivation for learning. Applied activism pedagogy differs from much of traditional education in ways that reflect the differences between theory Y and theory X views of human behavior in management studies (see e.g., Lawter, Kopelman, and Prottas 2015). Much traditional education reflects a theory X ideology as it frames students as unmotivated learners who are inclined to avoid educative responsibilities, require constant direction and supervision, and must be incentivized to acquire knowledge through the threat of unfavorable grade rankings. Assessment in this frame consists of compulsory course content reiteration to leverage positive market-ready evaluations from teachers. That reading of student motivation and learning, which I believe is accurate in most instances, emerges from the routinized (and often lifeless) system of essentialist pedagogy and lifeless memorization that students have been forced to endure throughout their schooling.

Conversely, activism pedagogy reflects a theory Y ideology as it frames students as motivated learners who are inclined to pursue educative opportunities tied to their social cause passions, desire supportive direction, take creative ownership of their problem-solving work, require minimal supervision, and are incentivized to acquire knowledge based on their advocacy passions and experiences. Assessment in this frame provides opportunities for students to pursue advocacy work in a field that deeply matters to them and it offers supportive feedback on their creative collaborations in that field. That reading of student motivation and learning, which I believe is accurate in most instances, emerges from the alternative system of progressive action pedagogy and infectious learning that occurs when students work in communities to alleviate suffering and help solve social problems.

Activism Course Assessment

The grading structure in the activism course is a standard breakdown. I am not a fan of rubrics, so I avoid them. In my experience, students often perceive them as a means of gaming courses by completing minimal rubric requirements and then arguing for the corresponding grade. Instead, I strive to construct clear assignments that inspire student work and I encourage students to dialogue with me about their grades if they do not agree with my assessment. I do not (currently) see standard grades as inherently negative; instead, for me, their value and effect depend on why and how educators use them.

The fourteen weekly discussion posts are worth 25 points each and the final mentor letter assignment is worth 100 points, for a total of 450 points. Assessment of the core course assignment, the activism project, is spread out across both the discussion posts, as students complete their project in weekly stages, and the mentor letter final assignment. All assessment consists of written feedback to students, generally extensive responses to each submission, on Canvas.

My approach to grading in the activism course—in particular, my evaluation of the mentor letter and the advocacy work it summarizes—is consistent with justice education directives. I outline below three general questions (and related subset questions) that I employ when evaluating student work in my activism course. Because learning in activism contexts is inductive, situated, and adaptive, its assessment is less formulaic, rigid, and quantitative than traditional assessment designs. Instead, as I grade student work, I employ criteria that are context-driven, flexible, and qualitative. The assignment and course letter grades I assign reflect the quality of student work relative to the below criteria.

1. *How and how well did students take ownership of their social cause and their collective, creative work to contribute to that cause?* Justice movements consist of individuals who are willing to take personal ownership of a social cause by familiarizing themselves with the problem and regularly contributing to a cause-related community. Subsequently, activism educators (who are progressive by nature) insist that students take an active role in engineering the focus and fabric of their own learning (e.g., Shor 1992). Glennon (2004), for example, suggests that, "in teaching and learning about social justice, the learner should be actively involved in shaping the purpose and direction of the learning that takes place" (32). The activism course provides that opportunity as it directs students to choose a social cause, teach the class about its unique features, and engineer their own fieldwork and activism projects. Student fieldwork also presents them with opportunities to build relationships in which ideas and tactics are discussed, social support is provided, and networking opportunities emerge. Hildyard (2016) suggests that relationships are a vital, often overlooked, source of learning in social movements.

As I evaluate student work, I am attentive to their commitment level and the creative methods they employ to achieve outcomes. Their level and methods of social cause ownership shape not only their own learning gains, but also their impact on the social cause arena. Most students take zealous ownership of their social cause and their contributory work; others less so, and their commitment level shapes the nature and the level of impact they make in their fieldwork and activism. Subset questions I ask here include: How do students take initiative in the study of their social cause and in connecting to and working with others in their social cause field? How ardent are the student's efforts to creatively solve problems and work with others? In what ways do students build relationships with others in their fieldwork and what outcomes stem from those relationships?

2. *How and how well did students apply their study of the problem, its solution initiatives, and activist tactics to their advocacy work?* Activists who know how to research and analyze social problems and who have a working

knowledge of advocacy tactics can contribute much to social movements. The activism course helps students locate resources and develop the knowledge and analytical skills that will allow them to become more informed and able activists. Moreover, the course helps students build that knowledge, not simply to contemplate or to restate on a test or paper, but precisely so they can apply that knowledge in their fieldwork and activism. Glennon (2004) suggests that "in the case of teaching and learning about social justice, a praxis (action-reflection) model provides a more qualitative experience for learning about social justice than reading about social justice" (32). Students weekly reflect on and receive feedback about their fieldwork, an ongoing process that generates insights into how the course content directly connects to their fieldwork experience. Research on formative assessment has clearly established it as one of the strongest positive influences on achievement when students can immediately apply that feedback (see e.g., Irons 2007).

As I evaluate student work, I pay close attention to how they apply their course-based knowledge to their fieldwork. How, for example, did they employ their research of the problem and its organizational field to identify and connect to relevant regional organizations? How well did they apply their knowledge of the problem to their organizational fieldwork? Did their activism project reflect apt knowledge of the problem and its established solution goals? How did they apply their knowledge of organizing tactics to their fieldwork and activism project? How did their study and experience of the social cause field translate into their mentor letter?

3. *How and how well did students co-build knowledge in their fieldwork and apply that knowledge to organizational operations and social cause goals?* Scholars suggest that social movements are vital cultural spaces for collective knowledge production and learning (e.g., Choudry 2015; Choudry and Kapoor 2010). Each social problem and organization-based connection to that problem constitutes a unique and fluid set of circumstances from which students gain understanding and to which they make contributions. The student's fieldwork provides them with opportunities to learn about both the formal and informal tactics involved in social cause work, ideas to which they contribute as they adapt those tactics and their own ideas to unfolding circumstances. One thematic example entails students using their social media proficiency to expand their organization's event marketing tactics. Another common example is when students expand the nature and scope of an organization's resource drive. The activism project in particular constitutes a protracted exercise in students working with others to adapt plans and organizing efforts to emergent challenges and fluid conditions.

As I evaluate student work, I am attentive to how students co-produce relevant knowledge and skills that they, in turn, apply to their fieldwork. Were

150   *David L. Palmer*

students open to learning what others and their experiences were trying to teach them throughout their fieldwork experience? How did they apply what they were learning in the field back into their fieldwork? To what extent did they adapt their ideas and talents to their organizational work and activism? How well did they adapt to challenging circumstances and failure? How well did they communicate what they learned in their fieldwork and activism in the mentor letter?

CONCLUSION

The mentor letter has proven to be an effective teaching, learning, and assessment tool that supports my activism course goals. The letter is a flexible assignment that justice educators can readily adapt to their course designs. Having current students write letters to future students is an inspiring exercise for the former and a valuable resource for the latter, and a means for them to further bond to social causes. Tailoring mentor letters to a course requires having a purpose and-or cause to connect former and new students. That purpose will shape the letter content and provide insight into how it can support course goals. A key consideration in this process is ascertaining how inbound students will utilize the information and advice that veteran students outline in the letter. In my activism course, for example, the mentor letter enabled me to draw upon the experiences of veteran students to inform and inspire inbound students as they navigated their weekly fieldwork and engineered their activism projects. Unlike traditional assessment forms, which reinforce individuated and competitive market ideals, the mentor letter encourages the collective and supportive work that justice advocacy entails.

Grading justice requires that students produce subjects for evaluation that are connected to and/or are constitutive of justice. For activist educators, that process often entails having students produce assessible projects that are grounded in the living work of justice. The activism project and mentor letter assignments are small yet vital initial steps that my students take toward justice advocacy. Because justice requires social change engineered through collective advocacy, educators should help citizens see themselves not as passive observers of history, but as active change makers; they must realize that justice rarely is granted from above, but instead results from the extensive hard work of grassroots initiatives. My activism course admittedly makes a small (and hopefully resonating) contribution to the broad system of advocacy organizations and activist communities. We must imagine, however, and continue to work toward, a future when similar courses are an integral part of

APPENDIX A: MENTOR LETTER ASSIGNMENT

a systemic activism education field that is helping train generations to forge a more just world.

APPENDIX A: MENTOR LETTER ASSIGNMENT

The final paper will become a letter to a student in this course next fall who wants to get involved in your social cause area. I will provide students who want to get involved in your cause area with this letter as a way for you to help teach them about your journey as a helpful guide on theirs.

For the first part of the paper, answer the following questions: (a) Say hello and tell the person a bit about yourself and your passion for this social cause. (b) What general advice do you have for someone who is getting involved in this social cause? (c) What are 2–3 things you did this semester that worked really well that you would tell the future student: definitely DO these 2–3 things? (d) What did you do and-or not do this semester that you would do differently? (e) What have you learned about activism and yourself as an activist after completing this course? Finally, (f) Give the student a word of encouragement to stick it out when times get tough.

For the second part of the paper, provide substantive responses to the following questions. Feel free to import your ideas and text from your earlier discussion posts.

1. What is the name of your social cause? What inspired you to get involved in this social cause?
2. Outline a general overview of the problem or issue, including its underlying causes. What resources for studying this social problem/cause do you recommend?
3. Outline a general overview, including a brief history of the social cause that addresses that problem. If relevant, what are some of the core national organizations that have developed in response to this social problem? What are some of the core solution initiatives that have been implemented to help solve this problem and with what success? What are the primary problems that still need to be addressed?
4. Who did you contact and how did you get involved? Tell us about involvement strategies you tried that did and did not work. What did you learn from your successful and frustrating experiences about getting involved in this social cause?
5. What specific organizations that you contacted were responsive and helpful? What specific organizations that you contacted were not responsive and helpful?

6. Give a brief overview of your across-the-semester participation in this social cause.
7. What sort of activism project did you design and why? What did you want to have happen a result of this project? How was communication a central feature of the event orchestration process?
8. Tell us about the project. How was the event set-up? What transpired? How was communication a central feature of the event?
9. What impact (no matter how big or small) do you hope this project had in the service of helping to solve this social issue and-or serve this social cause? Did the event meet and/or fail to meet your expectations? Explain.
10. What core lessons did you learn from your social activism project? If you could plan, orchestrate, and execute your activism project all over again, would you do anything differently? Why?
11. Moving forward, what must be done to help solve this social problem? In other words, what will it take to mobilize effective solutions to this social problem? How would this social cause benefit from more people getting involved? How would this social cause benefit from social policy changes (i.e., new laws, regulations, etc.)?

APPENDIX B: EXAMPLE MENTOR LETTER

*This letter has been rendered anonymous.

Dear Fellow Activist and Compassionate Human,
    Hello! My name is Andrea and I am a graduate student at the University of _____ in the Communication Department. I have a young daughter and I work as a marketer for a local restaurant in [my town]. I graduated with my undergraduate degree in Communication Studies in May of 2019 and went straight into the graduate program. I'm very passionate about helping others and improving not only our community but our world through small and big acts whenever possible.
    Being the parent of a young daughter, I am hyper-aware of scary issues facing women and I want to work to change them. I hate that we live in a world where women have to have a weapon on them for protection if we go for a run, we can't travel alone, and we are constantly looking over our shoulder in our everyday lives for predators. Predators in the form of other humans. I don't want my daughter growing up with these fears, so I am extremely passionate about changing this atmosphere and these threats for women.
    When I first heard about [Helping Liberate Women] and heard their amazing founder, Gina McCabe, speak at a local business meeting I was at, I knew

I wanted to get involved. I just didn't know how. We exchanged information and the process pretty much stopped there. But when I started this wonderful Social Activism class and we were told we needed to pick a cause and organization to work with, I not only immediately knew I wanted to work with [Helping Liberate Women], I was excited too. I had not been able to find the time before this class to volunteer and the class was the exact urging in the right direction that I needed. I feel so blessed to have been able to volunteer with [Helping Liberate Women] for an entire semester and I hope to be able to keep working with the organization and for the cause.

The general advice I have for someone getting involved with sex trafficking is to be prepared to be both sad and angry often. Reading the stories of the girls manipulated into this enslavement and the stories of the men barely punished for doing so is pretty awful. But if you don't know how awful it is you won't have the fire to fight to change it.

There were many things I did this semester that I feel worked really well. First, make sure you not only pick a cause and organization early but also that you contact them early. These organizations are very busy with little funding and support for fighting the good fight and may take extra time to get back to you or [to bring you] onboard as a volunteer. I contacted my organization the second week of school and it took until the fourth week to start volunteering, and that was with me immediately turning in my volunteer application. Give yourself time to get your volunteer time and school/ work/life set up for the semester, but make sure you give the nonprofit time to place you in the best volunteer position possible for both you and them for the semester as well. Next, communicate [about your cause] as much and as often as you can. The more you talk about your cause and your event, the more you will educate the community around you and the more support you will get when the time for your event comes. If you are not continually discussing the cause you are passionate about, that passion stands a good chance of dwindling. Keep that fire alive; keep the conversation going. And finally, be patient. Be patient. Be patient. Life is busy and crazy, and we live in a world of instant responses. You will not get instant responses from the organization you are working with. They are busy making our world a better place, give them a few days to respond to you without giving up or getting frustrated. If I could have done anything differently this semester, it would have been to be more patient and understanding with [Helping Liberate Women]. I was expecting them to communicate in the time I expected, not the time they needed. This would have relieved a lot of stress and frustration for me. I would have been patient and thankful that the reason they weren't responding immediately was because they were too busy helping women escape the world of sex trafficking.

154   *David L. Palmer*

After completing this course, I have realized that activism takes resilience, patience, passion, courage, and time. Nothing changes overnight. Big changes often don't even happen in a year. But we should never give up. We should always start and continue any conversation about the cause we are passionate about, and we should always involve ourselves with the work to help the causes we care about no matter how much time we think we do or do not have. I realized that I have more time and talents to donate than I might think I do. Just because I think my schedule is impossible to work with doesn't mean that it is and there are SO many ways to volunteer and make a difference. I learned not to count myself out before I even start to fight and ask how I can volunteer my time for the things that matter to me, no matter how big or small of a time commitment it may be. When times get tough, remember that this world needs your big heart. One of my favorite quotes is, "fall down seven times, stand up eight." Keep standing up for what is right no matter how many times this harsh world might make you fall down. Your cause is worth the fight, and your cause is worth standing up for.

Godspeed and keep standing up,

Andrea

1. What is the name of your social cause? What inspired you to get involved with this social cause?

Sex Trafficking. I am part of a group in [my town] named Women, Business, and Civic Life. This group meets once a month and contains anywhere from 50 to 100 local businesswomen. In July of 2019, the focus of the meeting was sexual violence and trafficking in our area and the nonprofit organizations working to combat these issues in our community. Three groups spoke at this specific meeting, one of which [was Helping Liberate Women]. I chose this cause for two reasons. First, seeing the founder, Gina McCabe, speak at a Women, Business, and Civic Life meeting I was attending was very inspiring. She herself is a survivor of domestic sex trafficking, she went back to school after this happened to her, and she started a non-profit to save young girls like herself when there was no one there to save her. Second, I have a young daughter and I don't want her to grow up in a world where she has to be aware, scared, or exposed to traffickers. I want to help destroy this threat and help girls who are currently enslaved to escape and get their lives back.

2. Outline a general overview of the problem or issue, including its underlying causes. To someone who is just starting to study this issue, what core academic and other resources do you recommend?

According to many studies, it has been shown that those most likely to be targets of sex trafficking are, "individuals who have [had] previous experiences of psychological trauma, histories of family violence or child sex abuse, drug dependency, homelessness, and social isolation. Individuals with limited economic resources, minors and individuals with limited educational opportunities, work opportunities, or family support are also at a heightened risk of trafficking" (Institute for Women Policy Research 2017). Once a target is located, the highest rates of those targeted from the above group include women, children, and those from other marginalized groups, the pursuer then begins to manipulate them. "Traffickers exploit economic vulnerabilities through force, fraud, and coercion luring victims with promises of work, shelter, food, and support" (Institute for Women Policy Research 2017). The Polaris Project additionally found that many victims of sex trafficking turn to traffickers due to, "sustained unemployment, unpaid debt, and desperation to provide for themselves and their children" (Polaris Project 2015). Many feel that this option is their only way to find financial stability, whether they are lured into it or involved with the trafficker romantically. There has always been a major pay gap between men and women in the United States; it's getting better, but right now there is still a female to male earning pay gap of 0.805. Also, just in the US, we have 39.7 million people living below the poverty line, and through the last census conducted, the only group that had a decrease in poverty were those who had a bachelor's degree (US Census Bureau 2019). Young people looking to find jobs are having an extremely rough time finding them and are becoming desperate. These socio-economic factors [contribute to] sex trafficking in the United States. Beyond that, the main underlying cause for sex trafficking is the continued existence of sex traffickers; in particular, each trafficker's "willful decision to profit by compelling people to work or prostitute . . . human trafficking is not a natural occurring phenomenon, it's a choice" (Richmond 2017).

For someone who is just starting to study this issue, I would recommend visiting The Polaris Project website, the END IT Movement website, the [Helping Liberate Women] office and boutique if possible, and/or any SAVA (sexual assault victim advocacy) location or their website.

3. Outline a general overview, including a brief history, of the social cause that addresses that problem. If relevant, what core national organizations have materialized in response to this social problem? What basic solutions have been applied to help solve this problem and with what success? Explain.

Sex trafficking is a form of slavery where people, mostly women and minors, but also men, are sold over and over again by pimps or traffickers for income. These victims are taken and brainwashed to believe that their lives, and often the lives of their loved ones, are at risk if they do not do as the pimp or trafficker says. Those most at risk are those "experiencing economic instability, young runaways . . . [and girls] with a history of childhood abuse. . . . College students are another vulnerable population" (Reeder 2018). The Polaris Project, a data-driven nonprofit that seeks to disrupt the sex trafficking industry, states what sex trafficking is perfectly, "the business of stealing freedom for profit" (The Polaris Project 2019). Although slavery was abolished in 1863, through the Emancipation Proclamation, slavery is not gone in our country. Sex trafficking is a form of slavery because people are being forced to work against their will and give their earnings to their "boss." The Trafficking Victims Protection Act (TVPA) was put into place in the year 2000 which, "was the first federal law to address sex trafficking and labor trafficking in the United States" (Jesionka 2013). In 2012, leaders from several organizations around the United States met for the Freedom Summit to discuss change. From this meeting in Atlanta came the END IT Movement, which was started for awareness as many Americans did not and still do not know that sex trafficking is happening domestically. The first step to solving a problem is admitting there is one (END IT Movement 2019). This was what started the movement to officially work towards ending sex trafficking in the United States and since this time many nonprofit groups have emerged focused on ending the cause, including The Polaris Project, Urban Light, and The Code. The basic strategies these groups use to deal with, combat, and hopefully put an end to sex trafficking is through the use of 24/7 national hotlines where those seeking escape can call for help and trauma support. Collecting data about sex trafficking in the United States [is] difficult since the operations are very private and survivors are afraid (The Polaris Project 2019). These efforts are gaining more and more success each year but, due to fear and the underground nature of this cause, it's difficult to measure the exact success being accomplished over time.

4. Who did you contact and how did you get involved in this social cause? What "getting involved" strategies did and did not work? What did you learn from your successful and frustrating "trying to get involved" experiences?

I got involved [with] this social cause by using my resources to contact them. I made immediate contact with the [Helping Liberate Women] founder when I first heard of them at our Women, Business, and Civic Life meeting and I made sure we immediately exchanged business cards. I had her information from this meeting. She instructed me to go to the [Helping Liberate Women] website and apply to be a volunteer. This was a fairly short process and the most difficult part was getting them a background check on myself. Usually a background check costs $50, but I had just had one done at my daughter's school, so I forwarded that information to them. I didn't really run into any instances of "getting involved" that didn't work since I had already

Student-Activist Mentor Letters as a Form of Social Movement-Building   157

networked and connected with the founder, but it did always take several days if not a week to receive any communication back from [Helping Liberate Women]. My volunteer application took almost two weeks to be accepted and I couldn't start any volunteering until it was, so that was frustrating. But, from the success and the frustration, I just learned to be very patient when working with any nonprofit group, especially [Helping Liberate Women].

5. What specific organizations that you contacted were responsive and help-ful? What specific organizations that you contacted were not responsive and helpful?

Honestly, I got very lucky and had success with the only organization that I did contact, [Helping Liberate Women]. They were excited not only to provide me with information but also to have me as part of the team volun-teering. They were the first and last organization I reached out to and worked with, and all of my other work was done remotely through online resources.

6. Give a brief overview of your across-the-semester participation with this social cause?

When the semester began, I was concerned that I would not have the time or availability necessary to volunteer. [Helping Liberate Women] was wonderful and worked with my hectic schedule so that the majority of my volunteering was able to be done remotely. After completing my volunteer application and having my background check cleared, I began working on administrative work, mostly revamping their volunteer excel sheets. Their old sheets were incomplete and did not include all of the information they needed. I recreated the sheets to be color coded and included the informa-tion they needed. Then, I worked on transferring all of the old and current volunteer information into the new spreadsheets. We also discussed having me work with their newer intern to help them contact Free Trade companies to get donations for the [Helping Liberate Women's] boutique, The Good Samaritan, but unfortunately, we were never able to properly schedule this. We did discuss it over email with some good practices and the best verbiage for the intern to use when contacting these companies.

7. What activism project did you design and why? What roadblocks, if any, did you encounter as you tried to plan and stage this event? How was com-munication a central feature of the event orchestration process?

The activism project I designed was a "Dine to Donate" night for [Help-ing Liberate Women] at [my restaurant] because I am in charge of marketing for [my town's restaurant] and know how successful these fundraisers are. I do several of them throughout the year and knew this would be the best way for me to efficiently give money back to the organization and educate the community. The main roadblocks I encountered, since I was planning the fundraiser for school and work, came from the members of [Helping Liberate Women] taking days to weeks to respond to me. Many times, I would need a "yes" or "no" answer to continue with setting up and planning the event on my end, but because of the long gaps in communication, it made finishing preparations very difficult. I also had an impossible time getting [Helping Liberate Women] to create a Facebook event in advance to invite their supporters to. They never created the page, so I did, and I invited as many people as I could. They did send out an email to their database the day before the event, but this roadblock, I feel, caused the event to not be communicated enough to the community before the single night of the event. I feel we could have had more support if this was orchestrated differently on their end, but, having said that, I know they are extremely busy helping women in trouble, which was more important than a one night only fundraiser.

8. Tell us about the project. How was it set-up? What transpired? How was communication a central feature of the event?

At [my Dine-to-Donate] event, any guest that dined in or ordered take out and mentioned they were there to support [Helping Liberate Women] or showed the flyer I created for this event had their receipt saved. At the end of the night, I added all of the receipts together and gave 10 percent of the total of these combined receipts back to [Helping Liberate Women]. This event was set up by agreeing on a date between [my restaurant] and [Helping Liberate Women] to host the event. Then, I made three different sizes of flyers with the information regarding fundraiser and printed over 100 copies of the three combined sizes. I then distributed these around campus, the community, and at The Good Samaritan. I went on to create an event for the fundraiser on Facebook and invited anyone I could as well as ask anyone I knew to invite their friend list. The event was also posted on [my restaurant's] Facebook page and the message was sent out via email to the [Helping Liberate Women] database. The night was a success and I was able to donate just under $200 to [Helping Liberate Women]. Communication was a central feature of this event because information of the fundraiser had to be [disseminated] before the event night in order to get a return on support from the community. Under Colorado law, businesses are not allowed to hand out or distribute flyers for these events at the door or inside the business on the night(s) of the event because it is considered solicitation of guests. Without active and constant communication of the event to anyone I could speak to before the night, it would have been a failure and could have been a legal issue had I tried to communicate too late.

Student-Activist Mentor Letters as a Form of Social Movement-Building   159

9. What impact (no matter how big or small) do you hope this project had in the service of helping to serve this social cause? Did the event meet and/or fail to meet your expectations? Explain.

I hope this event helps to keep [Helping Liberate Women] working hard and successfully in our community and [helped] to educate the community. I know that my work and event both [made] small impacts for the big fight against sex trafficking, but I hope that I was able to fund sending a care package to one or two women and bringing them hope and that I was able to encourage others to help this cause. I know that many people I spoke to at the event had no idea that sex trafficking is an issue in our area or how poor of a job our legal system is doing to punish the pimps running the operations. The event met my expectations. Usually, when I do a fundraiser, I run them for three nights and feel they are successful if we are able to donate $100 to $400 from those combined nights. So, having a one night only fundraiser that I almost single handedly communicated to the community raise just under $200 was a major win.

10. What core lessons did you learn from your social activism project? If you could plan, orchestrate and execute your activism project all over again, would you do anything differently? Yes and-or no: explain.

The core lessons I learned from my social activism project were to be patient when working with nonprofit organizations, communicate the cause(s) closest to your heart as often and to anyone that you can, and be okay with large or small impacts you can make. If I could plan, orchestrate, and execute my activism project all over again, I don't think I would do anything different. I started early, I contacted as many people as I could, and I handed out all but maybe ten of the flyers I made. I was very proud of the work I did and the outcome of my activism project.

11. Moving forward, what will help solve this social problem? In other words, what will it take to mobilize effective solutions to this social problem? How would this social cause benefit from a lot more people getting involved? How would this social cause benefit from social policy changes (i.e., new laws, regulations, etc.)?

Moving forward, I believe that the answers to solving this social problem are awareness and harsher punishments for the pimps in charge of these women. So many people are unaware of the sex trafficking not only going on in the world but in their own communities. If more people are aware of how serious the problem is, I believe more people would mobilize to work toward a solution. Additionally, pimps involved in sex trafficking need [to be] sentenced to much more than one to nine years of jail time. This [offense] needs to be treated as the violent and heinous crime it is and these men should get twenty-five years or more for each woman they are enslaving. If more people would get involved to educate and fight for harsher laws, less women would be taken into these awful situations and the legal system would have to adjust how they are punishing this crime. Putting these men away for longer periods of time gives women time to escape and get the help they need rather than just being passed from pimp to pimp in the short time their pimp is in jail.

WORKS CITED

END IT Movement. 2019. "END IT Movement: #enditmovement." https://endit movement.com/.

Free Our Girls. 2019. "Free Our Girls." http://www.freeourgirls.org/.

Institute for Women Policy Research. 2017. "The Economic Drivers and Consequences of Sex Trafficking in the United States." September 2017. https://iwpr.org/wp-content/uploads/2017/09/B369_Economic-Impacts-of-Sex-Trafficking-BP-3.pdf.

Jesionka, Natalie. 2013. "What's Being Done to Stop Human Trafficking?" *The Muse.* February 1, 2013. https://www.themuse.com/advice/whats-being-done-to-stop-human-trafficking.

Reeder, Jen. 2018. "Yes, There's Sex Trafficking in Northern Colorado." *NOCO Style.* January 25, 2018. https://nocostyle.com/2019/04/30/yes-theres-sex-trafficking-in-northern-colorado/.

Richmond, John. 2017. "The Root Cause of Trafficking is Traffickers." *The Human Trafficking Institute.* December 19, 2017. https://www.traffickinginstitute.org/the-root-cause-of-trafficking-is-traffickers.

The Polaris Project. 2015. "Sex Trafficking in the U.S.: A Closer Look U.S. Citizen Victims." https://polarisproject.org/sites/default/files/us-citizen-sex-trafficking.pdf.

The Polaris Project. 2019. Polaris. https://polarisproject.org.

The White House. 2018. "President Donald J. Trump Is Taking Action to End Human Trafficking." October 11, 2018. https://www.whitehouse.gov/briefings-statements/president-donald-j-trump-taking-action-end-human-trafficking.

US Census Bureau. 2019. "Income and Poverty in the United States: 2017." April 16, 2017. https://www.census.gov/library/publications/2018/demo/p60-263.html.

REFERENCES

Banks, James A. 2004. "Teaching for Social Justice, Diversity, and Citizenship in a Global World." *The Educational Forum* 68 (4): 296–305. https://doi.org/10.1080/00131720408984645.

Bettez, Silvia Cristina, and Kathy Hytten. 2013. "Community Building in Social Justice Work: A Critical Approach." *Educational Studies* 49 (1): 45–66. https://doi.org/10.1080/00131946.2012.749478.

Britt, Lori L. 2014. "Service-Learning in the Service of Social Justice: Situating Communication Activism Pedagogy within a Typology of Service-Learning Approaches." In *Teaching Communication Activism: Communication Education for Social Justice,* edited by Lawrence R. Frey and David L. Palmer, 139–166. New York: Hampton Press.

Burand, Michael W., and O. Maduka Ogba. 2013. "Letter Writing as a Service-Learning Project: An Alternative to the Traditional Laboratory Report." *Journal of Chemical Education* 90 (12): 1701–1702. https://doi.org/10.1021/ed400215p.

Carey, Christopher. 2014. "Ground-Truthing a Timber Sale: Teaching Environmental Communication Activism in the Mt. Hood National Forest." In *Teaching Communication Activism: Communication Education for Social Justice,* edited by Lawrence R. Frey and David L. Palmer, 261–290. New York: Hampton Press.

Chafe, William H. 1980. *Civilities and Civil Rights: Greensboro, North Carolina, and the Black Struggle for Freedom.* New York: Oxford University Press.

Choudry, Aziz. 2015. *Learning Activism: The Intellectual Life of Contemporary Social Movements.* Toronto, Ontario: University of Toronto Press.

Choudry, Aziz, and Dip Kapoor, eds. 2010. *Learning from the Ground Pp: Global Perspectives on Social Movements and Knowledge Production.* New York: Palgrave Macmillan.

Choudry, Aziz, and Salim Vally, eds. 2018. *Reflections on Knowledge, Learning and Social Movements: History's Schools.* New York, NY: Routledge.

Desai, Dipti. 2019. "Social Justice–Looking Forward: Art and Activism: Moving Between and Beyond Aesthetic Objects to Organizing." In *Art, Culture, and Pedagogy,* edited by Dustin Garnett and Anita Sinner, 273–282. Leiden, Netherlands: Brill Sense.

Fredericksen, Elaine. 2000. "Letter Writing in the College Classroom." *Teaching English in the Two-Year College* 27 (3): 278–284.

Frey, Lawrence R., and David L. Palmer, eds. 2014. *Teaching Communication Activism: Communication Education for Social Justice.* New York: Hampton Press.

Foley, Griff. 1999. *Learning in Social Action: A Contribution to Understanding Informal Education. Global Perspectives on Adult Education and Training.* London, UK: Zed Books Ltd.

Glennon, Fred. 2004. "Experiential Learning and Social Justice Action: An Experiment in the Scholarship of Teaching and Learning." *Teaching Theology and Religion* 7 (1): 30–37. https://doi.org/10.1111/j.1467-9647.2004.00188.x.

Hartnett, Stephen John, Novek, Eleanor, and Jennifer K. Wood, eds. 2013. *Working for Justice: A Handbook of Prison Education and Activism*. Champaign, IL: University of Illinois Press.

Hildyard, Nicholas. 2016. *Licensed Larceny: Infrastructure, Financial Extraction and the Global South*. Manchester, UK: Manchester University Press.

Irons, Alastair. 2007. *Enhancing Learning through Formative Assessment and Feedback*. New York: Routledge.

Kelley, Robin D. G. 2002. *Freedom Dreams: The Black Radical Imagination*. Boston, MA: Beacon Press.

Kilgore, Deborah W. 1999. "Understanding Learning in Social Movements: A Theory of Collective Learning." *International Journal of Lifelong Education* 18 (3): 191–202. https://doi.org/10.1080/026013799293784.

Klandermans, Bert, and Dirk Oegema. 1987. "Potentials, Networks, Motivations, and Barriers: Steps Towards Participation in Social Movements." *American Sociological Review* 52 (4): 519–531. https://www.jstor.org/stable/2095297.

Lawter, Leanna, Kopelman, Richard J., and David J. Prottas. 2015. "McGregor's Theory X/Y and Job Performance: A Multilevel, Multi-source Analysis." *Journal of Managerial Issues* 27 (1–4): 84–101.

McLaren, Peter, and Joe L. Kincheloe, eds. 2007. *Critical Pedagogy: Where Are We Now?* New York: Peter Lang Publishing, Inc.

Moore Jr., Barrington. 2015. *Injustice: The Social Bases of Obedience and Revolt*. New York: Routledge.

Osnes, Beth, and Jason Bisping. 2014. "Theatre for Energy Justice." In *Teaching Communication Activism: Communication Education for Social Justice,* edited by Lawrence R. Frey and David L. Palmer, 461–484. New York: Hampton Press.

Palmer, David L. 2014. "Communication Education as Vocational Training and the Marginalization of Activist Pedagogics." In *Teaching Communication Activism: Communication Education for Social Justice,* edited by Lawrence R. Frey and David L. Palmer, 45–76. New York: Hampton Press.

Richardson, Kayliegh, and Ana Kate Speedy. 2019. "Promoting Gender Justice within the Clinical Curriculum: Evaluating Student Participation in the 16 days of Activism Against Gender-Based Violence Campaign." *International Journal of Clinical Legal Education* 26 (1): 87–131. http://dx.doi.org/10.19164/ijcle.v26i1.823.

Routledge, Paul, and Andrew Cumbers. 2009. *Global Justice Networks: Geographies of Transnational Solidarity*. Manchester, UK: Manchester University Press.

Rowley, Rick, and Jill Friedberg, dir. *This Is What Democracy Looks Like*. 2000; United States: Corrugated Films.

Shor, Ira. 1992. *Culture Wars: School and Society in the Conservative Restoration*. Chicago, IL: University of Chicago Press.

Snowden, Michael, and Tracey Hardy. 2012. "Peer Mentorship and Positive Effects on Student Mentor and Mentee Retention and Academic Success." *Widening Participation and Lifelong Learning* 14, 76–92. https://doi.org/10.5456/WPLL.14.S.76.

Chapter Six

Love Letters Gone Wrong

Complicating the Romantic Ideal of Democratic Processes in the College Classroom

Londie T. Martin and Kristen A. McIntyre

Our southern metropolitan campus features an honors program in which students take a tailored set of core general education classes, including two sequenced courses in written and oral communication. In the first half of this two-semester sequence, students focus on reading and writing in response to several books that address the relationships among education, critical thinking, and self-actualization. One of these texts, Paulo Freire's (1993) *Pedagogy of the Oppressed*, specifically emphasizes the role of mutuality and co-creation in liberatory spaces of learning:

> Through dialogue, the teacher-of-the-students and the students-of-the-teacher cease to exist and a new term emerges: teacher-student with students-teachers. The teacher is no longer merely the-one-who-teaches, but one who is himself taught in dialogue with the students, who in turn while being taught also teach. They become jointly responsible for a process in which all grow (80).

This emphasis on the critical role of mutuality offers a potentially meaningful and exciting connection to the honors program as it uses a collaborative team-teaching model in most of its core courses, including the sequenced written and oral communication courses. Yet, as practitioners of democratic pedagogies know well, engaging in democratic co-creation in the classroom is not without its challenges. How do enthusiastic and committed instructors invite students into a learning partnership that often requires risk-taking and shared vulnerability? Moreover, what perhaps unseen fields of emotional labor might arise in classrooms designed around democratic pedagogical practices?

When we were invited by the honors program to co-teach the second course in the two-semester sequence, we were both hopeful about the collaborative opportunity to try something that our honors students had likely

164 *Londie T. Martin and Kristen A. McIntyre*

never encountered: a collaborative, democratic classroom focused on personal and communal knowledge-sharing through creative communication, self-reflection, and self-assessment. Londie, coming from the Rhetoric and Writing Department on campus, had previous experience team-teaching the course; however, her co-teacher from English was unable to return the following year. Kristen, from the Department of Applied Communication, was approached about stepping in to team-teach the course with Londie. Kristen, having facilitated a few communication workshops in the past for the program, had limited experience working with the honors program students.

WHAT WE BROUGHT TO THE TEAM-TEACHING TABLE

To get a sense of what each of us brought to our team-teaching experience, we want to share both the background and key aspects of our pedagogical practice. Londie was trained in rhetoric and composition, and early in her scholarly journey she fell in love with critical pedagogy and multimodal communication. In the almost thirteen years that she has been teaching in university contexts, whether in first-year composition courses or graduate-level design and digital communication courses, she has worked to emphasize critical thinking in all aspects of the composition experience. Central to this process is a commitment to collaboration and the co-creation of a classroom space that affirms all students as creators and holders of knowledge who can offer up their storytelling and communication as tools for self-reflection, growth, and community engagement in the classroom and beyond.

When Londie was first invited to co-teach the course for the honors program, she was cautious and curious. She had never co-taught a class before, and the opportunity to collaborate, learn, and teach alongside a fellow instructor was exciting. Having never taught in an honors context, she was also cautious about investing energy in a program that separates honors students from their fellow university classmates. Seen in the broader context of a US university system that often marginalizes students according to race, gender, sexuality, citizenship status, and/or disability, the further separation and identification of some students as "honors students" was cause for concern. In what ways might the honors classroom further reify the marginalization of some student identities and ways of knowing? How might this particular form of institutionalized difference manifest in the classroom, and what new approaches would it take to co-create a space of collaboration and engaged learning? Though a detailed discussion of Londie's first year co-teaching for the honors program is outside the scope of this chapter, it is important to note that the experience was, overall, a positive one.

The practice of co-teaching turned out to be invigorating and worthwhile. Student evaluations from the course were evenly divided between those students who appreciated the course's emphasis on memoir writing and collaborative multimedia projects and those who did not. Londie came away from the experience with a desire to learn more about best practices for building sustainable co-teaching relationships, and she also gained a more nuanced perspective on the honors student experience. The competition, the aggressive argumentation, the anxiety about grades—these challenges were intense in the honors classroom but not quite discouraging. Londie wondered if it were possible to co-create an honors classroom as a space where students could explore their interests, values, and stories outside of their heightened concerns about performance and grade point averages. When she was invited to teach the course again, this time with Kristen, it seemed like a good opportunity to learn more about democratic pedagogical practices that de-center assessment models based on teacher-driven critique and instead embrace self-actualization and collaborative assessment.

Kristen earned her doctorate in communication, with an emphasis in communication Education, and had taught for nineteen years at the time she teamed up with Londie for their most excellent team-teaching adventure. Twelve of those years were at their current institution, and of those twelve, Kristen had spent the last seven years using a MacGyver-ed form of competency-based learning in her upper level classes.

Feeling frustrated with the superficially transactional nature of traditional grading (assigning points and weighted percentages to assignments in the hopes of communicating the importance and value of the learning-related work being produced), Kristen realized that the learning, for students, always seemed to be beside the point—de-centered as a sad consolation prize with the almighty points being what students felt was the true reward. Students ranted and they raved, haggling and pleading for their precious points, all the time misunderstanding what the points represented—that they had room to stretch and grow in their thinking and skill-building. To lose a point, though, was to fail. And failing was not OK for students. Surely there was a better way to situate a curriculum that created and valued process so that students could re-focus on the real prize, their learning and the inevitable failure that comes with the pursuit of it. Competency-based learning seemed to be the best bet.

Competency-based learning (CBL) is essentially *keep doing it until you get it right* pedagogy, with "right" representing the basic understanding or skill enactment of what competency looks like, with an emphasis on developing needs that are practical and useful to society (Grant 1979). The focus on valuing process, from a CBL approach, resonated with Kristen, so she gutted her current grading practices in her upper level public speaking course and built a curriculum that no longer used points on individual assignments. Instead, some assignments were designated as complete/incomplete because they were important practice in evaluating, analyzing, and/or creating key material in the course. Other assignments were in the pass/revise category—assignments that needed to demonstrate basic competencies. These assignments were process-related pieces, foundational to the success of the larger product being created, as well as the final products, such as each major speech. On pass/revise assignments, students had to engage in the revision process until a "pass" was earned for the work or they were not eligible to pass the class.

A final formal self-assessment portfolio was used to assign final grades in the course. In the portfolio, students were tasked with arguing that they had not only met the learning outcomes for the course, but also the other expectations established by the instructor, such as engagement in the revision process, quality of work, support of classmates, ethical communication, etc. The first time the new curriculum was rolled out students rolled their terrible eyes and gnashed their terrible teeth. Not having points left them lost and scared, and the fear often manifested itself as anger. But everyone, Kristen included, persevered through the tears and uncertainty. By the end of the semester, when survival, nay, success was imminent, the students no longer thought that not having points was all that bad. Many of them came back when invited to help prepare the next class for the strange and uncomfortable class experience the new, unsuspecting students were about to embark upon.

For several years, up until this very moment dear reader, Kristen shepherded students through a no-point curriculum, weathering the inevitable ups and downs as students wrestled with being accountable for their own learning. The prospect of working with honors students to truly co-create a more democratic learning experience based on direct participation and growth-oriented accountability was at the forefront when Kristen sat down to talk with Londie. Also sitting with her, however, was some discomfort with the antithetical concept of honors programs and the illusion of intellectual elitism they often perpetuate. In time, Kristen would learn that Londie shared these precise concerns, too.

WE DREAMED A DREAM OF DEMOCRATIC PEDAGOGY

During our initial conversations about the possibility of co-teaching a course, we discovered that we shared similar pedagogical values about the place of critical thinking in the classroom as well as the relationship between learning objectives and meaningful assessment practices. In particular, we were excited to find a shared interest in critical pedagogy and more democratic assessment methods as ways to encourage student agency and critical thinking. In our conversations, we learned that we both embrace what Freire refers to as "problem-posing education" or a kind of pedagogy in which "people develop their power to perceive critically *the way they exist* in the world *with which* and *in which* they find themselves; they come to see the world not as a static reality, but as a reality in process, in transformation" (83). Drawing on Freire's understanding of critical pedagogy as a way of being in and with the world, bell hooks, in *Teaching to Transgress: Education as the Practice of Freedom*, articulates an engaged pedagogy that is, at its heart, collective. She argues that students—so many of whom experience and grow accustomed to more conventional, teacher-centered models of classroom learning—can thrive within a truly "radical pedagogy" informed by "an ongoing recognition that everyone influences the classroom dynamic, that everyone contributes" (8). Yet, what is sometimes lost in the practice of this kind of problem-posing and collective critical pedagogy is the specific context—the lived experiences of colonialism, marginalization, and oppression—from which these liberatory practices emerge.

For Freire and hooks, pedagogy becomes liberatory when we resist the thought-action binary through praxis and actively commit ourselves, in coalition with others, to uncover and contend with the roles we play—as colonizer, as colonized, as sometimes both. This commitment to putting theory and thought into action is, of course, difficult work, and asking students to co-participate (teachers always included) in this kind of uncomfortable transformation process is sometimes a tall order. Personal reflection can quickly become a perfunctory task, something we perform uncritically for authorities rather than something we engage intentionally as a set of practices for ethically naming, negotiating, and re-naming our place in the world. As we continued to share our ideas about critical pedagogy and our dreams of co-teaching, we wondered: Is it possible to co-create a learning space outside of assessment models that seem to be primarily driven by the centralized authority of teachers and larger academic institutions? Could we create a course that would encourage students to practice reflection not just as a tool for self-assessment but also as a mode of knowledge production? What would such a course look like? We decided to move forward together to see what we could build.

The semester before the class, we met regularly and dreamt together of all the ways we could lovingly craft a course that invited our students to play with ideas, to feel safe enough to fail, and to engage in the co-creation of learning with us. We created a Google Team Drive and named it *Pedagogy Playground*—here we dared to playfully imagine the shapes and weights of a curriculum neither one of us had yet built in our respective courses. Our past experiences with the honors program led us to construct a humble scholar frame, a guiding frame that worked to value humility and other-centeredness in our learning. We used Big Questions (Bain 2004) to articulate this frame in the learning outcomes of our course:

- *What counts as knowledge?* Students will explain how different contexts constrain and enhance what counts as knowledge.
- *How do we create knowledge?* Students will articulate why knowledge creation is always collaborative.
- *How do we share knowledge?* Students will analyze the inherent power dynamics of knowledge expression.

We developed these questions to help us all recognize and contend with the ways in which people, communities, and institutions understand and wield "knowledge." When, where, how, and by whom is knowledge conceptualized as a tool for liberation? For oppression?

To explore these Big Questions, we invited students to try out two major projects—a written and spoken flash memoir assignment (see Appendix A and Appendix B) and a group multimedia project informed by qualitative research practices and presented publicly on campus (see Appendix C). Throughout both major projects, we scaffolded the curriculum to engage students deeply in the processes of reflection and revision of their own and each other's work, and we situated these experiences within a larger and ongoing class conversation about the problematic role of grading in liberatory learning environments (Strommel 2017) and the constraints of prescriptive rubrics for assessment (Kohn 2006). We integrated in-class activities that would encourage our students to engage with tricky concepts playfully while building each assignment—to try out different approaches and skills, to sometimes be silly in their exploration and adaptation of concepts, and to resist or re-think perhaps rigid or singular notions of what it means to create and share knowledge.

At midterm and at the end of the semester (see Appendix D), we used single point rubrics (Gonzalez 2015) as a starting point for class conversation about learning goals and outcomes, and we also incorporated more traditional assignment materials to help our students self-assess not only their ability to meet expectations set by us and the class but also the grade they could best support with the work they generated. Moreover, we encouraged students to see the rubrics and assessment guidelines as points of departure for conversation; in other words, if a student disagreed with a particular assessment guideline, it was entirely okay for them to offer a thoughtful, well-supported argument for something different.

Just as importantly, in this self-assessment, we also encouraged them to identify and celebrate their areas of growth from the start of the class as well as their goals for continuing forward with their learning. In this way, we hoped the course would create space for students to identify moments of struggle or challenge (perhaps identified as "failure" in other educational contexts) and instead reflect on those moments as opportunities for knowledge production. Here, we understand the challenges and failures as moments of potentially productive disorientation where, as Sara Ahmed argues, the point is not to dwell on the existence of failure or disorientation. Instead, she suggests that "[t]he point is what we do with such moments of disorientation, as well as what such moments can do—whether they can offer us the hope of new directions, and whether new directions are reason enough for hope" (Ahmed 2006, 158). We imagined our honors students might, over the course of the semester, grow into the kind of hope Ahmed describes and open themselves up to the idea that failure can be productive, valuable, perhaps even desirable.

Our partnership as team-teachers was tentative at first, an awkward seventh grade dance of sorts, both of us not quite sure about how we could and should do the teaching togetherness. Quickly, though, we negotiated an all-in approach. While we divided and conquered drafting tasks, we decided everything—from lesson plans to emails sent—should be blessed by both of us before they were shared with the class. We knew this path entailed a significant amount of labor and time, but we made this decision to be fully collaborative with each other because we valued each other's insights and respected each other as equals in the process. And after all of this collaboration and dreaming, we were proud of the course we so carefully built together. On the first day of class—feeling vulnerable, apprehensive, and hopeful—we offered the class to our twenty-one students as a potential "brave space" where power dynamics would be thoughtfully and openly explored (Arao and Clemens 2013), along with two dozen doughnuts for good measure. The semester that followed was challenging in ways neither of us had yet experienced in our years of teaching.

WHEN DREAMS BECOME REALITY: NEGOTIATING STUDENT ANXIETIES IN THE DEMOCRATIC CLASSROOM

Inspired by Brian Arao and Kristi Clemens's (2013) theorizing of the "brave space" as a sometimes more democratic and socially just model for classroom ethics and participation, we began the course with a desire to co-construct classroom agreements with students. We imagined that these agreements would encompass not just how students talk with each other, but how everyone in the classroom—teachers included—engaged with others via both verbal and nonverbal communication cues.

To help introduce the concept of "brave spaces," we asked students to read Arao and Clemens's article for the first week of class, and we engaged students in a discussion of their take-aways and insights. Specifically, we invited them to think about the difference between the terms "safe" and "brave" in our current classroom context. As instructors, we approached this conversation (which unfolded over two class periods) "not as a prelude to learning about social justice but as a valuable part of such learning" (Arao and Clemens 2013, 142). Concerned with students' ability and willingness to explore issues around social justice, marginalization, oppression, and privilege, teachers sometimes lean on "safe space" pedagogy to create classrooms that encourage vulnerability and attempt to offer psychic, physical, and emotional protection by establishing (sometimes co-created) ground rules or guidelines for engagement and discussion. Arao and Clemens (2013) recognize, however, that participants often interpret safe space guidelines as being founded on comfort—that there is "a conflation of safety with comfort" (135).

As a reflective practice, brave spaces are designed to question this conflation, and Arao and Clemens offer an analysis of commonly voiced guidelines that can be problematic (e.g., "agree to disagree"). In our class conversation about the Arao and Clemens article and about our potential brave space guidelines, students expressed some discomfort but still seemed hopeful and enthusiastic about the direction of the course during these first few class periods. Our democratic approach to guideline development seemed to bring more students into the conversation and alleviated some of the tension students were feeling. After class conversations, we asked students to write down their top five classroom guidelines, and then we used a pair-and-share approach to facilitate small group conversation about the patterns they saw in their writing. We then collected the top eighteen guidelines (comprised of the top three responses from each of the six small groups) and developed an interactive online poll which allowed students to anonymously vote for their top ten guidelines. You can see the results of this polling in figure 6.1.

In hindsight, a look at the most popular course guidelines helps us make sense of some of the student behaviors we experienced in the classroom and how they align with what we know about honors education, in general, at the college level. While there were guidelines that could be seen as emphasizing empathy (i.e., "being kind," sharing "authenticity" and "vulnerability," having "humility," and being open to "different perspectives"), they were the least popular. We were a little surprised to see that the top five guidelines

Love Letters Gone Wrong　　　　　　　　　　　　　　　171

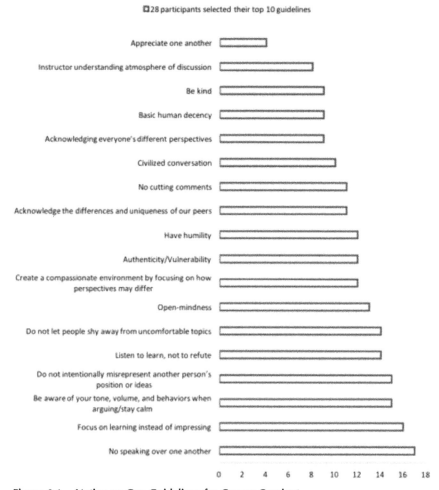

Figure 6.1. Voting on Our Guidelines for Course Conduct

seemed to focus explicitly on controlling or managing uncomfortable, aggressive, or competitive emotions (i.e., "no speaking over one another," "focus on learning instead of impressing," "listen to learn, not to refute"). As instructors, we were prepared to encounter students who identified as high-achievers and who saw the educational environment as a competitive one (though our actual experience in the classroom far surpassed our preparedness), and we pursued democratic exercises (such as the Brave Space voting) as well as a rubric and reflection-based self-assessment model of evaluation as a way of providing some of the structure that honors students crave while also inviting creativity and encouraging students to heighten their critical thinking skills.

We found, however, that employing a more democratic and self-reflective grading model in a context of extremely heightened grade anxiety and competition required a tremendous level of affective labor that was quite different from anything we had experienced in previous university classrooms.

Scholars who participate in and study honors education often suggest more democratic pedagogical strategies to help students find relief from their anxiety about competition, grades, and evaluation, but few discuss the emotional labor required to encourage the bravery, self-reflection, and critical thinking necessary for some honors students to flourish within these more open models. In his thorough survey of assessment issues faced in honors programs, Larry Andrews (2007) acknowledges "the often excessive concern over grades among honors students" (27) and offers alternative assessment opportunities that could help students think about learning as a lifelong process and not a competition that solely defines their self-worth. Participating in rubric construction, self-evaluation, and portfolio grading are good alternatives to more traditional and authoritarian assessment models, Andrews (2007) argues, yet "our conscientious students will often rebel if they do not receive clear, ongoing, quantitative signals of how they are performing" (27). We certainly experienced this rebellion in response to our decision to provide students with detailed self-reflection tools and guidance as they learned to assess their own work and find meaning beyond a quantifiable, teacher-assigned grade. In a similar vein, Annmarie Guzy (2007) describes the disheartening moments when students flip past the comments lovingly left on their writing only to zero in on the letter grade at the end of the assignment that they believe quantifies their performance. Guzy (2007) taps into their concerns when she remarks, "Who are they if not the students who earn straight As?" (34).

To help students recognize and manage their anxieties, we developed playful exercises to de-emphasize competition while also encouraging them to practice skills related to their major semester projects. For example, to help students practice the self-reflection and dynamic storytelling necessary for their Flash Memoir with Critical Selfie project (see Appendix A), we designed a Twitter Flash Nonfiction exercise that brought together short form personal writing with creative photography. During week three, students took time in and out of class to author a Twitter-length (280 characters) story of their life, and they worked together in pairs to visually interpret each other's life stories through portrait photography using their smartphones. It was a fun exercise that energized the learning space and helped us all think more deeply about the subjectivity and power dynamics involved in interpretation and knowledge sharing through different modes of creative expression.

To further allay student grade anxiety in a more grounded way, we followed the Twitter Flash Nonfiction exercise with a guest visit from one of

Kristen's former students who had experienced the kind of self-reflection- and portfolio-based assessment we were practicing and who was also a student in the same university honors program. We framed the visit as an open Q&A event where our students could ask one of their peers anything and everything about what it would be like to assess themselves and argue for their own course grade. The conversation was student-directed, candid, and lively, and most students reported (verbally in class and in their midterm reflective writing) that this visit was helpful; it offered them evidence that what we were inviting them to do was indeed possible and perhaps even worthwhile.

Yet, anxieties continued to emerge as more formal discussions of the midterm self-assessment set them on edge. After Kristen's former student left, we transitioned to dedicated class discussion time to review the midterm portfolio assignment and the rubric. We allotted twenty-five minutes or so for this housekeeping task and ended up needing the entire seventy-five-minute class period. The level of anxiety in the room was palpable and neither of us was prepared for the amount of emotional labor needed to manage the feelings of uncertainty and fear that erupted. The conversations about grade anxiety and the midterm reflection seemed to hinge on their feeling that the class we had designed lacked structure. We offered them a different perspective: *there is a structure, but we understand that it is not one with which you are familiar.* Our goal, then, was to help them see the structure: two major projects; readings, practice exercises, and peer response sessions to scaffold their growth; and midterm and final semester self-assessment portfolios and conferences with us to reflect on all that the student was experiencing in the course and in their own collaborative and self-directed learning.

Try as we might to relieve their worries, the concept of assessing themselves was so overwhelming that inviting them to negotiate the rubric criteria with us, as we had planned, would have been disastrous. As we both lacked the bandwidth to emotionally invest in what more than likely would have been a highly contentious discussion, we had to let this piece of our democratic process dream slip away. It was clear during the review of the midterm assignment that our students were unable to conceptualize the criteria as being shared, something that we were trying to create together in the class. The structures familiar to them situated us, the teachers, as owners of the measuring stick. And our role, as wielders of that stick, was to ruthlessly evaluate how each of them measured up. In light of Guzy's (2007) insight about the extent to which honors students base their identity on performance measured by grades, we now better understand that the productive, hopeful disorientation of failure that Ahmed theorizes was much further from our grasp. When you have held onto failure as so deeply antithetical to your own sense of self, what do you do when failure, in some ways, becomes the goal?

But we always remained hopeful because we cared deeply for our students and wanted them to succeed by their own thoughtfully crafted measures. It was difficult and draining to so frequently engage directly with such high anxiety, but, as co-teachers, we were able to lean on each other for pedagogical and emotional support, which continued to fuel our ability to remain flexible and cautiously optimistic. In a moment of particularly exciting hopefulness, we designed what we thought would be a quick, meaningful icebreaker exercise that would feed into their midterm self-assessment work and playfully turn our collective attention to self-care and a more loving approach to learning. During week seven, we wanted students to take a moment to document their current understanding of the Big Questions we were exploring in the class, but in a perhaps more lighthearted way that might ease some of the tension they were feeling. This documentation would give each student a quick snapshot of their current understanding that they would be able to compare with their understanding at the end of the semester (thus, focusing our collective attention on growth and process). Our idea was, we thought, simple: "Take five minutes to freewrite a love letter to yourself in which you talk about where you are currently in your understanding of our Big Questions."

We began the class with our usual lively chatter and greetings, but some students noticeably tensed up as soon as we invited them to take out a sheet of paper. "We'd like you to freewrite a little love letter to yourself . . . " We could not even finish the brief instructions; the rebellion was so vocal and immediate. *What do you mean a love letter? How do I write to myself? How do we address this letter? What even is a love letter?!* We were both shocked at how intensely and immediately their worry about performance and evaluation rose to the surface. To practice our commitment to shared understanding and engaged self-reflection, we worked with students to process their feelings in conversation: *Where is this anxiety coming from? What is making you feel uncomfortable or vulnerable right now?* The process, as it mostly is when human beings are involved, was messy. Initially, students met our questions with a flurry of responses, irritations, and nervous laughter, with one student even responding to the question "Why do you think you can't write yourself a love letter?" with a jarring exclamation, "Because we hate ourselves!" That moment was shocking not just because it pained us to witness such anguish, but also because many other students in the class seemed to identify with this feeling.

Later, in our reflections on the course, we recognized this moment in class as indicative of the heightened tension students were experiencing as they were called to think critically about their own identities and contend with the incongruence that can emerge in the process. Moreover, from this conversation we began to better understand how our different perceptions and intentions were colliding. Our offer to play and write freely out of love and self-care was, for them, just another moment of pop-quiz reckoning as soon as we uttered the words, "Take out a sheet of paper."

The response to our playful love letter activity was shocking and disorienting. However, midterm student conferences allowed us to clearly see that most students were beginning to understand this new invitational structure and how to make it work for them. To prepare for the conferences, we each individually reviewed students' midterm portfolios and completed a feedback form (see Appendix E), merged our responses on the feedback form, and printed them off for each student. We took great comfort in finding that we were both responding similarly to the work in terms of the grades for each scoring area as well as feedback on their memoir project. We were even more comforted to see that our assessments and our students' self-assessments were very closely aligned. Both of us attended every twenty-minute student conference held in Kristen's purple, unicorn-bedazzled office. We took turns taking the lead on getting the conferences started, asking students about the semester in general and then the class more specifically, and finally talking through the feedback form. As we discussed and compared our individual grade assessments, we tried to make it very clear that the grade assessments we offered each student were a starting point for conversation and not an authoritative or final grading of performance in the course. We tried to encourage students to see our grade assessments as data for them to reflect on as they crafted their own self-assessment.

Despite all the vocalized anxiety and angst, during these conference discussions the majority of our students were able to successfully apply the letter grade criteria in their arguments to the work they had created and the choices they had made in the course (though they struggled, or refused, to use the individual memoir assignment rubrics to add additional support to their grade argument) and identified similar areas of progress and growth. We learned that some students did not believe that they would *really* get to argue for the grade they thought they deserved, even though we said this repeatedly in class and on all course documents (i.e., assignment sheets, syllabus materials). We learned that some students assumed, based on other college course experiences, that we would curve the class grades (none of our materials mention curved grading), placing each student in direct competition with each other. In other words, several students believed that trickery was afoot!

Conference after conference, we encountered how students were internalizing their fears about evaluation and manifesting them in their own unexamined choices, behaviors, and assumptions about the course, their role in it, and our teaching practices. We began to more deeply understand the extent to which their difficulty seeing and trusting the unconventional evaluation structure we offered them was deeply connected to their years of experience in honors education contexts. The affective labor required to help them think and feel outside of these contexts was, we found, intense and exhausting in ways we had never quite experienced in other classrooms. After conferences, we had a much better understanding of the affective labor necessary to help this group of honors students make their way toward a growth-oriented understanding of academic evaluation, and this realization informs the lessons we learned and continue to learn from the experience.

LESSONS LEARNED OR HOW WE TRIED TO STOP WORRYING AND LOVE THE EXPERIENCE

On the final day of class, we met with our students, offering fresh baked muffins, homemade cheesecake, and a fruit platter. We circled up and randomly handed out slips of paper with individual discussion questions on them to help decenter the semester debrief session:

- What went well?
- What are you proud of?
- What would you like to do differently?
- What advice would you give to future honors students about approaching the collaborative project and the public event?
- What did you enjoy about each other's projects?
- What did you enjoy about working with your team members?
- How will what you experienced during the public project-sharing event impact how you think about yourself and your identity?

We ate and listened while they talked about what they had learned and how they felt about it. The discussion was, overall, fine—polite and safe. Several of the students shared seemingly sincere reflections of powerful learning and the challenges they had experienced in the course, with many of them commenting that this was the first positive group work experience they had. Additionally, students shared that they enjoyed and learned from the self-reflection memoir project that helped them recognize and appreciate aspects of their identities outside of their status and performance as high-achieving honors students. We left the classroom understanding that, though some students had negative feelings about the course, a significant portion of the class was able to find value in what we created together.

Later, when the course evaluations were shared with us, it felt, after all of the anxiety we had attempted to manage that semester, like a weirdly expected sucker punch. We say "expected" because we are both familiar with research on the ineffectiveness of course evaluations in a variety of assessment contexts, including tenure and promotion cases (Lawrence 2018), and we are particularly familiar with research on the problem of gender and racial biases in student evaluations (Flaherty 2019; Laube, Massoni, Sprague, and Ferber 2007). Furthermore, the honors program administrators had cautioned us earlier in the year that honors students are known to write sometimes scathing evaluations.

Yet and still, upon the first read-through Kristen wanted to print them off just so she could set them on fire, and Londie had to lean fairly hard on her conscious breathing techniques lest a panic attack bubble to the surface. Reading student course evaluations has never been an easy thing for either of us to do (even when the results are usually overwhelmingly positive), but it had been a long time since we had read evaluations with comments that were so pointedly mean-spirited and unhelpful: "I really hope something is done because I hated having to waste my time on busy work that provided no knowledge," "Happy to go," "The language of the course was not accessible to most students . . . a lot of people found the class to be sort of a joke because of the way information was presented," and "This class was an absolute waste of my time and everyone else's." It was particularly jarring because none of the students in face-to-face interactions communicated any hint of this kind of hostility—discomfort and irritation, for sure—but nothing that would have prepared us for what we read.

To help temper the sting and allow us to really see what all the voices were saying, not just those few who clearly disliked the class, Londie created beautiful graphs and charts to help quantify a few of the ten open-ended responses (see figure 6.2). Based on this more abstracted, quantitative perspective, we could see that the majority of our students felt the workload was appropriate for an honors course, that we presented the material well, and that we, as instructors, seemed interested in them and their contributions. They also felt strongly, and unsurprisingly, that the feature that needed the most changing was the structure and grading of coursework. Student responses included: "Could use more structure," "Clear structure and better explaining," "The structure," and "I want them to grade my work." A very small percentage of our students identified self-assessment as the best feature of the course with the majority naming the second major project as their favorite. We did have some lovely, parting comments though: "Thank you for teaching the class and helping me grow as a student," "A class based on love and friendship," and "*Love* this class. Thanks for the life advice." From these evaluations, we left with a clearer understanding that valuable learning had occurred, but it was not a comfortable experience for many of them, or us.

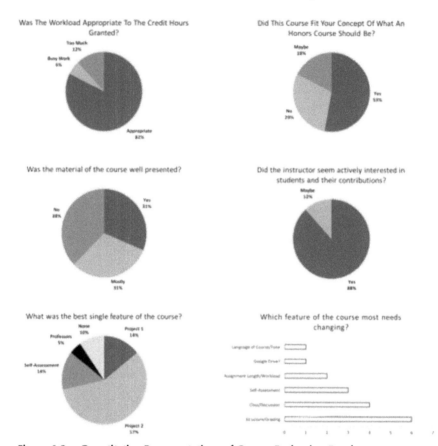

Figure 6.2. Quantitative Representations of Course Evaluation Results

When the opportunity landed in Kristen's inbox to submit a chapter proposal for this book, she paused for a moment before she forwarded the call to Londie. Teaching this course was one of the most difficult teaching experiences she had ever had. It was possible that writing about it could be cathartic. It could also be incredibly painful. But, it was an opportunity to potentially make sense of our experiences and share them with interested colleagues, so off the email went and here we are. The writing of this has indeed been cathartic—but also some of the most difficult and painful academic writing we have both experienced. Upon reflecting on the course, the choices we made, and what we tried to create, we identified things we could do better, things we felt we did right, and a whole lot of learning for both of us.

Understanding the gendered academic training, perpetuated by a patriarchal education system, our students brought with them into our course could have better prepared us for both anticipating and mitigating the resistance and anxiety our students expressed. After the first few class sessions where we tried to approach learning as play, free from traditional assessment, it was clear that the majority of our students understood our pedagogical choices within a gendered dichotomy; they perceived collaboration and co-creation as more feminine practices (thus, less valuable) and actively desired a more masculinist approach to learning—adversarial and grounded in an agonistic view of competition and communication.

Within this dichotomy, we could better understand their resistance to anything detached from points and their discomfort with seeing this self-assessed labor as valuable to their learning process. Without points and a constant measuring against each other, they seemed to teeter on the edge of an identity crisis of sorts. As honors students, so much of their identity was entwined with grades—they are "A" students. In a class with no points, with no grades, what were they? Who were they? How could they affirm their identity in the absence of points and measurements?

Our students perceived themselves as our academic equals, yet they functioned within an adversarial frame—they needed us to be the "experts" so they could replicate the structure that was familiar to them. They had been groomed to challenge, to question, to critique by default. They needed to challenge us, and in doing so, regain their identity by showing that they were smarter than us. But, as collaborative feminist academics, we very mindfully constructed our class to be invitational and not combative. We offered them a playground and some of them wanted, perhaps needed, a cage fight.

In hindsight, we can see this tension at play in the results of our Brave Space voting (see figure 6.1); in their responses and voting, students were trying to tell us: *some of us think that knowledge sharing has to be combative, and we know it's a problem, but we might not know how to solve it.* Our students felt they could not trust us, that we were somehow tricking them with our invitations to explore and try out ideas without penalty should those ideas not work out as planned. Or, our framing of learning as play, what we had labored over so carefully, meant it could not be real learning and we, consequently, could not be real teachers. Thus, some of them played the game they had been trained to play without genuinely engaging in play; and, for this reason, it was difficult for us to trust that they were ever really being authentic with us. There is a deep sadness that comes with this realization.

In light of this realization, we now understand that students who identify as "honors students" or "high achievers" (through their own identification and/ or perhaps through the influence of authority figures like teachers, parents, etc.) might benefit from a blending of democratic and more traditional assessment methods to help support the level of self-reflection necessary to find meaning outside of solely quantitative measures. Or, rather than attempting an entire course or blended course in democratic processes, start small with one negotiated assignment and see how students respond, holding the design of the rest of the course lightly so it can unfold in ways that better match where students are in their self-assessment journey. It is also clear that teachers will need to both teach and practice self-care as a matter of regular course engagement in honors classrooms. Having a co-teacher with whom to process the day's events was extraordinarily helpful, but it was equally helpful to model this kind of processing and ethical communication in the classroom. In this way, we offer students communication tools that go beyond the advice to simply "not be a jerk."

Moreover, it is important to recognize that the ethical communication practices and shared vulnerabilities and responsibilities that support a democratic classroom might not be reflected extensively in the overall honors program. From our experience, we now understand how important it is to learn as much as possible about the culture and ethos of the larger program so that, as instructors, we can better anticipate and work through the tensions that emerge when democratic pedagogies co-exist with more traditional pedagogical approaches. We wonder, too, if teachers might have more success cultivating democratic learning environments when their courses are housed in local departments where teachers (hopefully) have a more direct input in collectively shaping culture and best practices.

Additionally, we want to hold space for the moments of joy we experienced—both in the build up to the course and in the classroom itself. As we designed the course, we relied on a power-sharing model of democratic collaboration fueled by our feminist commitments to loving candor, honest vulnerability, and mutual respect. When anxieties were high in the classroom, it was this relational foundation that helped us work together to solve problems and remain hopeful. The relationship we developed as friends and co-teachers also helped us make sense of and celebrate those moments of joy in the classroom—for example, the sincere support students offered each other when they shared their personal writing and the excitement most students experienced when they collaboratively identified a research focus that was meaningful in the context of their own lives and the communities they cared about. Overall, our experience led to the creation of a course we love, and we hope to someday offer it as a cross-listed course between our two departments, where students have more experience and practice with democratic pedagogical processes.

Our experience affirmed for both of us that employing democratic processes in the classroom, though undoubtedly a labor of sometimes unrequited love, is indeed worth the time and energy. We worked to co-create an experience with our students where they could not only imagine justice as conceivable but could participate in its creation. In doing so, we hoped to empower our students to put thought into action and to live democracy, not just study and critique it, and engage with it critically on conscious terms—mindful that the aspects of democratic processes that made them hugely uncomfortable also make others, outside the walls of our classroom, hugely uncomfortable. Even as they struggled and continue to struggle, to make sense of our class experience, we feel strongly that in our toil together we have planted the justice seed.

We returned to our respective departments more committed than ever to practice our critical pedagogy carefully, thoughtfully, and reflectively with our students. Thinking back to Freire's (1993) "teacher-student with students-teachers" (80), we believe that we did achieve a mutuality where, through our collaborative democratic processes and labors of love, students and teachers in our course were indeed "jointly responsible for a process in which all grow" (80). Our experience created an amazing team-teaching opportunity that stretched and strengthened our individual pedagogies as we worked to develop an even deeper appreciation for the important work we did in this course as well as the work we do in our home departments. We recognize that team-teaching might not be feasible or equitable in some institutional contexts, but creating shared spaces (for example, the cloud-based "Pedagogy Playground" we built) with others can help challenge and grow the design and integration of democratic practices while also cultivating the vital emotional and professional support needed to navigate the sometimes tumultuous affective landscape of classrooms that attempt to exist outside of more traditional grading ecologies.

APPENDIX A

Project 1
Flash Memoir with Critical Selfie

Big Questions

- How do we create knowledge?
- What counts as knowledge?

Purpose

Memoir offers us the opportunity to reflect on specific memories and use what we learn to craft a "true" story about ourselves. When we combine flash nonfiction and memoir, we open ourselves to personal insights illuminated by what Moore describes as the "urgency" of "an abbreviated frame." In your writing, craft energetic prose by experimenting with dialogue, setting, time, character, vivid sensory description, metaphor, and carefully chosen details. For this assignment, you will submit a rough draft and a final draft of about 700–900 words. But words are just one mode of expression. To explore possibilities for meaning-making beyond linguistic expression, submit a "critical selfie" along with your writing. A "critical selfie" is a photographic self-portrait that makes creative use of lighting, setting, color, shape, angle, and materials or props to amplify, extend, and/or contrast the meaning and subject you develop in your flash memoir. Your critical selfie will serve as your backdrop for your extemporaneous presentation (see the Flash Memoir Presentation assignment sheet for details).

Project Focus

So, what should you write about? What should your critical selfie focus on? Following our course theme and our "Big Questions," your project should focus on your developing sense of identity. We are asking you to think about how we create knowledge about the self and what counts as knowledge when the self is the subject of our inquiry. To reflect on these larger questions, you might focus your project on a moment or series of moments when you:

- . . . questioned something that you long believed was true.
- . . . recognized something you once took for granted.
- . . . reconsidered the credibility or authority of someone central to your life.
- . . . recognized or rejected how someone else perceives you.
- . . . learned something that shifted how you understand yourself and/or your relationships with others.

Evaluation

A creative and effective flash memoir will study one moment of time or one ultra-concentrated period of time. There is not enough room in a flash piece to go too broad; stay focused up-close and concentrate on the details of that moment or period of time to make your reader feel immersed in it. Use sensory details to help your reader feel the moment with you: sights, sounds, smells, textures, etc. Your flash memoir should include that lightning strike moment of insight or understanding: what truths might be glimpsed in the brief memory you are studying? Your goal for the flash memoir should be to accomplish those two things—immersing your reader intimately in the moment with you and reflecting on the truth or truths that could be known in that one moment.

A creative and effective critical selfie will offer a representation of the self that approaches, but does not solidify, a "truth" about the self. In other words, no single photo can encapsulate all of *you*, but a single photo can offer one story—a part of the whole. Your selfie should offer a meaningful combination of image, color, shape, perspective, perhaps words, maybe objects, kinesics (use of body, facial expressions, gestures, etc.), personal artifacts (how you adorn yourself), and possibly filters. The combination of these design choices should connect to the specific memories, details, and tone of your flash memoir. You can use your choice of camera (digital, smartphone, 35mm, etc.), but the final presentation should be digital (.png, .jpg, or .pdf). If you want to explore photo editing options, this Tutorials and Resources list features several image editing programs.

Just as your writing should be your best work (edited for grammar and correctness), the design of your image should be your best work (quality images, no pixilation).

Getting Started

For the flash memoir, begin by making a list of those movie clips of memories that often play through your mind. Which memories feel salient and full of gravity or intensity for you? Choose one and examine it closely: What does the memory feel like and look like? What stands out brightly in the memory, and what is cast into shadow? What questions and ideas emerge when you try to poke around in those shadows?

For the critical selfie, you can try associative thinking. What are the key details in your flash memoir? What objects, colors, or images do you associate with those details? How might you represent (or evoke) those details visually?

Deadlines

February 1:	Rough draft due in class
February 8:	Final draft due in class
February 20 & 22:	Presentation days

Delivery

To submit your work for this project, please use your personalized "Flash Memoir" folder on our class Google Drive space. Use this folder to submit your (clearly marked/labeled, please) rough draft, your final draft, your critical selfie, and your extemporaneous outline.

184 *Londie T. Martin and Kristen A. McIntyre*

APPENDIX B

Project 1
Flash Memoir Presentation

Big Questions

- How do we create knowledge?
- What counts as knowledge?

Description: Using your flash memoir piece, translate your story of a pique identity moment into an extemporaneous presentation (not a performance) for a live, public audience.

Rationale: There is a strong relationship between how we approach the process of our writing and our public speaking. However, it is important to understand that they are separate beasts in terms of how we adapt to the respective rhetorical situation of each. Learning how to transition our papers to public speaking situations is an invaluable skill that will serve you well academically and professionally. Additionally, this assignment connects us to our ancient oral storytelling roots. Before we wrote stories, we were telling them to each other to entertain one another, to learn from one another, to connect with each other—to create and share knowledge.

Requirements:

Time: 5 to 7 minutes (firm)

Content: Adapted from flash memoir paper and organized using a narrative pattern that reflects coherence and fidelity as theorized in Fisher's (1985) "The Narrative Paradigm: An Elaboration": qualities of *coherence* (the internal consistency of the story) and *fidelity* (the values embedded in the story). A formal outline of the presentation will be developed prior to rehearsal.

Visual Aid: Static *Critical Selfie* slide to support story

Delivery: Extemporaneous (speaking outline: key-word notes, one piece of paper, one-sided)

Audience: peers, Dr. Martin and Dr. McIntyre

Question and Answer: Each speaker will need to facilitate their own 2–3 minute Q & A session after their presentation.

Deadlines

February 13:	Presentation Formal Outline (due at the beginning of class for peer workshop)
February 15:	Presentation Speaking Outline (due at the beginning of class for small group rehearsals)
February 20, 22, & 27:	Presentation days

Delivery

To submit your supporting documents, use our team drive to upload your revised, final formal outline and speaking outline.

APPENDIX C

Project 2
Self, Knowledge, Community—Exploring Multimodal Expression

Big Questions

- How do we create knowledge?
- What counts as knowledge?
- How do we share knowledge?

Purpose

Building on what we learned from project one, this group project offers us the opportunity to more deeply consider how we create and share knowledge. In small groups, define a specific project focus grounded in an issue you care about and a key question about identity (e.g., truth, privilege, credibility, perception, transformation, belonging), and identify community members who can offer you potential insights about the relationships among identity, communication, and knowledge creation/sharing. We will generate research questions and invite our community partners to participate in interviews designed to foster understanding, encourage positive communication, and unearth realizations about worldviews. Specifically, we want to learn more about how worldviews inform, shape, and drive identity and how identity informs, shapes, and drives worldviews.

As a group, you will work together to invent and create a multimodal representation of your research findings, and you will share your work with a live audience. Here, "multimodal representation" refers to a text that moves beyond alphabetic expression (i.e., the written word) and instead weaves together multiple modes of expression (i.e., linguistic, visual, aural, gestural, and spatial). The final project should draw on the affordances and limitations of different modes of expression to underscore, amplify, or otherwise emphasize the meaning and insights you gained through your collective research and reflection. The final form of these projects will vary depending on topic, focus, and research, but some options you might consider: a photo essay, an interactive website, a podcast series, a set of infographics, a zine, a reader's theater script/performance, a short film, etc.

While the group will work together throughout this process, each group member is responsible for conducting their own interview and for creating a specific piece of the final group project that reflects insights gained from that interview. For example, if the group decides to create a zine, individual group members should compose their own work to publish in the group zine. If the group decides to create a short film, individual group members should create brief vignettes that the group can weave together into a cohesive film project. But these are just examples. Your group should rely on imagination and rhetorical invention—grounded in your research and the meaning you draw from it—to guide the development of your multimodal project.

Overview of Project Process

This is a group project, and we will work together to co-create our groups based on the *Flash Memoir with Critical Selfie and Presentation* assignment. Groups will need to work together to:

- Create a team communication contract
- Invent a research question
- Design an interview protocol
- Identify participants
- Compose a multimodal project proposal
- Interview participants
- Make sense of interviews
- Deliver a public presentation of multimodal project with artist statements

Evaluation

This project has many pieces, and some will be evaluated at the group level, others at the individual level.

Group-level evaluation includes:

- Team Communication Contract
- Project Process Work

- Draft research question related to identity question (e.g., truth, privilege, credibility, perception, transformation, belonging) and issue. (pass required)
  - Prep for interviews (identify participants, develop informed consent form and questions, and potentially co-facilitate).
  - Make sense of interviews (thematic analysis).
- Multimodal Project Proposal (pass required)
  - Justify connection between research and modes of expression and delivery.
  - Articulate relationship between individual contributions and the larger group project.
  - Present proposal orally for instructors and classmates.
  - Public presentation of multimodal project with artist statements

Individual-level evaluation includes:

- Interview facilitation and transcription
- Individual multimodal product (i.e., the thing you made)
- Artist statement
- Group communication self-assessment and peer-assessment

Deadlines & Important Dates

March 8:	Group Contracts
March 13:	Research Question & Annotated Bibliography
March 15:	Team Proposal Draft
March 27 & 29:	Proposal Panels
April 3:	Interview Protocol Draft
April 24 & 26:	Public Presentations of Multimodal Project

Delivery

Whenever a deliverable is due, you will submit your work through Google Drive. However, remember that you will share your final multimodal presentation at a public venue for a live audience.

APPENDIX D

Midterm Reflection: Formal Self-Assessment

Directions: Your mission is to create a well-reasoned, well-supported formal self-assessment based on the provided criteria. While effort is important, evidence and results will help you make your learning and growth *visible*. Therefore, as you craft your assessment paper keep your audience in mind: Dr. Londie and Dr. M. We need to be convinced, beyond a shadow of a doubt, that you have (1) met the criteria that best aligns with your self-assessment and (2) demonstrated substantial growth since the beginning of the semester.

Format of Assessment:

1. A Google Folder containing all materials, a Google Document with embedded links to supporting materials, *or* a paper supported by a binder of materials.

2. Please use the first person perspective in your writing. We want this to be a meaningful, reflective journey of what you have learned and the choices you have made as a learner. You cannot have too much in this paper. However, you can have too little. Most papers are about 10 pages long (or longer).

3. Use formal essay structure using headings and the template we provide. Using the criteria for the grade you feel you've earned (see the rubrics below), explicitly address the questions for each section in the template. You should have dedicated paragraph(s)/page(s) for each letter grade criterion. Example:

Section 3. Revision Process
What role has revision played in your learning so far this semester? How have you approached revision in and out of class? What has your process been like? What, if anything, would you like to be different about your process?

While I have evidence of multiple versions of my Flash Memoir (hyperlinks to drafts), according to the rubric, I have earned a B in "Revision Process" for the following reasons . . .

4. Specific references to the work you have created (with examples from that work) should be used to support your assessment at all times. Additionally, referencing peers' work may also be appropriate. *Work* includes discussion posts, peer response activities, in-class exercises and experiments, major projects, engagement in readings, emails, etc.

Table 6.1. Midterm Reflection: Self-Assessment Criteria

	A Refined	B Well Developed	C Adequately Developed	D Underdeveloped	F Absent
Big Questions/ Learning Outcomes	Supports with evidence and outstanding explanations the achievement of the course learning outcomes by making meaningful connections between the course supporting materials and coursework (in-text citations required), class discussions/assignments when answering the questions. Provides insightful explanations for the importance of meeting each outcome.	Supports with evidence and satisfactory explanation the achievement of the course learning outcomes by making clear connections between the course supporting materials and coursework (in-text citations required) when answering the questions. Provides well-developed explanations for the importance of meeting each outcome.	Supports with evidence and adequate explanations the achievement of the course learning outcomes by answering the three "big" questions but lacks consistent connection to course supporting materials and coursework / citations. Demonstrates adequate understanding of the relevance of the questions.	Unable to adequately address the achievement of one or more of the course learning outcomes via course supporting materials and coursework and/or explanation. Attempts to answer the three "big" questions but does not demonstrate understanding of the relevance of the questions.	No attempt to address the achievement of course learning outcomes. No attempt to answer the three "big" questions.

(*continued*)

Table 6.1. (*continued*)

	A *Refined*	B *Well Developed*	C *Adequately Developed*	D *Underdeveloped*	F *Absent*
Revision Process	Effectively engages in the revision process, producing evidence of multiple drafts of work. Thoroughly explains how feedback from peers and instructor was integrated in each revision. Articulates, in depth, the value of the revision process.	Engages in the revision process, producing evidence of multiple drafts of work. Clearly reflects on how peer and instructor feedback was used. Articulates clearly the value of the revision process.	Engages in the revision process, producing evidence of multiple drafts of work. Adequately reflects on how peer and instructor feedback was used.	Engages minimally in the revision process, only producing the required posts/ assignments. Does not reflect on how peer and instructor feedback was used.	Fails to provide evidence of engagement in the revision process.
Work Quality	Quality not only meets expectations but demonstrates superior skill and thoroughness in the work produced, as indicated by peer feedback and instructor rubrics. Work is nuanced, grounded in the assigned course materials as well as personal experience, reflects the intention of the assignments, and is well-written.	Quality of work demonstrates above average competence as indicated by peer feedback and instructor rubrics. Work is well developed, grounded in the course material, respects the intention of the assignment, and is well-written.	Quality of work is adequate as indicated by peer feedback and instructor rubrics. Work is adequately grounded in the course material, generally aligns with the intention of the assignment, and is written clearly.	Quality of work repeatedly demonstrates an inability to grasp the material. Work does not demonstrate a grasp of the material beyond the obvious and fails to make meaningful connections across course materials. Work does not reflect attention to writing.	Work turned in meets the criteria for academic dishonesty (plagiarism, etc.).

Engagement in Work	Enthusiastically engages in the assigned course material via meaningful participation/ reflection in class, online, and outside of class. Completes 100% assigned work on time as time stamped by Team Drive.	Engages in the assigned course material via well-developed participation/ reflection in class, online, and outside of class. Completes all assigned work and 80% of work is completed on time as time stamped by Team Drive.	Engages in the assigned course material by doing only what is required with regard to participation/ reflection in class, online, and outside of class. Completes all assigned work and 70% of work is completed on time as time stamped by Team Drive.	Minimally engages in the assigned course material by responding sporadically OR demonstrates a lack of serious effort. Fails to complete 50% of assigned work as time stamped by Team Drive.	No evidence of engagement in the assigned course material in or outside of class. Fails to complete 50% or more of the assigned work as time stamped by Team Drive
Classmate Support	Actively engages classmates in supportive ways above and beyond required feedback.	Engages classmates in supportive ways via required feedback that follows assigned guidelines.	Engages classmates via required feedback that follows assigned guidelines.	Engages classmates via required feedback, but the feedback does not reflect the required guidelines.	Fails to provide required feedback.

192   *Londie T. Martin and Kristen A. McIntyre*

APPENDIX E

Student:

Midterm Reflection Self-Assessment Criteria Checklist

Table 6.2.   Student's Overall Grade Assessment

	Dr. Londie					Dr. Kristen					
	A	B	C	D	F	A	B	C	D	F	Growth Goals
Big Questions/ Learning Outcomes											
Revision Process											
Work Quality											
Engagement in Work											
Classmate Support											

We offer the following advice in the spirit of revision. However, if you choose to use your energy in other ways, we will expect that you transfer the suggestions to your Project 2 work.

Memoir Writing Goal:

Memoir Speaking Goal:

REFERENCES

Ahmed, Sara. 2006. *Queer Phenomenology: Orientations, Objects, Others*. Durham, NC: Duke University Press.

Andrews, Larry. 2007. "Grades, Scores, and Honors: A Numbers Game?" *Journal of the National Collegiate Honors Council* Spring/Summer, 23–30. https://digital commons.unl.edu/nchcjournal/41/.

Arao, Brian, and Kristi Clemens. 2013. "From Safe Spaces to Brave Spaces: A New Way to Frame Dialogue Around Diversity and Social Justice." In *The Art of Effective Facilitation: Reflections from Social Justice Educators*, edited by Lisa M. Landreman, 135–150. Sterling, Virginia: Stylus.

Bain, Ken. 2004. *What the Best College Teachers Do*. Cambridge, MA: Harvard University Press.

Fisher, Walter R. 1985. "The Narrative Paradigm: An Elaboration." *Communication Monographs* 52 (4): 347–367.

Flaherty, Colleen. 2019. "Teaching Evals: Bias and Tenure." *Inside Higher Education*. May 20, 2019. https://www.insidehighered.com/news/2019/05/20/fighting -gender-bias-student-evaluations-teaching-and-tenures-effect-instruction.

Freire, Paolo. 1993. *Pedagogy of the Oppressed*. New York: Continuum Books.

Gonzalez, Jennifer. 2015. "Meet the Single Point Rubric." *Cult of Pedagogy*. Accessed December 15, 2019. https://www.cultofpedagogy.com/single-point-rubric.

Grant, Gerald. 1979. *On Competence: A Critical Analysis of Competence-based Reforms in Higher Education*. San Francisco, CA: Jossey-Bass.

Guzy, Annmarie. 2007. "Evaluation vs. Grading in Honors Composition or How I Learned to Stop Worrying about Grades and Love Teaching." *Journal of the National Collegiate Honors Council* Spring/Summer, 31–36. https://digitalcommons .unl.edu/nchcjournal/35.

hooks, bell. 1994. *Teaching to Transgress: Education as the Practice of Freedom*. New York: Routledge.

Kohn, Alfie. 2006. "The Trouble with Rubrics." *English Journal* 95 (4): 12–15. https://www.alfiekohn.org/teaching/rubrics.pdf.

Laube, Heather, Massoni, Kelley, Sprague, Joey, and Abby L. Ferber. 2007. "The Impact of Gender on the Evaluation of Teaching: What We Know and What We Can Do." *NWSA Journal* 19 (3): 87–104.

Lawrence, John W. 2018. "Student Evaluations of Teaching are Not Valid. *Academe* 104 (3). https://www.aaup.org/article/student-evaluations-teaching-are-not-valid.

Strommel, Jesse. 2017. "Why I Don't Grade." Accessed December 17, 2019. https:// www.jessestommel.com/why-i-dont-grade/.

Chapter Seven

Are We *Just* Grading or Grading *Justly?*

Adventures with Non-Traditional Assessment

Kristen C. Blinne

In this chapter, I offer five different social justice-inspired approaches to grading and assessment, which I have developed and utilized in my communication courses over the last decade, in an attempt to embody the spirit of grading justice as outlined in this edited collection. Throughout this chapter, I hope to model the process-based pedagogy I enact in both my teaching and learning practices. By doing so, I invite readers into my experience, experimenting with various grading systems, illustrating a range of assessment methods designed to reframe student success—not against student failure as articulated in traditional modes of grading and assessment—but instead as practices aimed at grading justice. As part of this discussion, I shall provide some background regarding my teaching-learning journey to set the stage for what follows. Next, I shall explore conversations surrounding alternative or "non-traditional" approaches to grading and assessment. Finally, I round out this chapter with a detailed discussion of a range of grading and assessment methods I have experimented with in my communication courses, offering resources for further reflection and implementation.

SETTING THE (TEACHING-LEARNING) STAGE

Even though I am a fourth-generation teacher, I have *always* been a creatively maladjusted student (see Blinne 2014b). To be honest, grades never really motivated me to learn differently or better. For whatever reason, in early high school, I have a vague memory of consistently receiving the lowest quiz and assignment grades in my geometry course, which at the time, appeared to be a point of pride. It is not that I did not care about learning, I just did not have the passion, the wherewithal, nor readiness to successfully navigate

196   *Kristen C. Blinne*

the requirements and expectations of that subject area. As I progressed in my studies, my dissatisfaction with traditional approaches to education grew, inspiring me to drop out of high school at the beginning of my junior year, opting instead to take the G.E.D. and apply for college two years early.

While I hoped that attending college would offer the respite I was seeking from the "business-of-education-as-usual" approach to education I had come to know in K–12 environments, unsurprisingly, college did not depart that significantly from this model (for me, anyway). Eventually, I attended three different undergraduate institutions, taking a gap year after my first and second years to try to figure out my place in these educational systems to which I did not quite seem to belong. Graduating with my Bachelor of Arts in liberal studies in three years, it took me five years from start to finish to complete the process. To be honest, I now believe the only reason I ever actually graduated from college was because I eventually attended Goddard College in Plainfield, Vermont.

For those not familiar with Goddard, it is a progressive (and non-competitive) college that emphasizes self-direction, utilizing a tutorial system, wherein students work directly with one faculty member each semester, crafting a plan of study, and then engaging various projects during a semester-long credit block. Goddard functions without the role of standard courses or classes, in addition to operating without conventional modes of grading (numeric or letter grades), instead utilizing learner-centered self-evaluation and instructor-focused narrative assessment. For me, Goddard's approach revolutionized my learning experience because for the first time in my life (as a student), I was able to take almost complete ownership of my *process* with the support and guidance of a faculty co-facilitator who was equally invested in my success. In addition to learning *with* and *from* my mother, a career English teacher, it was at Goddard that I truly believe that I gained my most important pedagogical training, although at that moment in my life, I had no intention of ever becoming a teacher.

Some six years after graduating, I decided to pursue advanced graduate studies overseas at the Universiteit van Amsterdam (UvA), culminating in a Master of Arts in medical anthropology. My small cohort included learners from diverse corners of the globe, each with remarkable stories and interests, which also dramatically shifted my understanding of learning and the world at large. This program employed a modular or block design, taking one course at time as a kind of intensive meeting all day and throughout the week for a specified period (depending on the credits). At UvA, assessment occurred on a numeric scale ranging from 4.0 (equivalent to an "F" grade) to 9.0 (equivalent to an "A+" grade). The scale itself actually goes as low as 1.0 and as high as 10.0, utilizing descriptors such as *excellent* (9.0 /A+), *good*

(8.0/A- or 8.5/A), *satisfactory* (7.5/B+, 7.1/B, 6.8/B-, or 6.5/C+), *sufficient* (6.0/C), and *fail* (5.0/D or 4.0/F). Within this system, at least as I understand it, grades at the 7.5 or higher level were extremely uncommon. Because I already did not put much stock into the value of numeric or letter grades as a student, I was able to integrate into the expectations of this system with little challenge.

Returning to the United States several years later to attend a doctoral program in communication at the University of South Florida (USF), I once again found myself immersed in traditional or conventional modes of grading and assessment with my feet straddling two worlds—one as a graduate student and the other in my role as a graduate teaching assistant, serving as the instructor of record for a range of courses throughout my studies. My doctoral program offered little to no training for graduate student teachers, particularly in the realm of grading and assessment of the courses they were offering, so I found myself experimenting with every approach I could to better grasp how to tackle this required element of my teaching process.

It was not until I began working with Mariaelena Bartesaghi, the then supervisor of our interpersonal communication courses and later my advisor, that I was offered a pathway out of the limiting assessment frameworks so often employed in college courses. Later in this chapter, I dive more deeply into the structure of USF's interpersonal communication courses, designed by Bartesaghi, to illustrate the many ways that my learning from this teaching experience has shaped my current understandings of teaching and learning. For now, however, I will note that our interpersonal courses were writing-intensive, utilizing process pedagogy that centered on contract grading, portfolio project design, and consensus-based workshops. It was *within* this alternative assessment structure that I was first able to find a way to *belong* as a teacher because I was able to experiment with and adapt this approach to de-emphasize the power of grades within my courses, while also attempting to share grading power with students.

During this pivotal time, I began to develop my passion for a wide variety of pedagogical approaches, resulting in a range of publications focused on the scholarship of teaching and learning. My exploration started with a project published in *Communication Teacher* (Blinne 2012) titled, "Making the Familiar Strange: Creative Cultural Storytelling within the Communication Classroom," which presents a storytelling activity designed to assist students with looking critically at an everyday experience, creating a story that re-languages this practice performatively. Next, my teaching experimentation resulted in a short article for *College Teaching* (Blinne 2013) titled, "Start with the Syllabus: HELPing Learners Learn through Class Content Collaboration," which discusses the benefits of incorporating learners' input into classroom content design, starting with the syllabus, to invite a more democratic learning process.

Moreover, I developed a feedback process, which I present in an essay titled, "Performing Critical Pedagogy Through Fireside Chats," which was published in the *International Journal of Critical Pedagogy* (Blinne 2014a). In this piece, I introduce fireside chats as a critical pedagogical practice, which can strengthen students' compassion and contemplation by enhancing communication practices and opening discussion about students' learning ideas, dreams, reflections, questions, and fears while changing hierarchical communication patterns between teachers and students. After completing my doctoral studies, I began teaching at the State University of New York College at Oneonta, a small public liberal arts institution in central New York. Moving from a large and quite diverse urban college community to a more regional comprehensive one afforded me the opportunity to continue to explore innovative pedagogies with a different student population. In both instances, I have been able to work with many first generation college students, international students, and students with a wide range of socio-economic backgrounds, abilities, and needs.

After working with fireside chats at both institutions, I was further inspired to embrace contemplative pedagogies sharing my experiences in an article titled, "Awakening to Lifelong Learning: Contemplative Pedagogy *as* Compassionate Engagement," which explores the role contemplative practice could play in both teaching and learning, published in *Radical Pedagogy* (Blinne 2014b). Finally, prior to this chapter and edited collection, I wrote an academy commentary titled, "Applying (Com)passion in the Academy: A Calling . . . A Vow . . . A Plea . . . A Manifesto," which was published in *Departures in Critical Qualitative Research* (Blinne 2016). This essay examines the question—*What is the cost of caring in the academy?*—reflecting on the challenges of doing engaged scholarship by starting with the question: What is the cost of caring in the academy? I explore this question by considering how we, as academics, can better continue this conversation by daring to care about our own and others' work and by not silencing but compassionately supporting each other's voices and passions regarding our work and lives.

Reflecting on my teaching and learning journey, I wholeheartedly believe that communication teachers can be the educational change agents the world needs, helping individuals learn to engage more peacefully, nonviolently, and compassionately with each other. Within my teaching, I am always striving to answer the questions: *How can we better understand and negotiate cultural differences, and how can we teach and learn to engage more peacefully, compassionately, and nonviolently with each other so that at least one person might suffer less each day.* Within my teaching, grading justice, as

I understand it and engage with this idea within my teaching and as part of the collaborative assessment practices I employ in my classrooms, can be conceptualized as a framework that dares to imagine what a social justice approach to grading and assessment might be to assist instructors with intervening into and potentially disrupting unjust modes of teaching and learning by creating more just practices and policies.

To this end, like Berila (2016), I start with the premise, "We have to literally *unlearn* oppression: examine our role in it, dismantle deeply held ideologies, and create alternative, more empowering, ways of relating to one another" (3). As part of this process, it is imperative that we continuously examine education as "a social system in which we all *participate*" (Berila 2016, 3). In doing so, all of my courses place a strong emphasis on building awareness of social inequalities so we might collaborate to create more just structures together. As Frey and Palmer suggest (2014), "Education, of course, offers one of the best opportunities for challenging and changing unjust systemic structures and practices" (1). For me, grading justice operates in alignment with the commitments of critical communication pedagogy (Fassett and Warren 2007, 2008; Rudick, Golsan, and Cheesewright 2017), as well as with communication activism pedagogies (Frey and Palmer 2014); contemplative pedagogies (Zajonc 2006; Miller 2006; Grace 2011; Blinne 2014; Berila 2016; Kaufman 2017); decolonizing pedagogies (Diversi and Moreira 2009; Pirbhai-Illich, et al. 2017); critical pedagogies more broadly as advanced by Paulo Freire (1994, 1998, 2000), Ira Shor (1997, 2009), bell hooks (1994), Henry Giroux (1983), Peter McLauren (2006, 2015), Ernest Morell (2008), Antonia Darder (2011, 2016), and Joe Kincheloe (2008, 2010), among others. In the following section, we shall discuss these connections and commitments.

CRITICAL APPROACHES TO ASSESSMENT

In exploring the relationship between critical pedagogy and assessment, Linda Keesing-Styles (2003) contends that a critical pedagogy of assessment must involve "an entirely new orientation" centered on "dialogic interactions" (9). As part of this, she argues that ultimately this orientation must also "reinterpret the complex ecology of relationships in the classroom to avoid oppressive power relations and create negotiated curriculum, including assessment, equally owned by teachers and students" (10). A primary mode of enacting assessment from the vantage point of critical pedagogy, per her view, involves sharing ownership with students, putting the collective power in their hands when generating assessment criteria (13). Keesing-Styles makes a compelling case for not assessing students against established learning outcomes on the grounds that these outcomes represent and reproduce a "prescribed standard," which is then applied (most often inequitably) to all students (14). She contends that this approach "focuses students' attention on assessment rather than on learning" (14). To illustrate this notion further, she shares her experience with removing learning outcomes from courses and instead being more thorough in detailing course content so that students are assessed against the aim of the course rather than particular learning outcomes (15). Finally, she advocates for the integration of peer review and self-assessment as additional tools that can reflect the goals of critical pedagogy. In all of these examples, Keesing-Styles suggests that,

> The intention here is to try to equalise the power relations between students and teachers, to encourage autonomy and ownership of their learning and work, to help in the development of truly reflective practice and to equip the students better to address issues in their everyday work outside of the classroom and after graduation (15).

Similarly, in an article written by Stacey Gray Akyea and Pamela Sandoval (2004), which explores assessment through the lens of feminist pedagogy, the authors discuss the complexities associated with sharing power with students, in addition to "how demanding a democratic classroom can be" (2). Examining the challenges associated with grading and assessment, they ask the following questions: "Is giving grades just a judgment? Or does giving grades provide feedback to students, so they may improve? Or do students really earn their grades?" (4). Asking these questions inspires reflection on the ways in which educational inequalities occur through both *overt* and *covert* forms of discrimination as they contend that "blanket interpretations of shared power in the sense of issuing grades" may not account for the wide range of experiences of learners in a classroom setting (e.g., underrepresented students, first generation students, among other historically disadvantaged groups) (4). As such, they urge teachers to reflect on the ways in which they may be intentionally (or not) reinforcing imbalances of power within their classrooms as part of their grading and assessment practices ("traditional" or otherwise).

David Kahl, Jr. (2013), in his article which discusses the relationship between critical communication pedagogy and assessment, argues that "assessment procedures that reflect the goals of critical communication pedagogy can be developed to assist educators in reaching critical goals in the classroom," working in contrast to the "prescriptive, objective tenets of neoliberal assessment" (2615). As he contends, the goal of assessment more broadly is to "determine the degree to which students are actually learning what instructors want them to learn," and he further suggests that "assessments themselves are not inherently problematic" (2616). In other words, the problem is not the use of assessment but instead how to develop assessments that reflect critical agendas (2617). While he does not offer prescriptions for how teachers might embrace or design "critically minded assessments," he suggests that instructors start with their course design, namely their syllabi and associated course materials (2618). Moreover, Kahl contends that "assessment should be free of prescription," citing Freire (1970) who states:

> One of the basic elements of the relationship between oppressor and oppressed is *prescription*. Every prescription represents the imposition of one individual's choice upon another, transforming the consciousness of the person prescribed into one that conforms with the prescriber's consciousness (2620).

Embracing this notion, Kahl advocates for helping students understand the ways in which hegemony functions to marginalize groups and individuals as a tool to heighten their awareness of assessment processes and society at large. In this spirit, he further contends that assessment can help teachers determine "whether they are helping students become more critically engaged in society" while also illustrating the degree to which students are learning course content and how this can be applied to enacting justice within society (2625). For me, Kahl (2013), Akyea and Sandoval (2004), and Keesing-Styles (2003) all offer important considerations when one is attempting to enact grading justice in their teaching. Similarly, I fully embrace dialogic and consensus-based approaches to teaching and learning (Campbell and Kryszewska 1992; Wolk 1998; Bruffee 1999; Sartor and Young Brown 2004). Central to this discussion, as follows, includes the ways in which various process pedagogies that utilize contract grading and assessment have shaped my understandings of grading justice (Danielewicz and Elbow 2009; Shor 2009; Moreno-López 2005; Cunningham et al. 2017).

ASSESSING PROCESS AND PROCESSING ASSESSMENT

Danielewicz and Elbow's (2009) hybrid contract grading system outlined in their essay, "A Unilateral Grading Contract to Improve Learning" has greatly influenced and inspired my approach to assessment. Danielewicz and Elbow primarily utilize this approach to teach writing within first-year courses through honors sections. Their rationale for utilizing grading contracts centers on striving to reduce unfairness, while also attempting to radically reduce the role of grading in their teaching by working to decouple evaluation from feedback with the goal of improving student learning. Because instructors are still required to assign a "one-dimensional qualitative score," which is meant to "represent the quality of each student's performance in a course," they utilize grades and no grades as one of the main features of their hybrid grading contract (244).

To provide more context for Danielewicz and Elbow's system: students are guaranteed a "B" grade based on the completion of specified activities, not on the evaluation of the quality of students' written work. Put differently, if students complete all of the required course activities, they can count on receiving a "B" grade regardless of instructor feedback. The motivation behind this system is to assess students on what they "do" via their effort and active participation. Thus, "B" grades serve as a baseline for student's conscientious investment and effort, not the "quality" of their work, though they are required to follow the instructions to meet the criteria for a "B" grade.

Danielewicz and Elbow state they have found this form of contract grading reliable for producing "B" quality writing along with meeting the following criteria: attending class regularly, arriving on time, and not missing more than the pre-determined amount of absences determined by the teacher; meeting the due dates for all assignments; following the instructions provided on the assignment rubrics for each requirement; actively participating in all in-class exercises and activities; completing all informal and formal assignments; working collaboratively and giving thoughtful peer and group feedback; sustaining effort and investment on all in-progress projects; making substantive revisions when assigned to revise (not just editing or touching up); copyediting all final revisions; attending meetings with the instructor to discuss progress; and, finally, submitting one's midterm and final projects (245–246).

Because they do not distinguish final course grades until the end of the semester, they utilize three assessment markers during the term to help students understand their progress, including: *not satisfactory for a B, satisfactory for a B,* and *better than a B* (Danielewicz and Elbow 2009, 246). As previously referenced, within this system, Danielewicz and Elbow basically ignore the quality of writing for grades up to a "B"; however, grades higher than a "B" do rest on the judgment of the instructor, taking into account the student's final project and participation throughout the semester. In reflecting on their approach, they state they "don't hold back on teacher evaluation and judgement," offering evaluative feedback on strengths and weakness; however, they do work to "decouple those judgments from *grades* (up to B)" (247).

To better situate their system, it is important to note that Danielewicz and Elbow's approach is "unilateral," meaning they do not give students power over course policies or rules. In other words, as they state, "We don't mask the large power differential between us and our students, but we're not inviting negotiations about it either. In general, we're side-stepping conflict—especially by not putting grades on papers at all, since grades are a prime source of conflict" (248). Even so, central to their process is engaging students in on-going conversations about the what constitutes "high-quality" work. They aptly argue that this approach disrupts conventional grading, resting on two principles, which they believe to be "patently false," the first principle being that instructors have common standards for grading, the second being that the "quality of a multidimensional product can be fairly or accurately represented with a conventional one-dimensional grade" (249). Danielewicz and Elbow further contend that conventional grading "helps induce student compliance by obscuring analogous structures of unfairness," insomuch that they are "supposed to accept without question that a one-dimensional form of evaluation is rational and just" (248).

In an attempt to craft a grading system they believe to be more just and fair, Danielewicz and Elbow offer four primary reasons for giving a "B" grade based on behavior, while focusing on the quality of each individual's work for higher grades (250–251). Of the reasons, first they contend that for most students, the quality of each person's writing improves enough over the course of the term to warrant a "B" grade by semester's end if they have met the outlined behavior components of the contract. Second, they feel that the disparities surrounding "B" quality work offers the final grade of a "B" to a wider range of abilities. Third, they believe that behavior and one's quality of work interact differently at varying levels of a grading scale. In other words, behavior has the capacity to pull a student's grade up or down, depending on the instructor. Fourth, they argue that this approach works against grade inflation because it relies on excellence for grades higher than a "B."

To determine grades higher than a "B," Danielewicz and Elbow maintain students who do not fulfill the contract are thereby disqualified from earning higher grades, whereas for grades lower than a "B," the flexibility of contract grading allows instructors to make individual judgements, based on each individual's unique circumstances. Ultimately, as they state, they are trying to "badger and cajole *every* student into getting a B," by doing everything they specify in their contract (254). In summary, Danielewicz and Elbow's focus on evaluative feedback is based on decoupling evaluation from grading (up to a "B"), contending that "a B should be available for *every* student" (258). They argue that this approach not only reduces their record keeping, but also that it increases student motivation and work output. By focusing on "process" as a primary grading tactic, they have crafted an approach that is both simple and radical (in some instructors' views), designed to reduce the impact of grading by allowing students to make behavioral choices, based on feedback (peer and instructor) to better the quality of their work throughout the semester.

Before I discuss how my philosophies and practices of grading and assessment intersect with and depart from Danielewicz and Elbow (2009), I turn to Ira Shor's (2009) response to their essay, which he titled "Critical Pedagogy is Too Big to Fail." Like Danielewicz and Elbow, Shor also utilizes grading contracts within his teaching. Unlike Danielewicz and Elbow, Shor *does* grade the quality of student writing, using traditional A–F letter grades throughout the semester. In analyzing the differences in their approaches, Shor describes Danielewicz and Elbow's system as attempting to take the suspense out of grading, assessing student work in both a *quantitative* and *performative* manner (8). Similarly, Shor also proposes minimum work levels for each letter grade category (e.g., one absence for an "A" grade; different lengths of papers; and/or more or less active participation). He states that he mostly gives one of three grades on written work, namely A, B, or C, "earned first by meeting quantitative minimums for each grade" as well as by his judgment of the "quality" of the work (8). Work that is considered to be lower than a "C" grade is given the marker "R" or "Rewrite Required, No Credit," (most closely linked to a "D" or "F" grade). Students are thus encouraged to rewrite the paper for a new grade; however, if they choose not to hand in a revision, they will receive a "D" or "F."

Shor states that Danielewicz and Elbow's "better than a B and less than a B" are comparable to his "A" grade (better than a B) and his "C" grade (less than a B) (9). To assist students with understanding this approach, Shor offers a "teacher's proposed plan" for earning A, B, and C grades at the start of the course, inviting them to negotiate the grading proposal as well as the larger syllabus, as opposed to providing a "unilateral protocol." In my view, Shor's approach to contract grading offers additional nuance to my own views as he fully discusses the pitfalls associated with utilizing a "B" grade as the benchmark, especially in educational contexts where students may lack "B-minimum skills" or where they may interpret "guaranteed a B" as akin to just "showing up" (or "blowing off" the tasks at hand). Additionally, a major difference between these two approaches focuses on the ways in which power is negotiated and shared between teachers and students.

For Shor, at the beginning of the course, he initiates what he terms a "constitutional assembly," designed to give students the opportunity to negotiate grading *and* course policies so they may engage in a *"co-authoring of mutual obligations"* (13). He goes into the depth about his views regarding the term "contract" as a kind of "meeting of the minds," suggesting that Danielewicz and Elbow's unilateral contract functions more like a "seller's warranty to consumers" versus a "covenant of explicit understandings between all parties affected by the terms" because a teacher's presentation of non-negotiate rules "unilaterally obliges another to abide by the terms to which the second party did not formally consent" (13). Building on this idea, Shor explores the role the syllabus plays as a kind of contractual relation, which is typically authored solely by an instructor, who then distributes this contract on the first day of the course as a teaching requirement that also operates as "an archived document perused by outside accreditors and by inside promotion committees" (16). Citing Fish, Shor situates the syllabus as a "contractual guarantee for professional services that teachers will render in exchange for the tuition" that students pay for each course, while also arguing that a unilateral syllabus and grading contracts are "paper representations or bills of lading specifying goods and services guaranteed to buyers" (16). Per this view, teachers specify the terms of exchange with students situated as the customers in this interaction. As Shor contends,

> As customers, students can exercise consumer agency: they can drop a class if disappointed and apply for a refund. Truly savvy consumers will size up the situation and simply not buy in the first place (not register for the class), taking their business elsewhere (a different class or instructor), shopping around for a better deal. The problem is that market relations such as these tilt the field to the sellers. Customers, especially the working-class majority in college, cannot nimbly shop around for a better syllabus, a better grading plan, a better teacher, or even a better college (16).

Because of this all-too-common reality, Shor offers students "protest rights" so they can contest his grading of the quality of their work (17). He also offers a "rewrite provision," allowing students to revise any piece "as often as they like for a higher grade" (18). Shor utilizes two other primary tools to share grading power with students such an "A-B-C grading proposal sheet," offered for discussion and negotiation at the beginning of the term, in addition to what he refers to as an "After-Class Group," which involves student volunteers who assist with evaluating each class session, holding him accountable for his choices while also providing immediate feedback regarding his teaching (18).

As part of Shor's discussion of critical pedagogy and his use of grading contracts, he states, "grading is a social practice in a public place, the classroom" (21). Moreover, he contends that "Grading is one practice which forms us into the people we become," (21) and because all modes of evaluation involve the negotiation of power, he asserts "co-authorship in the classroom is an alt/dis for the downward distribution of authority in a time when power and wealth are rushing to the top" (19). Considering this further, in these two instances, it becomes clear that Danielewicz and Elbow attempt to reduce the impact of grading by giving up as much grading power as possible, yet they maintain the power over course requirements, whereas Shor shares power with students to shape both course and grading policies but maintains power when assigning grade categories, though he has created a variety of tools to disrupt or unsettle this power and share it with students.

Before moving to forward with our discussion, I would like to offer three additional examples to help contextualize the possibilities of contract grading as well as other approaches aimed at sharing grading power with students. The first example focuses on Isabel Moreno-López (2005), whose work with contract gradings is cited by both Danielewicz and Elbow (2009) and Shor (2009). In situating her own approach, Moreno-López suggests that "Sharing authority sets the ground for a bilateral learning process in which students and teacher negotiate the class procedures, structure, content, grading criteria as well as their own roles in relation to each other" (1). She draws on the work of Paolo Freire and Henry Giroux, along with Lev Vygotsky to illustrate the ways in which contract grading can help both teachers and students examine the purpose and meaning of education, in addition to the roles they play in this process, asking, "What are the implications of sharing authority among students and their teacher?" as well as "What are students' reactions when they participate in the course decision-making process?" (2).

Within this conversation, Moreno-López utilizes her intermediate-advanced Spanish course as an example to illustrate how she approaches contract grading, stating upfront that she worked collaboratively with students to develop the contract system to assess student's performance. Similar to Shor (1996), she disrupts conventional approaches to grading by engaging in a negotiation process with students, designing a system or proposal which is then presented to students at the beginning of the semester. Students are then able to determine which grade category they wish to "sign" for (or work towards), based on the negotiated criteria. To facilitate this process, she dedicates class-time to discussing both the syllabus and grading system so that students may ask questions, make amendments, or provide comments on the initial proposal (5). After the criteria is agreed upon by the group, each student then signs the grading contract, based on the grade they are working towards earning. Throughout the semester, students continue to negotiate this process, discussing their final grade with her at the end of the term. Within this process, the grade may be in alignment with their contracted grade category or not, depending on their performance.

As part of this negotiation process, Moreno-López allows students the opportunity to discuss the proposed grading criteria while she is not present in the classroom. Thus, she steps outside of the space so that they can share their questions and concerns with each other first (p. 6). When the students have completed discussing any changes they hope to make, she is invited back into the classroom space and the negotiation process continues until the group reaches an agreement. Moreno-López states that in the case of this course example, the negotiation primarily focused on the proposed attendance policy (7). Finally, at the end of the semester, she meets with students individually, asking them to evaluate their work and assign a final grade to their process, based on their signed contract. Reflecting on this experience, she states "Among the 24 students who remained in the course at the end of the semester, 23 had initially signed for an A and one for a B. The final grades as decided by each student were twelve As, eight Bs, three Cs and an Incomplete. I agreed with each of the students' grade decisions" (7).

Moreno-López contends that by inviting students to help develop the course by redesigning the syllabus and related grading policies, they are able to "take responsibility for their own education by becoming independent, active learners" (8). One of the pitfalls she encountered, however, was that students often demanded that she play the role of the traditional teacher. Additionally, it is important to note as part of her approach that she developed criteria for a "student committee," outlined in her syllabus, which would only be created if students wished to challenge her assessment criteria (9). In such a case, the student committee would meet to discuss the grades of the student who requested review. Unsurprisingly, she found that many students were hostile to the idea of having a student committee operate in this manner. Part of the reason for this, she explains, is that students feared that the committee would be stricter in their assessment. Even so, overall, Moreno-López states that her students appreciated the opportunity to engage in these discussions and to have policies in place that allowed them to question her criteria.

By the end of the semester, Moreno-López comments that "Participants reproduced and rejected, at different moments, the traditional roles of the teacher as an authority figure and of students as passive consumers of knowledge" (14). As such, she recognizes that regardless of how much a teacher attempts to share the power with students some "may prefer and thus respond better to the more teacher-controlled classroom to which they are accustomed" (14). Ultimately, Moreno-López contends that contract grading is one approach teachers can utilize to reinvent the role of power in their courses, sharing authority with students and designing a teaching-learning process that allows them to analyze, criticize, and question the material they are studying and how they are studying this content (2).

At the conclusion of her article, she offers a contract sample in an appendix that outlines course expectations as follows: For an "A" grade, students must have no more than 2 absences; 2 late arrivals or early departures; "A" quality written work (all handed in on time); and very active class participation. For a "B" grade, she specifies 3 absences; 3 late arrivals; 1 early departure from class; "B" quality written work; 1 late assignment; and active class participation. For a "C" grade, students can have 4 absences, 4 late arrivals, 2 early departures, "C" quality written work; 2 late assignments; and little class participation. For a "D" grade, students will have 5 absences; 5 late arrivals; 3 early departures; "D" quality written work; 3 late assignments; and no class participation (17–18). Each of these categories has a tiered number of assignments. For instance, for an "A," a student must complete 5 journal entries and 12 hours of work outside of class meetings, whereas for a "C" grade, students must only complete 3 journal entries and 9 hours of outside work.

Finally, it is important to note that Moreno-López offers these additional stipulations: If the teacher's criteria is questioned, a student committee will be elected to review written assignments to determine what A, B, C, or D quality means, as well as deciding how to evaluate the different levels of participation, if necessary (18). She allows students the opportunity to rewrite papers for a higher grade, if revisions are handed in within one week of receiving feedback from her. Students in Moreno-López's example are able to rewrite as many times as they would like for a higher grade within a one-week period. Within these expectations, she states that for "borderline grades," the student committee will help to establish if the student has met the criteria between categories, based on the outline criteria.

Asao Inoue (2019), too, employs a grading contract system referred to as "labor-based grading," which calculates final course grades solely based on students' labor with zero judgments regarding the quality of their writing. Inoue states that while labor-based grading integrates feedback about writing quality, these conversations do not impact a student's course grade. Inoue critiques the grading contract approaches of Danielewicz and Elbow (2009) and Shor (2009) on the grounds that they integrate "quality" judgments within their systems to determine higher course grades. Inoue argues that labor-based grading, as an alternative contract grading approach, offers *all* students access to the entire range of final course grades (3). In doing so, Inoue seeks to resist grading and assessment practices that "uphold singular dominant standards that are racist, and White supremacist when used uniformly" (3). Inoue invites educators to explore their own complicity within unfair grading and assessment systems and to think seriously about changing these systems, stating "It is compassionate to suffer with others, like the suffering that so many of our students feel when a standard that is not of their own is used against them" (6).

Inoue describes labor as the "work the body does over time," contending that students must labor to learn (129). While he recognizes the term itself might call forth negative connotations, ultimately he argues that labor-based grading is one way he is able to enact a social justice agenda within his teaching. He suggests that typical grading systems rarely account for students' labor, instead focusing on judging the outcomes of the labor and the perception of the labor's quality. Within this approach, Inoue creates a set of social agreements with the entire class regarding how final grades will be determined for everyone (130). The resulting contract is negotiated at the beginning of the term and then revisited midway. Like Danielewicz and Elbow (2009), Inoue, too, utilizes the default grade of a "B," if students complete the labor requested (regardless of the quality of this labor). In attempting to separate course grades from how students learn, Inoue assumes that all students are doing the labor. Higher grades, then, result from doing more labor with no attention to the labor's "so-called quality" (130). To assist students with this process, all labor is quantified (e.g., words read, time spent writing, and so on). Inoue offers the expected time needed to complete each activity per step. He only records information regarding this labor process when students do not turn something in, or if they turn something in late or incomplete.

All assignments are calculated equally and the criteria for each is considered to be met if the assignment is turned in when requested. Students are responsible for documenting their labor process, not the products (133). Inoue offers instructions that provide information about the description of the assignment, a statement of goals of the labor, and a step-by-step process for completing the labor (133). In keeping with other contract grading systems, labor-based grading is still behavior-based as students that do not participate fully, consistently turn in assignments late, or do not follow the instructions will likely receive a lower grade (331). Even so, within the labor-based grading approach, Inoue outlines the following as examples of different grade categories. For a "B" grade, a student must fully participate 84 percent of the time (i.e., 26 out of 31 scheduled sessions); miss no more than 5 classes (university-sponsored activities or documented illnesses are considered independently of this policy); come late more than 1–2 times; engage in sharing and collaboration; and have no more late or incomplete work than the contract stipulates for each letter grade or point category (331–333). For Inoue, late or incomplete work refers to work that is turned in after the deadline but within 48 hours of when it was due. "Missed work" refers to work that was turned in after the 48-hour mark, resulting in a more serious mark, and "ignored work" refers to work that is unaccounted for or not on record. In other words, as part of labor-based grading, the expectation is that work will be completed on time, though Inoue does offer opportunities for revision as well as a plea or "gimme clause" once a semester to allow for the unexpected (140).

To improve one's contracted grade, one must engage in more labor. Not only must they complete the labor asked in the spirit it was asked, but also they must engage in labor that helps or supports the class (333). Students have the option of raising their "B" grades (3.1) by .3 grade points for each additional labor item they complete (e.g., journal essay, extra assignments, lesson activity handout, a bigger project, or some other labor that benefits the group) (334). Thus, if one completes additional assignments, they can move their "B" or 3.1 incrementally as follows: one (3.4), two (3.7), three (4.0). Adding labor also has the capacity to move "C" contracted grades (2.1) or lower by adding .3 grade points for each additional assignment (334). Students in this category are able to complete more than three assignments to change their grade. In all cases, the main output of the assessment process is creating a labor log, which is a spreadsheet tracking the time spent on each task, providing the following information: duration in minutes, date of session, description, type of session (e.g., reading), start time and end time, location, engagement rating on a scale of 1–5, number of slacks, and the week of the semester (339).

Inoue also tracks the number of non-participation days, late assignments, missed assignments, and ignored assignments, offering criteria for each letter grade category. For example, an "A," a student cannot have more than 5 non-participation days, 5 late assignments, 1 missed assignment, and 0 ignored assignments; whereas, for a "C" grade, a student may have 6 non-participation days, 6 late assignments, 2 missed assignments, and 0 ignored assignments (335). As previously mentioned, Inoue offers a "gimme/plea" that may be used for any reason to make alternative arrangements regarding conduct, attendance, or workload; however, the use of this plea does not mean that the work is not completed but is instead for situations or circumstances that are out of the student's control (335). Finally, within labor-based grading, to perform "exemplary labor," students will have missed *no* classes, participated in *all* activities, have *no* late, missed, or ignored work, *and* also not used the "gimme" (335).

While I have no experience implementing Inoue's labor-based grading within my own grading and assessment practices, I do see some basic commonalities with my "Pick-A-Grade-Plan" approach, insomuch that I require more work per letter grade category; however, within my system, students work collaboratively to determine the criteria for what exemplifies "A" work and so on for each assignment category. Moreover, as part of my approach, students are not able to do additional work to raise their grades; however, in some courses, I allow students to revise their work until they reach their desired grade category. Instead, all work functions on a complete/incomplete basis for the "B" grade and thereafter collaborative assessment is utilized or higher course grades. I discuss this system in more depth in the next section. Reflecting on Inoue's claim that labor-based grading is a more socially just method to produce course grades, I have some concerns regarding the implications of a system focused on quantifying time spent as an indicator of meaningful learning.

I personally do not believe that doing more work equates to more learning. Moreover, asking students to create detailed labor logs to account for their effort also seems like it has the capacity to take time away from other learning opportunities involving self-assessment or inquiry. Because calculating late, missed, and ignored work plays a pivotal role in this system, it is my belief that beyond the offered "gimme" opportunity, this approach could be harnessed in quite unjust ways (also true of other contract systems), mirroring the reward or punishment aspects of traditional grading systems. Finally, another concern I have regarding labor-based grading is that it would best benefit those with lower labor commitments. In other words, students taking heavy credit loads to graduate early due to finances, students caring for sick loved ones, students working multiple jobs, or those that are time- disadvantaged could be negatively impacted by such a system.

I now offer an example that takes me back to where I started my own teaching journey—the University of South Florida. In a collaboratively written article by Summer Cunningham, Mariaelena Bartesaghi, Jim Bowman, and Jennifer Bender (2017) focused on process pedagogy, situated as "an interpersonal dynamic that includes ongoing grading, writing to learn, and the portfolio method," this had the capacity to "shift the power dynamic of the classroom by disrupting students' expectations for evaluation and shifting the learner's orientation from product to process" (381). For this example, their focus centers on teaching interpersonal communication, situating communication more broadly as an "embodied and situated relational practice," emphasizing "learning as on-going interaction" which "emerges in the praxis of multiple, reflexive and ongoing conversations" (381).

Within this course structure, designed by Bartesaghi, writing is situated as relational and emergent and not for a grade but functions as the connecting thread among class peers—in other words, the stuff of interpersonal communication. Through peer review, workshops, and consensus building, the goal is for students to become accountable to and for each other as a shared learning community, while at the same time improving their writing (382). Key to this process is the use of portfolio project design and the hybrid grading contract. In keeping with the previous examples offered, Cunningham, et al. do not utilize points, percentages, or exams; instead, they lean on Danielewicz and Elbow's (2009) "unilateral grading approach." Similarly, within this adaptation, students "begin the class with a "B" and are guaranteed a "B" at the end of the semester as long as they participate fully in class and complete all assignments" (382). For students to earn grades beyond the "B" level, they must demonstrate substantial revision for their final portfolio.

The assignments that make up their portfolio project include 4 short (2–3 page essays), which are reworked over the course of the semester as part of

212 *Kristen C. Blinne*

consensus-based workshops. Each of these workshops, which occur on the day papers are due, involve the creation of evaluation criteria for an "A" grade, along with peer review of draft papers (383). The goal of this process is to foster dialogue that attempts to illustrate that "writing is communication meant for others," and, moreover, to highlight that the group can work together to "build consensus and accountability as to what counts as criteria for revision" (384). From herein, the "collaboratively generated evaluation criteria" becomes the context for feedback, but also for revision (384). Further, each portfolio may also include items such as journal entries and/or a reflexive essay, which invites students to contemplate their choices throughout the course. By the end of the term, the portfolio creates a "tangible record of the semester-long process and progress as well as an artifact that makes an argument for their desired grade" (385).

Cunningham et al. contend that the process-oriented portfolio project shifts the dynamic of the communication classroom by "placing the onus of the grade on the student as part of a relational dynamic" wherein the "student (as part of a learning community) is always in control of their grade" (386). Moreover, they state that this "nontraditional grading schema—the grading contract—disrupts students' expectations for evaluating, shifting the learner's orientation from product to process" (386). It is important to note that they suggest that their focus is not solely on seeing improvement in students' writing but also on the ways in which this process helps "constitute interpersonal relationships," which is manifested in the "embodied experience of a cohesive classroom community—a knowledge community—and lasting relationships among students" (386).

Based on my explorations of these contract grading approaches as outlined by Moreno-López (2005), Danielewicz and Elbow (2009), Shor (2009), and Cunningham et al. (2017), in addition to my own communication commitments, I have experimented with a variety of assessment strategies, aimed at practicing grading justice in my teaching and learning, which I discuss in the next section.

ADVENTURES WITH "NON-TRADITIONAL" ASSESSMENT

As part of this adventure, I offer five different social justice-inspired approaches to grading and assessment I have implemented in a range of educational contexts. Each of these approaches serve as examples of "nontraditional assessment" insomuch that they differ from "traditional grading systems" that utilize points-based scoring to arrive at a final percentage, which translates to a letter grade (Percell 2014). Before exploring these ideas in detail, however, it is important to state the following: 1) I do not determine grades until the end of the semester so I can look at the entire journey of each individual learner, in addition to allowing time and space for the group to develop collaborative assessment criteria before and *after* completing each project; 2) I do not *ever* utilize *any* tests or quizzes in my courses because I personally feel that this approach prioritizes what is meaningful to me regarding the course concepts versus the larger learner community; 3) Every course involves revision of some sort so that learners have the opportunity to improve and refine their ideas and projects *together*; 4) A wide range of feedback is offered as the primary means for assessing work "in-progress" and our overarching "process"; and, 5) As part of my commitment to exploring more just modes of grading and assessment, I am *always* willing to adapt our model throughout the course, allowing for opportunities to change course at any time. It is important to note that even though these approaches are based on "contract grading," I never actually have my students sign a contract, nor do I utilize the language of a "contract" in discussing each model with my students.

The "Guaranteed 'B' Grade" Approach:

As previously discussed, I truly started my teaching journey with alternative assessment practices with Bartesaghi's design of the University of South Florida's interpersonal communication course (Cunningham et al. 2017), based on Danielewicz and Elbow's (2009) hybrid grading contract, which utilizes a "B" grade standard for organizing the course. When utilizing this model, like Danielewicz and Elbow (2009), I do not give letter grades for individual assignments and instead use markers such as: "Meets criteria for a B," "Does not meet criteria for a B," or "Exceeds Criteria for a B." When I first started with this approach, I utilized the markers: √, √+, or √-, but I found that students were more confused and anxious, focusing less on my feedback and more on the value of the symbol (and its assumed meaning). Other markers I have used to signal feedback, based on this approach, include: Excel (similar to "exceeds criteria"); Accept (equivalent to "meets criteria); and Decline (which suggests that the work "does not meet criteria" to a significant degree). Below are two brief statements from my syllabi, which articulate this approach:

> Have you ever taken a class where you received an "A" and learned nothing or one where you received a low grade but learned a lot? Unfortunately, both of these scenarios are all too common in the college classroom. In my opinion, grading systems, as they are currently constructed, turn students into grade

214   *Kristen C. Blinne*

grubbers, panhandling for points and percentages, placing the emphasis on performance goals and outcomes rather than lifelong learning.

I see learning as a path, not a goal. Thus, until colleges and universities do away with grading and more towards being gradeless, pass/fail, or evaluative assessment systems, I am still required to enter an alphabetical measure onto your record. To this end, we shall work with a grading system designed to help you reframe your relationship with grading with these easy-to-follow steps. Think of it like the "Easy-Bake Oven" guide to grading. Within this system, you are *guaranteed* a "B" grade if you do the following:

- Attend class regularly, arrive on time, and do not miss more than __ classes.
- Arrive late to class or leave class early no more than __ times.
- Meet all assignment due dates, following the instructions.
- Actively participate (via reading, writing, listening, and speaking) in all in-class exercises and activities.
- Complete all informal (in-class activities) and formal assignments.

Please note: I *shall not* distinguish grades higher than "B" until the end of the semester when you complete your final project. In this course, earning a "B" grade is based on the choices you make throughout the semester, regarding your participation and effort. Grades up to a "B" *will not* be based on an evaluation of the quality of your work; however, you must show that you took the assignment seriously in alignment with the requirements. You will not receive a "B" if you do not do the readings, do not actively participate in class discussions or activities, or do not work towards improving your projects. Engagement is key. If you do not plan to attend class, you cannot hope for a "B" grade or to pass this class.

Grades higher than a "B," however, do rest on my evaluation of your final project. To earn a "B+," "A-," or "A" grade, you show improvement over the course of the semester, integrating my feedback, peer feedback, and your self-evaluations into your projects. You will have opportunities to work with me one-on-one as well as with your peers. To earn an "A," you must be engaged, have all assignments turned in on time, and show improvement, insight, and creativity in your work. Consider this an invitation for you to consider your work as "in progress." Should you ever feel confused about where you stand grade-wise, please ask yourself the following questions:

- How many classes have I missed? How often do I arrive late or leave class early?
- Have I turned in all of the assignments? On time? In the assigned format?
- Have I secretly (or not so secretly) been using my cell phone in class for unrelated work, or been engaging in other disruptive behaviors such as talking while others are talking (e.g., side chit chat), and so on (see creating common ground)?

Are We Just *Grading or Grading* Justly? 215

- Have I actively participated in improving our classroom community by both listening and engaging in class discussions?

As you can see, this system does not eliminate grading entirely, but it is my hope that this grading approach radically reduces stress so you can focus on learning. To help demystify this process, I will use three markers to keep you informed about your progress: "Meets criteria for a B," "Does not meet criteria for a B," or "Exceeds Criteria for a B" with detailed feedback on how to improve your work. If you miss four or more classes, do not turn in assignments, nor participate in class, your work will likely only qualify for a "C" or lower grade.

I have utilized this approach for courses that are writing, presentation, group work, and/or creative activity-focused, and I have found that once students process their initial shock about a course with no quizzes, tests, or grades until the end of the semester, they are actually able to relax into the system. Of course, there are always students that are not able to make the leap to a model that has this type of structure, which is why I place a strong emphasis on scheduling meetings with students so I have the opportunity to speak with them one-on-one about their progress. Appendix A contains a sample handout for students that attempts to explain this approach in action. For my second example, I straddle the space between Danielewicz and Elbow (2009) and Shor (2009), in that I still utilize non-letter grade markers; however, I typically focus my overarching course grade on the culminating project.

Grading: I shall not distinguish grades higher than a "B" until the end of the semester when you complete and turn in your final projects. If you miss numerous classes, do not turn in assignments, nor participate in class, your work may only qualify for a "C" or lower grade. Consider this an invitation for you to think of your work as "in progress." If your work meets the assignment requirements, then your work will likely fall within the "B" range. You are responsible for keeping *all* of your returned work with feedback, which is needed to complete your final project. Your final project will be the determining factor in moving your "B" grade to an "A" or lower grade, and should, thus, reflect substantial improvement from earlier work submitted in the semester.

Instructor Feedback/Evaluation: To help you understand your progress throughout the term, I shall utilize revision markers. Generally speaking, when individuals submit their writing and research to peer-reviewed journals for publication consideration, these drafts generally undergo a rigorous review process, wherein authors are given feedback to improve the quality of their work. It is rather uncommon for even the best writers to receive an "accept," requiring no changes to their submitted drafts. More commonly, authors receive "decline" notices or what journal editors refer to as "revise and resubmit," which requires the author to address a range of feedback before the article would be reconsidered for

216 *Kristen C. Blinne*

publication. Published articles often do not show the role reviewers and editors have played in shaping the final text; thus, using this style of assessment not only highlights the intertextuality of texts but also helps you experience writing as a relational process. Because this course is writing-intensive and requires you to engage in revisions, if needed, I will employ the following journal publication designations regarding your assignment drafts:

Accept—Drafts that are marked "accept" do not require further revision; however, they can still be selected for substantial revision for your final project.

Revise & Resubmit (Minor Changes)—Drafts labeled "R & R-Minor" may require you to do revisions that focus on minor editing changes (e.g., grammar, word choice, or organization) or they may require you to include additional information to meet the assignment criteria.

Revise & Resubmit (Major Revision)—Drafts marked as "R & R-Major" need to undergo substantial revision. Furthermore, these drafts may require major editing changes (e.g., grammar, word choice, or organization) and require information to be added, deleted, or moved. Papers that do not follow the assignment criteria, including page length, format, or topic/theme, may fall into this category or be declined (see below).

Decline—Papers will be declined if they contain substantial content and style errors; do not meet the assignment criteria, including page length, format, or topic/theme; or are turned in late. Papers marked "decline," which are still turned in on time, are still eligible for revision.

*Papers marked *accept* are most equivalent to "A" papers; those marked *revise & resubmit-minor* are most equivalent to "A-/B+" papers; those marked *revise & resubmit-major* are most equivalent to "B to C+" papers; and *decline* papers most likely convey "C or lower" equivalency.

With this approach, I highlight to my students that often revision feedback may exist *between* grade categories, especially when multiple reviewers are involved. Though I offer a rough grade equivalent, I encourage them not to assume that their paper is a specific grade as sometimes I also utilize the markers: *Accept/Revise & Resubmit Minor, Revise & Resubmit Minor/Major, or Revise and Resubmit Major/Decline.* Most recently, I found that one of my courses was struggling with writing beyond the "B" level; thus, at the end of the semester, we decided to shift our course assessment approach. Near the end of the term, we collectively negotiated a new assessment system, based on a range of options and a series of conversations (see Table 7.2 in Appendix B for course materials related to this example).

Per my view, Moreno-López (2005), Danielewicz and Elbow (2009), Shor (2009), and Cunningham et al.'s (2017) approaches are quite open for adaptation to learning communities' unique needs and context. While I have employed these approaches *unilaterally,* designing the course content and policies (less social justice-focused, in my view), I prefer to work with collaborative assessment, meaning that learners are active participants in the construction of grading categories and criteria. As I have previously stated, I personally believe that learners are better equipped to determine criteria after they have engaged in a project, not before doing so. Additionally, with the "Guaranteed a 'B' Grade Approach," I find that the way Shor's (2009) and Moreno-López (2005) work to share power with students, in regard to developing content, policies, and assessment criteria, along with avenues for revising these components, is more in alignment with how I understand grading justice.

The "Pick-A-Grade-Plan" Approach:

Within my courses, I also often utilize a tiered project completion structure, which I refer to as one's "grade plan." As you will see, this "grade plan" is a further adaptation of the "Guaranteed a 'B' Grade" approach. Within this model, "Plan A" will require the most work. Depending on the course, the plans lessen in work requirement as the grade categories move down. Thus, if a student fails to turn in an assignment, they automatically drop grade plans. Students may also opt to complete a lesser amount of work (e.g., "Plan B" requires five essays, whereas, "Plan A" requires seven). In each case, picking a plan does not automatically guarantee that the student will receive the grade of that plan. Attendance and feedback are crucial to this assessment process. Students can drop to a less work intensive plan at any time, but they can only move up to a more intensive work plan if the first assignment deadline has not passed for the plan they seek to add. No late work is accepted (unless accommodations are made in advance) and missing the work for one plan automatically drops one into the next, lesser grade plan. Thus, students only qualify for their chosen plan if they complete all work on time. Any missing or incomplete items disqualifies them from whatever higher grade plan they have chosen (unless revisions are allowed). Over time, I have noticed that many students feel more comfortable with this approach than the "Guaranteed a 'B' Grade Plan." This is probably because, at first glance, the system seems less ambiguous and/or mysterious. To illustrate this approach-in-action, I offer the following description from my syllabi:

> By the end of this course, you will have completed a range of assignments designed to encourage you to reflect upon your understanding of [topical focus], depending on the plan you choose.

218 *Kristen C. Blinne*

Table 7.1. Sample Grade Plan

Plan "A"	Complete all assignments (7 ECDA, *cultural writes,* big question essay); Miss no more than one class. Arrive late or leave early no more than two times; Turn in all assignments on time, following the instructions. Please note: Completing all assignments does not guarantee an "A" grade.
Plan "A-/ B+"	Complete (6 ECDA, *cultural writes* [missing no more than two], big question essay); Miss no more than one-two classes. Arrive late or leave early no more than two times; Turn in the above on time, following the instructions. Completing this does not guarantee an "A-/B+" grade.
Plan "B"	Complete (5 ECDA, *cultural writes* [missing no more than three], big question essay); Miss no more than three classes. Arrive late or leave early no more than three times; Turn in three assignments on time, following the instructions. If your work meets the criteria for Plan "B," you are guaranteed a "B" grade in the course. *Please note: Plans up to a "B" grade are based on your engagement. Grades higher than a "B" are based on my judgment regarding your effort beyond the criteria for a "B" grade.
Plan "B-/C+"	Complete (5 ECDA, *cultural writes* [missing no more than four], big question essay); Miss no more than three-four classes. Arrive late or leave early no more than four times; Turned in assignments that primarily meet the "B" requirement but may lack some organization or reflection (or may be below the "B" requirement).
Plan "C" or Lower	Miss four or more classes; arrived late or left more than four times; Turned in assignments with missing, late, or unfinished work and/or turned in work that does not meet the "B" requirement.

Please Read the Fine Print: The grade you earn will be based on what you do through your conscientious effort and active participation, depending on the plan you choose. Regardless of which grade you hope to achieve, all plans require that you show that you took the assignment seriously through your investment and effort. If you do not do the readings, do not actively participate in class discussions or activities, or do not follow the assignment guidelines and deadlines, you will only qualify for the "Plan B-/C+" or the "Plan C or Lower" option.

I shall not distinguish plan grades until the end of the semester when you complete your final project. Therefore, this is an invitation for you to consider your work as "in progress." As you move through the term, I shall provide feedback regarding your work and am happy to answer any questions or concerns you might have regarding your plan status. The purpose of providing a range of plan options is two-fold: First, it allows you the flexibility to do your work to the best of your ability based on your semester obligations. Many of you are taking numerous classes, have jobs, care for others, or have generally busy and stressful lives. As a result, you might opt to do a plan that requires slightly less work so you can maximize your effort to create quality work. Regardless of the plan you choose, the following applies to everyone:

- Picking a plan does not automatically guarantee that you will receive the grade of that plan. Engagement is crucial to keep you on track with your plan. To help with this, we will check-in over mid-term and assess your progress. You can meet with me one-on-one anytime. Also, you can drop to a less work intensive plan at any time. You can only move up to a more intensive plan if the first assignment deadline has not passed for the plan you are adding.
- Only work submitted when something is due will be counted for credit. Unless prior consultation or accommodation occurs, work that arrives during or after class counts as late. Do not wait until you arrive to class to discuss this with me. Work submitted after the assigned day will not count towards your plan. If you are absent, your work is still due. All work must be uploaded to our course management system by the deadline.
- Missing the work for one plan automatically drops you into a different plan (unless accommodations are arranged). Thus, you only qualify for your chosen plan if you complete all work on time. Any missing or incomplete items disqualifies you from whatever plan you have chosen.

Comparatively, within this example, you can see that this plan places a greater and more explicit emphasis on course attendance; however, this aspect can be amended if attendance policies are discouraged or not utilized by an instructor and instead replaced with a participation or engagement clause or removed entirely to focus solely on work output. As with the previous approach, this tiered-model can function unilaterally or be built into a collaborative structure that students participate in the design of the work load itself, in addition to the criteria for each grade category. Typically, I work with my students to develop detailed criteria and plan expectations for each assignment. Students do not have to alert me to which plan they are selecting; however, at the end of the course, I ask them to identity which plan they feel that they have met. Along the way, I offer them feedback regarding work that meets the criteria for a "B" grade, so that they are aware of their plan progress.

The "100% Participation/Engagement" Approach

This grading and assessment approach grew out of my experiences with the "Guaranteed a 'B' Grade" and the "Pick-A-Grade-Plan" models, and it

220 *Kristen C. Blinne*

is also inspired by Moreno-López's (2005) approach. This plan is entirely based on engagement. In other words, the course is assessed on 100 percent participation though I use the term "engagement" instead. Within this model, I work with each class to develop a consensus around what "engagement" and "participation" means within the context of our course. We revisit our initial agreements halfway through the semester, and again at the end of the term. In some versions of this model, I ask students to do a thorough self-evaluation each week (see Appendix C for a sample "self-assessment" chart), discussing both their in-class participation and out of class work. A central component of this model involves the requirement that students must meet with me one-on-one two times during the semester to discuss their self-evaluations (process and progress). Prior to these meetings, the whole group develops criteria for the various grade levels, and then I discuss each person's self-evaluation in relationship to the group's criteria, integrating my feedback on each student's progress with their own experience and understanding. The following example is what is stated in our course map (syllabi) regarding this approach:

Warning: The only certainty in this course is that you will have a series of weekly assignments. Otherwise, I hope you will experience our time together as a place of possibility—a living laboratory—an opportunity to learn, grow, and share your insights and observations with others. As I am sure you have already noticed, this is not an "ordinary" syllabus wherein I prescribe our course policies, assignments, and grading/assessment strategies. Instead, I have treated this document like a course map, which serves to guide our exploration into uncertain, uncharted territory. Inevitably, this design will make some of you uncomfortable due to the lack of structure or pre-determined path. Others of you may feel a greater sense of freedom due to this heightened flexibility. In either case, I believe a fully sketched plan limits our ability to explore. Thus, I, too, do not have a set itinerary for our journey. Instead, I have series of spaces, places, and experiences to offer in-class and outside of class, depending on our group dynamic and individual interests. Each week, my goal is to let these experiences emerge and unfold through a wide range of activities.

Grades for this course will be entirely based on your relational assessment of your active and committed engagement, including all in-class and out-of-class activities. Your weekly assignments will serve as the primary record of your engagement. Because our path is uncertain and our itinerary has not yet been set, I do not believe it would be beneficial to prescribe a pre-determined grading scheme to follow. Instead, after we have a sense of our direction, we shall work together and discuss self-assessment and group-assessment criteria. To better guide your journey, I shall meet with each of you individually two times over the course of the term to check-in about your progress. Remember: The spirit of this course is one of exploration and your grade will be based on your engagement; thus, I invite you to engage fully in each class meeting, asking yourself weekly:

How engaged was I in today's class? Was I listening? Did I actively participate in all in-class activities? Did I bring the required assignments and materials? Was I late or did I leave early? Did I work collaboratively with my partners or group? Was I open to trying new experiences? Did I respect others' views even when they differed from my own? Did I communicate my learning needs to the group? Have I actively contributed to creating the class I want, while being mindful of others' needs, too? Have I shared my insights, observations, questions, comments, or concerns? Have I allowed space for others to share their insights, observations, questions, comments or concerns? Have I taken responsibility for the choices I have made in regard to coming to class, turning in my work, and engaging fully with the course content? Finally, and perhaps most importantly, what would the group have missed had I not been in class?

As this excerpt indicates, within this approach, I do not pre-determine grade categories, course content, or policies, nor do I offer a weekly schedule regarding what will be explored within the boundaries of our time together. Depending on the course, I provide jumping off points in the first few weeks to get the ball rolling, and then the group itself begins to build content and design the structure of their course around their shared interests. Later in the semester, after everyone has engaged in numerous weekly assignments and some self-assessment, we then start to build our criteria to determine final course grades based on our constructed ideas of "engagement" before each person's first meeting with me. To offer an example of what this looks like in practice, one semester the group determined the following grading scheme:

A   Attended every class, completed every activity, participated in discussion, handed in work on time that thoroughly answered prompts, engaging in all of them. Turned in a complete practice chart and thorough self-assessment.

A-   Missed a class or was late/left early several times. Participated in discussion and completed every activity. Handed in work on time (one may have been late), and thoroughly answered / discussed every prompt. Turned in a summarized discussion of the practice and/or self-assessment.

B+ Missed a class, participated in discussion some of the time. Completed weekly work on time (one may have been late) but did not always thoroughly answer/discuss every prompt. Turned in a summarized discussion of the practice and/or self-assessment.

B   Missed two classes, participated in discussion some of the time. Completed weekly work but may have turned in one or more late. Did not always thoroughly answer/discuss every prompt. Turned in an incomplete discussion of either the practice requirement or self-assessment.

B- Missed two or more classes or came late/left early multiple times. Participated in some discussion, but not regularly. Handed in work that was either incomplete or late multiple times. Did not thoroughly complete the practice, discussion, or self-assessment.

C Missed three or more classes. Did not hand in work (or has multiple late work). Did not complete the practice chart or self-assessment.

In the case of this group, they decided that "C or lower" grades could be determined at my discretion, in consultation with the impacted student. After engaging in numerous discussions regarding these grade categories with various classes, I have been consistently impressed with the nuance and complexity regarding how they discuss and understand grading and assessment practices. Sure, at first, some wished to hand over the authority to me and these conversations sometimes caused exhaustion. However, as you can see from this example, it was the students that created the more narrow attendance policy. Because once-a-week assignments (of any variety) form the basis of this approach, based on a series of prompts or instructions, the assessment itself focuses primarily on whether or not someone "engaged" with all of the required pieces versus the quality of the engagement. In keeping with my focus on the importance of revision as students near the end of the semester, they focus more significantly on one aspect of their process, building on and refining their understanding of some aspect of our course that they find most meaningful.

At first glance, this might seem like the most laborious of the approaches offered; however, for me, without a doubt, it is my favorite approach as I learn a tremendous amount of information about students' relationship with evaluation in the context of my course and more broadly. To implement this successfully, one does need to dedicate multiple class sessions to discussing assessment criteria, which I typically do in conversation with readings such as Ron Pelias' (2000) piece, the "The Critical Life," or John Tagg's (2004) "Why Learn: What W May *Really* Be Teaching Students." In regard to "grading" the weekly assignments, I do not offer *any* grade markers, only feedback based on the content. I consider my feedback as an opportunity to have a one-on-one conversation with each student about their process. On my end, once the collective assessment criteria has been established, I start to keep brief notes regarding each individual's engagement, in anticipation of our one-on-one meetings. At these meetings, I have a hard copy of the criteria, which I ask each student to discuss with me as to where they see themselves within these categories. Very rarely do I have students that argue for categories they do not actually come close to meeting. When this does occur, I am able to discuss their unique case in relationship to fairness or just assessment as it relates to the larger whole (e.g., "Do you think it would be fair to give you an "A" for the course when you did not complete all of the required weekly assignments? If so, why?).

In almost all cases, we are able to have an honest conversation about engagement, whereby I ultimately let them decide their grade with my feedback serving as only one component of the assessment process. In this manner, final course grades are decided on the spot at each student's second one-on-one meeting, requiring no further grading work on my end as I read their final weekly assignment prior to the meeting. To conclude my discussion of this approach, of the models I work with, this one is definitely the most "radical" (or innovative, depending on which language one prefers). It also offers the most opportunity for conversation about assessment, as well as the most hands-on involvement for the group as a whole. As you can see, this approach takes us in a totally different direction than the first two options, and in my view, has the capacity, depending on implementation, to be the most democratic and/or social justice-focused of the approaches.

The "Group-Focused" Approach:

Similar to the "100% Participation/Engagement" model, this approach focuses on group versus individual assessments. I primarily utilize this approach with courses centered on group work or those that involve numerous group projects. In my syllabi, I state, "Part of our group process will be to collaboratively determine our grading criteria and assessment goals. Instead, after we have a sense of our direction, we shall work together as a group to determine our grading criteria and what counts as an 'A,' and so on. To better guide our process, I shall meet with each group individually over the course of the term to check-in about your progress. Remember: Grades for this course will be entirely based on your active and committed engagement, including all in-class activities and required group papers and projects." Thus, this approach does not determine grades until the end of the semester when each group completes their final projects. Throughout the semester, I offer feedback to assist each group with refining both their written and oral work, including peer feedback and self-evaluation along the way. Near the end of the semester, I provide a thorough self-assessment package for each individual group member, which states the following:

> In this assessment package, I am inviting you to both assess yourself and reflect on the contributions of the group members you worked with throughout the semester. As you know, peer assessment is complicated, especially because

224   *Kristen C. Blinne*

it may be biased and unfair, depending on the group's dynamic, particularly in scenarios where relationships have become strained or in cases where one or more people have done the majority of the work. Also, in regard to self-assessments, generally speaking, people may have an inflated sense of their own effort. To combat these potentially unfair assessment endings, the purpose of this self-assessment package is for you to honestly assess yourself, writing a critical evaluation of your participation in comparison to how you envision the efforts of the other members of your group and your group as a whole.

Let's look at this more deeply: For instance, you might have landed in a group and developed great relationships with everyone, but you may have contributed far less to the overall workload than the other members of your group. If I graded you on your relationships via your peer assessment, you might have gotten an "A." In reverse, someone might have completed all of the work for a group but not had positive relationships with the members; therefore, the group might have graded this person more harshly. Moreover, with peer assessments, all too often people tend to give higher grade feedback to avoid conflict versus providing realistic assessments. *Please note:* My intention/goal is not to use these assessments as part of a grade average but instead to serve as a tool for me to contextualize my own observations of each group's dynamic, which is only one part of our assessment process. The primary mode of assessment for this course will be based on the assessment option selected by the majority of the class, outlined at the end of this packet.

Once I receive everyone's assessment package, I will review this information along with my feedback for your projects over the course of the semester, determining grade categories thereafter, based on the option selected. I shall then send this information to each of you individually, providing feedback about this process.

At the conclusion of the self-assessment packet, students are asked to rank the following group assessment options, based on their experiences during the course, along with their perception of assessment fairness (1—being most fair/desirable and 5—being least fair/desirable):

All group members in a group should receive the same grade, regardless of each member's contribution, determined through peer feedback, self-evaluation, and instructor evaluation.

Each group member should be given an individual grade, based on their unique contribution to the group, determined through peer feedback, self-evaluation, and instructor evaluation.

All group members in a group should receive the same grade, regardless of each member's contribution, based solely on instructor evaluation of member dynamics and project output.

Are We Just *Grading or Grading* Justly? 225

Each group member should be given an individual grade, based on their unique contribution to the group, determined through instructor evaluation of member dynamics and project output.

Each group member should be given an individual grade, based on their unique contribution to the group, determined through peer feedback and self-evaluation, focusing only on group dynamics; instructor evaluates only the group projects (no other components).

More often than not, most classes select the option: *Each group member should be given an individual grade, based on their unique contribution to the group, determined through peer feedback, self-evaluation, and instructor evaluation.* This option allows for sharing the grading power, while still utilizing instructor input. Unsurprisingly, the second most selected option is: *All group members in a group should receive the same grade, regardless of each member's contribution, based solely on instructor evaluation of member dynamics and project output.* In this case, complete grading authority rests with the instructor. In many ways, these two options exist on separate ends of the grading spectrum. When working with the first option, I assign grades to each project, focusing solely on the collaborative product regardless of group dynamics. I then turn to peer feedback and self-evaluation to understand more about each group's process, based on the following prompts for each project:

I encourage you to utilize this opportunity to provide honest feedback about your own and others' contribution to your group process and projects and overall participation in this course. The provided forms are the required template for this process. There is no required word count for each form.

Please note: These forms will remain completely confidential and will not be reported to your group members at any point. Thus, there is no reason to report inaccurate information regarding your group's process. I have spoken to many of you over the course of the term, so I do have some insight into various group dynamics in addition to my own observations. So, please provide honest and constructive feedback, as these reflection forms are only one layer of the assessment process for this course.

Each member's primary contribution to the completion of the [project title], including: [description of requirements]:

1. In discussing each member's primary contribution to this assignment, please also consider the following questions: Did they attend group meetings (in class or outside)? Did they show up late or leave early? Did they contribute meaningfully to group discussions? Did they complete tasks on time, preparing quality work in a collaborative manner? Did

they demonstrate a supportive and cooperative attitude? Did they take an active and equal role in ensuring the group's success? How so and/ or why not?

2. Please also note if any particular member took on a leadership role in this assignment, providing some specific information to support this claim.

3. Finally, please reflect on each member's overall performance on this assignment, using *one* of the following markers: *Excellent, Good, Average, Below Average, Poor.*

Each individual is also asked to utilize the above reflection prompt when discussing their own contribution to the project, describing any issues they feel need to be addressed (#1); their relationship to group leadership with this project; and how they would assess their contribution overall (#3).

In short, this assessment approach most often blends peer-feedback, my feedback, and group consensus to determine individual grades. At the conclusion of the course, once final course grades are offered, if numerous people raise concerns about their grades, in the past I have provided the following follow-up choices: Please select the assessment option you feel would most fairly resolve any grading concerns you have:

Option A: Each of you would be allowed to reassess yourself, writing a critical evaluation of your participation in response to your assigned course grade. If you feel your course grade was fair, you may "opt out" of this requirement and let your grade stand.

Option B: Each of you may keep your assigned course grade as first assigned.

Option C: I eliminate the collaborative assessment course grade, and I then solely assess the final projects to determine grades, giving each group member the same grade per project.

Option D: Everyone returns to their initial groups and collaboratively comes up with your group grade (everyone gets the same or you decide on the variation), providing an accompanying letter to support your group reasoning. In this scenario, each group must take into account your current course grade (based on collaborative assessment). In your letter, each group is required to discuss who and how the grading process will be organized step-by-step, including: each member's grade or the group grade and how you determined this (based on what components). If I have concerns with the assigned grades, I shall meet with each group to discuss this further.

Only on one occasion did I need to move to this follow-up assessment scenario. In this case, the entire class had to reach a consensus on which of the four options they would pursue. Option D was ultimately selected, and only two groups out of eight decided to complete the follow-up process. To sum up this approach, in almost all cases, the grade categories have been determined based on each group's alignment with the required prompts for each assignment, making this system very similar in orientation to the "100% Participation/Engagement" approach but instead with a group focus.

The "Select-An-Assessment-Plan" Approach:

Finally, for this approach, I ask each student to complete a learning inventory (see Appendix D for a sample), sharing their responses with each other and having a whole class conversation about learning and assessment to determine which assessment approach the group would like to utilize for the course. I have also been successful implementing the learning inventory at the group level versus asking for individual responses. With this approach, I typically dedicate an entire class session to determining our grading strategy, presenting all of the above approaches previously discussed (1-4) and integrating ideas from each group. In this way, the "Select-An-Assessment" approach functions as a kind of "determine your own assessment adventure." Beyond the approaches I offer each group, I also open space for new approaches to emerge. More often than not, however, amendments are made to existing approaches.

Another variation to this approach that I have successfully implemented in my courses involves creating a unique assessment plan for each student, based on a wide range of final project options. Put differently, the whole group creates criteria for some basic assessment categories related to attendance, participation/engagement, or other related work. After this, each student then does the following: proposes a final project from a wide range of options; creates a collaborative assessment guide for said project with me; completes the project; receives my feedback and peer feedback; and then collaboratively assesses their grade based on the agreed-upon collective grade categories in conversation with their developed assessment guide and feedback. We then decide together what their final course grade is based on these various components (see Appendix E for an example of a "build-a-final-project" assessment form).

Finally, I would like to share another option in this category, which I feel merits further attention. In an article written by John Dorroh (2019) for *Edutopia,* he discusses integrating student choice into his assessment practices for his sciences classes (at the K–12 level). He was inspired to shift his approach

228   *Kristen C. Blinne*

because he started to notice the varying ways that students excelled in his courses, motivating him to create seven ways students could be evaluated in his course, including: journaling, lab work, oral reports, written work (drama, fiction, poetry, and/or essays), small group work artwork, and written tests. Once determining these possible assessment avenues, he told students that each of them would choose three modes from this list.

Once they selected their choices, the caveat was that they had could not change them during the grading period for the course. Thus, during the course, Dorroh *only* evaluated students on their selected options. For both his written work and artwork options, he also required "fact sheets," wherein students identified the relationship between the project and the course concepts. He also utilized specific questions to help guide each of the assessment areas, giving credit if the questions were addressed with the various modes of project presentation. Not surprisingly, he reported, very few students decided to be assessed by tests (only 6%). Dorroh commented that the most common choice combination included lab work, small group work, and journaling, which he states seems well-tailored for a science course. This variation to the "Select-An-Assessment-Plan" could be widely tailored to a variety of projects, employing either unilateral contracts or collaborative assessment practices. I share Dorroh's example because I believe that it has promise for college courses as it allows students to take ownership over their assessment process while still operating within a collaborative system of choices. Moreover, this approach sets the stage for the current grading and assessment system I employ in my teaching, which is the subject of chapter 8 in this volume.

GRADING MYSELF AND MY ASSESSMENT PRACTICES

My approach to grading and assessment has been hugely impacted by the range of educational settings from which my own learning path has carried me. I have structured my courses around themes related to "self-study" as a tool to enhance relational awareness, utilizing process-based pedagogy through a variety of revision-centered projects. Because of this, I have the opportunity to see students' work vastly improve over the course of the semester regardless of whether the project is written, spoken, performed, or arts-based. Reflecting on this further, I cannot help but relate my experiences to Tagg (2004), who explores how taking a performance goal approach to learning aligns with the ways in which grades structure a student's learning identity. As such, he encourages teachers to build courses that support learning goals, which are goals for personal change and growth. In order for learners to embody this approach, he argues, that learning must become a part of you versus engaging in learning merely to produce a satisfactory performance (e.g., grade, GPA), which he deems as a more surface approach.

Throughout this chapter, I have introduced my adventures with grading and assessment, striving to cultivate learning goals versus performance goals through a range of practices involving reflection and self-inquiry, building collaborative course content and policies, helping students understand the relationship between grading student learning and assessing or improving student learning, and integrating portfolio and revision projects to transform learning. In attempting to embrace process over product-based learning, ultimately, my grading systems have focused heavily on student improvement, involving them in the analysis of their behavioral choices, along with their own learning and effort. As a result, comparatively, my grades tend to average slightly higher than my department or college. Regarding "A" grades, most recently my average per semester was around 26.48; whereas, the department's averages at 26.26, which is in alignment statistically. Interestingly, both of these averages are slightly less than the college average for "A" grades, which is around 29.1. In the "A-" range, I average 3.4 more than the department, and 8.35 more than the college. At the "B+" level, I average 9.07 more than the department, and 12.04 more than the college. Finally, within the "B" category, I average 1.29 more than the department, and 1.09 more than the college. I attribute my higher grade distributions in the "A-" and "B+" range to my use of revision projects, allowing students to better their work over the course of the semester.

Considering my grade distribution in relationship to student evaluations of my teaching, I believe that the category which explores whether the course "provided a valuable learning experience" is worth examining to help make sense of this data. My average in this category is a 3.84/4.0 as compared to the department's 3.61 mean and the college mean, which is 3.50. Following in the footsteps of the many educators who actively attempt to involve learners in content collaboration, I believe that my average score in this category directly relates to my attempts to integrate students into all aspects of the course, striving to make learning relevant and valuable for their lives. I contend that students invest in their work differently, elevating their grades as they improve their writing process and participation throughout the course.

In students' qualitative responses, they speak about becoming stronger writers, in addition to stating comments like "this class was extremely beneficial for me"; "this class was the most unique class I have ever taken in my entire life"; "this course helped me battle/overcome internal struggle"; "allowed me to personally grow"; "this is the first course at Oneonta I feel actually benefited me as a full person, not just as a student"; "words cannot express how much I gained from this class"; "she helped me grow as a person for the first time in a college class"; "I am a better person after taking this class"; "loved the personal growth involved in the class," among other related comments. Each of these examples illustrates my attempt to cultivate learning goals based on personal growth and change versus focusing on producing a satisfactory performance, based on grade categories. Based on this, I have truly come to understand and hopefully embody Ernest Morell's call to stop measuring students' success against failure, which is so common in traditional modes of grading and assessment.

Moreover, within my qualitative responses, of the 524 comments (during a two-year period), 48 responses (around 9.25%) commented about "grades" or "grading." Of these, 18 responses were positive, with students stating they liked the freedom and creativity this grading system allowed. Several stated the grading was fair or extremely fair. One stated the "whole world should" grade this way, whereas another stated they "appreciated the modern approach" and one other stated they found the grading "progressive and motivating." Several responded they liked or loved the grading system, and one other mentioned that they liked that the course "focused less on grades and more on learning." The 30 students (of the 48) who expressed some confusion about their "grades" or the "grading system" made comments that suggested they felt "unclear" or "unsure" of their grades. Some described the grading system as confusing, suggesting there is a need to know one's grade or one did not know their grade. Others stated they wished they got grades back sooner or more frequently or that they wished they had a better understanding of their grade. The overall theme of the comments seemed to request a clearer understanding of one's individual grade or the grading system more broadly.

Other patterns of response in my qualitative, written feedback includes comments about my courses being "insightful," "engaging," and "fun." Many comment on my teaching methods, style, or practices with colorful descriptors such as "unorthodox," "weird," "avant guarde," "unique" or "different," suggesting I am passionate about the courses I teach, working to create discussion-based courses that are "open" and "respectful." Approximately 57 comments (of 524) focus on the idea of "openness," suggesting that the course was "eye-opening" (10); "opened my eyes" (13); "openness of the class" (9); "open discussions/communication" (5); students feeling more "open-minded" after taking the course (11), referring to the classroom space as open and "honest," "safe," and "comfortable" (3); speaking about me as open (3); and two other comments focused on being "open to new possibilities" or "open to individual needs." Other patterns of comments speak about

Are We Just *Grading or Grading* Justly? 231

real world application or being able to apply concepts to one's life, in addition to a focus on "learning" versus memorizing content. In reflecting on the landscape of responses, the greater majority echo some of my own learning commitments, insomuch that I attempt to cultivate a compassionate community within each of my courses that attempts to inspire and motivate students to be engaged classroom citizens and lifelong learners.

At this stage in our conversation, you may have some additional questions I may not yet have addressed. First, for me, each of the grading and assessment approaches that I utilize in my courses operate as my attempt to create some form of grading justice in my teaching. Having worked with these models with a variety of learners over the years, I can attest to both the rewards and challenges of engaging with these modes of evaluation. Like the scholars referenced in this chapter, I continuously adapt these systems to attempt to meet the unique needs of the individuals and groups I encounter in my courses, integrating more flexibility into my process as I move forward. For additional context: Within my current institution, faculty teach seven courses per year unless they receive a reduction for service or scholarship. My courses on average have between twenty-six to thirty-two students; however, I know that these "non-traditional" grading and assessment approaches can be and have been successfully employed in large course formats as well.

In regard to my own process, earlier in my journey, I was much stricter about attendance and late work than I am now. As such, over the course of some semesters, I have not included an attendance policy at all to see how this impacts these models. What I have learned in the process is that it can go either way. I have had semesters where it had virtually no impact, and others where it significantly reduced the engagement among students. Based on this, I personally feel that allowing students to dictate the terms of attendance is where the balance can be found. This is also true of "late work" as I often reflect on ways in which I can "undo" this aspect of my process to allow more openness. Part of how I have successfully tackled this issue has been resolved by *some* assignments being due at the end of the semester versus throughout. There is no doubt that some students do the work last minute, but overall, I have seen a much stronger engagement with the concepts with this flexibility. Regardless of the policy in play, I always make space for accommodating students' unique circumstances regarding assignment deadlines, involving the larger group to create umbrella policies to help me navigate this terrain. More and more, I offer the learners in my courses the option to talk about items without my being present in the classroom. I have found this to be quite successful in allowing them to hash out ideas without my gaze, producing many fruitful discussions thereafter.

In further reflecting on my adventures with non-traditional grading and assessment practices aimed at grading justice, I invite you to consider a few possible tools that could be implemented in your own process, if you are not doing so already. The first involves crafting a grading system that eliminates points and percentages—what Percell (2013) describes as the value of a "pointless education." As he suggests, when assigning point values to assignments, teachers may actually be unintentionally hindering learning possibilities as points often exist as a "means to an end," serve as "extrinsic rewards," or create "misleading value" to learning processes. Per his view and mine, moving to a "no-points grading system" is one method among many to start to disrupt students' habitual commitment to traditional grading systems, based on neoliberal ideologies. Second, I personally believe, as Danielewicz and Elbow (2009) contend, that it is crucial for teachers to begin to de-couple evaluation from grading, employing feedback as a mechanism for illustrating the messy, "in-progress" processes that come with learning. To this end, I also agree with Percell (2017) that feedback should be informative, personal, encouraging, constructive, concise, conversational, *and* informal. Employing feedback in this manner has the capacity to assist students with moving from a "grading orientation" to a "learning" one.

It is probably quite clear, but if not, it is important for me to state that I would do away with grading completely if I were able. In my view, a student's grade tells me little to nothing about their learning. Instead, it tells me more about how successfully (or not) they are able to navigate an educational system. Because grades are how teachers communicate their view of a student's "learning," serving as a powerful symbol that both rewards and stigmatizes, it is not surprising that student identities become deeply entrenched in assessment systems, even though it is quite clear that these indicators reduce "the full-color relief map of the student's understanding into a two-dimensional, black-and-white cartoon" (Tagg 2004, 4). But since most of us cannot fully go "gradeless," we can to the best of our abilities attempt to "ungrade" by changing our relationship with these oppressive educational structures, asking ourselves: What purpose does our grading serve and for whom? What do grades actually mean? In other words, what is a grade's overarching value? What would teaching and learning look like without grades? How might we change our own relationship to grades and grading as well as our students?

For those of you who work in educational settings that require a standardized approach to grading, you may feel helpless to make broad or drastic changes to your grading system. It is true I have had the opportunity to work in institutions that have allowed me to disrupt grading and assessment systems. Additionally, as a White, recently tenured faculty member, I am able to act from a privileged position not equally available to other faculty members. However, it is important to note, that my experimentation with these approaches existed prior to tenure, starting in graduate school. Nonetheless, I recognize that we do not all have the same opportunities to enact these approaches, nor would they operate in the same way if we did, based on our different positionalities, teaching styles, scholarly commitments, and learner communities. Further, embracing "non-traditional" approaches to grading and assessment can be met with scorn and/or distrust by hiring, renewal, or tenure and promotion committees, requiring more risk and labor on the teacher's part to unpack and explain the value of these methods. Finally, I will also state that even at this length, my discussion of these approaches is impossibility incomplete. I have attempted to offer a baseline for inspiration, including what I thought would best help paint a picture of the possibilities. To fully dive into the potential pitfalls would require another chapter.

In this spirit, however, if I were to grade my own efforts at embodying and enacting grading justice through these various non-traditional grading and assessment approaches I have employed in my teaching, I believe I could make a strong case for either a "B+" or "A-" grade on the grounds that I have put forth considerable efforts to find creative ways to attempt to share power with students through collaborative assessment, involving peer feedback, self-evaluation, and revision-centered projects. In doing so, I have diligently worked to disrupt traditional grading systems, which rely on points and percentages to convey information about student performance, instead favoring in-depth feedback. At this moment, I am leaning more towards assessing myself with a "B+" grade because even though I have considerably de-centered the role of grades within my courses, I still find that students struggle with understanding the purpose and transformative potential of shifting away from performance goals to learning goals. While I receive very few grade "complaints," "appeals," or "grievances," I often wonder if this is because of the power dynamic (and imbalance) that can only be slightly reduced but not eliminated between us.

Building on this idea, writing this chapter has provided a vital opportunity for me to deeply reflect on how closely my grading and assessment approaches align with how I understand grading justice. As I pen these words, I continuously ask myself: Am I *just* grading or grading *justly?* Honestly, after careful consideration, I realize that sometimes the line between these two possibilities is more blurred than I hoped or imagined. Over these many assessment adventures, inspired by contract grading systems, I often wonder if focusing on the learning choices students make, including behavior, effort, and improvement, is actually less just versus more. Put differently, in what way has requiring students to work within the limitations of the grading and assessment approaches (unilaterally or collaboratively constructed) actually continued to keep them trapped in a cycle of performance goals versus learning goals? As Kohn (1999) contends, any grading system can serve as an "instrument of control" that impacts how students learn, whether they show up to class, or turn in their work, among other variables. Thus, even with "non-traditional" grading and assessment approaches, one can still fall into the same pitfalls of "traditional" systems such as diminishing students' interest in what they are learning, creating a preference for engaging in the easiest possible tasks, and also reducing students' critical and creative thinking about the content and learning more broadly (Kohn 2011).

By attempting to decouple grading and evaluation, I have utilized a wide range of feedback markers to assist students with understanding my interpretation of the "quality" of their work, as discussed in this chapter. It is this aspect of my journey that I feel has done the greatest disservice to my pursuit of grading justice in my courses; hence, why I would award myself a "B+" grade for my choices, effort, and attempted improvement with these various grading systems. Per my view, my assignment of this grade to myself is both subjective and, for the most part, uninformative as a kind of "evidence" that measures my learning in any significant manner. Moreover, the value and meaning of the "B+" grade category for me likely differs considerably from how you understand it or the grade you might assign for my efforts. The arbitrary nature of this evaluation is further complicated by the line between what would have constituted an "A-" grade effort versus a "B+" (or other grade).

I could have instead given myself an alternative or "non-traditional" marker such as *"exceeded criteria for a B"*; "excel," *"revise and resubmit major/minor"* or simply a √ or √+; however, none of these labels would tell either of us much about the learning as to which processes I have engaged to arrive at this moment. Due to this, I now believe, as Kohn (2011) suggests, "It's not enough to replace letters or numbers with labels (*exceeds, expectations, meets expectations,* and so on). If you're sorting students into four or five piles, you are still grading them" (31). Is that not the purpose of grades anyway—to sort learners into categories and rankings which then determine grade point averages and class rank, along with determining college entrance (or exit), scholarship opportunities, among other consequences built of both grade-based reward and punishment? Collaborative assessment is one strategy I have engaged to try to move away from grading as a practice of reward or punishment. Whether I have been successful in this endeavor or not remains to be known.

Of the markers I have employed to convey information to students regarding their "in-progress" work, for me, if one must employ such labels, I feel that the terms associated with revision (e.g., *revise and resubmit minor*) have been the least problematic of makers of which I have experimented. Even so, these marks still pile student work into categories, based on my interpretation as the overarching authority on "quality," as I am the one who must enter the grade in the system at the end of the term, regardless of whether I wish for this power or not. There is no doubt that my beliefs about assessment have informed my grading practices, shaping the ways in which grading policies are constructed in my courses, which, in turn, have further impacted how assessment is carried out in my courses as a result (Percell 2014). Each of these models has been developed with the goal of intervening into and potentially disrupting unjust modes of teaching and learning by attempting to create more just practices and policies, aimed at dismantling traditional modes of grading and assessment that serve to reinforce oppressive educational structures. All have offered opportunities to engage in deep reflection and dialogue with a wide range of learners about the role of grading and its impact on learning. In this way, while there is still much work to do to fully embody and enact grading justice, I see each approach as a seed planted in a crack of cement. In the chapter that follows this one, I introduce the philosophies and practices of *awareness pedagogy*, an approach to teaching and learning that has blossomed as a result of my adventures with grading and assessment over the last decade, which most closely embodies grading justice at this moment in my journey.

Please note that I welcome queries and am always happy to share materials and offer advice, in addition to my desire to learn about your unique approaches and methods aimed at grading justice. I now close with words from Tagg (2004), which I hope will inspire further reflection and action in your own teaching-learning journey:

> Indeed, it is not just the instructor's classroom policies that we should examine in seeking to place responsibility, but also the policies of our colleges. Most of the assessment that places a value on student work reduces it to quantifiable points, and the student with the most points wins the best grade. The only thing the college preserves about the student's work in the class is the grade. Thus, when students become grade-oriented they are merely responding to the incentives of their environment (9).

To wrap up this chapter, I invite each of us to continue to ask ourselves are we *just* grading or grading *justly* and what does this look like in practice? For me, it is an ever-evolving process and adventure.

APPENDIX A

"Guaranteed a 'B' Grade" Approach Handout Example

Grades for this course will not be determined until the end of the semester; thus, I ask that you view your work as "in progress."

You are *guaranteed* a "B" grade if you do the following:

- Attend class regularly, arrive on time, and do not miss more than __ classes
- Arrive late to class or leave class early no more than __ times
- Meet all assignment due dates, following the instructions
- Active class participation (via reading, writing, listening, and speaking) in all in-class exercises and activities
- Complete all informal (group work, writing activities) and formal (final project) assignments, including revisions, peer feedback, and self-evaluations
- Give thoughtful peer feedback during class workshops and work with your group on other collaborative tasks (e.g., sharing papers, commenting on drafts, peer editing, on-line discussion boards, answering peer questions)
- Complete "B" quality written work, making substantive revisions when required

Thus, you earn the grade of "B" entirely on the basis of what you do through your conscientious effort and active engagement. The "B" grade does not derive from my evaluation of your work; however, you must show that you took the assignment seriously through your investment and effort. You will not receive a "B" if you do not do the readings, do not actively participate in class discussions or activities, or do not work towards improving your projects. Engagement is key. If you do not plan to attend class, you cannot hope for a "B" grade or to pass this class. Grades higher than a "B," however, do rest on my evaluation of your final project.

To earn a "B+ to an A" grade you must meet the criteria for a "B" grade plus:

- Have excellent attendance, missing no more than one class
- Arrive late to class or leave class early no more than one time
- Very active participation (via reading, writing, listening, and speaking) in all in-class exercises and activities
- "A" quality written work (Accept); "A-/B+" (Revise & Resubmit-Minor)
- Shown improvement through revision and creativity in the presentation of your work

Are We Just *Grading or Grading* Justly?

- Go above and beyond what is required, integrating class discussions, reading, and other course learning opportunities in your final project/portfolio.

Grades in the "B- to C-" range are earned as a result of:

- Missing more than two classes
- Arriving late or leaving early more than two times
- Little class participation via reading, writing, listening, and speaking) in all in-class exercises and activities
- Turning in informal or formal assignments late
- "C" quality written work (Revise & Resubmit-Major or Decline in the first draft stage)
- Not following assignment instructions
- Not participating in peer review and/or self-evaluation
- Not participating in class (speaking, listening, reading, writing) or working collaboratively with others
- Consistent technology use unrelated to course discussion or content

Please note:

1. Failure to fulfill the above expectations will result in a grade of "D" or lower
2. For borderline grades, that is, if you wrote "A quality" papers but did not fulfill two of the other requirements for an A, you may be asked to do additional work to receive an "A" range grade; otherwise, your grade will only qualify for "B to B+" grade.
3. Your final grade will be based on our collaboratively established criteria.

238   *Kristen C. Blinne*

APPENDIX B

Sample Collaborative Self-Assessment Materials

Sample of Collaborative Assessment at the Assignment Level

*Students were tasked to work with a partner or in a small group with a blank chart to determine each grade category, based on the project instructions. The following is what the group determined after having completed these assignments as a revision guide for their final projects.

Relational Development Paper:

Project Instructions: For your second paper, you will watch the film, *Lars and the Real Girl* (in class). Based on the concepts discussed thus far, you will write an essay that explores one or more of the themes from the course in conversation with the story/characters of this film. You may choose to focus on any combination of course concepts presented thus far.

Criteria for an "A"

- Organizes essay in a manner that makes sense to the reader (intro, body, conclusion)
- Creates a detailed, engaging introduction, hooking the reader
- Clearly connects course concepts and movie details with examples to show understanding, focusing on an identifiable relationship (or relationships) within the story/film
- Avoids summarizing the film and instead synthesizes key film examples to illustrate course concepts, using specific theories (e.g., five features, relationship models, etc.)
- Includes an analysis/reflection of the connection between related themes present in the movie and our course
- Includes transitions and an identifiable thesis statement
- Includes correct citations/references when integrating course concepts
- Contains minimal grammatical errors or spelling mistakes
- Meets and exceeds basic requirements for substantial revision

Criteria for a "B"

- Writing contains some organization but does not flow as smoothly as it could
- Evokes a feeling of the film's story or characters' relationships (including some details) and/or the paper may be doing more summarizing work versus course connection
- Contains some discussion of course concepts in relationship to specific examples within the film, but may lack specifics, clarity, or detail
- Contains some grammatical and spelling errors
- Analysis/reflection may be lacking in depth or specific examples
- Includes non-specific references/citations
- Features only minimal revisions, or meets the basic requirement for substantial revision

Criteria for a "C" or Lower

- Story is disconnected and does not follow a recognizable pattern or sequence and/or does not have a clear structure (intro, body, conclusion)
- Creates an incomplete picture, including sketchy or irrelevant details of the film/characters
- Merely summarizes the movie without providing an analysis/reflection, and/or does not discuss book concepts and only contains minimal examples from the movie
- Does not show an understanding of course concepts as applied to the film
- Contains numerous grammatical errors or spelling mistakes
- Includes incorrect references or content is not referenced
- Little to no revision

Sample Checklist for a Final Project Focused on a Cumulative Paper

Final Paper Checklist

Paper Components:

_____*Title* (grabs attention and makes readers want to know more)

_____*Abstract* (150 words or fewer, indented and single-spaced): Introduces your topic and writing style *and* previews the theme, goals, purpose, and/or argument

_____*Introduction* (how readers enter your story—sets the tone for moving forward): Ask yourself: Why am I telling this story? What do I hope others will learn? How might I creatively introduce my experience/ theme? How am I writing/organizing?

_____*Story* (shares your personal experience): Does the story have creative/ aesthetic merit? Is it relatable to others?

_____*Reflection/Analysis* (discussion of writing style/method): Discusses your writing process including the value of storytelling/writing. Discusses any obstacles, insights, and/or ethical dilemmas you encountered. States explicitly what you learned from the story. Does your reflection include a discussion of your writing style? Why is your story important for better understanding communication?

_____*Connection/Contribution* (integrating support citations and connecting with readers) Did you include three sources? Are the sources cited consistently? Did you include a specific takeaway for readers, situating your story as important to understanding interpersonal communication with the goal of contributing to better understanding relationships?

_____*Works Cited* (if including references/citations from sources not included in course)

Self-Assessment/ Course Assessment:

_____*Relational Understanding*
Does your story/paper make some contribution to people's understanding of relational life? In other words, your story should be both uniquely specific and also connected to broader social issues.

_____*Innovative Writing/ Thematic Delivery*
Does your paper include some creative/aesthetic merit/thoughtfulness in organization, presentation, and flow?

_____*Reflection/Analysis*
Does your paper illustrate your process of self-reflection, in so much that you showcase the ways in which you hold yourself *account-able* and *response-able* for the telling of this tale?

_____*Connection with Reader/Audience*
Does your paper actively attempt to create a relationship with the audience/reader, inviting connection and introspection?

Are We Just *Grading or Grading* Justly?   241

Sample "Re-Vision" Cover Sheet for a Final Written Paper

Name: Final Paper Cover Sheet

Use this as the cover sheet for your final, revised paper. Please check the materials you have included. If you are missing items, please write a brief note next to the item such as "not included."

A.) *Section One: Journals*

_____Completed journals in hardcopy form. If uploaded to Blackboard, please note this.

_____ Total number of journals included out of nine

Note:

B.) *Section Two: Revised Essay*

_____One substantially revised course paper. This paper should be typed, 12 pt. font with 1 inch margins. You can employ any citation style as long as it is consistent. Please include a complete works cited list as well if your paper utilizes sources not discussed as part of this course.

_____Original draft of your essay with my comments, including cover sheet and peer reviews.

Note:

Substantial Revision Notes:

*All papers should revise grammar, check spelling, look for typos, and improve sentence coherence.

Check all that apply:

_____Added new content/ideas

_____Rewrote confusing passages and/or paragraphs

_____Reorganized essay, including rearranging paragraphs and/or sentences

_____Cut irrelevant sentences and/or sections

_____Reworked introduction and/or conclusion

_____Integrated an easy-to-recognize thesis statement

_____Added transitions (linked content and ideas)

_____Re-analyzed or reframed my use of book content/course concepts

_____Utilized creative writing devices

_____Created enhanced connections within content

_____Additional changes that give more meaning to the assignment, including (describe below):

Additional Information/Comments for Assessment:

242 *Kristen C. Blinne*

Sample Final Paper Self-Assessment Form

*On the date students turn in their "final" revised paper in hard copy (the primary basis of their final course grade), I ask them to assess their work with the following map, adding symbols in their paper to identify the various required components.

ABSTRACT

- If the abstract is indented, single-spaced, or set out from the rest of the text, place a * by the content.
- Within your abstract, underline your primary story *topic* and place a #A1 above it.
- Next, underline your decription of your *writing style* and place a #A2 above it.
- If you have also previewed your *theme*, underline it and place #A3. If you have previewed your goals, purpose, or primary argument, underline the key word and place a #A4 above it.

Example:

    #A2   #A1

In this autoethnographic reflection, the author narrates her family's struggle with meaning after learning that her sister experienced a near-fatal car accident.

THEMATIC ANCHOR

- In the first occurrence or reference to your thematic anchor, circle the primary keywords or content that illustrates this for a reader.

REFLECTION/ANALYSIS

- Place [ ] around the content that discusses your *writing process*, adding #R1 at the beginning of the sentence.
- Place [ ] around the content that defines your *writing style*, adding #R2 at the beginning of the sentence.
- Place [ ] around the content that discusses any obstacles/insights you encountered in the process of telling this story, adding #R3 at the beginning of the sentence.
- Place [ ] around the content that explicitly states *what you learned from the story,* adding #R4 at the beginning of the sentence.

Example:

#R3 [Writing this story has helped me process the "pain, confusion, anger, and uncertainty" I experienced (Author, 2012).]

CONNECTION/CONTRIBUTION

- Locate each of your references/citations (to total three). Underline the name of each author, identifying them as #C1, #C2, and #C3. If you have more than three citations, just signal to the required three.
- Locate the content that explicitly states what you hope the reader gains from reading your story. Place → ← at the beginning and end of the statement(s).
- Locate the content that attempts to make some contribution to people's understanding of relational life, connecting your personal story to broader social issues. Place * * at the beginning and end of the statement(s).

SELF-ASSESSMENT

Based on the above components, I would assess my paper with the following grade _____.

Creative/Aesthetic Merit

Briefly describe why you organized your story the way you did, speaking specifically to how readers enter your story, in addition to your paper organization, presentation, and flow of ideas.

Theorizing Relationships

Briefly discuss the following questions: *Why is your story important for better understanding communication?* Moreover, *how does your story help us better understand and theorize about interpersonal relationships?*

Table 7.2. Sample Assessment Plan Amendment Opportunity

Current Assessment Plan	Additional Assessment Plan Options	Additional Assessment Plan Options
Participation at the "B" level:	Based on our current assessment plan, we have the following alternative options:	*Option 3:* Turn in all papers (either during the peer review session or within the extended revision timeline unless accommodations were requested/made):
Meet all assignment due dates (e.g., no late work), following the instructions;		
Semi-active class participation (via reading, writing, listening, and speaking) in all in-class exercises and activities;	*Option 1:* Turn in all papers (either during the peer review session or within the extended revision timeline unless accommodations were requested/made):	• Do not engage in a final paper revision, accepting a grade average for your papers, based on your revision makers.
Complete all informal (group work, writing activities) and formal (final project) assignments, including revisions, peer feedback, and self-evaluations; Provide peer feedback during class workshops and work with your group on other collaborative tasks (e.g., sharing papers, commenting on drafts, peer editing, on-line discussion boards, answering peer questions);	• If turned in, you are guaranteed a "B" regardless of what revision markers were given. • Substantially revise one paper to move beyond the "B" grade. • Complete all nine journals, showing effort, understanding/synthesis, and engagement with the course. • Semi-active class participation (via reading, writing, listening, and speaking) in all in-class exercises and activities.	• Complete all nine journals, showing effort, understanding/synthesis, and engagement with the course.
Complete "B" quality written work, making substantive revisions.		

To earn a "B+ to an A" grade, you must meet the criteria for a "B" grade plus:

Very active participation (via reading, writing, listening, and speaking) in all in-class exercises and activities;
"A" quality written work (Accept); "A-/B+" (Revise & Resubmit-Minor, Revise & Resubmit Minor/Major);
Show improvement through revision and creativity in the presentation of your work; Go above and beyond what is required, integrating class discussions, reading, and other course learning opportunities in your final project.

Grades in the "B- to C-" range are earned as a result of:

Little class participation via reading, writing, listening, & speaking) in all in-class exercises and activities; Turning in informal or formal assignments late; "C" quality written work (Revise & Resubmit-Major or Decline in the first draft stage); Not following assignment instructions; Not participating in peer review and/or self-evaluation; Not participating in class (speaking, listening, reading, writing) or working collaboratively with others; Consistent technology use unrelated to course discussion or content.

*This option differs from our current assessment plan because it does not utilize the revision markers when assessing your overall course grade.

Option 2:
Turn in all papers (either during the peer review session or within the extended revision timeline unless accommodations were requested/made):

• If turned in (as above), assessment of your work is based on the revision markers; however, you still have the opportunity to raise (or lower your grade), based on your final revision.
• Substantially revise *two* papers to raise revision markers.
• Complete all nine journals, showing effort, understanding/synthesis, and engagement with the course.
• Semi-active class participation (via reading, writing, & speaking) in all in-class exercises and activities.

*This option differs from our current plan because it allows for the substantial revision of two papers (versus one).

Semi-active class participation (via reading, writing, listening, and speaking) in all in-class exercises and activities.

*As a pair or small group, please discuss these options, offering amendments or feel free to propose other options below:

APPENDIX C

Sample Self-Assessment Chart

Questions for Reflection: How engaged was I in today's class? Was I listening? Did I actively participate in all in-class activities? Did I bring the required assignments and materials? Was I late or did I leave early? Did I work collaboratively with my partners or group? Was I open to trying new experiences? Did I respect others' views even when they differed from my own? Did I communicate my learning needs to the group? Have I actively contributed to creating the class I want, while being mindful of others' needs, too? Have I shared my insights, observations, questions, comments, or concerns? Have I allowed space for others to share their insights, observations, questions, comments or concerns? Have I taken responsibility for the choices I have made in regard to coming to class, turning in my work, and engaging fully with the course content? Finally, and perhaps most importantly, what would the group have missed had I not been in class?

*Please keep an accurate record of your engagement with class activities and weekly assignments.

Table 7.3. Sample "Self-Assessment Chart"

Date/week	In-class	Weekly Assignments	Assessment
Week 1 – 1/21			
Week 2 – 1/28			
Week 3 – 2/4			
Week 4 – 2/11			
Week 5 – 2/18			
Week 6 – 2/25			
Week 7 – 3/3	Individual Meetings		
Spring break	No class	3/5 – 3/13	
Week 8 – 3/17			
Week 9 – 3/24			
Week 10 – 3/31			
Week 11 – 4/7			
Week 12 – 4/14			
Week 13 – 4/21			
Week 14 – 4/28			
Week 15 – 5/5			

Are We Just *Grading or Grading* Justly?

APPENDIX D

Sample Group Learning Inventory

Context Questions:

- What, if anything, excites each of you about studying communication, especially in regard to this course?
- What, if anything, concerns or confuses each of you about studying communication, especially in regard to this course?
- When you leave this class, what do each of you hope to have gained?

Content Questions:

- What types of in-class activities do each of you find the most useful/beneficial and why?
- What types of assignments do each of you find the most useful/beneficial and why?
- The following activities/assignments/teaching approaches often cause us to lose interest, motivation, or focus. Please explain why/how.
- In your group's view, "participation" means:
- Your group feels most engaged in a class when:
- To your group, a great class discussion/session involves the following:
- As learners in this course, we expect the following from our classmates:
- As learners in this course, we expect the following from the instructor/ course:

Assessment Questions:

- In our view, "grades" should be determined by:
- To us, earning an "A" typically involves or means that:
- To us, earning an "A-/B+" typically involves or means that:
- To us, earning a "B" or "B-" typically involves or means that:
- To us, earning a "C or Lower" typically involves or means that:

Additional Questions/ Comments:

[Completed Individually]

Name:
Email:
Major:
Year/Classification:

Career goals/plans, if any:

To help me better understand your semester, please let me know how many classes you are taking, number of jobs/hours worked per week, club, sport, or other commitments, and/or anything you would like to share to paint a picture of your time constraints this term.

Tell me one unique thing about yourself (like a job, or hobby, or experience, etc.), so I can get to know you a little bit better:

As a learner in this course, what do you expect from yourself?

Are We Just *Grading or Grading* Justly?

APPENDIX E

Name(s):   Build-A-Final-Project Rubric

Final Project Description (including form of project and topical focus):

Table 7.4.   Proposed Assessment Categories and Grade Range Requirements

Category Examples	"A" Range	"B Range"	"C or Lower Range"
Design & Layout			
Content & Message			
Audience Engagement			

250 *Kristen C. Blinne*

REFERENCES

Berila, Beth. 2016. *Integrating Mindfulness into Anti-Oppression Pedagogy: Social Justice in Higher Education.* New York: Routledge.

Blinne, Kristen C. 2016. "Applying (Com)passion in the Academy: A Calling . . . A Vow . . . A Plea . . . A Manifesto." *Departures in Critical Qualitative Research* 5 (1): 92–101. https://doi.org/10.1525/dcqr.2016.5.1.92

Blinne, Kristen C. 2014. "Performing Critical Pedagogy Through Fireside Chats." *International Journal of Critical Pedagogy* 5 (2): 131–144. http://libjournal.uncg .edu/ijcp/article/view/556.

Blinne, Kristen C. 2014. "Awakening to Lifelong Learning: Contemplative Pedagogy *As* Compassionate Engagement." *Radical Pedagogy* 11 (2): 1–30. https:// www.academia.edu/8134359/Awakening_to_Lifelong_Learning_Contemplative_ Pedagogy_as_Compassionate_Engagement.

Blinne, Kristen C. 2012. "Making the Familiar Strange: Creative, Cultural, Storytelling within the Communication Classroom." *Communication Teacher* 26 (4): 216–219. https://doi.org/10.1080/17404622.2012.700722.

Blinne, Kristen C. 2013. "Start with the Syllabus: HELPing Students Learn Through Class Content Collaboration." *College Teaching, 61* (2): 41–43. https://doi.org/10 .1080/87567555.2012.708679.

Bruffee, Kenneth. 1999. *Collaborative Learning: Higher Education, Interdependence, and the Authority of Knowledge.* Baltimore: John Hopkins University Press.

Campbell, Colin, and Hanna Kryszewska. 1992. *Learner-Based Teaching.* Oxford: Oxford University Press.

Cunningham, Summer, Bartesaghi, Mariaelena, Bowman, Jim, and Jennifer Bender. 2017. "Re-Writing Interpersonal Communication: A Portfolio-Based Curriculum for Process Pedagogy and Moving Theory into Practice." *International Journal of Teaching and Learning in Higher Education* 29 (2): 381–388. https://files.eric .ed.gov/fulltext/EJ1146274.pdf.

Danielewicz, Jane, and Peter Elbow. 2009. "A Unilateral Grading Contract to Improve Learning and Teaching." *CCC* 61 (2): 244–67. https://scholarworks.umass .edu/eng_faculty_pubs/3.

Darder, Antonia. 2016. *Culture and Power in the Classroom.* New York: Routledge.

Darder, Antonia. 2011. *A Dissident Voice: Essays on Culture, Pedagogy, and Power.* New York: Peter Lang Publishing.

Diversi, Marcelo, and Claudio Moreira. 2009. *Betweener Talk: Decolonizing Knowledge Production, Pedagogy, and Praxis.* Walnut Creek, CA: Left Coast Press.

Dorroh, John. 2019. "Bringing Student Choice to Assessment in Science Classes: What Happens When Students Can Opt to Skip Tests and Instead Give Oral Presentations or Create Art to Show What They Know?" *Edutopia,* November 13, 2019. Accessed December 25, 2019, https://www.edutopia.org/article/bringing -student-choice-assessment-science-classes.

Elbow, Peter. 1998. *Writing Without Teachers.* New York: Oxford University Press.

Fassett, Deanna L., and John T. Warren. 2007. *Critical Communication Pedagogy.* Thousand Oaks, CA: Sage.

Fassett, Deanna L., and John T. Warren. 2008. "Pedagogy of Relevance: A Critical Communication Pedagogy Agenda for the 'Basic' Course." *Basic Communication Course Annual* 20 (6): 1–34. https://ecommons.udayton.edu/bcca/vol20/iss1/6.

Freire, Paolo. 1998. *Pedagogy of Freedom: Ethics, Democracy, and Civic Courage.* Lanham, MD: Rowman & Littlefield Publishers, Inc.

Freire, Paolo. 1994. *Pedagogy of Hope: Reliving "Pedagogy of the Oppressed."* New York: Continuum.

Freire, Paulo. 2000. *Pedagogy of the Oppressed.* New York: Continuum.

Frey, Lawrence, and David Palmer, eds. 2014. *Teaching Communication Activism: Communication Education for Social Justice.* New York: Hampton Press.

Frey, Lawrence R., Pearce, W. Barnett, Pollock, Mark A., Artz, Lee, and Bren A.O. Murphy. 1996. "Looking for Justice in All the Wrong Places: On a Communication Approach to Social Justice. *Communication Studies* 47 (1–2): 110–127. https://doi.org/10.1080/10510979609368467.

Giroux, Henry. 1983. *Theory & Resistance in Education: A Pedagogy for the Opposition.* New York: Bergin & Garvey.

Grace, Fran. 2011. "Learning as a Path, Not a Goal: Contemplative Pedagogy—Its Principles and Practices." *Teaching Theology and Religion* 14 (2): 99–124. https://doi.org/10.1111/j.1467-9647.2011.00689.x.

Gray Akyea, Stacey, and Pamela Sandoval. 2004. "A Feminist Perspective on Student Assessment: An Epistemology of Caring and Concern." *Radical Pedagogy,* 1–15. http://radicalpedagogy.icaap.org/content/issue6_2/akyea-sandoval.html.

hooks, bell. 1994. *Teaching to Transgress: Education as the Practice of Freedom.* New York: Routledge.

Inoue, Asao B. 2019. *Labor-Based Grading Contracts: Building Equity and Inclusion in the Compassionate Writing Classroom.* Fort Collins, CO: The WAC Clearinghouse.

Kahl Jr., David H. 2013. "Critical Communication Pedagogy and Assessment: Reconciling Two Seemingly Incongruous Ideas." *International Journal of Communication* 7, 2610–2630. https://ijoc.org/index.php/ijoc/article/view/1897.

Kaufman, Peter. 2017. "Critical Contemplative Pedagogy." *Radical Pedagogy,* 14 (1), 1–20. https://www.academia.edu/31097956/Critical_Contemplative_Pedagogy.

Keesing-Styles, Linda. 2003. "The Relationship Between Critical Pedagogy and Assessment in Teacher Education." *Radical Pedagogy,* 5 (1): Accessed December 23, 2019. https://radicalpedagogy.icaap.org/content/issue5_1/03_keesing-styles.html.

Kincheloe, Joe L. 2008. *Critical Pedagogy Primer.* Second edition. New York: Peter Lang Publishing.

Kincheloe, Joe L. 2010. *Knowledge and Critical pedagogy: An Introduction (Explorations of Educational Purpose).* Springer.

Kohn, Alfie. 2011. "The Case Against Grades: When Schools Cling to Letter and Number Ratings, Students Get Stuck in a System that Undermines Learning." *Educational Leadership* 69 (3): 28–33. https://www.alfiekohn.org/article/case-grades/.

Kohn, Alfie. 1999. "From Degrading to De-Grading." High School Magazine. https://www.alfiekohn.org/article/degrading-de-grading/?print=pdf.

McLauren, Peter. 2006. *Life in Schools: An Introduction to Critical Pedagogy in the Foundations of Education.* 5th Edition. Pearson.

McLauren, Peter. 2015. *Pedagogy of Insurrection: From Resurrection to Revolution (Education and Struggle).* New York: Peter Lang Publishing.

Miller, John P. 2006. *Educating for Wisdom and Compassion: Creating Conditions for Timeless Learning.* Thousand Oaks, CA: Corwin Press.

Morell, Ernest. 2008. *The Art of Critical Pedagogy: The Promise of Moving from Theory to Practice in Urban Schools.* New York: Peter Lang.

Morell, Ernest, Duenas, Rudy, Garcia-Garza, Veronica, and Jorge, López. 2013. *Critical Media Pedagogy: Teaching for Achievement in City Schools.* New York: Teachers College Press.

Moreno-López, Isabel. 2005. "Sharing Power with Students: The Critical Language Classroom." *Radical Pedagogy* 7 (2). http://radicalpedagogy.icaap.org/content/issue7 2/moreno.html.

Pelias, Ronald J. 2000. "The Critical Life." *Communication Education* 49 (3): 220–228. https://doi.org/10.1080/03634520009379210.

Percell, Jay. 2019. "Democracy in Grading: Practicing What We Preach." *Critical Questions in Education* 10 (3): 180–190. https://academyedstudies.files.wordpress.com/2019/06/percellfinal.pdf.

Percell, Jay. 2014. "Essentially Point-Less: The Influence of Alternative, Non Points-Based Grading on Teachers' Instructional Practices" PhD diss., Illinois State University, 2014, https://ir.library.illinoisstate.edu/etd/196/.

Percell, Jay. 2017. "Lessons from Alternative Grading: Essential Qualities of Teacher Feedback. *The Clearing House: A Journal of Educational Strategies, Issues and Ideas* 90 (4): 1–5. https://doi.org/10.1080/00098655.2017.1304067.

Percell, Jay. 2013. "The Value of a Pointless Education." *Educational Leadership* 71 (4): 1–5. http://www.ascd.org/publications/educational-leadership/dec13/vol71/num04/The-Value-of-a-Pointless-Education.aspx.

Pirbhai-Illich, Fatima, Pete, Shauneen., and Fran Martin, eds. 2017. *Culturally Responsive Pedagogy: Working Towards Decolonization, Indigeneity and Interculturalism.* New York: Palgrave Macmillan.

Rudick, C. Kyle, Golsan, Kathyrn B., and Kyle Cheesewright, K. 2017. *Teaching From the Heart: Critical Communication Pedagogy in the Communication Classroom.* San Diego, CA: Cognella Academic Publishing.

Sartor, Linda, and Molly Young Brown. 2004. *Consensus in the Classroom: Fostering a Lively Learning Community.* Mt. Shasta, CA: Psychosynthesis Press.

Shor, Ira. 2009. "Critical Pedagogy is Too Big to Fail." *Journal of Basic Writing* 28 (2): 6–27. https://www.goucher.edu/learn/academic-centers/hispanic-and-latinx-studies/documents/Shor.pdf.

Shor, Ira. 1997. *When Students Have Power: Negotiating Authority in a Critical Pedagogy.* Chicago and London: The University of Chicago Press.

Shor, Ira, and Caroline Pari, eds. 2000. *Education is Politics: Critical Teaching Across Differences, Postsecondary.* Portsmouth: Boynton/Cook.

Tagg, John. 2004. "Why Learn? What We May *Really* be Teaching Students." *About Campus*March/April, 2–10. https://eric.ed.gov/?id=EJ791236.

Wolk, Steven. 1998. *A Democratic Classroom*. Portsmouth: Heinemann.

Zajonc, Arthur. 2006. "Love and Knowledge: Recovering the Heart of Learning Through Contemplation." *Teachers College Record* 108 (9): 1742–1759. http://www.arthurzajonc.org/publications/love-and-knowledge-recovering-the-heart-of-learning/.

Chapter Eight

"Ungrading" Communication
Awareness Pedagogy as Activist Assessment
Kristen C. Blinne

In this chapter, I build on my experimentation with grading and assessment discussed in the previous chapter, "Are We *Just* Grading or Grading *Justly*?: Adventures with Non-Traditional Assessment" (Blinne, this volume). In doing so, I shall introduce *awareness pedagogy* as an approach that aims to cultivate *grading justice* through its associated philosophies and processes, having the capacity to serve as a kind of activist assessment, which could be utilized and adapted both within communication and broader interdisciplinary courses. Moving through this chapter, we shall first explore how I am situating awareness broadly before delving into its more specific application as related to awareness pedagogy and grading justice. Thereafter, I offer a sample course map to illustrate these ideas in-action, rounding out this conversation with some concluding reflections on how one might embody and enact these principles within their own teaching and learning journeys.

CULTIVATING AWARENESS

If you want to understand the beauty of a bird, a fly, or a leaf, or a person with all his complexities, you have to give your whole attention which is awareness. And you can give your whole attention only when you care, which means that you really love to understand—then you give your whole heart and mind to find out (Krishnamurti 1969, 32).

Krishnamurti's words provide a wonderful starting point for this conversation, suggesting that awareness, as an idea, practice, and/or process involves our whole presence and attention, which is linked to both our capacity and willingness to build understanding, but also to show care for learning and change, giving our whole being to the effort. I cannot imagine an idea that better captures my sentiments about learning as well as the transformative possibilities of teaching and studying communication. Similarly, I situate *awareness* broadly as a type of self-observation that involves observing, witnessing, and reflecting on one's interactions as a tool to gain perspective, encourage empathy, and cultivate doubt while also building relational awareness, as a form of heightened understanding of one's focus of attention at any given moment.

In this way, cultivating awareness is an invitation to embrace the unknown, to be ready to understand, listen, observe, and question and challenge our knowing. Per this perspective, with awareness, we can begin to study ourselves in interaction, exploring our world, which brings about multiple perspectives, moving us from our individual views to a more complex and interrelated space, paying attention to the judgments me make, how we present ourselves, the stories we tell, how we account for our actions, the afterlives of our conversations, and our coordinated actions—who is doing what to whom and why. From here, we can question what we think we know and where our knowing originates, by becoming more aware of what makes us able to live together in harmony or in disharmony with each other.

Ultimately, this approach invites us to un-learn how we approach each other and construct difference, or as Rodriguez (2010) also contends, through our communication, we must nurture a feeling of doubt so we are willing to see our most sacred truths as fallible—so we recognize that certainty puts us in conflict with each other by convincing us that our differences are the cause of conflict versus our lack of willingness to catalyze communication by embracing uncertainty. Without uncertainty, Rodriguez argues, we would have no reason nor need to try to understand anything. In other words, awareness invites us to look at the bigger picture by examining the social worlds we create, inhabit, and travel among, noticing the contexts we co-create so we might adapt and coordinate with other worlds, imagine new possibilities for interaction, and respond compassionately to the expectations and actions of others. In other words, "Being mindful of how our actions affect others' experiences of joy and suffering ought to encourage feelings of care. And being mindful of how human action creates the world ought to give us hope that we can make the world a better place" (Schwalbe 1998, 205). Only when we see the patterns we live within, occurring between and among us, will we be able to disrupt and change the impact they have on our lives. In other words, as Krishnamurti (1969) suggests,

> I lead a certain kind of life; I think in a certain pattern; I have certain beliefs and dogmas and I don't want those patterns of existence to be disturbed because the

disturbance produces a state of unknowing and I dislike that. If I am torn away from everything I know and believe, I want to be reasonably certain of the state of things to which I am going (42).

To this end, Anthony De Mello (1992) challenges each of us to consider: "Would you rather act and not be aware of your actions, talk and not be aware of your words? Would you rather listen to people and not be aware of what you're hearing, or see things and not be aware of what you're looking at?" (39). Thus, for me, I believe that we enlarge our understanding of what is possible when we begin to build awareness of our learning, engaging in practices of un-learning aimed at creating a more just world together. In like manner, Rodriguez offers an emergent definition of communication, defined as a process of being vulnerable to the humanity of others, which greatly inspired my development of awareness pedagogy.

As Rodriguez suggests, with this vulnerability, we come to know that our humanity is bound to the humanity of others and that being vulnerable means being open to mystery, complexity, and ambiguity, thereby offering new ways of seeing and being in the world. To do so means we must become aware of the suffering we cause as well as the suffering we experience. While vulnerability might be considered by some as a sign of weakness, I truly believe that vulnerability is our greatest strength. But what does it mean to be vulnerable? *Vulnerability,* as a term, suggests that we are capable of being wounded or hurt. Based on this definition, how then can vulnerability be harnessed for good? By situating communication as a practice of vulnerability, as Rodriguez contends, we enlarge "our moral and ecological obligation to each other by highlighting our own capacity to influence the condition of the world by how we engage the humanity of others" (xi). If we take seriously the notion that communication is a process wherein we can become vulnerable to others, then communication becomes something more than something *we do to each other.* Instead, it becomes something *we are to one another.* It is in this space between *you* and *me* that we can harness our capacity for compassion and understanding. Vulnerability as Rodriguez suggests, "means being open to the interpretations, experiences, understandings, and even confusions and frustrations of others" (14). Opening ourselves to this idea also means we are capable or susceptible to getting hurt or wounded in our interactions, situating the importance of an ethic of care.

Rodriguez's definition of communication has important implications for better understanding the transformative possibilities of communication, including all of the ways in which we can acknowledge and celebrate our differences. By recognizing each other's vulnerability, we are invited to abandon or reinvent our ways of seeing and being in the world. Stated another way, "Diversity is about communication, finding new ways to understand each other especially when such understanding seems impossible"; therefore, the "success of communication depends on how constructively we manage and negotiate our differences" (xii). Ideally, by attending to each other in a more vulnerable manner, we can move towards developing more just and humane worlds *together* through our communication one conversation at a time.

First, however, to better understand how awareness pedagogy can assist us with this endeavor, we must ask: *What is communication?* and *Why is being aware of one's communication important?* While communication scholars have created a variety of definitions to explain what communication is and how it functions in people's day-to-day lives, I find Barnett Pearce's (2007) idea that communication is everything people say and do together, which he relates to the content and quality of the conversations as well as their "afterlives" as a great starting point for this discussion. Considering the afterlife of a conversation means we take into account the effects our words and actions have on each other "as the afterlives from many such conversations extend and intertwine, they comprise the social worlds in which the people involved in those conversations—you and I—live" (31). By considering communication in this way, Pearce asks us to look at communication, via paying attention to the critical moments whence we make and manage meanings and coordinate our actions.

Though humans constantly manage and make our worlds of meaning together—meanings about culture, language, time, relationships, identities, environments and space, politics, belief systems, and so on—each of our worlds is distinct to us even within our shared, consensual realities. In order to connect to each other, we have to first be aware of the meanings we construct about the nature of our own realities as well as trying to find common ground with the realities and meaning-worlds that others are also making. The way we make sense of our lives is an ever-changing, meaning-making process, and often miscommunication is a response to how closely (or not) our worlds of meaning *relate.* Throughout our lives, we learn and create meanings, which shape the very social worlds we live in by what we do together. Because we all experience social worlds differently, we are called upon to try to understand each other's vantage points. In other words, because we are making these worlds together, none of us controls the outcomes of our interaction, but we have the power to continue or end the conversation—building relationships or dissolving them. Pearce examines these ideas through a framework of coordination, looking at the ebbs and flows of our conversations or instead how our interactions are put together and the meaning-making we apply to understand these encounters. Pearce contends that we can begin to construct richer stories together so we might better understand ourselves and others, moving beyond frameworks of "us" and "them" to "we," by considering the following four questions: *What are we making together? How are we making it? What are we becoming in the making?* and *How can we make better social worlds?* He discusses this further by asking,

> But what if the things we take as important are not so much the *objects* that we perceive but the *meanings* we make of them, and the *actions* we take on the basis of these perspectives? If we *act* on the basis of how we perceive things, those actions are things in the universe and they have an afterlife (43).

In other words, what we define as real becomes our reality through our worlds and actions, continuously and collaboratively coordinated through meaning-making practices within our interconnected social worlds. It is within the experiencing of our diverse social worlds that we come to understand our differences and how we handle them, which relates to Rodriguez's assertion that how we negotiate our differences has a direct impact on the quality of our communication (xii). Or as Pearce similarly contends,

> Things get more interesting when we are open to the possibility that our social worlds differ not just because we think differently about the same things, but also because we think similarly about different things. That is, people in different social worlds may be honorable, but each may deem honorable that which the other finds dishonorable or simply incoherent. It may be impossible to translate one social reality into another; or, better said, to understand someone else, it may be necessary for us to adjust our horizons. In a sense, engaging and understanding another social world means becoming, to some extent, another person (44).

Kimberly Pearce (2012), in discussing her father's work, describes our experience of humanness as consisting of three interlocking realities: our need to tell stories to counter and illustrate our suffering and struggles so we know how to move forward (coherence); our coordination with others within our everyday actions (coordination); and how we make and manage meanings through our experiences of mystery. In this case, mystery is described as a quality of our experience measured by our willingness to celebrate and embrace uncertainty, cultivate open-mindedness, and embrace a sense of awe and wonder, recognizing and acknowledging the limits of the stories we tell and expanding our capacity for tolerance, forgiveness, and compassion. Because our social worlds are complex, always-changing, and multilayered, we must start to bring awareness to our stories—the judgments and assumptions we make about ourselves and others as well as the contexts within which these arise. Once we are able to bring awareness to these reactions and our responses to them, it is imperative we also contemplate the context and consequences in order to discern what actions to take so we might see these "critical moments" from a place of compassionate engagement. Doing so highlights our ability to care deeply about others' lives, experiences, and worlds, recognizing that our interactions are journeys together to something better versus a set destination.

Maria Lugones (1994) beautifully articulates this notion with the metaphor of world-travel. In describing what she means by "worlds," she suggests that each world is inhabited by embodied beings as well as imaginary ones and that worlds are only ever partially constructed in that these worlds may construct us socially in ways we may not understand, and at the same time, we may still embody and perform these constructions. Moreover, we often inhabit multiple worlds, share worlds, and travel between worlds at the same time. As such, our worlds offer a description of our experiences as well as opportunities to "travel" among worlds, thus making us "world-travellers." Traveling among each other's worlds may be conscious or unconscious; hence, she advocates for developing a sense of playful travel and being at ease in the world so one can cultivate a loving attitude in order to experience an opening to uncertainty and mystery. As we enter each other's worlds, we begin to identify with "others" through a playful curiosity so we might understand what the world looks like through someone else's eyes/experience. By doing so, we move away from a communication framework positioning our world as right, good, moral, and so on, and others' worlds as wrong, evil, or amoral. We instead attend to the in-between, recognizing the potential for creating new worlds together.

Per each of these views, with awareness, we can begin to critically reflect on the field of consciousness containing all of our processes, desires, pleasures, motives, hopes, and longings, better understanding what Krishnamurti refers to as our "extraordinary complexity," which we must discover by examining our landscape of response and reaction with our complete and total attention –the goal of awareness pedagogy.

We Are the World (Café):
Teaching & Learning to Keep the Conversation Going

I like to imagine my classroom as a kind of *World Café*, a collaborative process developed by Juanita Brown and David Isaacs (2005), in which conversation (or rather communication) is centered as the primary means for building awareness and accessing our collective intelligence, which is vital to understanding ever-evolving social injustices. Within this space, my goal is to bring people together to share their everyday experiences, stories, and dreams through reading, writing, speaking, and listening so each of us can develop into (com)passionate conversationalists and communication leaders, hopefully carrying these conversational streams far beyond the boundaries of class to the world at large through the following aims built from my experiences as a learner first and also as a teacher:

Because I value teachers who have *clarified the purpose and set the context of our time together,* as an instructor, I situate awareness pedagogy as working in tandem with learner-based teaching strategies, enabling me to create my classes *with* students, not *for* them. Most of my students indicate they learn best when provided with structures they can build on or adapt; thus, I integrate feedback loops into my courses as tools to explore and engage what is meaningful to the group as a whole as well as to each individual student. In other words, as my students and I mutually engage as learners and teachers, I am able to more successfully serve as a guide, not dictating information, but instead facilitating discussions that offer opportunities for shared inquiry designed to inspire compassionate action (Blinne 2013). As such, I first embrace the premise that each learner wants to be *heard.* They want to know their ideas and input matters and they can influence class direction. Second, learners want to be *excited* about what they are learning; hence, content should reflect their interests and make meaningful connections to their daily lives. Third, they want to be *liked.* Most students want their teachers and classmates to support their contributions, recognize their work and participation within the course, expressing care if they do not engage. Finally, learners want learning to be *personal.* They want their teachers to know their names, to tell their stories, and to approach learning in their own style.

Because I thrive when teachers have worked to *create a hospitable space,* as an instructor, I situate awareness pedagogy as a process and practices of learning that strive to be lighthearted, humorous, stress-free, yet challenging and engaging, encouraging students to feel inspired to experiment, play, and sometimes fail, as teachable moments. To create a warm, welcoming, and collaborative learning community based on the above ideas, I organize my classes around the following guiding questions: *What topics are of greatest interest to us as a group? How can we best connect our reading, writing, conversations, and activities to our lives both inside and outside of the classroom? In what ways do we learn best and how can we integrate diverse learning practices into our course?* Perhaps most important to creating a hospitable space is exploring how we can best adapt our environment to be more conducive to discussion. In other words, should we sit in a circle, go outside, dim the lights, or experiment with some other model? In response to student feedback, I developed a process I call "fireside chats" (see Blinne 2014a), inviting students to sit in a circle around a mock campfire (decorated with Christmas tree lights) to discuss our learning goals, readings, assignments, or various course themes.

Because I enjoy teachers who have wanted to *explore questions that matter* to me personally, as an instructor, I work diligently to create a classroom environment where relationships can emerge between all individuals involved in the learning process (myself included), providing opportunities for building friendships as a vital component of awareness pedagogy. Because each dynamic is different, I work collaboratively with each group to build all or part or our course map (a term I prefer over a syllabus), develop group consensus regarding our course content and policies, and discover our shared interests in each topical area, employing a wide range of engaged learning strategies to support multiple and individual learning styles such as mapping, visual art, performance and role-playing, games, poetry, journaling, and movement. In each of these instances, all assignments and activities are grounded in self-exploration with the goal of enhancing students' relational awareness. Key to this approach is also highlighting that learning is a lifelong process and one's work, whether it be writing, a performance, or other project is always "in-progress."

Because I respect teachers who want to build an environment that *encourages everyone's contribution,* as an instructor, I employ a wide range of processes aimed at cultivating contemplation and collaboration as key components of awareness pedagogy. Because not every learner learns best by vocalizing in class, I also employ solo, partner, and group activities, involving self-evaluation, peer feedback, and small group decision-making, designed to bring students into conversation with themselves, each other, and me. I also integrate informal, low stakes writing and arts-based exercises, as well as an "interaction board," for students to pose questions, make suggestions, plan, map ideas, issue a challenge, and engage with course material and "connector groups," three to four people leading the group discussion based on their shared interests. Additionally, I often conclude many of my class sessions with a "closing" ritual with each student invited to offer a closing statement, thereby formalizing the opportunity for all individuals to participate and reflect on each day's theme and discussion.

Because I am inspired by teachers who have attempted to *connect diverse perspectives,* as an instructor, I encourage conversation as dialogue as a necessary component of cultivating cultural understanding through awareness pedagogy, encouraging learners to build awareness of the identity work they "do" together, while also practicing with communicating across group differences, engaging in dialogue about difficult subjects, also working collaboratively and compassionately to address conflict and develop practical skills for cultivating empathy, inspiring action, and intervening in unjust discourses as agents of change. By doing so, I hope to celebrate each person's unique perspective and their ability to impact the community/world, incorporating the power of storytelling as a means to travel into each other's worlds with openness, curiosity, and a willingness to learn from and be changed by each other.

Because I feel safe with teachers who listen deeply and empathetically, as an instructor, my goal is to cultivate space for us to *listen together for insights.* To do so, central to awareness pedagogy is integrating a series of activities into my courses, designed to highlight the ways in which we construct, maintain, and simultaneously negotiate our shared realities and worlds. By engaging in these exercises, students have an opportunity to learn to sharpen their abilities to look closely and listen more fully as they travel into each other's worlds as well as to better understand their own beliefs, assumptions, and interactions that make up their worlds. Integral to this process is taking the time to listen for patterns and connections while also slowing down, pausing for reflection, and embracing moments of silence together.

Because I value teachers who care about *sharing collective discoveries*, as an instructor, I invite each learner to continuously reflect on the following questions as an important mode of awareness pedagogy self-assessment: How engaged was I in today's class? Was I listening? Did I actively participate in all in-class activities? Did I bring the required assignments and materials? Was I late or did I leave early? Did I work collaboratively with my partners or group? Was I open to trying new experiences? Did I respect others' views even when they differed from my own? Did I communicate my learning needs to the group? Have I actively contributed to creating the class I want, while being mindful of others' needs, too? Have I shared my insights, observations, questions, comments, or concerns and created space for others to do the same? Finally, and perhaps most importantly, what would the group have missed had I not been in class? By reflecting on these questions, my hope is that each learner will come to recognize that they are response-able and play an important role in shaping the world (café) we create together through our conversations. Moreover, as part of this process, my goal is to help each learner build awareness about what they learned and what they found meaningful within the course; what surprised them about their process; what they feel their most vital contributions were to the community; which work they are most proud of and why; what processes worked best for them to accomplish their own learning goals; what obstacles did they face; what might they do differently if embarking on this journey again; and, finally, what help might I offer them to continue their process moving forward.

Each of these conversational components, when combined, set the stage for the ways in which awareness pedagogy aims to enact grading justice by emphasizing the importance of developing a "social justice sensibility," which Frey et al. (1996) describe as:

> A social justice sensibility entails a moral imperative to *act* as effectively as we can to do something about structurally sustained inequalities. To continue to pursue justice, it is perhaps necessary that we who act be personally ethical, but that is not sufficient. Our actions must engage and transform social structures (111).

A core element of this idea involves not only employing communication to promote social justice, at the same time raising awareness about injustices, but also intervening into oppressive educational practices (as one layer among many), and in doing so, modeling the importance of questioning and critiquing course content and teacher-learner roles, in addition to *all* policies and practices. In doing so, within my teaching I strive to illustrate the importance of harnessing "communication knowledge and skills to intervene to attempt to reduce oppression and achieve justice," by first building "social justice awareness" (Simpson 2014, 87) and then cultivating a "social justice sensibility" that informs daily interactive choices. Simpson (2014) discusses five components vital to helping students build awareness of injustices, including: *communication as constitutive*, defining "what is possible and expected"; *knowledge and power,* understanding the relationship between these systems; *material realities,* conceptualizing how people live and the consequences of our interactions; *agency and structure,* how choices individually and collectively shape our daily communicative interactions; and finally, the *desirability of the public good and justice,* embracing the importance of a common good (88–89).

Helping individuals and communities of learners see how studying their own communication can transform their understanding of themselves and others, in addition to enhancing relationships and the quality of their lives, is for me, a practice of building an awareness of how our words and actions impact each other, which is at the heart of my understanding of the relationship between communication and community, in addition to realizing the importance of not only serving others with and through communication but also our willingness to intervene in unjust discourses (we create, experience, and maintain) are central components of awareness pedagogy, and per my view, grading justice.

INTRODUCING AWARENESS PEDAGOGY

My approaches to grading and assessment have emerged from the teaching and learning practices I have been developing over the last decade as part of a pedagogical process I refer to as *awareness pedagogy*. Building on our previous sections, I define *awareness* as a field of consciousness whereby we become conscious of ourselves, others, and our environment (including communicative contexts), building heightened understanding through self-observation as our interactions unfold in any given moment. Further, *pedagogy*, in my view, is not limited to merely being the study and practice of teaching but instead serves as a process of living our learning. Thus, when combined, awareness pedagogy is both a tool for self-exploration but also an approach for expanding our "we consciousness" in classroom settings (and beyond).

Awareness pedagogy, inspired by universal design for learning, culturally-sustaining, critical, feminist, queer, anti-racist, indigenous, decolonizing, and communication activism and social justice pedagogies, focuses on five, broad learning awareness practices that are integrated into all of my courses, including: contemplative engagement, cultural understanding, critical exploration, collective action, and creative application—each of which involves the goal to foster compassionate action through everyday communicative micropractices, designed to cultivate awareness through what I refer to as *living-our-learning-awareness practices:*[1]

- *Contemplative Engagement:* Cultivating awareness of the value of self-reflection and inquiry: learning to pay attention to what we are paying attention to at any given point in time so we can cultivate presence, listen deeply, and also witness ourselves in our interactions as they unfold within our lives.
- *Cultural Understanding:* Cultivating awareness of our role in culturing processes (e.g., how we "do" culture via our communication), including understanding the value of equity and justice: learning to engage cultural differences with compassion, empathy, and kindness.
- *Critical Exploration:* Cultivating awareness of multiple perspectives and diverse points of view: learning to understand, evaluate, and apply communication concepts to address everyday social issues and injustices.
- *Collective Action*: Cultivating awareness of the value of relationships: learning to engage ethically and collaboratively with others.
- *Creative Application:* Cultivating awareness of the importance of creatively exploring the choices that inform our actions (what we say and do): learning to select the appropriate modalities and technologies to accomplish communicative goals for diverse audiences across a range of contexts.

It is important to note the following: First, within my courses, there are no exams or quizzes, nor do we utilize points or percentages as part of our assessment practices; instead, we focus on offering feedback as the primary means

266 *Kristen C. Blinne*

of understanding and offering guidance on "in-progress" work. Second, when we develop collaborative assessment criteria, we do so *after* the work has been completed not before, situating self-assessment as the primary mode of feedback and evaluation. Additionally, awareness pedagogy involves the following guiding principles that work in alignment with our living-our-learning-awareness practices:

- *Relational Inquiry:* At its core, this portion of our process involves asking questions such as: Who am I in relationship to you? Who are you in relationship to me? Who are we together? Who do we become as a result of our interaction? Central to this exploration is cultivating an environment where each of us can learn from and potentially be changed by each other's points of view (critical exploration) as a tool to enhance relational awareness (cultural understanding) through our engagement (collective action) with our unique ways of seeing and being in the world (contemplative engagement and creative application). This process comes to life as we engage in self-evaluation and peer feedback practices, including collaborating on course content design and policies as well as when working with partners and in groups to offer feedback and support, in addition to building awareness of our communication processes and patterns.
- *Re-Visioning Work:* Within this aspect of our process, we situate all of our coursework as "in-progress" (contemplative engagement). Doing so allows us to fully embrace the possibilities of relational inquiry, insomuch that we lean on each other to refine our own visions and explore new possibilities by seeing our contributions through other people's eyes (critical exploration, cultural understanding, and collective action). Regardless of whether our contributions to a course are centered on written work, creative projects, presentations or performances, our goal is to re-vision our project by crafting a larger project through small steps, taking one project among many and substantially revising after receiving feedback; or in collectively creating something, we situate all our work as "unfinished" and "messy" (creative application) versus constructing our contributions as "one and done" and never to be revisited (or, in this case, re-visioned) again.
- *Collaborative Creation:* Building on our focus of relational inquiry and re-visioning work, we work together to recognize and embrace the value of "not-knowingness" as a tool for on-going reflection (contemplative engagement), sharing learning collective discoveries focused on the varying learning processes in play. To this end, we spend a great deal of time exploring the possibilities associated with uncertainty (critical exploration), recognizing the value of ambiguity (cultural understanding), while also

engaging in shared decision-making to create criteria that attempts to be fair, just, and equitable for the whole (collective action and creative application) (e.g., what constitutes a meaningful group discussion; do we need an attendance policy, what does course engagement mean, what would constitute an uninspiring or disruptive learning environment, among other guiding questions). In doing so, we collaborate on course policies to create a guide for how we might understand letter grade categories at the conclusion of the term. This aspect of our process will be discussed in more depth later in this chapter.

- *Self-Assessment and Advocacy:* Central to this component of our process, we engage in on-going conversations about the relationship between *grading* student learning and *assessing* or improving student learning, trying to reframe student success as a practice of lifelong learning, versus measuring it against each other's failure or operating in comparison to one another. As part of this, each learner is engaged in extensive self-evaluation, in conversation with other forms of feedback focused on making connections between course content and the living-our-learning-awareness practices. In this way, they reflect on their own learning process (contemplative engagement), based on their unique experiences (cultural understanding), building insights about group learning processes (collective action) and diverse points of view (critical exploration), creating an individual plan to illustrate what learning they found to be most meaningful for their lives (creative application).
- *Collective Response-ability*: By engaging in communicative micropractices aimed at social justice (contemplative engagement), we embrace processes aimed at building community (collective action) by opening up spaces for dialogues across differences and developing cultural awareness and empathy (critical exploration and cultural understanding). In doing so, our goal is to embrace creative opportunities that help us keep the conversation going (creative application). However, as part of this process, we each must be willing to be response-able for our words and actions, recognizing the impact that we have on each other. Collective response-ability is a key component of relational inquiry, re-visioning work, and collaborative assessment.

Within communication studies, awareness pedagogy has the capacity to help individuals examine their communication patterns as well as their relational routines and personal habits; observe their reactions within their interactions; explore their relationship with self-care (and/or what nourishes them); consider their impact (on themselves through embodied listening, their relationships with others, and the world at large); practice gratitude (along with compassion and empathy), and finally, to discover their own perspectives on communication.

Awareness pedagogy in practice can be best articulated as a teaching and learning approach, aimed at cultivating awareness across five broad-communication focused living-our-learning-awareness practices, which are then tailored to act in alignment with specific course content. Courses that utilize awareness pedagogy are designed to be discussion-based, utilizing dialogue circles, and other conversational methods. Within this practice, as already mentioned, tests and quizzes are not part of the process. Instead, each learner works to create an individualized plan to accomplish building heightened understanding or awareness in each of five learning practices across the landscape of the semester. Thus, even in situations where each student partakes in the same assignment, as part of this process, each student may focus on illustrating their awareness of different living-our-learning-awareness practices.

By the end of the semester, each student must illustrate some level of awareness in each of the five learning awareness practices. The student then meets with the instructor at the end of the term to finalize their course grade, based on extensive self-assessment of each assignment, in conversation with the instructor's feedback. Throughout the semester *no grades* are given— only feedback. Within this system, I do not record grades or evaluate the quality of work. Instead, I offer feedback designed to help the student build heightened awareness and understanding of each of the living-our-learning-awareness practices, in conversation with the course concepts as applied to their overall life. It is important to note that in cases where students complete an assignment, which meets none of the awareness practices, they are able to redo the work until they illustrate one of these practices-in-action. Moreover, a student might self-assess their work as one practice; however, my feedback might suggest that the works meets a different awareness practice instead. If a student decides not to complete an assignment or does not choose to "re-vision" an assignment that did not meet any of the criteria, they are then required to reflect on this in a self-assessment, accounting for their decision-making process. We then discuss this in-depth during our final meeting.

When I say that no grades are given or recorded until the end of the semester, I mean none. Zero. Also, awareness pedagogy does not utilize points or percentages, nor markers, labels, or numerical formulas to sort students or their work into hierarchical categories (e.g., excellent, average, etc.) *ever.* Instead, I work with specific assignment options (e.g., an identity project), inviting students to explore each project through *any* of the learning awareness practices. When I present the assignment, I typically offer students the option to do a written paper, a presentation or performance, visual work (e.g., video, poster, or other multimedia option), audio work, a partner or group project, or a teaching activity, though I am open to other options, depending on their interests. Once the assignment form is selected, students are then guided to consider how they will link specific course content with one or more of our learning awareness practices. As part of this discussion, continuing with the example of an "identity project," we fully consider the range of possibilities for exploring identity (in conversation with course content) through contemplative engagement, cultural understanding, critical exploration, collective action, and/or creative application. Once they are clear on their direction, we work together to tailor a process for their unique approach to the assignment.

Furthermore, in this approach, I do not have set project deadlines. Instead I give students an end date near the conclusion of the semester by which each assignment must be finalized. However, I do encourage them not to wait until the last minute as then they will not have the option for do-overs, if needed. Again, students who decide not to turn something in as required are simply asked to complete a self-assessment form thereafter accounting for their decision process, which is then discussed in-depth at the end of the semester when finalizing their course grade in our one-on-one meeting. Depending on the semester, I invite students to meet with me at the beginning or middle of the semester to check their progress, and all students must meet with me at the end of the term to finalize their grade. Not setting concrete deadlines allows student to work at their own pace, avoiding the complications associated with "late work." Only with certain presentations or group work do I schedule a specific timeframe for consistency and ease of engagement. Moreover, I do build in peer review sessions during the semester, which require students to come to class with their "in-progress" projects. While this is not a "hard" deadline, it does help students have some structure to work with in regard to our project scheduling. It is also important to note that as part of each student's self-assessment process, they must provide evidence that attempts to illustrate how they have engaged with the living-our-learning-awareness practice they are attempting to claim awareness of in each assignment. In most cases, I also offer students the opportunity to work alone, in pairs, or small groups to accomplish these tasks.

At first glance, how awareness pedagogy approaches grading and assessment might appear slightly similar in aim to "competency-based learning" (Townsley 2014; Schaef, 2016), "standards-based grading" (Guskey 2000, 2001; Marzano 2000; Cox 2011; Owens 2015) or "mastery grading" (Guskey and Bailey 2001); however, it departs in significant ways due to its strong alignment with and integration of ideas from critical communication pedagogy (Fassett and Warren 2007, 2008; Rudick, Golsan, and Cheesewright 2017), as well as with communication activism pedagogies (Frey and Palmer

270 *Kristen C. Blinne*

2014) and contemplative pedagogies (Zajonc 2006; Miller 2006; Grace 2011; Blinne 2014b; Berila 2016; Kaufman 2017).

"Competency-based learning" (CBL), designed to be "learner-centric," focuses on students' mastery of skills and the application of knowledge. As part of this approach, students work without time constraints, creating artifacts that best represent the competencies they have accomplished while also reflecting on their achievements. In this case, competencies refer to sets of skills or capacities, which are grouped according to related skills, receiving feedback on their work to demonstrate mastery and growth (Townsley 2014). CBL emphasizes application advanced through content based on proficiency versus time spent with a focus on multiple means of assessment, extending beyond the confines of the classroom. As a result, CBL creates opportunities for students to proceed at their own pace, starting with well-defined outcomes which students utilize to track their progress.

Similarly, "standards-based grading" focuses on the notion of mastering learning concepts, based on predetermined learning outcomes, with students working to achieve a certain "standard." Within this approach, which diverges from traditional A–F grading, all of the course assignments are built to help students demonstrate the standard. Work is scored with nominal numbers (with no ordinal value), utilizing a 4- or 5-point rubric, which indicates the mastery of the standard or objective (e.g., 5 = mastery, 4 = an acceptable level of competence, 3 = developing towards competence, and 2 or 1 as indicating an emerging or limited level of mastery or lack of it) (Percell 2014). Most often associated with the "Common Core" curriculum embraced in K–12 educational contexts, "standards-based grading," as Kohn (2011) suggests, is also used to denote "grading that is aligned with a given set of objectives" or may refer to "criterion-based testing" depending on the context (31). Thus, even though "standards-based grading" attempts to move us into new grading and assessment territory, it still adopts some of the means associated with traditional grading systems such as extrinsic motivation and numerical ratings that sort students and rank them (Kohn 2011).

"Mastery grading," like "standards-based grading" allows for students to engage in "do-overs" until mastery is achieved or the standard is met; however, with this approach, points are not utilized as part of the criteria to show proficiency (or lack of). Even so, within "mastery grading," as Percell (2014) states, "there is a definitive cut-off between mastery and 'non-mastery'" (44). Regardless, as part of this process, students are given multiple chances to achieve mastery as part of their progress. This assessment practice has grown out of "mastery learning" as advanced by Bloom (1968) and has been expanded by Lalley and Gentile (2009), Guskey (2010), and Percell (2013, 2014). Percell (2013), in advocating for the value of "no-points grading systems," based on mastery learning, utilizes a four-tiered rubric to assess students' work qualitatively, employing the following markers: *E* (Exceeds), *M* (Meets), *A* (Approaches), or *B* (Far Below). These tiers are then translated into letter grades. For example, "To earn a final letter grade of *A,* students needed top-tier work in three categories and mid-tier work in the fourth" (Percell 2013). The categories, in this case, refer to specific assignments (e.g., performance objectives, written assignments, literary terms, and journals). While I applaud Percell's "no points" approach as an attempt to decouple points from grading with the goal of fostering "authentic mastery learning" with the hopes of increasing "students' intrinsic motivation," like Kohn (2011), I, too, believe "At best, these prescriptions do nothing to address the fundamental problems with grading" and at worst "they exacerbate those problems" (31).

In further reflecting on "standards based grading" and "mastery grading," from a communication standpoint, I take issue with the language choices associated with both of these systems. To start, for me, I want to move far, far away from standardization within my teaching, instead prioritizing in-dividualized learning processes. Additionally, the term "standard," in my view, speaks to a norm and/or an outcome versus a process, serving to sort students into piles based on achievement of the standard (or lack of). As such, in Blommaert and Varis' (2013) terms, it reinforces the idea that students must acquire and/or perform "enough" of the emblematic features of the standard to be granted access to the categories they represent. Thus, students still remain trapped in a cycle of "enoughness," which is ultimately judg-ment of their worth or value (even as it purports to be solely focused on their capacity to demonstrate a standard). Similarly, for me, "mastery" suggests that learning happens in a neatly packaged, tiered-manner, and that one can clearly demarcate where mastery has occurred or has not—still a judgment of "enoughness" on the evaluator's part. Building on this, I am not striving for my students to become "masters" of anything as mastery typically suggests a level of achievement that requires no further growth once reached.

Of these three systems, awareness pedagogy most closely mirrors the goals of "competency-based learning," by encouraging learners to work at their own pace, creating projects that illustrate their engagement with our learning awareness practices throughout the semester. However, a significant differ-ence between CBL and awareness pedagogy centers on the elimination of as-sessment hierarchies based on the notion of "competency," "proficiency," or "mastery" on the grounds that perceptions surrounding these notions can eas-ily reinforce further learning inequities. Instead, awareness pedagogy seeks to encourage students to take risks and explore learning possibilities, which do not require them to "advance" through various tiered practices.

In other words, by situating awareness as the process-goal, students work to build awareness skills in each learning awareness area through various practices, rather than being assessed on the outcome or product of each of these practices. For instance, if students are attempting to develop awareness in the realm of creative application, they engage in self-assessment regarding what they learned about the project choices they made in completing an assignment; in addition, they learn to tailor the project to a particular audience and context versus being assessed on the final project itself (e.g., for example, the design of a textbook cost educational campaign aimed at faculty). While I give feedback on the final project as a learner myself, I ultimately focus on their learning progress and the awareness skills developed in the process. Although this might seem like a subtle difference, it is an incredibly important one as I wish for students to see their process as dynamic, messy, partial, unfinished, and, if anything, I hope they will adopt a non-expert stance, which values the power of "not-knowingness" to ease the toxic certainty that can accompany meeting a specific competency, standard, or attempting to gain mastery.

To this end, while I understand the appeal of trying to create innovative approaches to assessment that attempt to map learning *differently*—the entire focus of the previous chapter, which discuses my adventures with grading (Blinne, this volume)—I now recognize more than ever that for me to truly embody and enact grading justice within my teaching, I have to join the many educators that are advocating for "ungrading" or "no-grading" such as Kohn (1999, 2011), Hunt (2008), Bower (2010a, 2010b), Sackstein (2015), and Blum (2017), among many others. Each of these educators enacts "ungrading" in different ways within their teaching in a range of educational contexts; however, what they share in common is a commitment to decentering the role of grading within the learning process. Of the alternative and non-traditional grading and assessment approaches that I have experimented with and researched, it is my belief that those engaging in "ungrading" come as close to how I understand grading justice as a kind of collective social justice movement, which is particularly illustrated by the Facebook group with over 10,000 members titled, "Teachers Throwing Out Grades." Awareness pedagogy builds on the momentum created by this "ungrading" movement, focusing not only on the decentering of grades but also on the centering of social justice, a core component of its approach. The educational network, "Teachers Going Gradeless," offers a wealth of resources for those interested in exploring the possibilities of gradeless teaching as does the "Human Restoration Project," aimed at changing mindsets and school systems through a variety of means.

As Dave Tomar (n.d.) contends, "Education is complex and nuanced. Grades are simple and arbitrary"; even so, grades are deeply entrenched in our educational system to such a deep level that "it would take an absolutely enormous systemic change in American education to come up with, let alone implement, something new." In his essay, "Eliminating the Grading System in College: The Pros and Cons," he does not argue to abolish the grading system; however, he does suggest that its "unchecked authority" is long overdue for reconsideration. Some of the "pros" he presents for eliminating grading include: the movement towards learning for learning's sake; the impracticality of grades for the development of practical skills; the inherent subjectivity of grades (rendering them arbitrary and meaningless even though still highly consequential in application); and, finally, the notion that grades are easy to "fudge," in which he discusses debates about grade inflation. Tomar, conversely, discusses the associated "cons" of eliminating grades and grading on the following grounds: learners are deeply entrenched in the grading system, so much so that they may not know how to learn without them; grades continue to carry weight in the "outside world"; teachers would lose authority; and, last, educators can improve grading systems without throwing away grades.

While Tomar clearly states that letter grades merely quantify learner abilities, presenting the "illusion of qualitative assessment," he also recognizes that not only do professors "draw a significant amount of institutional power from the ability to assign grades," but also that the "grading system's capacity to dole out punishments is among its strongest features." Even in recognizing these limitations, he contends that we do not need to trash grades altogether, while at the same time arguing that they offer instructors "clean lines of demarcation between types of performance, types of students, and types of future outcomes." In my view, from a grading justice standpoint, this is exactly the reason grades could be and should be eliminated as it is this type of categorization which only serves to reinforce inequity and injustices within, between, and among learners, while at the same time, moving learners further away from the learning. In his argument, Tomar does provide this awareness about the potential for grading injustice stating:

> But grades don't tell us how to help, how to cultivate talent, or how to push students beyond the bare minimum. All we know is who to reward and who to punish. But punishment should have no place in college. College is meant to challenge students, to help them look for deeper meaning.

Awareness pedagogy holds this exact aim to quest for heightened understanding, or rather deeper meaning and connection to learning itself. Tomar ends his essay suggesting that educators challenge themselves to provide richer, more meaningful evaluative feedback as one step forward in this hotly debated realm of teaching and learning. This edited collection is designed to contribute to these on-going conversations, bringing the discipline of communication into the mix, in addition to foregrounding the importance of social justice within teaching and learning processes, practices, and philosophies. I consider this effort to be the start of "The Grading Justice Project," which at its core hopes to disrupt traditional approaches to grading and assessment by creating more humane and just practices aimed at social justice within educational contexts and more broadly as well.

In this manner, I argue that awareness pedagogy functions as activist assessment due to its social justice focus, which prioritizes the pursuit of sociocultural and educational equity, regardless of a person's intersecting identity categories or group membership, diligently working against the perpetuation of marginalization and oppression. Thus, for me, awareness pedagogy, when practiced, is a form of "communication activism for social justice," which involves engaging in communicative practices to promote social justice (Frey and Blinne 2017) that also seeks to educate for social action (Del Gandio and Nocella 2014), engaging in communicative practices aimed at un-learning and disrupting social realities that reinforce injustices. As I have previously stated, I wholeheartedly believe that communication teachers and students can be the educational change agents the world needs, helping individuals learn to engage more peacefully, nonviolently, and compassionately with each other.

In the realm of grading and assessment, grading justice can be conceptualized as a framework that dares to imagine what a social justice approach to grading and assessment might be to assist instructors with intervening into and potentially disrupting unjust modes of teaching and learning by creating more just practices and policies through awareness pedagogy. To help you conceptualize what this looks like on paper, I offer a sample interactive course map (the term I utilize in place of syllabus), based on these ideas. For the sake of space, I shall not include the week-by-week calendar (as this is often built with students), nor my particular institution's required college policies within this example. It is also important to note that this course map only contains short explanations of the proposed assignments because within many of my courses, I often create a separate project guide which includes collaboratively shaped project categories, instructions, and prompts.

GENDER COMMUNICATION

(Sample Syllabus/Interactive Course Map)
Professor: Kristen C. Blinne, Ph.D.
Department: Communication and Media

About Your Professor: I came to the study of communication because I wanted to be a better communicator, hoping to enhance my relationships, and, as a result, the quality of my life. Thus, I am primarily interested in studying how communication can transform our understandings of ourselves and others. With a focus in feminist communication studies and listening, I examine communication and the construction of difference, in addition to having a strong passion for sexuality studies. My goal as an instructor is to provide a space for you to discover your own passion for communication studies, and, in the context of this course, for you to consider how gender is impacting your life by reflecting on your own unique gender story.

Questions about me?

About You: I would love to learn more about your career goals/plans, in addition to more about your hobbies or general interests or anything you would like to share "about you" so that I might get to know you better! Also, please let me know how to best address you (name and pronouns) and anything else that can help me to help you succeed in this course.

Gender Play

In your view, how many categories of "gender" exist? →
   Explain:

In your view, how many categories of "sexual orientation" exist? →
   Explain:

Do you believe the terms "sex" and "gender" can be used interchangeably? →
   Explain:

Do you believe individuals communicate differently because of their gender? →
   Explain:

Do you believe you can "see" someone's gender? →
   Explain:

276   *Kristen C. Blinne*

Has anyone ever criticized you for your gender? →
  Explain:

How closely do you believe you align with stereotypes associated with your gender? →
  Explain:

If your gender were a fruit, which would it be and why? →

If your gender were a car, which would it be and why? →

If your gender were an animal, which would it be and why? →

If your gender were a color, which would it be and why? →

Course Description: This course will examine the relationship between gender and communication, analyzing multiple and varying gender theories and the discourses through which we understand gender dynamics and issues. This course further investigates gender stereotypes and gendered cultural patterns of interaction within a range of contexts. After participating in this course, it is my hope you will gain a better understanding of and respect for a diversity of gender theories/stories and the role these play in shaping our everyday lives. To guide our process, we shall focus on the following questions: Do various gender identities communicate differently? If so, what does this difference "do" relationally and socially? Also, if not, how can our communication expand our ability to connect and relate versus limit this potential? Further, what does it mean to be gendered, to communicate about gender, and/or communicate in a gendered manner?

Based on the above description, what, if anything, excites you about studying communication, especially in regard to this course?

What, if anything, concerns or confuses you about studying communication, especially in regard to this course?

When you leave this course, what do you hope to have gained?

What questions about gender and communication do you hope this course will answer?

Course Structure: The structure for this course is different from many other gender and communication courses, insomuch that in studying a broad range of theories and perspectives, the ultimate goal I hold is for you to determine your own perspective about gender, while also being able to recognize the gender theories that inform other perspectives, research studies, and lived realities. As such, this course is designed to increase your understanding of gender as it is constructed, performed, evaluated, and negotiated through communication. As part of our time together, I hope that we shall:

- Participate in a robust conversation about gender that increases your awareness of the factors that impact the construction and performance of gender as a process, practice, and product of communication.
- Become more conscious about how you construct and perform your own gender stories and encourage you to make more deliberate and conscious choices about your gender stories and performances.
- Gain a better understanding of and respect for the multiple gender stories presented to you by others.

To assist our collaborative effort to create a welcoming and supportive learning environment where we can explore questions that matter, encouraging everyone's contribution so we can listen for insights and share our collective discoveries. Please reflect on the following:

As a learner in this course, what do you need from your classmates to feel welcomed and supported, especially when discussing difficult topics?

As a learner in this course, what do you need from me, the instructor, to feel welcomed and supported, especially when discussing difficult topics?

Finally, as a learner course, what do you expect from yourself, in regard to your contribution to this effort:

My Promise to You: I realize many of you have multiple classes, jobs, families you care for, and other obligations; therefore, I shall work to be mindful of my demands on your time. Please be mindful that I also have many responsibilities, and I shall work diligently to return and provide feedback on your work in a timely manner. Further, I promise not to keep you in class beyond our scheduled time. I shall respect each of you as individual learners with unique needs and interests and not assess you by comparison. I shall send you weekly emails to update you about our schedule. Additionally, I am

278   *Kristen C. Blinne*

always available to meet with you to discuss your work and progress as well as my interpretations of your process. I shall remain flexible so we can adapt our schedule, classroom space, readings, activities, assignments, media, and course content to reflect the needs and interests of the group; however, I reserve the option to revise the course material, classroom policies, and schedule as necessary to facilitate what I deem to be the most beneficial process for the overall course. However, my goal is always to work collaboratively to find a mutually agreeable direction for proceeding, in the event that changes must occur. Please discuss any concerns you have with me as well as needs related to accommodations, religious observances, and so on.

To help me better understand your semester, please let me know how many classes you are taking, number of jobs/hours worked per week, club, sport, or other commitments, and/or anything you would like to share to paint a picture of your time constraints this term.

Your Promises to Me: [Students write content here]

Course Texts: [Book titles go here]

What is your relationship with reading? Do you love it, hate it, or something else entirely?

Learning Opportunities:

Gender Aha! Moment(s) (x5)—Due by Week 12: As part of this course, various gender aha! moment entries will be due. Your entries should highlight a specific page, passage, quote, idea, or concept within one of the session's readings, course discussions, or your personal experiences as they relate to the class which: A) inspired or intrigued you, *or* B) confused you, *or* C) angered, frustrated, or bothered you. You do not need to address all three points. Most importantly, please provide some information about an aspect or idea or concept that spoke to you and why. Over the course of the semester, you will turn in *five* of these entries. These entries may take a variety of forms, in consultation with me including: poems, short stories, original songs, conceptual maps or diagrams, cartoons, questions, videos,

"Ungrading" Communication   279

posters, letters, among other options. *See our course project guide for more information.*

Gender Artifact Presentation (x1)—Week 9: Over the course of the semester, you will engage in one short presentation (10 minutes), working with a partner, and selecting *three* gender artifacts that illustrate specific gender theories from our readings. Your artifacts might be a scene from a movie or TV show, a song or poem, an article from a magazine or newspaper, a website or advertisement, an excerpt from a book, a greeting card, photograph, painting, or comic strip, or a description of a personal experience with accompanying documentation. Your artifact presentation must also include a typed explanation (details to follow). All artifacts must be posted to the course Facebook page as a comment on the thread. If you do not have a FB account, you may email your artifact to me and I will post it on your behalf. Currently, there are numerous examples of artifacts on FB. Please check to make sure you are not duplicating the artifact of another pair. Each pair must also upload a typed 1–2 page explanation of the artifacts selected, following the assignment prompts. *See our course project guide for more information.*

Language Observation/Awareness Experiment (x1)—Due by Week 12: For this assignment, we shall explore the persuasive power of gender through one of its most obvious forms: language. In other words, we shall examine identity-marking language, which shapes and is shaped by our everyday communication practices and processes.

Film Writes (x5)—Due by Week 12: During this course, we shall watch five documentaries focused on gender and communication. As part of this process, you will be responsible for completing a related form, which examines the (C) core concepts of the film; the target audience (A); any links you make to the course and your life (L); and what "meaning" or "message" (M) you feel the film is conveying, including its significance. *These can be typed or handwritten and will be due at one time, utilizing only one self-assessment form.

Gender Reflection/Self-Assessment (x9)—Due w/ Projects: Each time you turn in an assignment, you will be asked to complete a short self-assessment of your work. Moreover, halfway through the term as well as at the conclusion of the course, you will complete more in-depth self-assessments that speak to your broader course contribution.

Build-A-Final-Project—Due Week 14: **See our course project guide for more information.*

- *Step One:* The associated course project guide offers a series of suggestions to inspire you to begin brainstorming what type of final project you want to complete for this class. You can pick one of my examples, mix and match ideas, or propose something entirely new.
- *Step Two:* Once you have selected your project, I urge you not to take Ellen DeGeneres' advice to "Procrastinate now, don't delay," and instead start working on gathering resources, researching your topic, and outlining your ideas.
- *Step Three:* We shall work together to create a self-assessment plan for your project.
- *Step Four:* You will include a thorough self-assessment, which includes a detailed explanation of your project process, which will be determined by your final project format.
- *Step Five:* You will turn in your final project and self-assessment at the conclusion of the term. If you are doing a performance, presentation, art installation, teaching activity, or other interactive process, we shall schedule class time for this to take place in the last week of the term.

Learning Opportunity Brainstorming Space

A Few of My Favorite Things: I do not want you to waste important learning time trying to figure out how to make me happy; however, in the spirit of transparency, below is the scoop about a few of my favorite things and how you can brighten my day:

Knowing you care about learning. I love learning, and as Joseph Joubert states, "To teach is to learn twice"; thus for me, it is an honor to be able to spend this time exploring the beauty and complexity of communication with you. That said, I find it quite sad when I encounter learners who seem to be completely uninvested in being part of a learning community. While every group dynamic is different, each of us contributes to the whole in our own unique way. Therefore, it is vital that you actively work to find what is meaningful to you within the context of our course.

Seeing you in class. I know that life happens and you cannot always be present; however, your contribution is vital to our group. It brings me great joy to see you when class starts, and it can be really disruptive to our group dynamic if your on-going contribution is to come in late, leave early, or disengage while present.

Compassionate conversations. Please come to class on time, prepared with materials, ready to engage and participate. If your tendency is to contribute frequently to class discussion, take a step back to allow others to step up. If your tendency is to contribute infrequently to class discussion, I encourage you to step up! It is vital you respect others' opinions even when they differ from your own so we can create a compassionate environment where each individual can express their own opinions, beliefs, values, and ideas. Sharing diverse ideas and worldviews is important to the success of this class; however, I ask that you please be mindful of any language or behavior that you feel might denigrate another person or group.

A Few of Your Favorite Things?

What types of in-class activities do you find the most engaging//beneficial and why?

What types of activities/assignments/teaching approaches cause you to lose interest, motivation, or focus? Please explain why/how.

In your view, "participation" and "engagement" mean:

In your view, a great class discussion/session involves the following components.

A Philosophy of (Un)Grading

It is well-established within educational research that grades do not provide adequate information about what someone has learned, especially given that learning may continue far beyond the last meeting of a course. What then are we to glean about one's learning from a grade, especially since it is quite possible to receive an "A" in a course where you feel you have learned very little? Moreover, it is entirely possible that one could receive a "C" grade for a course in which they learned a great deal. Susan Blum offers the following example to illustrate this in-action:

> Is a student who enters already knowing a lot and continues to demonstrate knowledge at a high level, but then misses an assignment because of a roommate's attempted suicide and ends up with a B-plus, the same as someone who

282   *Kristen C. Blinne*

> begins knowing nothing, works really hard, follows all the rules, does quite
> well and ends up with a B-plus? What information is conveyed? What about
> someone who loves biology and excels in those classes, but who loathes history,
> bombs in history classes and ends up with a 3.0 GPA, compared to someone
> who muddles through every class with a similar GPA, yet with no passion, ex-
> cellence or highs or lows? What do we learn from the GPA? What does a course
> grade mean? (Blum 2017).

No two professors would grade an exact assignment in the same manner, *and*
even if they did, the grade category might mean something completely different to each. As such, it is unsurprising that many learners find grades and
grading systems confusing, arbitrary, and inconsistently (and often unfairly)
applied. To illustrate this further, one need only do a quick survey of various
syllabi, examining different policies on late work, absences, participation,
and extra credit, among other variables. Unfortunately, these discrepancies
force learners to spend more time attempting to navigate the wide-ranging expectations (i.e., what the professor wants) versus focusing on finding what is
most meaningful for learning application to one's life. Studies also conclude
that this greatly impacts creativity and risk-taking, keeping learners trapped
in a cycle of reward and punishment.

*What is your relationship with grades? Grading? What does it feel like to be
graded?*

Do you feel like grades accurately portray your learning (why or why not)?

How do you feel about participating in a course that employs "ungrading"?

"Ungrading" Communication

WHAT IS MY GRADE?

A Self-Assessment Survival Guide

Grades will not be determined until the end of the semester. Another way of saying this is that you will receive *no grades* on any of your assignments throughout the term—only feedback (i.e., asking questions, offering advice, sharing discoveries, and engaging in conversation with you about your process, not evaluating it). To this end, I, too, will not be keeping *any* records that resemble letter grades, points, or percentages. This practice is referred to by many as: *ungrading*. Second, our course will not feature *any* tests or quizzes because I personally feel that this approach prioritizes what is meaningful to me regarding the course concepts versus what is meaningful to you as a unique learner. *All* work, in my view, is "in-progress" and is part of a learning philosophy that values collaboration and revision.

Grades are not assigned until the end of the semester. Why?

I understand at some point in the semester, you may begin to wonder about your grade, which is normal given how grades function in most college courses. Even so, the purpose of this approach is to de-center grading to instead emphasize your entire learning experience—not the individual parts.

This is confusing. Why do you grade like this?

I realize this grading system might be unfamiliar to you, but it is designed to mirror performance review practices in work environments, which, generally speaking, are based on feedback *and/or* periodic reviews—not grades. Put differently, what matters "on the job," in most cases, is showing up prepared and on time (presence), taking initiative (participating and working well with others), meeting deadlines when set, and finding something meaningful you can connect to your life in some manner.

How will my grade be determined after I complete all of my projects and self-assessments?

Throughout the semester, we (you and I) shall work together to determine an individualized assessment plan for you. After each project, you will complete a self-assessment form that provides information regarding your process. I shall offer feedback both on your projects and on your self-assessments. At the conclusion of the term, we shall meet one-on-one to finalize your grade, based on our collaborative assessment of your process, in conversation with

284 *Kristen C. Blinne*

criteria for each letter grade category determined by the whole group. As part of your individualized assessment plan, you will be able to set the majority of your project due dates throughout the semester.

But seriously, how does this work? What about attendance and participation?

As a class, we shall work together to determine some base criteria regarding engagement and attendance, creating collaborative criteria to help shape your individual assessment plan. Throughout the semester, we shall revisit and refine our criteria to better meet the needs of the whole group, working to create the most fair and equitable policies possible. While you are not required to contact me when you will not be present in class, please do contact me if you find that you will not be present for a long period of time so that we can make accommodations, if possible, for you regarding our individual work.

Questions, confusion, or concerns regarding self-assessment?

LIVING-OUR-LEARNING-AWARENESS PRACTICES

All self-assessment and collaborative assessments will focus on five, broad learning awareness practices vital to the study of communication, including: contemplative engagement, cultural understanding, critical exploration, collective action, and creative application, which are described as follows:

- *Contemplative Engagement:* Cultivating awareness of the value of self-reflection and inquiry: learning to pay attention to what we are paying attention to at any given point in time so we can cultivate presence, listen deeply, and also witness ourselves in our interactions as they unfold within our lives.

  Example: Language awareness tracking of one's daily use of "you guys"

- *Cultural Understanding:* Cultivating awareness of our role in culturing processes (e.g., how we "do" culture via our communication), including understanding the value of equity and justice: learning to engage cultural differences with compassion, empathy, and kindness.

  Example: Attending a cultural event on campus and analyzing it using gender concepts

- *Critical Exploration:* Cultivating awareness of multiple perspectives and diverse points of view: learning to understand, evaluate, and apply communication concepts to address everyday social issues.

  Example: Conceptual map of divergent views regarding circumcision

- *Collective Action*: Cultivating awareness of the value of relationships: learning to engage ethically and collaboratively with others.

  Example: Working with a classmate to illustrate gender performance in action

- *Creative Application:* Cultivating awareness of the importance of creatively exploring the choices that inform our actions (what we say and do): learning to select the appropriate modalities and technologies to accomplish communicative goals for diverse audiences across a range of contexts.

  Example: Creating a gender-focused educational workshop for a target audience

286   *Kristen C. Blinne*

Each of your assignments *must* focus on one of these learning awareness practices, providing reflection on how your work illustrates this practice-in-action as related to our course concepts and gender and communication more broadly. While you will not be required to show awareness of multiple practices per assignment, you are invited to engage with more than one practice. That said, my preference would be for you to focus more deeply on one versus a more surface treatment of multiple. Together, we shall determine if the learning awareness practice has been engaged in your work. By the end of the term, you must show some indication of each learning awareness practice, illustrated through your uniquely constructed projects. As we move through the semester, we shall work with these practices in-depth, continuing to create applied examples and indicators of awareness and learning in each.

How do you understand each of these practices? Do you have any questions or concerns regarding assessing yourself and your work this semester? Explain.

SAMPLE SELF-ASSESSMENT FORM

Name:

Project:

Guiding Questions:

Table 8.1. Awareness Self-Assessment

Learning Opportunities	Evidence of Learning-Awareness-Practices-In-Action	X/O
Contemplative Engagement		
Cultural Understanding		
Critical Exploration		
Collective Action		
Creative Application		

*X means that you believe you have illustrated the practice-in-action, and O means you are not attempting to illustrate evidence of this learning opportunity.

Table 8.2.   Semester Self-Assessment Guide

	Contemplative Engagement	Cultural Understanding	Critical Exploration	Collective Action	Creative Application
Journal Entries					
Language Awareness					
Artifact Presentation					
Film Writes					
Final Project					

AWARENESS PEDAGOGY IN PRACTICE

As my interactive course map example hopes to illustrate, the pursuit of awareness is multifaceted, relational, complex, and continuous. To pedagogically commit to creating learning opportunities that foreground the importance of awareness as a transformative place of encounter, whereby understanding becomes heightened through self-observation as part of our *relating* to and with each other, we must open space within our teaching practices for this process to emerge. To assist others with this effort, should they be interested in experimenting with this approach, I offer the following seemingly simple, yet still complex commitments at the heart of awareness pedagogy:

- Cultivating awareness is the primary purpose, process, and practice, as well as the goal of learning within awareness pedagogy. What one is attempting to build awareness of depends on the learning desired, in addition to one's unique positionalities, lived experiences, content and context of the learning experience, in addition to the relational dynamics between individuals and among the learning group. Within this pedagogical approach, awareness involves infinite possibilities that can be further catalyzed by embracing uncertainty, while also learning to keep the conversation going across our differences as well as within difficult dialogues. In this way, awareness cannot be measured, reduced, nor quantified because it is dynamic, on-going, and always "in-progress"—just as we are as we move through our lives.
- Because awareness cannot be quantifiably measured, only qualitatively communicated, awareness pedagogy does not grade nor assess learning by utilizing letter grades, points, percentages, or numeric formulas. Further, this system does not employ tiered or hierarchical categories of evaluation (or judgment) that aim to rank, sort, standardize, or ascribe mastery or competence (or lack of it) on the learner or learning process. Instead, the overarching focus is on communicating feedback between co-learners (i.e., the learner and the facilitator/instructor). Within this process, per my view, the instructor has little to no right to inform the learner about whether they have become "aware" of something or not. Instead, their role is to help guide the learner in deepening their awareness, based on their own learning experiences by asking questions, offering advice for further exploration, and most importantly, listening to what the learner has found to be meaningful for them in their own process. Additionally, within this approach, awareness pedagogy seeks to disrupt traditional educational practices that situate specific project deadlines, late work, extra credit, or other incentives that reward or punish academic

or non-academic behaviors or choices, instead prioritizing processes for learners to collaboratively learn at their own pace and in their own manner (but still together).

- To assist instructors with helping to guide learners to expand and cultivate awareness as applied to specific communication concepts, awareness pedagogy embraces five broad living-our-learning-awareness practices to help carve a connective path among experiences. These practices are then tailored to the unique context of the course (and units of exploration continued therein) as well as the needs and interests of the individual learner, who exists in relationship to the larger learning community (or co-learners, including the instructor). As part of this approach, course content operates in support of each awareness practice, offering specific examples to illustrate the possibilities of putting these practices into action. By the end of the course, the hope is that at minimum, learners will have a heightened understanding through self-observation of these practices-in-action so they may continue to expand their awareness within their daily lives by embracing contemplative engagement, cultural understanding, critical exploration, collective action, and creative application, making their own unique contributions to each as they apply them to their lives. It is important to note, however, that even though awareness pedagogy as I practice it is based on these five learning awareness practices, I also see awareness pedagogy as something each teacher can tailor to their own unique commitments. Thus, instructors are also invited to create their own learning awareness practices within this system.
- Because awareness is vital for action, within awareness pedagogy, central to the embodiment and enactment of whatever living-our-learning-awareness practices are in play, is understanding the role of difference, including how it is constructed within communicative interactions, especially the role it plays in conflict (e.g., moments when our differences are interpreted as a communicative obstacle), including how constructions of difference can serve to marginalize and reinforce oppression in one's daily words and actions. Central questions for exploration in this realm include: How can we better understand and negotiate our differences *and* how can individuals and communities teach and learn to engage more peacefully, nonviolently, and compassionately with each other to create more humane and just worlds together? Further, how might we practice a style of communication which creates less suffering in our own life as well as the lives of others?
- Exploring the above questions and pursuing grading justice within awareness pedagogy feedback, including self-assessment and self-advocacy, serves as the primary means of communicating one's awareness of each

living-our-learning-awareness practices, in conversation with the unique learning content and context in play. This means that each assignment is assessed by the learner first, then responded to by the instructor, who seeks to assist the learner in deepening their awareness (not evaluating their current level of it). At the conclusion of the course, both co-learners meet one-on-one to discuss the collaborative learning process, including any and all awareness that has been cultivated as a result. For those instructors that are required to enter a formal grade into the learner's record at this time, the learner and instructor then determine the grade based on this conversation, in consultation with the self-assessments (and other feedback processes) created throughout the course. As previously discussed, elements that can help shape the determination of the final letter might include group consensus surrounding specific course policies (e.g., attendance, disruption, engagement, and so on).

In the spirit of these commitments, I return to where we started, reflecting on Krishnamurti's words—the seeds planted to open the space for awareness pedagogy to bloom, wherein I first presented awareness as an idea, practice, and or process involving our whole presence and attention, which is linked to both our capacity and willingness to build understanding but also to show care for learning and change, giving our whole being to the effort. As I previously stated, I cannot imagine an idea that better captures my sentiments about learning as well as the transformative possibilities of teaching and studying communication.

Within this view, he also contends, "There is no guide, no teacher, no authority. This is only you—your relationship with others and with the world—there is nothing else" (1969, 14). In claiming this, he urges us to stop and try living with ourselves so we become our own teacher, which requires a radical transformation of how we act in the world because it asks us to forget all that we have come to believe about ourselves so we can start fresh as if we knew nothing, re-learning to investigate and observe ourselves together. By letting go of the fear of failure (or certainty) so we can embrace the messiness, ambiguity, and complexity of life, he encourages us to question our conditioning, looking at life with new eyes, not agreeing or disagreeing, but attempting to understand ourselves in interaction with the world, stating:

> Most of us walk through life inattentively, reacting unthinkingly according to the environment in which we have been brought, and such reactions create only further bondage, further conditioning, but the moment you give your total attention to your conditioning you will see you are free from the past completely, that it falls away from you (Krishnamurti 1969, 28).

He offers the example of this by discussing an oak tree, suggesting that when we look at the tree, we immediately label it a "tree," perhaps even an "oak tree." In doing so, we call on our learning to name and categorize the tree. As a result, Krishnamurti contends that we never actually see the tree; we only see our interpretation of the tree. Similarly, once we assign a letter grade or numeric value to learning, we come to see the learner through this interpretation of their "learning." The more awareness we can build regarding grading injustices, the closer all of us as co-learners can come to embodying and enacting grading justice together one conversation at a time. To support this effort, As De Mello (1992) contends, we must challenge ourselves to question our most deeply held beliefs and assumptions about life. As a teacher, I find this to be particularly important within my teaching and learning life. In his words, "That's what learning is all about . . . unlearning almost everything you've been taught. A willingness to unlearn, to listen" (18). This is the purpose of awareness pedagogy—a process of (un)learning as a tool to build awareness, challenge injustices, engaging "ungrading" practices to create learning (and grading) justice.

NOTES

1. At my current institution, our department has adopted a variation of these learning awareness practices as student learning outcomes for our overarching communication studies major.

REFERENCES

Berila, Beth. 2016. *Integrating Mindfulness into Anti-Oppression Pedagogy: Social Justice in Higher Education.* New York: Routledge.

Blinne, Kristen C. 2016. "Applying (Com)passion in the Academy: A Calling . . . A Vow . . . A Plea . . . A Manifesto." *Departures in Critical Qualitative Research* 5 (1): 92–101. https://doi.org/10.1525/dcqr.2016.5.1.92.

Blinne, Kristen C. 2014a. "Performing Critical Pedagogy Through Fireside Chats." *International Journal of Critical Pedagogy* 5 (2): 131–144. http://libjournal.uncg.edu/ijcp/article/view/556.

Blinne, Kristen C. 2014b. "Awakening to Lifelong Learning: Contemplative Pedagogy *As* Compassionate Engagement." *Radical Pedagogy* 11 (2): 1–30. https://www.academia.edu/8134359/Awakening_to_Lifelong_Learning_Contemplative_Pedagogy_as_Compassionate_Engagement.

Blinne, Kristen C. 2013. "Start with the Syllabus: HELPing Students Learn Through Class Content Collaboration." *College Teaching* 61 (2): 41–43. https://doi.org/10.1080/87567555.2012.708679.

Bloom, Benjamin S. 1968. "Learning for Mastery." *Evaluation Comment* 1 (2): 1–12. https://eric.ed.gov/?id=ED053419.

Blommaert, Jan, and Piia Varis. 2013. "Enough is Enough: The Heuristics of Authenticity in Superdiversity." In *Linguistic Superdiversity in Urban areas: Research Approaches,* edited Joana Duarte and Ingrid Gogolin, 143–159. Amsterdam: John Benjamins Publishing Company.

Blum, Susan D. 2017. "Ungrading." *Inside Higher Ed.* Accessed December 12, 2019. https://www.insidehighered.com/advice/2017/11/14/significant-learning-benefits-getting-rid-grades-essay.

Bower, Joe. 2010a. Replacing Grading. Accessed December 15, 2019. http://www.joebower.org/2010/02/replacing-grading.html. http://www.joebower.org/2010/03/detoxing-students-from-grade-use.html.

Bower, Joe. 2010b. Detoxing Students from Grade-Use. Accessed December 15, 2019.http://www.joebower.org/2010/03/detoxing-students-from-grade-use.html.

Brown, Juanita, Isaacs, David, and the World Café Community. 2005. *The World Café: Shaping Our Futures Through Conversations That Matter.* San Francisco, CA: Berrett-Koehler Publishers, Inc.

Cox, Keni B. 2011. "Putting Classroom Grading on the Table: A Reform in Progress." *American Secondary Education* 40 (1): 67–87. https://www.jstor.org/stable/23100415.

Del Gandio, Jason, and Anthony J. Nocella. 2014. *Educating for Action: Strategies to Ignite Social Justice*. Gabriola Island, BC, Canada: New Society Publishers.

De Mello, Anthony. 1992. *Awareness: The Perils and Opportunities of Reality*. New York: Doubleday.

Fassett, Deanna L., and John T. Warren. 2007. *Critical Communication Pedagogy*. Thousand Oaks, CA: Sage.

Fassett, Deanna L., and John T. Warren. 2008. "Pedagogy of Relevance: A Critical Communication Pedagogy Agenda for the 'Basic' Course." *Basic Communication Course Annual* 20 (6): 1–34. https://ecommons.udayton.edu/bcca/vol20/iss1/6.

Feldman, Joe. C. 2018. *Grading for Equity: What It Is, Why It Matters, and How It can Transform Schools and Classrooms*. Thousand Oaks, CA: Sage.

Foss, Sonja K., Domenico, Mary E., and Karen A. Foss. 2013. *Gender Stories: Negotiating Identity in a Binary World*. Long Grove, IL: Waveland Press.

Frey, Lawrence R., and Kristen C. Blinne. 2017. "Activism and Social Justice." In *Encyclopedia of Communication Research Methods*, edited by Mike Allen. Thousand Oaks, CA: Sage. https://dx.doi.org/10.4135/9781483381411.n6.

Frey, Lawrence, and David Palmer, eds. 2014. *Teaching Communication Activism: Communication Education for Social Justice*. New York: Hampton Press.

Frey, Lawrence R., Pearce, W. Barnett, Pollock, Mark A., Artz, Lee, and Bren A.O. Murphy. 1996. "Looking for Justice in All the Wrong Places: On a Communication Approach to Social Justice. *Communication Studies* 47 (1–2): 110–127. https://doi.org/10.1080/10510979609368467.

Grace, Fran. 2011. "Learning as a Path, Not a Goal: Contemplative Pedagogy—Its Principles and Practices." *Teaching Theology and Religion* 14 (2): 99–124. https://doi.org/10.1111/j.1467-9647.2011.00689.x.

Guskey, Thomas R. 2000. "Grading Policies that Work Against Standards . . . and How to Fix Them." *NASSP Bulletin* 84 (620): 20–29. https://doi.org/10.1177/019263650008462003.

Guskey, Thomas R. 2001. "Helping Standards Make the Grade." *Educational Leadership, 59*(1), 20–27. http://www.ascd.org/publications/educational-leadership/sept01/vol59/num01/Helping-Standards-Make-the-Grade.aspx.

Guskey, Thomas R. 2010. "Lessons of Mastery Learning." *Educational Leadership,* 68 (2): 52–57. http://www.ascd.org/publications/educational-leadership/oct10/vol68/num02/Lessons-of-Mastery-Learning.aspx.

Guskey, Thomas R., and Jane M. Bailey. 2001. *Developing Grading and Reporting Systems for Student Learning*. Thousand Oaks, CA: Corwin.

Human Restoration Project. "Ungrading Resources." Accessed January 15, 2020. https://www.humanrestorationproject.org/ungrading-resources

Hunt, Lester H., ed. 2008. *Grade Inflation: Academic Standards in Higher Education*. New York: SUNY Press.

Kaufman, Peter. 2017. "Critical Contemplative Pedagogy." *Radical Pedagogy* 14 (1), 1–20. https://www.academia.edu/31097956/Critical_Contemplative_Pedagogy.

Kohn, Alfie. 2011. "The Case Against Grades: When Schools Cling to Letter and Number Ratings, Students Get Stuck in a System that Undermines Learning."

Educational Leadership 69 (3): 28–33. https://www.alfiekohn.org/article/case-grades/.

Kohn, Alfie. 1999. "From Degrading to De-Grading." High School Magazine. https://www.alfiekohn.org/article/degrading-de-grading/?print=pdf.

Krishnamurti, Jiddu. 1969. *Freedom from the Known.* San Francisco: Harper.

Lalley, James P., and J. Ronald Gentile. 2009. "Classroom Assessment and Grading to Ensure Mastery." *Theory Into Practice* 48 (1): 28–35. http://dx.doi.org/10.1080/00405840802577577.

Lugones, Maria. 1994. "Playfulness, 'World'-Travelling, and Loving." In *The Woman that I Am: The Literature and Culture of Contemporary Women of Color*, 626–638. New York: St. Martin's Press.

Marzano, Robert J. 2000. "Transforming Classroom Grading." Alexandria, VA: Association for Supervision and Curriculum Development. http://www.ascd.org/publications/books/100053.aspx.

Miller, John P. 2006. *Educating for Wisdom and Compassion: Creating Conditions for Timeless Learning.* Thousand Oaks, CA: Corwin Press.

Nicol, David J., and Debra Macfarlane-Dick. 2006. "Formative Assessment and Self-Regulated Learning: A Model and Seven Principles of Good Feedback Practice. *Studies in Higher Education* 31 (2): 199–218. https://doi.org/10.1080/03075070600572090.

Owens, Kate. 2015. "A Beginner's Guide to Standards Based Grading." *American Mathematical Society.* Accessed January 6, 2020. https://blogs.ams.org/matheducation/2015/11/20/a-beginners-guide-to-standards-based-grading.

Pearce, Kimberly. 2012. "Living into Very Bad News: The Use of CMM as Spiritual Practice." In *The Reflective, Facilitative, and Interpretive Practices of the Coordinated Management of Meaning: Making Lives, Making Meaning*, edited by Catherine Creede, Beth Fisher-Yoshida, and Placida V. Gallego, 277–295. Lanham, MD: Fairleigh Dickinson University Press.

Pearce, W. Barnett. 2007. *Making Social Worlds: A Communication Perspective.* Malden, MA: Blackwell Publishing.

Percell, Jay. 2019. "Democracy in Grading: Practicing What We Preach." *Critical Questions in Education* 10 (3): 180–190. https://academyedstudies.files.wordpress.com/2019/06/percellfinal.pdf.

Percell, Jay. 2014. "Essentially Point-Less: The Influence of Alternative, Non Points-Based Grading on Teachers' Instructional Practices." PhD diss., Illinois State University, 2014, https://ir.library.illinoisstate.edu/etd/196/.

Percell, Jay. 2017. "Lessons from Alternative Grading: Essential Qualities of Teacher Feedback. *The Clearing House: A Journal of Educational Strategies, Issues and Ideas* 9 (4): 1–5. https://doi.org/10.1080/00098655.2017.1304067.

Percell, Jay. 2013. "The Value of a Pointless Education." *Educational Leadership* 71 (4): 1–5. http://www.ascd.org/publications/educational-leadership/dec13/vol71/num04/The-Value-of-a-Pointless-Education.aspx.

Rodriguez, Amardo. 2010. *Revisioning Diversity in Communication Studies.* Leicester, UK: Troubador Publishing Ltd.

Rudick, C. Kyle, Golsan, Kathyrn B., and Kyle Cheesewright. 2017. *Teaching From the Heart: Critical Communication Pedagogy in the Communication Classroom.* San Diego, CA: Cognella Academic Publishing.

Sackstein, Starr. 2015. *Hacking Assessment: 10 Ways to Go Gradeless in a Traditional Grades School.* Cleveland, OH: Times 10 Publications.

Schaef, Sydney. 2016. "What is the Difference Between Competencies and Standards." *ReDesign.* Blog. Accessed December 19, 2019. https://www.redesignu.org/what-difference-between-competencies-and-standards.

Schwalbe, Michael. 1998. *The Sociologically Examined Life: Pieces of the Conversation.* Mountain View, CA: Mayfield Publishing Company.

Simpson, Jennifer S. 2014. "Communication Activism Pedagogy: Theoretical Frameworks, Central Concepts, and Challenges." In *Teaching Communication Activism: Communication Education for Social Justice,* edited by Lawrence Frey and David Palmer, 77–103. New York: Hampton Press.

Teachers Going Gradeless. Accessed January 5, 2020. https://www.teachersgoinggradeless.com/.

Teacher Throwing Out Grades. Facebook Group. Accessed January 5, 2020. https://www.facebook.com/groups/teachersthrowingoutgrades/.

Tomar, Dave. n.d. "Eliminating the Grading System in College: The Pros and Cons." *The Quad.* Accessed January 9, 2020. https://thebestschools.org/magazine/eliminating-grading-system-college-pros-cons/.

Townsley, Matt. 2014. "What is the Difference Between Standards-Based Grading (or Reporting) and Competency-Based Education?" *CompetencyWorks Blog,* November 11, 2014. Accessed December 23, 2019. https://aurora-institute.org/cw_post/what-is-the-difference-between-standards-based-grading/.

Zajonc, Arthur. 2006. "Love and Knowledge: Recovering the Heart of Learning Through Contemplation. *Teachers College Record* 108 (9): 1742–1759. http://www.arthurzajonc.org/publications/love-and-knowledge-recovering-the-heart-of-learning/.

Chapter Nine

Resisting the Detrimental Effects of Grade Inflation on University Faculty and Students through Critical Communication Pedagogy

David H. Kahl, Jr.

Many university faculty are dedicated to holistic student development, something many see as the primary goal of a university education (Kuh 2018). To accomplish this, educators challenge themselves with the goal of "educating the whole student, by addressing one's intellectual, social, emotional, ethical, physical, and spiritual attributes" (Kuh 2018, 52). Although the means by which to reach this goal differ, one constant is the need to maintain rigor and high academic standards in courses. Rigor can be defined in various ways and include the following: rigor can relate to the number of hours students must work to complete assignments (Arum and Roksa 2011); rigor can be operationalized as giving students large quantities of work (Campbell, Dortch, and Burt 2018); rigor can relate to providing students with material that is intellectually challenging. Finally, the assessment, or grading practices that instructors use in the classroom, can be utilized in ways that ensure rigor.

While the definition of rigorous grading practices can be operationalized in various ways, rigor in grading typically means that students earn high grades for high quality work and, similarly, students earn low grades for substandard work. Most faculty purport to maintain rigor in their classes that challenges students to think critically about subject matter and to apply course content in their studies and their lives. However, despite university faculty's efforts to maintain rigor and high expectations in their classrooms, that rigor tends to correlate less and less to students' grades. Specifically, students' grades continue to rise. Examining this problem of grade inflation from a historical perspective provides useful context. In the 1960s, 15 percent of university students received "As" and 35 percent received "Cs." By 2008, 43 percent received "As" and only 16 percent received "Cs" (Rojstaczer 2015). Further, as of 2008, approximately 90 percent of students received either an "A" or a "B" in their courses (Gray 2008). Research indicates that the issue of grade

297

increases is not due to students' gaining a better grasp of subject matter. To illustrate, 45 percent of university students who completed their first two years of coursework did not display a significant increase in important cognitive abilities such as analytic reasoning, critical thinking, or writing abilities. Additionally, 36 percent of students did not display any significant increase in these abilities after four years (Arum and Roksa 2011). Despite research indicating that students are not learning more/to higher levels, their grades are increasing.

Research shows that grade inflation is occurring on college campuses. However, there are various reasons that this troubling trend is occurring. The reality below the surface of the grade-inflation problem reveals that surreptitious forces exist that actively work to counter faculty's aspirations for holistic development and high standards. The primary force is the ubiquitous pressure of neoliberalism on the university and the students.

OVERVIEW OF THE CHAPTER

In this chapter, I will begin by discussing three aspects of neoliberalism: (1) how neoliberalism inculcates students to expect high grades for all completed work, (2) how neoliberalism influences universities to promote grade inflation, and (3) how neoliberal hegemony has deleterious effects for tenure-track faculty and the increasing number of contingent faculty who do not acquiesce to the pressure to inflate students' grades. Then, I will analyze these three aspects through the lens of critical communication pedagogy (CCP) and will offer ways in which faculty can resist the neoliberal pressure to engage in grade inflation. Following the tenets of CCP, I will discuss how instructors can challenge students to learn about the neoliberal system which has inculcated them to believe that profit, success, and individualism are the only measures of a meaningful life. I will also discuss how instructors can help students understand the importance of high academic standards. Overall, I will argue that in order for tenure-track and contingent faculty to be able to resist the pressure to inflate grades, instructors should dialogue with students regarding neoliberal ideology that promotes grade inflation. In so doing, students will begin to learn to engage in resistance behaviors to neoliberal power structures that marginalize them.

NEOLIBERALISM

Neoliberalism, the hyper-capitalistic state of our current economy, has existed since the 1970s (Kahl 2017). It has been described as "dominant and pervasive economic policy agenda of our times" (Venugopal 2015, 165) and "the most successful ideology in world history" (Anderson 2000, 17) because of its ability and success in inculcating the general public to reject the social contract in favor of means of individualism. Neoliberalism's rejection of any social safety net has duped the public to embrace policies that result in wealth creation for an infinitesimal percentage of society because the public naively believes that they have the ability to also reach the heights of economic stratification.

Universities, instructors, and students are not immune to the reaches of neoliberalism. Because of its unrelenting focus on profit over people (Chomsky 1999), neoliberalism teaches undergraduate students that personal growth is not necessary. Undergraduate students have been inculcated to resist the holistic education model that is/was the bedrock of the American university. Therefore, they tend not to think in terms of how rigorous assessments can benefit their affective and cognitive development, nor do they consider how they can use their knowledge to become civically engaged members of society. Instead, their focus is on what they need to do to earn a favorable grade (Draeger, del Prado Hill, and Mahler 2015). Instructors must face the challenge of teaching students who believe that learning to think critically is unimportant and that success and individualism are the only measures of a meaningful life. Because of this, the university is no longer a place in which students collectively gather to learn, think, be challenged, grow through failure, and build character. Neoliberalism has changed the landscape of higher education.

Neoliberal Effects on Students

Rather, neoliberalism has inculcated students to believe that they are paying for a credential (a bachelor's degree). The institutionalization of belief tells them that not only should they be trained for a job (not taught to critique ideas and the power that supports hegemony) but also that they should receive renumeration for their tuition dollars and work in the form of high grades. Students now largely believe that they university is merely a business from which they purchase a product—a degree. This producer-consumer mindset has created a deleterious situation for both students and faculty. Because students believe that they are purchasing a degree, they expect high grades to accompany their purchase. To them, high grades, coupled with their degree, are the academic currency with which they purchase a career. This student-as-consumer model has negative effects for learning: "The business model obscures the responsibility and involvement required by students in the learning process. Good students are responsible for reflecting critically, exploring ambiguities, and giving and receiving feedback. A customer does not have responsibilities beyond the economic" (Davis 2011, 88).

Neoliberal Effects on Universities

Exacerbating the problem of grade inflation is also the intense pressure that universities now feel to recruit and retain students. Universities have become increasingly reliant on tuition dollars as state funding for public colleges has dwindled (Woodhouse 2015). Neoliberal lawmakers perpetuate the fallacious belief that universities produce left-leaning students who are taught to challenge the free-market system which creates vast inequalities for Americans. For this reason, neoliberal ideology has influenced the public in such a way that it has changed its perception of universities and their role in society, most notably among conservatives. To illustrate, 58 percent of conservative voters, those who are more closely aligned with neoliberal principles, now believe that universities are detrimental to society (Fingerhut 2017). State governments, in turn, purportedly follow their constituents' wishes, continue to slash state support for their own universities. These changes have forced universities to do all that they can to lure students to their campuses and remain attractive to student "consumers." Many of these recruitment efforts for tuition dollars are overt and visible—student activity centers, lazy rivers at institutions such as the Universities of Alabama, Iowa, Missouri, and at LSU (Koch 2018), and even pets being allowed to live with students in dorms (Bruce 2019). Universities also exact pressures on their faculties to make the learning process amenable to tuition-paying students. As consumer-driven organizations, universities understand that students who receive higher grades are more likely to express satisfaction with the university and are less likely to transfer or drop out. Thus, faculty feel pressure to give students what they believe they are paying for—high grades. When students are treated as consumers, universities need to keep them satisfied. Thus, the neoliberal influence on the university has created a situation in which grade inflation is an expectation because negative evaluations of faculty equate to negative evaluations of the university.

Neoliberal Effects on Faculty

Faculty are also not immune to the reaches of neoliberalism and are placed in a precarious position because of this prevalent ideology. Neoliberalism places internal and external pressure upon faculty to reduce the rigor of their courses and/or artificially inflate the grades that students earn. When faculty and programs resist this model, they are punished. For example, when humanities departments at Wellesley College attempted to make a B+ the average grade in their courses, those courses suffered an enrollment loss of one fifth, and departments which placed this cap lost approximately one third of their majors (Nichols 2017). Although all faculty feel the pressure to conform to this neoliberally driven practice, it is especially problematic for tenure-track, non-tenure track, and other contingent faculty because their continued employment is, often to a large extent, dependent of student ratings of teaching effectiveness.

The grade-as-commodity model negatively affects all faculty, with some feeling the pressure to inflate grades more than others. For tenure-track faculty, teaching comprises a predetermined percentage of their work. This percentage is dependent on the type of institution at which they are employed. Thus, teaching ratings for faculty at a R1 institution, in which research is their primary concern, is less important than for faculty employed at a small liberal arts college, in which teaching is the primary job requirement. This situation is bad enough for tenure-track faculty; it is worse for contingent faculty. Contingent faculty, which the American Association of University Professors (AAUP) defines as "full-time non-tenure track, part-time, and graduate student employees" (2017, n.p.), now comprise 70 percent of all university faculty. This number has risen dramatically since 1975 (AAUP 2017).

Neoliberal forces have played no small role in the demise of tenure by instilling a corporatist ethic in which devalues employees. At many universities, pedagogical performance is measured almost exclusively by students through teaching evaluations. The performance-driven goals of the neoliberal project demand that consumers (students) evaluate frequently the performance of those providing them with a product (instructors). This practice is replete with problems—namely that students are not pedagogical experts. The practice of student evaluations, however, can cause them to believe that they are. The neoliberal pressures placed upon universities create a situation in which students "devalue respect for expertise" by evaluating the experts that educate them "as though they are peers" (Nichols 2017, 97). In doing so, "students (rate) professional men and women as though they're reviewing a movie or commenting on a pair of shoes" (Nichols 2017, 97). Thus, "the over-reliance on student evaluations as a metric for teaching effectiveness . . . generates a host of problems for contingent faculty whose performance reviews often include nothing else" (McConnell 2019). Often, students base their evaluations on the grades that they receive. Because of these pressures, faculty often feel that they must acquiesce to the (necessary) lowering of grading standards because they are directly evaluated by their students in the form of ratings of instruction.

O'Halloran and Gordon (2014) describe this dysfunctional model that treats students as customers. Under this model, professors are stripped of their

302   *David H. Kahl, Jr.*

role as subject matter experts who have studied tirelessly in their disciplines, attained advanced degrees, published research, and have served on editorial boards and as peer reviewers of others' scholarship. They have then taken this knowledge and translated it into effective pedagogy. Through the use of student evaluations, however, all of the expertise that accomplished faculty have accumulated becomes devalued. Through this model, expert faculty feel the institutional gaze of the colleges and universities in which they work that demand rigor, while concomitantly, encourage grade inflation to bolster student recruitment and retention. This set of circumstances places faculty in a precarious and untenable situation as they are reduced to being employees of the students who are allowed to evaluate faculty's performance and competence.

RESPONDING TO GRADE INFLATION PRESSURES THROUGH CRITICAL COMMUNICATION PEDAGOGY

Faculty are marginalized by neoliberal forces which reduce their vital roles as educators to that of merely facilitators who must reward students simply for the act of doing work, not for the quality of the work. If they do not, they are likely to be evaluated negatively by students. In fact, the grades that instructors give students significantly impact the teaching evaluations that they receive (Johnson 2013). Clearly, the neoliberal university has placed faculty in a precarious position regarding the relationship between grade inflation, student evaluations, and continued employment. Critical communication pedagogy (CCP) serves as an important form of resistance to these deleterious practices. Working at the intersections of pedagogy, critical scholarship, and communication, CCP functions to make students and teachers aware of power that exists in the classroom and in society (Fassett and Warren 2007). CCP provides a critical pedagogical lens by which instructors can work collectively with students to resist oppressive systems and, together, work toward the amelioration of hegemony in the classroom and in society. CCP is built on the Freirean (1970) principles of conscientization and dialogue. However, CCP is unique in that it focuses on the study of communicative messages. Specifically, CCP seeks to understand how communication is used by hegemonic forces to oppress and also how it can be used in counter-hegemonic ways to emancipate (Kahl 2015). Therefore, it places much importance on the analysis of messages to uncover ways in which power communicates.

In the present case, CCP provides faculty a means by which to resist the neoliberal pressure to pacify student consumers. CCP challenges faculty and students to communicate about ways in which they are being surreptitiously subjugated by neoliberalism. CCP invites communication regarding

Resisting the Detrimental Effects of Grade Inflation   303

movement toward the traditional mission of the university, which involves creating whole students, students who learn to be concerned not only with their own personal growth, but also with civic engagement by learning to act as critically engaged members of society (Kahl 2014). In doing so, CCP involves educating "students to be willing and able to engage the relationship between equality and social justice as fundamental to public life, and provide the conditions for educators to connect their teaching to broader social issues" (Giroux 2009, 669). Thus, for change to occur, resistance to neoliberal forces must include communicative interactions with students in the form of dialogue in order to reframe the idea of what grading should accomplish.

Implementing CCP to Facilitate Incremental Change

In order for instructors to resist the intertwined issues of neoliberalism, grade inflation, and student evaluations, instructors should engage in dialogue with students about these issues. Dialogic interaction is a crucial component in the quest to create a space in which mutual understanding and change can occur. Presenting dialogue as a direct response to hegemony in a learning environment, Freire (1970) views dialogue as horizontal communication in which instructors and students become co-learners in a pedagogical environment. Dialogue challenges instructors and students to interact regarding ideas that they have not previously considered, ideas they find uncomfortable, and ideas that conflict with their previously held beliefs. Specifically, dialogue, as a liberatory practice, allows interlocutors to be vulnerable by sharing their thoughts, feelings, emotions, and ideas about a topic. In this way, dialogue allows all involved to engage in active leaning and refine/change their deep-seeded ideologies and (possibly) develop a shared understanding that can lead to meaningful change.

My goal here is not to be prescriptive in how dialogue should look. Instead, I will lay out a vision for what they could entail. Unlike critical intellectuals who propose radical change, my belief is that change occurs by working at the grassroots level. In this case, I advocate for incremental change to begin in the classroom. In order for change to begin to occur to the neoliberal system of grading and evaluation, instructors should hold open and productive dialogue with their students to help them to understand the 1) the ways in which neoliberalism negatively affects students and 2) the ways in which neoliberalism negatively affects faculty, especially those working off the tenure track.

Dialoguing about neoliberalism's effects on students. First, to assist students in understanding the effects that neoliberalism has on them, instructors and students should engage in dialogue about the varied and nuanced issues that are involved in grading, student expectations, and faculty evaluation. In this sense, interlocutors are engaging in discussions about grading justice. This can be a difficult topic for instructors to discuss, namely because it opens them up to scrutiny regarding their grading practices and shows students that the practice of grading is actually more subjective process than many would care to admit. However, instructors do not have to hide this issue from students. Rather, open dialogue about what grading justice means for their class is important in creating a space in which this difficult issue can be brought to light. In this way, their dialogue provides students and instructors a means by which they can openly discuss what grading justice is and would look like if implemented in the classroom. Instructors and students can engage in discussions of what rigor means for their class, what instructors expect from students in regarding quality of work, what students believe reasonable expectations are, and what the effects that grade inflation, both positive and negative, have on instructors and students. The following paragraphs present a means of facilitating such dialogue.

Following the tenets of CCP, instructors can engage in dialogue about reframing the idea of grading. This dialogue can be initiated by utilizing Freire's (1970) notion of conscientization. Students should discuss the seemingly basic, but complex idea of what a grade symbolizes. Instructors and students need to understand each other regarding the notion of what a grade reflects and what requirements are necessary in order to achieve a certain grade. Because students have been inculcated to equate a high grade with mere participation, classes can have discussions about why they hold this belief and why such a belief will not benefit them in their lives after college. The following questions can help guide this dialogue.

1. Do professors maintain rigor and high standards in your classes? Do they grade accordingly? Why or why not?
2. Why does grade inflation exist?
3. What are the negative effects of grade inflation for you?
4. Do you earn high grades for quality work? What requirements are needed to earn a high grade?
5. How are you cheated when they are not held to high academic standards in a class?
6. Is an inflated grade the same as reaching competency in a subject?
7. Do you think that inflated grades accurately reflect your learning of course material?
8. Do rewarding careers come only to students who receive As?

Additionally, not all students are affected by grade inflation in the same ways. For example, students from privileged backgrounds have financial resources available to them, allowing them to afford academic tutors and other support systems that are not available to marginalized students. Because these students have resources in place that promote success, they demand success. Thus, grade inflation becomes a means by which universities pacify these students while cultivating satisfied consumers. As a result, these privileged students (consumers) and their families are more likely to become donors to the schools. Alternately, marginalized students, who are not the focus of universities' attention, may not be the recipients of inflated grades. These students who do not possess privileged backgrounds become further marginalized and cannot push back against another neoliberal practice that subjugates them.

Dialoguing about neoliberalism's effects on faculty. Second, to assist students in understanding the effects that neoliberalism has on faculty, instructors and students should engage in dialogue about student evaluations of instructors and the importance of evaluations for faculty job security and raises. These dialogues are important because students must understand the neoliberal university and the ways in which it forces students to act as arbiters of quality pedagogy. Many students are largely unaware that their evaluations hold such power over (some) faculty members. These discussions can help students to comprehend the plight of contingent faculty and to help them understand the power that they possess through their evaluations of teachers regarding tenure, raises, and continued employment. The following questions can help guide this dialogue.

1. Have you ever given a professor a low evaluation solely because you received a low grade in their class?
2. Are you aware that student evaluations are connected to professor job security, raises, and tenure?
3. Should the neoliberal university give students the power to evaluate professors?
4. Do you believe that students have the expertise to evaluate pedagogical performance?
5. When professors have high academic standards, does that affect how you evaluate the professor?

Although student evaluations are often cast as nefarious, engagement in the dialogues presented above help to remind all involved that students, just like instructors, are pawns in the neoliberal project that serves to subjugate all involved. Discussions about power, grade inflation, and student evaluations will not eliminate the hegemony that the neoliberal university holds over faculty. Even though students may be receptive to knowledge and dialogue about neoliberalism's hegemonic hold over the modern university, these discussions will not, on a macro level, eradicate the overreliance on teacher evaluations nor will it eliminate the pressure to inflate grades. However, following CCP, these initial steps provide a starting point for resistance of an inimical system that marginalizes students and faculty alike. These dialogic interactions can result in students beginning to comprehend the connections among grade inflation, student evaluations, and faculty performance. CCP provides a means by which instructors and students can analyze the neoliberal ideology that forces faculty to grade students in ways that are counter to effective pedagogy and learning. These dialogic interactions can lead to a mutual understanding of neoliberal power, the need for high standards, and the recognition of and response to neoliberalism. Doing so has the potential to make incremental steps toward the return to a university that values the development of the whole student.

REFERENCES

American Association of University Professors. 2017. "Trends in the Academic Labor Force, 1975–2015." Accessed December 10, 2019. https://www.aaup.org/sites/default/files/Academic_Labor_Force_Trends_1975-2015.pdf.

Anderson, Perry. 2000. "Renewals." *New Left Review* 1, 5–24. https://newleftreview.org/issues/II1/articles/perry-anderson-renewals.

Arum, Richard, and Josipa Roksa. 2011. *Academically Adrift: Limited Learning on College Campuses.* Chicago, IL: University of Chicago Press.

Bruce, David. 2019. "Pets Welcome this fall at Edinboro University." *Erie Times News,* March 4, 2019. https://www.goerie.com/news/20190304/pets-welcome-this-fall-at-dinboro-university.

Campbell, Corbin M., Dortch, Deniece, and Brian A. Burt. 2018. "Reframing Rigor: A Modern Look at Challenge and Support in Higher Education." *New Directions for Higher Education* 2018, 11–23. https://doi.org/10.1002/he.20267.

Chomsky, Noam. 1999. *Profit Over People.* New York: Seven Stories Press.

Davis, Tracy. 2011. "Have it Your Way U." In *Contested Issues in Student Affairs: Diverse Perspectives and Respectful Dialogue,* edited by Peter M. Magolda and Marcia B. Baxter Magolda. Sterling, VA: Stylus.

Draeger, John, del Prado Hill, Pixita, and Ronnie Mahler. 2015. "Developing a Student Conception of Academic Rigor." *Innovative Higher Education* 40, 215–228. https://link.springer.com/article/10.1007/s10755-014-9308-1.

Fassett, Deanna L., and John T. Warren. 2007. *Critical Communication Pedagogy.* Thousand Oaks, CA: Sage.

Fingerhut, Hannah. 2017. "Republicans Skeptical of Colleges' Impact on U.S., but Most See Benefits for Workforce Preparation." Pew Research Center. July 20, 2017. Accessed December 17, 2019. https://www.pewresearch.org/fact-tank/2017/07/20/republicans-skeptical-of-colleges-impact-on-u-s-but-most-see-benefits-for-workforce-preparation/.

Freire, Paolo. 1970. *Pedagogy of the Oppressed.* (M. B. Ramos, Trans.). New York: Herder and Herder.

Giroux, Henry A. 2009. "Democracy's Nemesis: The Rise of the Corporate University." *Cultural Studies <-> Critical Methodologies* 9, 669–695. https://doi.org/10.1177/1532708609341169.

Gray, H. Joey. 2008. "I'm Present, "A" Please: A Case Study Examining Grading Issues in a Recreational Curriculum." *Journal of Leisure Studies & Recreational Education* 23 (1): 43–60. https://doi.org/10.1080/1937156X.2008.11949609.

Johnson, Valen E. 2013. *Grade Inflation: A Crisis in College Education.* New York, NY: Springer.

Kahl, David H., Jr. 2015. "Analyzing Masculinist Movements: Responding to Antifeminism through Critical Communication Pedagogy." *Communication Teacher* 29 (1): 21–26. https://doi.org/10.1080/17404622.2014.985600.

Kahl, David H., Jr. 2014. "Basic Course Central Student Learning Outcomes: Enhancing the Traditional with the Critical." *Basic Communication Course Annual* 26, 34–43.

Kahl, David H., Jr. 2017. "Envisioning Instructional Communication Research as a Multi-Paradigmatic Response to Neoliberalism's Effect on Instruction." *Communication Education* 66, 481–483. https://doi.org/10.1080/03634523.2017.1341049.

Koch, James V. 2018. "No College Kid Needs a Water Park to Study." *The New York Times.* January 9, 2018. Accessed December 15, 2019. https://www.nytimes.com/2018/01/09/opinion/trustees-tuition-lazy-rivers.html.

Kuh, George. 2018. "Whither Holistic Student Development: It Matters More Today Than Ever. *Change: The Magazine of Higher Learning* 50, 52–57. https://doi.org/10.1080/00091383.2018.1509590.

McConnell, Kathleen F. 2019. "Teaching and Learning in an Age of Precarity: Toward a Pedagogy of the Transitory." *Communication Education* 68, 252–258. https://doi.org/10.1080/03634523.2019.1569248.

Nichols, Tom. 2017. *The Death of Expertise.* New York: Oxford University Press.

O'Halloran, Kim C., and Michael E. Gordon. 2014. "A Synergistic Approach to Turning the Tide of Grade Inflation." *Higher Education* 68, 1005–1023.

Rojstaczer, Stuart. 2015. "National Trends in Grade Inflation, American Colleges and Universities." Accessed December 15, 2019. http://www.gradeinflation.com.

Venugopal, Rajesh. 2015. "Neoliberalism as Concept." *Economy and Society* 44, 165–187. https://doi.org/10.1080/03085147.2015.1013356.

Woodhouse, Kellie. 2015. "Public Colleges' Revenue Shift." *Insider Higher Ed.* April 13, 2015. https://www.insidehighered.com/news/2015/04/13/report-shows-public-higher-educations-reliance-tuition.

Chapter Ten

Rate My Performance, or Just Sing Along

A Critical Look at Student Evaluations of Teaching

Summer R. Cunningham

To begin, I invite you to consider a song, a song comprised (almost) entirely of real excerpts from my student teaching evaluations.[1] Actually, can I ask you to sing it? I think it will be more fun that way. Just use the lyrics below and sing to the tune of Weezer's "Say it Ain't So."

SAY IT AIN'T SO (A SONG ABOUT STUDENT TEACHING EVALUATIONS)

[Intro]
Oh yeah
All right.
Feels good.
That's a lie.

[Verse 1]
I just want to thank you for giving me the chance
Simply to pass your class
Let's GIVE THIS WOMAN A FUCKING RAISE

[Interlude]
Amazing Women [sic]
She knows her shit
Teaches her shit
Kids learn the shit

309

310   *Summer R. Cunningham*

[Verse 2]
This one has pictures of some stick figures
Under the sun, Dr. C and me
I'm sure she'll know what that means?

[Chorus]
Say it ain't so a-woah-a-woah
My job can't be dependent on this?
Say it ain't so a-woah-a-woah
When we know that they are so biased.

[Verse 3]
I feel this instructor is good however
That's just now how I was raised
Well, this class should-be-a-gender-or-a-women's-studies-course-and-not-a communication-class!
It was Gender Comm

[Bridge]
The hardest 100-level class in the history of class
Too complicated, simplize [sic] projects, and we have homework twice a week
Let me tell ya 'bout mah girl Summer, she was kind've a bitch
Too much of a feminist
There's too much tuna in this class.

(Guitar or kazoo solo—imagine the instrument that feels most appropriate to you at this point)

[Chorus]
Say it ain't so a-woah-a-woah
My job can't be dependent on this?
Say it ain't so a-woah-a-woah
When we know that they are so biased.

INTRODUCTION

My friend is caught; my students are caught; I'm caught. Everyone is caught in the same critical grind, giving out and taking in comments designed to say how we are positioned, rated, ranked (Pelias 2000, 222).

Teaching and grading (seemingly) go hand in hand. All of us, okay *most* of us, grew up in an educational system where we were evaluated and assigned grades, and now *most* of us work as educators in a system where we are expected to evaluate and assign grades. Indeed, we evaluate our students regularly, assessing them formatively and summatively, judging the progress of their thinking, and determining if they meet the required learning objectives. We then assign a value to their performance in the form of a letter or a number. What are we grading exactly? Their ability? Their mastery? Their skill at demonstrating they have met a standard? That they can successfully follow directions and are thus compliant? What is the purpose of assessment? Perhaps we are measuring the fullness of their receptacles, which in turn, reflects our supposed effectiveness and successfulness as teachers to fill said containers (Freire 1979/2018). Are we being fair in our assessments? Are our grading practices just or discriminatory?

Indeed, there are myriad reflections, theories, and critiques to be made surrounding student grading and assessment, which is why a volume such as this exists; yet students are not the only ones who are evaluated, often unjustly, in college classrooms. As Pelias (2000) notes, "Judgment permeates the academy" (225). Since the latter part of the twentieth century instructors too have been evaluated, formally—by their students. In this chapter, I contemplate the role of student course evaluations in an educational system that relies heavily on banking and customer service models of education, considering how student and teacher evaluations might work in tandem to reinforce a system that devalues learning, thinking, and human connection in favor of productivity and compliance.

First, a confession: I have been procrastinating about writing this chapter on student evaluations of teaching (SETs), or as they are more rarely but perhaps more accurately referred to, student opinion surveys (SOSs). At my institution, they are called Student Perception of Instruction (SPIs, pronounced "spies").[2] I am procrastinating because reviewing my teaching evaluations makes me anxious.[3] Without fail, no matter how I prepare myself, the prospect of reading my student evaluations is never something I look forward to and rarely something that feels good on the whole. And this year, due to what I believe was a scantron-related error with last fall's completed evaluation forms, the Office of Institutional Assessment and Effectiveness at my college was unable to process the student evaluations via the typical automated method; it all had to be done manually. The manual processing created a delay; thus, I approached this summer with two sets of evaluations, fall and spring, to review at once. Awesome. Double the fun.

I ponder why this process inspires so much dread in me and wonder if there are any faculty out there who truly look forward to receiving their SETs each semester. It is not that I do not want to know what my students' experiences are like. I do. I care about how they feel in my classroom, and I am anxious to see what they have learned, but the numeric responses I receive on my SETs to items like "Overall, this class provided a valuable learning experience" and "Overall, how would you rate the instruction in this course?" does very little to help me meaningfully assess the content of the course I am teaching or to constructively improve my pedagogy. Further, I am pretty sure that items such as "Classes met regularly as scheduled," are just there to remind me that I am teaching in a panopticon where students are exploited to assist the academic disciplinary machine in surveillance; they call them SPIs for a reason.

Perhaps I hesitate to read my course evaluations because even though the majority of my feedback—qualitative and quantitative—is positive, the negative comments seem to stand out and stick with you.[4] There in the middle of all the "This was the best class I took this semester; this shaped the way I viewed life"; "This class really expanded my horizon on what communication means"; even the drawings (yes, for real, drawings) of hearts or of me standing with my students under a shining sun; the irrelevant "Love her hair!"; or those shining beacons of negativity and sexism: "She NEEDS TO GO!!! Save future students unnecissary and stress and agrivation [sic] " or "She was kind've a bitch."

But these are not the only reasons that I feel trepidation when approaching my student evils (I mean, evals, was that a Freudian slip?). It would be one thing (and bad enough) if that kind of bias showed up on course evaluations and teachers merely had to suffer through them, weighing such comments and responses with the fact that students are biased, are happily ignorant of the amount of training and preparation that goes into teaching a single college class, and do not themselves have enough awareness of the subject matter to know what they need to know about it. But it does not end there. Teachers are evaluated by students so that other faculty members and college administrators can use said evaluations to make further evaluations about faculty, evaluations that impact pay, promotion, and continuing employment. It is all very meta.

So, I procrastinate. I write songs using excerpts from my actual teaching evaluations in an attempt to vent and to process the trauma, but/and also to capture the complexity of the fucked-up-ed-ness of the whole process. I also procrastinate by reading and reviewing what others have said or learned about this process. There is actually a lot of research on SETs, and so, like a good academic, I turned to this literature to try and make sense of my experience and my feelings. And while I doubt it is possible to occupy any kind of teaching position in the academy without some awareness of these studies, I do think it is helpful to account for and review some of the major talking points in the conversation. Sooo . . .

LET'S REVIEW, SHALL WE?

Verbalistic lessons, reading requirements, the method for evaluating "knowledge," the distance between the teacher and the taught, the criteria for promotion: everything is this ready-to-wear approach serves to obviate thinking (Freire 1970/2018, 76).

A look into the literature on student evaluation of teaching quickly reveals many flaws in this practice. According to Wolfgang Stroebe (2016), SETs were first used by educational and learning psychologists in the earlier half of the twentieth century for the purpose of helping instructors understand students' perceptions of teaching, and arguably, students' opinions are truly the most major insight provided through this feedback (Hornstein 2017). Nevertheless, over the last century or so, the use of SETs in colleges and universities as a reliable and valid way by which to measure *teaching effectiveness* has steadily increased in popularity and pervasiveness. Indeed, this trend might be less troubling if somewhere along the way the purpose for employing them had not changed over time, moving from a desire to understand our students' perception to using them as a foundation for assessing *"teaching effectiveness"*[5] in which rankings (based on student opinions) are effectively used by administrators to make and/or justify decisions about pay increases, hiring, contract renewal, tenure, promotion, and other related personnel decisions. This practice continues despite the fact that scholars have historically and continually cautioned against employing them in this way (see Arbuckle and Williams 2003; Felton, Mitchell, and Stinson 2004; Hessler et al. 2018; Hornstein 2017; Lawrence 2018; MacNell, Driscoll, and Hunt 2015; Stroebe 2016). It is worth noting that while several if these critiques merely caution against using SETs as the sole measure of teaching effectiveness, some of them explicitly point to the fact that SETs cannot and do not, for many reasons, actually measure or reflect teaching effectiveness (for example, see Hornstein 2017). In what follows, I cover some reasons why it has been argued that SETs should be used cautiously if not discounted altogether.

Bias (is Not Sexy)

As it turns out, the literature shows that our students, not just my students, are biased, probably in all the ways you would imagine and more. For example, in a 2007 study entitled "Fudging the Numbers: Distributing Chocolate Influences Student Evaluations of an Undergraduate Course," Youmans and Benjamin found that students who were offered chocolate during the teaching assessment period tended to give higher evaluations than students who were not. It is probably not surprising then, that ten years later, Hessler et al. (2018) found that giving students cookies while they completed their SETs also resulted in higher ratings. The authors of the latter study note that it was likely the chocolate in the cookies that yielded such a result, but further studies would need to be done to be certain.[6] The common theme here, friends, is chocolate.

But if those studies are not sexy enough for you, perhaps Felton et al.'s (2004) Rate My Professors (RMP) study is more what you are looking for, a study that could have only been conducted back in the good ol' days when RateMyProfessors.com still featured the infamous chili pepper ranking. This study found that if you are attractive, smokin' hot like a chili pepper, your students would be more likely to perceive and rate you as a quality teacher and would also perceive you to be easier (grade-wise). Of course, I use "good ol' days" with sarcasm because, as BethAnn McLaughlin pointed out in the 2018 tweet that eventually led to the sacking of the chili pepper, "Life is hard enough for female professors. Your 'chili pepper' rating of our 'hotness' is obnoxious and utterly irrelevant to our teaching" (Flaherty 2018b). In July of 2018, in response to this tweet and the viral twitter storm that followed, Rate My Professors decided to drop their chili pepper rating. While this is good news overall in terms of potentially averting future sexism and objectification in online reviews, the brief existence of the chili pepper rating did prove useful in that it has helped us to see just how biased students are toward attractive teachers. Though their study looked at web-based student evaluations, Felton et al. (2004) argue that administrators need to consider that in-class teaching assessment surveys are likely also susceptible to types of aesthetic discrimination, which calls their validity into question.

But, can we go back to McLaughlin's tweet for a minute? Indeed, for various reasons "Life is hard enough for female professors," and one of those reasons are biased SETs. MacNell et al. (2015) argue that, "the continued use of student ratings of teaching as a primary means of assessing the quality of an instructor's teaching systematically disadvantages women in academia" (301). Indeed, research demonstrates that students have a particular image in mind when they think "professor" and those who do not fit that image, that is, those who have been historically marginalized in our culture and academic institutions, are more likely to receive lower ratings on student teaching assessments. For example, a 2010 study that looked at RMP ranking at the top twenty-five liberal arts colleges found that minority faculty, particularly Black faculty, were consistently rated lower than White faculty overall (Reid 2010), and a 2009 study at the University of Georgia found that women overall were rated lower than men, with female minority faculty receiving the lowest scores. In the same study, Black faculty received lower ratings than White and other minority faculty (Smith 2010). Smith concludes that, "Black faculty's assertion that their student ratings are lower than any other faculty has been confirmed by the data" (2010, 633). In sum, implicit bias is reflected in SET scores, those already on the margin culturally and within the academy receive lower scores due to this bias, and administrators subsequently use those rankings to make and/or justify personnel decisions and pay in a way that problematically reifies the present inequalities in the academic system by effectively continuing to support institutionalized racism, sexism, and other forms of discrimination.[7]

Anonymity, Hurtful Messages, Bullying

As anyone who has ever read the comments section on a YouTube video or an online news article knows, something terrible happens to *some* people when they have anonymity. Our students are no exception—it happens all over my teaching evaluations. Often when I read my qualitative comments and hear about the feedback that colleagues have received, I wonder if we are just granting free reign for bullying.[8] If we consider the definition of anonymity offered by Jordon (2019),"To be and/or do wrong and be protected against the consequences of the wrong" (42), perhaps we should not be surprised that when students are free to leave their feedback with no repercussions or accountability, we see an onslaught of messages that are racist, (hetero)sexist, ageist, ableist, and just plain mean. Of course, SETs are a mere reflection and perpetuation of our existing social structures. Thus, instead of giving me insight into what was working in my class and what was not, I suppose that what I am getting is insight into the sexism, ageism, racism, and insecurity that is pervasive in our culture. In that sense, perhaps student reviews are not totally invaluable. Nevertheless, it does not feel good. I wonder about the emotional toll some of the comments have, particularly for those already on the margin in the academy. My position as a White, able-bodied, straight-ish and presumably cisgender woman[9] who is not really young anymore but not quite older yet either, gives me a certain amount of privilege in the classroom, and yet without fail every semester I receive comments with blatantly sexist[10] content as well as more generally inappropriate comments about my appearance.[11] I imagine that many of my minoritized and marginalized colleagues receive comments that are easily more inappropriate and damaging.

A study by Carmack and LeFebvre (2019) confirms that I am not alone in feeling emotionally taxed by this process. The authors looked at the emotional impact of hurtful course evaluations and found that instructors commonly experienced negative emotions including sadness, anger, and fear in response to

316   *Summer R. Cunningham*

SETs. The study also found that encountering hurtful messages could thwart an instructor's ability to engage in constructive meaning-making around their SETs. To add to the stress, "instructors [are] not able to reconcile the comments specifically with students, and instead must spend time justifying their evaluation and continued employment in light of the comments" (365). In other words, the process we use for assessment affords no time and space for honest and open dialogue about the comments, which makes it extremely difficult for many instructors to use the feedback constructively. In this study, negative comments instilled a sense of failure for some and many instructors reported experiencing a high amount of stress as a result of hurtful teaching evaluations, particularly when they considered "the potential ramifications of course evaluation comments on instructors' livelihoods" (365), after all, our jobs are often contingent on this feedback. In all, this study suggests that the negative psychological impact is high, which prompts me to wonder what it means that instructors' health and well-being are not part of the equation when administration considers whether or not or how they will use of SETs in their institutions.

Carmack and LeFebvre recommend that positive spaces be created, both inside and outside of the academy, to help instructors process and dialogue about their feedback. I think this is important, I mean, I suppose that one of the outcomes I was hoping for with my song was such dialogue. Nevertheless, I find it problematic and odd that the recommendation is to encourage professors to deal with the negativity. While it is important to advocate for strategies that help people cope with stress, I worry that focusing on such an individualized solution obfuscates a critique of the structural issues that create this stress to begin with.

Misleading and Questionable Values

In Part 1 of their online series titled, "Evaluating Evaluations," for the Berkley Center for Teaching and Learning, Philip Stark and Richard Freshtat (2013) relate the following joke:

> Three statisticians go hunting. They spot a deer. The first statistician shoots; the shot passes a yard to the left of the deer. The second shoots; the shot passes a yard to the right of the deer. The third one yells, "We got it!"

The joke is supposed to illustrate one of the many flaws—the averaging of ordinal data—with the methods used to analyze quantitative teaching feedback. Teaching assessment surveys typically use Likert or other types of ordinal scales for data collection. While I realize that many who are reading this chapter are likely to be familiar with such scales, I think it is worth going into a bit of detail to explain how SET data based on such measurement can be misused when assessing teaching performance.

Variables on an ordinal categorical scale are ordered or ranked in a linear order, but the value between each category is not known or quantifiable. That is because the numbers on such scales do not have a true numeric value but are instead labels for categories. A Likert scale is one of the most common types of ordinal scales and is used to measure attitudes or opinions.[12] For example, the SETs at my institution use a Likert scale that assesses student opinions along a continuum of agreement. A variable in the form of a number is assigned to mark different levels of dis/agreement with a given statement (e.g., 1, 2, 3, 4 stand for *strongly disagree, disagree, agree, strongly agree,* respectively). In response to the statement "The instructor was well-prepared for class," a student is able to indicate how much they agree or disagree with that particular statement. While this numerical order might meaningfully suggest that a rating of 4 ("strongly agree") is better than a rating of a 2 ("disagree") and definitely better than a rating of 1 ("strongly disagree"), this scale cannot account for or measure a quantifiable distance between *strongly agree* and *agree*. On an ordinal scale, the actual value between the intervals is not known, thus, averaging such data becomes problematic.

Averages are not the only misleading aspects of quantitative scores on teaching assessments. Low response rates and low sample sizes can return data that are not statistically significant or truly representative of the opinion of the class, nor would it be reasonable, from a statistical perspective, to compare such scores across departments and campuses, particularly if we also consider that the content and requirements for many classes and subjects are simply incommensurable (see Stroebe 2016). Yet, these numbers are too often treated as though they are reliable and such comparisons often happen.[13] In short, even without the bias quotient, SETs as a form of measuring teaching effectiveness or even student opinion are quite ineffective. In short, you cannot shoot a deer with an average, but you can wound an instructor with your sloppy statistics.

Grade Inflation, Rigor, Thinking, and Learning

A final common theme I came across while reading the literature on course evaluations were discussions about the relationship between course evaluations and grade inflation, loss of academic rigor, and negative impact on student learning. For example, in a survey of the literature on SET and learning outcomes, Stroebe (2016) cites a number of studies that show a negative correlation between high course evaluation ratings and student performance

318   *Summer R. Cunningham*

in subsequent semesters. Stroebe also argues that "grading leniency is a major cause of grade inflation" and notes that leniency is frequently used as a "strategy to 'buy' positive teaching evaluations in exchange for assigning good grades without asking for great time investment" (2016, 810). Because instructors know that their future employment and livelihood are tied to high course evaluations, there is a great deal of pressure to produce high ratings. Further, instructors are also aware of students' preferences for less demanding coursework and high grades and act on these biases to protect their livelihood (Lawrence 2018). As Stroebe (2016) aptly notes, "There are many ways by which top ratings can be achieved and not all of them will also result in top learning" (814).

Recapitulation

Okay, so to recap, my review has yielded the following takeaways: Students like chocolate, easy As, and generally prefer their professors to be young (able-bodied, straight, cis-gendered) men who are sexy. Additionally, teaching evaluations can be negative and hurtful. Thus, teaching evaluations impact teachers emotionally and professionally (disproportionately depending on one's privilege/social status), and instead of helping instructors strengthen, improve, or develop their pedagogy, often result in paralysis and/or rejection of the feedback, and in other cases, a lowering of standards and rigor in order to appease students and earn higher evaluations. And do not forget, just because we like numbers and they are convenient, does not mean that they can accurately or actually measure things like teaching effectiveness.

Admittedly, my literature review was not exhaustive, but it was exhausting. I could have continued reading because there is plenty of material to peruse, but the overarching themes are clear and what it boils down to is that for the last three decades, academics have made countless studies and arguments that demonstrate the biases, statistical flaws, and structural inequalities connected to SET practices. Yet those arguments do not seem to matter; we are still doing this.[14] But why?

Something was missing from the arguments and criticisms I was reading, just like something was missing from my song. After reading through this literature, I found I had more questions than answers:

- Why are SETs, particularly the quantitative portions, still used pervasively as a means of gauging teacher effectiveness for the purpose of personnel decisions?
- More concerning, besides eroding rigor and contributing to grade inflation, what has this system, this customer service model of teaching, done to the

climate of our classrooms? Particularly in classes like the ones I teach, I feel the relationship I am establishing with my students is key. Many scholars have developed and/or suggested other methods to more fairly and justly assess teaching "effectiveness," but how do we cultivate, value, and reward pedagogy that aims to create the best climate for learning in a classroom?

- Finally, what does it even mean for one's teaching to be effective? What is the *effect* we are aiming for? The effects or desired outcomes of our teaching are course and discipline specific. Indeed, effectiveness might be *discipline* oriented in other ways as well. Should a measurement of what students have learned be used to gauge whether the teaching was effective? Judging effectiveness in this manner might be more realistic in classes where we have a set of standards that we are teaching to or a particular skillset we are trying to help students master, but such things do not necessarily apply or at least are often not the sole focus what I am teaching. And what about teaching *affective*ness? Why does that not matter?

- What kinds of relationships (student-teacher, student-student, group) are fostered and foreclosed on as a result of the evaluative practices we employ in our classrooms? How do evaluative practices such a student grading and evaluations of teaching work in tandem to reinforce the (flaws in our) existing educational system and social structures? What values and ideologies inform these practices? And how can students and teachers work together to critique, subvert, and/or transform such practices to cultivate meaningful educational experiences that transcend the classroom?

Teaching "Effectiveness" and Other More Ambitious Aims for Teaching

As I ponder the literature on SETs, I am prompted to reflect, not for the first time but newly, on what teaching effectiveness is and how that aligns with my aspirations and reasons for teaching communication. Personally, I would feel like I have done a quality job of teaching if:

- My students can see beyond the transmission model of communication and begin to understand and see the way communication is constitutive in their daily lives;
- If the work or practice in my classroom helps them to form a new friendship, prompts them to become more accepting of or to question aspects of their own identity, or expands their capacity for empathy;
- Ten years down the road a student of mine is in a management position and chooses not to abuse their privilege or power by reconstituting a problematic aspect of the status quo;

320 *Summer R. Cunningham*

- I am able to make and learn from mistakes and discover and question my own taken for granted assumptions.

I cannot easily measure or test for those things, and I really cannot imagine a set of SET questions, qualitative or quantitative, that could truly, fairly, and justly let me know that I am accomplishing them.[15]

Honestly, I am uncomfortable with measurement. Well, I am uncomfortable with measurement as a reductive way of interpreting the complexity of what is actually going on in a classroom. I teach because I want to do my part to make the world better. Because I want to teach people, particularly young people while the window is open for conversation, to question. Because I want *them* to go out into the world and make it better. As Elyse Pineau states, "Critical educators view education as a form of cultural politics and so commit themselves to teaching and learning in the service of social justice" (2002, 43). Thus, effective teaching is teaching that changes the world. A Likert scale cannot capture that.

I turn to Fassett and Warren (2006), and I am reminded that, "Critical communication educators embrace a focus on concrete, mundane communication practice as constitutive of larger social structural systems" (41). This is definitely an endeavor I am committed to in my classroom. I happen to teach classes like Gender and Communication and Intercultural Communication, and because I teach these classes from a critical perspective, I often ask my students to question things that they hold very dearly, like their beliefs and their privilege. And although I strive to do that with as much care and reflexivity as possible, many people do not respond positively to the kind of discomfort that arises when such questions are raised. I believe sincerely that having such conversations is critical to our democracy; necessary for eliminating the hateful divisiveness, oppression, and inequality that infect our culture; and key to cultivating better, stronger, and more loving relationships with one another. But, to be honest, asking students to question a gender binary construct that most have believed their entire lives is "natural" or asking them to consider the ways in which they are privileged or racist are not requests that are met with positivity 100 percent of the time. Teaching from a critical perspective involves not only questioning taken for granted assumptions, including the very power structures that might privilege certain students, but also requires that students reflect upon their own positions within such systems. Not only do such reflexive processes often make students uncomfortable because they call beliefs and values into question, but also because they veer from the traditional "banking" approach to education that so many of them have become accustomed to in their educational careers up to this point. Asking students to think about humanity, their humanity, and to think *differently* about the purpose of education is key to critical pedagogy. As Freire explains,

> The banking approach to adult education, for example, will never propose to students that they critically consider reality. It will deal instead with such vital questions as whether Roger gave green grass to the goat, and insist upon the importance of learning that, on the contrary, Roger gave green grass to the rabbit. The "humanism" of the banking approach masks the effort to turn women and men into automatons—the very negation of their ontological vocation to be more fully human (1970/2018, 74).

I know that often my teaching evaluations are simple reflections of those students who are resistant to an alternate approach to pedagogy. So, to a degree, I expect resistance, and in some ways, I feel that the benefits of employing critical pedagogy are worth the price of a few derogatory or sexist comments. Nevertheless, that price should end with those comments and not when it comes to my (or anyone else who teaches similar subjects) pay, promotion, or continued employment. Along those lines, I worry that Hornstein (2017) are right:

> Student evaluations with all the biases they embrace, put pressure on faculty to go slow and not rock the boat. In other words, do not push undergraduates to maximize their intellectual potential because that might fuel resentment, and do not confront the dominant political and religious beliefs of your particular subset of late adolescents even when such beliefs are patently false and when confronting them is supposedly part of the educational process and is course appropriate. Undergraduates might retaliate on evaluations (6).

If instructors are dissuaded from challenging students and asking them to think critically, then it is easy to see the purpose or at least one of the effects of the practice student course evaluations is that we are failing to produce critical thinkers.

Rate My Performance

Teaching is (a) performance.[16] Performance (theory) is also something that I teach. I perform. I teach. I teach performance. When I teach about performance in my classroom, I always make an effort to: a) help expand my students' understanding of what performance is, and b) emphasize that *all* performances are evaluated. It is critical for students to shake the idea that performance is a rehearsed *faking*[17] that plays out on a stage, critical that they understand that they, that *we,* are performing all of the time in our everyday lives and that we are also, often simultaneously, evaluating those performances—our own as well as those of the people around us. It is from here, this point of acknowledging the evaluative aspects of our everyday life, that we can begin to ask questions about our standards of evaluation: Where do they come from? What morals/ethics/ideologies are wrapped up in our judgments of ourselves and others? What larger systems and structures are reinforced through our performances and what freedoms and possibilities are policed through our evaluations? *What are the rules?* I ask my students. *And whose rules are they? Do you like them? Are they harmful or helpful? What would you like the rules to be?*

In his essay *The Critical Life,* Ron Pelias (2000) reminds us that, "judgments, whether given or received, seem to move inside the body. First and foremost, criticism is always felt. You wonder how often its effect is simply to harden us" (224). When I teach about performance in my classroom, I also emphasize to my students that performance theory uniquely aids our understanding of communication by orienting us toward embodiment, reminding us that we communicate, think, and learn from within a body, always, and that our bodies are also the place where we feel the judgment and evaluation of others. Bodies are material, the place where words take their toll, reminding us that evaluation has real consequences. As I reflect on Pelias' words in the context of this chapter, I am struck especially by the idea that evaluations harden us; that this is their effect. I do not think this is the sort of teaching effectiveness we are aiming for, but it does seem to be an outcome. Indeed, grading, for both students and instructors, hardens us and creates a distance as we close ourselves off to one another in acts of self-protection. I think about the difference between feedback and evaluation. Is there a difference? How do we make it so? Can we?[18]

In *Pedagogy of the Oppressed,* Freire cautions that "The capability of banking education to minimize or annul the students' creative power and to stimulate their credulity serves the interests of the oppressors, who care neither to have the world revealed nor to see it transformed" (1970/2018, 73), and I agree. But helping students see and understand this system also poses a challenge. Is it fair or even possible to expect my students to understand these dynamics? All these layers of power? But how can I *not* ask them to? How can I not ask them to dig into this complexity? To situate themselves, identify their positionalities? To question the way things work and to ask them how they really want them to be? Is my class, is their education, worth more than an arbitrary letter? Why are they here? What do they want? How do we have a real conversation about making *that* possible? This conversation about teaching evaluations is bigger than teaching evaluations, but it also becomes just one more thing that I am asking them to interrogate. And, as I stated earlier, it is not always easy to ask students to interrogate the systems and processes they have taken for granted their entire lives. Sometimes being creative helps. I suppose, in that sense, my teaching evaluation song was/is also an attempt to make this system visible, to make it accessible and digestible, creatively.

I want to return to my song. To that performance. In the "Critical Life," Pelias claims that he "writes to create an evocative resonance, to call together a company of voices who feel the burden and pain of criticism's sting. To open a space for dialogue" (223). I also want to open a dialogue about criticism, about these evaluations with my students (and perhaps beyond). I want them to know that I know how it feels to be evaluated, that I think about how it feels for them to be evaluated, and that I empathize both as someone who was a student for a long time and as someone who continues to be evaluated. I want them also to be critical about the biases that exist, and to question their own. I want them to know how important it is, given the power dynamic of a classroom, for them to have a space to air their grievances without fear of retribution, but also to be aware of the ways in which some students choose to exploit anonymity in unethical ways. I want them to understand that (even if I try to cultivate conditions otherwise) there is a particular power dynamic in the classroom that favors the instructor but also that all of us are subject to structures beyond this space, and that alignment with certain forms of institutionalized power (through sexist, racist, ableist, etc. comments, for example) has consequences as well, for some more than others.

After writing through this chapter, I think I know what is missing from my song. It makes visible *certain* flaws and biases of SETs and does it in a way that strikes a different chord than a research article, but it falls short of illuminating the larger systemic issues in an academic culture that teaches us that knowledge is a discrete entity that can be deposited into receptacles, reducing the value of education to the process of learning the skillsets that are most marketable and useful in a capitalist job market, using assessment practices to reward those of us, both students and teachers, who do the best job of holding up that status quo. In this way, student evaluations of teaching and teachers' evaluations of students go hand-in-hand. They discourage us from taking risks and asking critical questions while encouraging us to devalue each other, formally. I'm reminded of the subtitle of bell hooks's *Teaching to Transgress* (1994): "Education as the Practice of Freedom." But only if we make it so, and indeed, making it so is the challenge.

324   *Summer R. Cunningham*

FINAL THOUGHTS AND TAKEAWAYS

At the beginning of every semester, I ask my students to approach the class thinking about what they want their takeaway(s) to be. Takeaways are things that can be separate from the course learning objectives, something they learned or experienced in the class that is particular to their interests, needs, or desires. I ask them to consider this again when I debrief the class, and they are positioned to look back at the entirety of the material, concepts, and activities we have engaged together. Granted, when students first walk away from a class, they may not be able to fully account for everything they have learned—things are likely still marinating, and other ideas may only emerge or click later when they are context appropriate. Nevertheless, it feels better if you can walk away from a class with something tangible and *meaningful*. Likewise, I think it feels good to walk away from an essay that you have invested time in with something tangible and *meaningful*. And even though I imagine that each person reading this will come away with their own unique points of resonance (or dissonance), I want to close by offering some potential takeaways that are tangible. Thus, I leave you with a short list of ideas— potential strategies—for resisting, subverting, or perhaps even transforming student assessment of teaching.

1. *Talk about assessment with your students.* Such conversations could emerge in a variety of ways. For those already using nontraditional grading systems in their classes, having a conversation about grading and assessment with your students is probably a regular occurrence anyway, and it is likely that in helping your students understand why you grade differently than they are used to, you are already explaining some of the flaws or drawback with conventional grading in a way that asks students to consider the purpose of meaningful assessment. This might be the perfect time to open up to a larger discussion about evaluation and assessment and to help them understand some of the flaws in the SET system as well.

    Even if you are not using nontraditional grading in your classroom, we all spend some time at the beginning of the semester and at various points throughout explaining to our students how they will be evaluated. Why not use that as a jumping off point for explaining to students how *teachers* are evaluated? And, further, this conversation can then become a means for getting beyond assessment processes and delving into a deeper reflection about the purpose of evaluation. How do students feel when they are evaluated? Are their grades important to them? Why? What does a grade mean to them, and how does that coincide with their learning? What does valuable and/or meaningful feedback look like or feel like?

How would they like to be assessed? Do they have experiences of being evaluated unfairly? Have they been discriminated against? Are they concerned about the biases of those who evaluate them? Opening up a space for students to reflect and speak honestly about their assessment and evaluation experiences is valuable in its own right but it could also act as an important bridge to helping them understand evaluation and assessment from a broader perspective; perhaps it might even shape the way they go about their SETs.

2. *Collect more meaningful feedback.* For a variety of reasons, some discussed in this chapter, you may find the feedback you receive in your student evaluations is just not helpful in improving a class and/or your pedagogy. However, like me, you might also value perspectives and feel that it is important that students have the opportunity to provide anonymous feedback about their experiences. To facilitate meaningful feedback, if you are not doing so already, I recommend creating your own midterm and/or end-of-term assessments. I have conducted these in a variety of ways over my teaching career, but I find that it is most effective to ask specific, focused questions about the class. For example, in contrast to generic SET question that ask things like, "What were the strengths and weaknesses of the class," I like to ask, "Which assignments and/or activities did you find most valuable in developing your understanding of _____." I follow this question with a list of all the assignments and activities conducted over the course of the semester connected to the particular topic or learning objective I am asking them to assess. I then invite students to tell me *why* particular activities worked best for them or why they were meaningful. As with the SETs, this feedback can still be provided anonymously so students feel free to speak openly about their experiences.

   I also find it beneficial to ask students to provide individual feedback as the outcome of a conversation. For example, at the end of the semester, you might debrief and review your class in a way that reminds students of all the ground and activities you have covered that semester. During this conversation, you could ask students to volunteer feedback about the course as part of a class-wide conversation or break them into small groups so they can discuss the class together. After, you could then create an opportunity for them to provide individual, anonymous feedback. The purpose of having conversation first is that it opens up some space for recall and brainstorming that might not happen when students are placed in front of a blank document and asked to recall specifics.

3. *Change the system.* How is instruction assessed at your institution and what can you do to shift the culture or change the process and/or outcomes?

The National Academies of Science, Engineering, and Medicine recently convened a two-day workshop on the subject evaluating STEM teaching. Some of the major takeaways from the meeting include advocacy for the use of multiple measures to assess teaching and an emphasis on the importance keeping diversity and inclusivity at the forefront of any conversations about teaching evaluation (National Academies of Science, Engineering, and Medicine 2020). At my current institution, an ad hoc faculty committee is in the process of reviewing and revising both the quantitative and qualitative components of our student evaluations in an effort to collect student feedback that is more meaningful and less biased. Further, recent revisions to our renewal, tenure, and promotion process prompted campus-wide conversations about the role of peer evaluation in faculty development; of particular interest and concern in this discussion was the need to create a framework and process for evaluation that aligns with our institutional commitment to inclusive teaching. Are similar conversations happening at your campus or within your discipline? Could they be? And how might you become involved?

4. *Make a statement.* Systemic change can take time, so if you are looking for ways to counter bias within the existing system right now, you might consider providing a statement to accompany your classroom SETs that makes students aware of the bias that is common in student evaluations of teaching. A recent study by Peterson et al. (2019) found that such a simple intervention had a significant impact on gender bias against female faculty. While this is a single study and the authors conclude that more research could be done to further understand the effectiveness of such a statement, it might be worthwhile to conduct some experimentation on your own. If anything, you are giving students an opportunity to reflect and perhaps become aware of their own bias before it shows up on your evaluations.

5. *Bring them chocolate.* And, of course, you could always just give them chocolate—it is really a win-win. Not only does research indicate that this will likely improve your scores (see Hessler et al. 2018; Youmans and Jee 2007), most students could probably use a little dose of chocolate when they are in the throes of end-of-semester stress and chaos. You might also need some chocolate during this time.

If none of these suggestions are appealing to you, perhaps, like me, you would prefer to begin with song. Indeed, for the sake of visibility, dialogue, and perhaps a little levity, I invite you to consider my song again and rate my performance, sing along, and do your part to help me change the verse: "Say it ain't so, *our* jobs can't be dependent on this when we know that they are so biased."

NOTES

1. Italicized words reflect my commentary/responses to either: a) the content of the evaluations and/or b) the process, state, and implications of student teaching evaluations more broadly. All other lyrics are taken directly from my personal teaching evaluations. Most are quotes but there is an occasional bit of paraphrasing.

2. Some of these acronyms speak volumes in their polysemy, no? SOS? SPIs—you just cannot make this up!

3. Is this how my students feel when they read what I have written to them? Do they dread evaluation, too?

4. In addition to the comments I have received and shared with you in my song, you can find a seemingly unending series of examples on YouTube by conducting a simple search for "professors read reviews."

5. I use quotes here because I want to question the meaning of the term *teaching effectiveness,* which is a discussion I will broach a bit later in the chapter.

6. Which sounds like an invitation to me—if I could just get some funding for a SET pizza and ice cream taste test comparison, I am sure my scores might improve. Any grant writers out there?

7. Indeed, it seems as though SETs should be a key component of any campus discussions about diversity, equity, and inclusion, but in my own experience, I have not seen that this is the case.

8. Again, just check out some of those YouTube videos of professors reading their evaluations.

9. Look, my experience of my identity, particularly my gender identity, is complicated and perhaps fodder for a later essay, but I think the important thing here is despite the fact I try to make it complicated for my students, I am White and am typically read as a straight cisgender woman, and thus, I get all the privilege that comes with that.

10. For example, "There's too much tuna in this class."

11. For example, "Can't tell if she is trying to join the circus with that hairdue."

12. Perhaps also relevant and telling here is that Likert scales are commonly used in customer satisfaction surveys. Because, you know, what are students if not customers and what is education if not a for-profit consumable good?

13. At my institution, I am required to include and compare my global SET scores to the averages of the scores in my department, school, and college.

14. Although most institutions of higher education use some form of SETs, there are schools such as the University of Southern California that have expressly stopped using them to make merit, promotion, and personnel decisions, while other schools like the University of Oregon have discontinued the use of traditional quantitative SETs in favor of more holistic approaches. See Flaherty (2019), "Teaching Eval Shake-Up," for further details.

15. I recently had a student come up to me and hug me at a local establishment and proceed to explain that he met his best friend through an assignment in my interpersonal communication class, and that their friendship was the forged as a part of that

class. I really cannot think of a better outcome for a communication course focused on relationships.

16. See, Pineau (2005), "Teaching is Performance: Reconceptualizing a Problematic Metaphor."

17. Performance scholar, Dwight Conquergood (1998), imparts that our everyday performances are constitutive, the makings of our very reality.

18. The fact that schools like USC and University of Oregon have changed the way they use and think about student evaluation of teaching indicates that there are extant models for how we might make such distinctions. See Flaherty (2019), "Teaching Eval Shake-Up." In my classes, I try to help students distinguish between evaluation and feedback by using contract grading systems that allow me to focus on providing *meaningful*, course-specific feedback to them in a way that avoids reducing their work, ideas, and efforts to a letter, percentage, or number. To help students provide meaningful feedback to me about my teaching and the course, I integrate guided and focused feedback opportunities into the curriculum that prompts students to reflect on specific experiences, assignments, and ideas. Finally, I also use workshops to *teach* and allow students to *practice* giving peer feedback to each other in a way that is meaningful and constructive.

REFERENCES

Arbuckle, Julianne, and Benne D. Williams. 2003. "Students' Perceptions of Expressiveness: Age and Gender Effects on Teacher Evaluations." *Sex Roles* 49 (9/10): 507–516. https://link.springer.com/article/10.1023/A:1025832707002.

Carmack, Heather J., and Leah E. LeFebvre. 2019. "Walking on Eggshells": Traversing the Emotional and Meaning Making Processes Surrounding Hurtful Course Evaluations." *Communication Education* 68 (3): 350–370. https://doi.org/10.1080/03634523.2019.1608366.

Conquergood, Dwight. 1998. "Beyond the Text: Toward a Performative Cultural Politics. In *The Future of Performance Studies*, edited by Sheron J. Dailey, 25–36. Blackburg, VA: NCA.

Fassett, Deanna L., and John T. Warren. 2006. *Critical Communication Pedagogy*. Thousand Oaks, CA: Sage.

Felton, James, Mitchell, John B., and Michael Stinson. 2004. "Web-Based Student Evaluations of Professors: The Relations Between Perceived Quality, Easiness and Sexiness." *Assessment & Evaluation in Higher Education* 29 (1): 91–108. https://doi.org/10.1080/0260293032000158180.

Flaherty, Colleen. 2018a. "Teaching Eval Shake-Up." *Inside Higher Ed.* May 22, 2018. https://www.insidehighered.com/news/2018/05/22/most-institutions-say-they-value-teaching-how-they-assess-it-tells-different-story.

Flaherty, Colleen. 2018b. "Bye, Bye, Chili Pepper." *Inside Higher Ed.* July 2, 2018. https://www.insidehighered.com/news/2018/07/02/rate-my-professors-ditches-its-chili-pepper-hotness-quotient.

Freire, Paolo. 2018. *Pedagogy of the Oppressed: 50th Anniversary Edition*. New York, Bloomsbury Academic.

Hessler, Michael, Pöpping, Daniel M., Hollstein, Hanna, Ohlenburg, Hendrik, Arnemann, Philip, H., Massoth, Christina, Seidel, Laura, Zarbock, Alexander, and Manuel Wenk. 2018. "Availability of Cookies During an Academic Course Session Affects Evaluation of Teaching." *Medical Education* 52, 1064–1072. https://doi.org/10.1111/medu.13627.

Hornstein, Henry A. 2017. "Student Evaluations of Teaching are an Inadequate Assessment Tool for Evaluating Faculty Performance." *Cogent Education* 4 (1): https://doi.org/10.1080/2331186X.2017.1304016.

hooks, bell. 1994. *Teaching to Transgress: Education as the Practice of Freedom*. London: Routledge.

Jordan, Tim. 2019. "Does Online Anonymity Undermine the Sense of Personal Responsibility?" *Media, Culture & Society* 41 (4): 572–577. https://doi.org/10.1177/0163443719842073.

Lawrence, John W. 2018. "Student Evaluations of Teaching are Not Valid." *AAUP*. May-June. https://www.aaup.org/article/student-evaluations-teaching-are-not-valid#.X6hFjy2ZN2Y.

MacNell, Lillian, Driscoll, Adam, and Andrea N. Hunt. 2015. "What's in a Name: Exposing Gender Bias in Student Ratings of Teaching." *Innovative Higher Education* 40 (4): 291–303. https://doi.org/10.1007/s10755-014-9313-4.

National Academies of Sciences, Engineering, and Medicine. 2020. "Recognizing and Evaluating Science Teaching in Higher Education: Proceedings of a Workshop in Brief." Washington, DC: The National Academies Press. https://doi.org/10.17226/25685.

Pelias, Ronald J. 2000. "The Critical Life." *Communication Education* 49 (3): 220–228. https://doi.org/10.1080/03634520009379210.

Peterson, David A. M., Biederman, Lori A., Andersen, David, Ditonto, Tessa M., and Kevin Roe. 2019. "Mitigating Gender Bias in Student Evaluations of Teaching." *PLOS ONE* 14 (5): e0216241. https://doi.org/10.1371/journal.pone.0216241.

Pineau, Elyse Lamm. 2002. "Critical Performative Pedagogy: Fleshing Out the Politics of Liberatory Education." In *Teaching Performance Studies*, edited by Nathan Stucky and Cynthia Wimmer, 41–54. Carbondale, IL: Southern Illinois University Press.

Pineau, Elyse Lamm. 2005. "Teaching is Performance: Reconceptualizing a Problematic Metaphor." In *Performance Theories in Education: Power, Pedagogy, and the Politics of Identity*, edited by Bryant Keith Alexander, Gary L. Anderson, and Bernardo Gallegos, 15–39. Mahwah, N.J.: Routledge.

Reid, Landon D. 2010. "The Role of Perceived Race and Gender in the Evaluation of College Teaching on RateMyProfessors.Com." *Journal of Diversity in Higher Education* 3 (3): 137–152. https://doi.org/10.1037/a0019865.

Smith, Bettye P. 2009. "Student Ratings of Teaching Effectiveness for Faculty Groups Based on Race and Gender." *Education* 129 (4): 615–624. Accessed January 17, 2020. https://eric.ed.gov/?id=EJ871612.

Stark, Philip B., and Richard Freishtat. 2013. "Evaluating Evaluations, Part 1." *Berkeley Center for Teaching & Learning.* Accessed January 20, 2020. https://teaching.berkeley.edu/news/evaluating-evaluations-part-1.

Stroebe, Wolfgang. 2016. "Why Good Teaching Evaluations May Reward Bad Teaching: On Grade Inflation and Other Unintended Consequences of Student Evaluations." *Perspectives on Psychological Science* 11 (6): 800–816. https://doi.org/10.1177/1745691616650284.

Youmans, Robert J., and Benjamin D. Jee. 2007. "Fudging the Numbers: Distributing Chocolate Influences Student Evaluations of an Undergraduate Course." *Teaching of Psychology* 34 (4): 245–247. https://doi.org/10.1080/00986280701700318.

Chapter Eleven

The Seven Lesson Faculty Member

Outlining Assessment's Harm to Faculty

C. Kyle Rudick

Workshop Facilitator: Does assessment drive education?

Me: Of course not. Education happens all the time, in all sorts of places, and doesn't require assessment. Assessment is an institutional prerogative that tries to capture the process of learning.

Facilitator:

Me:

Facilitator: So, we're going talk about how to create high-impact learning goals for university-wide assessment . . .

Call it assessment,[1] evaluation, grading, or some other jargon dreamt up by some bureaucrat in the hopes of hitting it big in the next Ted Talk, it all comes down to the same thing—the institutional prerogative to claim to know the direction society should go and the institutional power of rewards and punishments to force students to follow that path. Whether formative or summative, with letters or numbers, minimum or zero-policy, scholarship consistently demonstrates that the process of assessment is antithetical to the learning. For example, Kohn (2012) noted social scientific research about grading and learning shows:

- Grades tend to diminish students' interest in whatever it is they are learning.
- Grades create a preference for the easiest task possible.
- Grades tend to reduce the quality of students' thinking. (144)

That these findings have been known for over one hundred years (Rugg 1918; Starch 1913) demonstrates a puzzling, yet deep, investment into an antiquated, erroneous practice. Assessment, whether conducted at the individual, classroom, department, or institutional level is a sickness, transmitting a set of logics (often White, masculine, and Eurocentric), justifying those worldviews as normal or neutral, and infecting each successive generation of students with beliefs enforced by the blunt instrument of a number or letter next to their name.

Although certainly assessment is an act of violence against students' epistemological, axiological, and ontological horizons,[2] what interests me in this essay is not to decry assessment for its effects on students. A reader interested in this work can find it in the writings of Kohn (1999, 2011), Guskey (2002, 2011), and hundreds of others (e.g. Bennett and Brady 2014; Blasco 2015; Murtonen, Gruber, and Lehtinen 2017). Rather, I am interested in describing the effect that assessment has on faculty. If, as we know, assessment constitutes the mechanisms by which students are socialized into certain ways of being or knowing, then what are the effects of assessment on faculty? Interestingly, I could find little writing that systematically addressed this question. Tangentially, critical scholarship concerning the deskilling of teachers (e.g., making teachers use rubrics, standards, or objectives without their input; see Giroux 2010) touches on how assessment and grading practices serve to make teachers interchangeable cogs in the machine that produces compliant students and diminishes teacher autonomy and expertise. However, this work often does not systemically or specifically address the effect a culture of assessment has on instructors; instead, remaining at a level of abstraction beyond the day-to-day grind of workaday life. Here, I would like to spend time to address what kind of *instructor* one becomes through the process of assessment. In other words, I am interested in understanding how assessment as a practice is performed, practiced, and perfected within an institutional culture, and how the normalization of this ritual constitutes a form of organizational socialization. That is, assessment, and the logics that animate it, are often unreflexively carried out within and beyond the institution—meaning that the hidden curriculum of assessment for instructors is just as pressing a problem as it is for students (Gatto 2005).

One wonders what animates the lack of scholarly attention on the socializing effects of assessment on faculty. The most benign reason is that most faculty are caring, other-oriented people, and their writing about the deleterious effects of assessment for students comes from a place of concern. The relative lack of attention on how it affects teachers, then, is an omission rooted in the hope that our scholarship can save students, even if we are too far gone to save ourselves. A more ominous reason is that faculty enjoy the ability to differentiate ourselves from each other by what type of language we use to talk about assessment: "Oh, I don't do traditional assessment! My practices are grounded in [insert: authentic learning, dialogue, high impact, real experience, or social justice]." As higher education becomes more entrenched in neoliberal forms of governance and culture, faculty uses assessment language as a way to brand themselves as cutting edge or unique—despite the fact that all assessment fulfills the institution's prerogative to create a subjectivity that acquiesces to the horrors and vagaries of the nearly-imminent economic and environmental meltdown. The most sinister reason is that faculty, for all of our decrying of assessment, really do enjoy the petty power of evaluating others. We are monitored and measured by administrators, legislators, journalists, and parents—certainly it feels good to be the one who assesses rather than the one assessed. Perhaps it is a mixture of these reasons, or something beyond. Regardless of the reasoning, my argument is that the relative lack of scholarship addressing this issue speaks to a need for scholarly intervention into the process.

My purpose in this chapter is to outline seven lessons[3] that assessment teaches faculty. In doing so, I wish to point to both the empirical horizons that future scholars may pursue (e.g., "What kind of instructor habits/dispositions/practices are influenced by, or are produced by, the socializing elements of assessment?") as well as a normative argument against the culture of assessment. As a critical scholar, I find every act of assessment an act of violence against faculty, an attempt to cut off those parts of ourselves that make us most creative, happy, and whole. It creates a person who is drained—not just of their professional skill (i.e., deskilling)—but of their very life essence through the unending grind of attending to institutional prerogatives that are often far removed from human learning, joy, or fulfillment. Despite the general tone of this book, and the larger trajectory of critical communication pedagogy (Fassett and Warren 2007; Fassett and Rudick 2018) describing the importance of retrieved assessment as a critical practice (see Kahl 2013), I maintain there is no practice of assessment—no buzzword, philosophy, or ethic—that can undo the violence inherent in its practice. Thus, I end this essay with advice on how to resist and undermine culture of assessment within higher education.

THE SEVEN LESSONS OF ASSESSMENT

1. Confusion

There is in every social formation a particular branch of production which determines the position and importance of all the others, and the relations obtaining in this branch accordingly determine the relations of all other branches as well.

334 *C. Kyle Rudick*

It is as though light of a particular hue were cast upon everything, tingeing all other colours and modifying their specific features (Marx and Engels 2004, 146).

The first lesson assessment teaches is confusion. By confusion, I mean a sense of disequilibrium that is brought on when a person knows that something that should be straightforward and simple is made violently byzantine. Assessment achieves confusion in two ways. First, the very process of assessment is one that is at odds with human nature. Setting aside our postmodern qualms about such a loaded term for one moment, we might say that humans offer feedback on the world around them as a natural part of their being. That is, if a person sees a sunrise, they will immediately think about it in terms such as beauty (e.g., "Oh, look at the colors!), practicality (e.g., "That looks like clouds on the horizon; I better seek shelter"), or science (e.g., "The red glow is from poisonous chemicals left in the atmosphere by a largely un-regulated petroleum industry"). The process of feedback, and its reception/negotiation, can be tacit or explicit. When offered, for example, to children, feedback is often given by parents or appointed adults (e.g., close kin) for how to act, think, or believe. A smile and "good job" or a frown and "stop that!" at the right (or wrong) time can have an incredibly high impact on children's emotional and psychological development. Adults, too, offer and process feedback tacitly and explicitly. Ostracism from group or community membership can be just as much of a deterrent for some behaviors as a letter of reprimand or threat of being fired. Humans cannot not react to the world around them and will, whether given to another or internally, evaluate the state of affairs in which they find themselves within any given time.

Assessment violates this natural order of things by dictating a set of pre-scribed criteria that may be (and often is) removed from faculty members' interests, intentions, or goals. The beauty of a poem is reduced to a five-point Likert like scale; a painting is reduced to a 100-word narrative; or an engineering marvel is reduced to its ability to be patented and monetized. Whatever a person may wish to create and receive applause or condemnation based on the natural interactions that emerge from their contemporaries is, instead, replaced by the institutional prerogative to name what is important or necessary. The feedback that is so freely and naturally given between humans is usurped by the parasitic function of the neoliberal institution, which takes that natural impulse and channels it toward institutional goals. This function, in turn, inculcates a sense of confusion to faculty who are left to throw their hands up in despair as not just their professional but their ontological under-standing of offering feedback is usurped by institutional prerogatives.

Second, confusion is guaranteed by the never-ending cycle of updates, re-visions, and complete overhauls of the assessment program. The fluid nature of assessment programs is due to the competing federal, state, institutional, and departmental whims that inform assessment practices. I say "whims" because that is exactly what they are—no one quite knows why this year's assessment practice is better than the last, what criteria would be used to make such a judgement, or how much institutional resources are expended in the transition. Instead, the new assessment practice is imposed, often with an appeal to some outside group (e.g., accreditation company or legislature), who is supposed to be pleased or impressed with the institution's ability to jump through the new set of hoops. The fact that the goals and measurements of assessment change so frequently forces faculty into a sense of intellectual precariousness. That is, as soon as a set of skills is mastered, the rules of the game change, forcing faculty to spend ever more cognitive resources to meet the new goals. The only people who are able to navigate this system are those who completely give themselves over to the confusion—often either those members who benefit the most from the system (i.e., administrators tasked with assessment for their university or accreditation companies) or those who (despite all evidence that should inform them differently) have an almost religious faith in the culture of assessment.

Assessment inculcates confusion to faculty by inserting itself as the most important obligation of the institution even though its practice is educationally detrimental. Faculty resources are not infinite and investment into achieving better results through or in assessment is almost always counterproductive. The arbitrariness of assessment, no matter its type or stripe, forces faculty into a paradox wherein they know that their dedication to the craft of teaching is the most important task, and yet they are continuously bombarded with mind number drudgery foisted off as education. Such a culture only creates a sense of confusion and dis/ease.

2. Professional Position

> It is with man as with commodities. Since he comes into the world neither with a looking glass in his hand, nor as a Fichtean philosopher, to whom "I am I" is sufficient, man first sees and recognises himself in other men. Peter only establishes his own identity as a man by first comparing himself with Paul as being of like kind. And thereby Paul, just as he stands in his Pauline personality, becomes to Peter the type of the genus *homo* (Marx 1887, 45).

Assessment is a way for institutions to evaluate, rank, and reward departments and instructors who are willing to "play the game." And, although certainly it is not a very fun game, assessment is akin to one in that it has rules, norms, and (above all) winners and losers. Assessment teaches faculty their position within the institutional structure in two ways. First, and most obviously, those instructors, departments, or universities that do well in their assessments (whether the annual Learning Outcomes Report or US College Rank List) are given accolades and, conversely, those who do not do well are punished. Although it might seem a bit counterproductive that those who do less well on their assessment are barred from resources that would increase their chances for success, it remains a staple of the US assessment culture. The penchant in US higher education to make sure that the haves and have-nots are clearly demarcated (whether between Ivy-league and two-directional institutions or between different departments) and those boundaries rigorously enforced and (re)produced is one of the ways that assessment drives a sense of positionality within the system.

Assessment makes the goal of education to do well on assessment, rather than, say, the goal of creating an educated society. Of course, assessment loving pedants will argue, "How can we know if we are educating society without assessment?" It is almost as if they believe no learning occurred prior to the invention of grading assignments in the eighteenth century. Doing well on assessment is relatively easy: How many times have you heard (or said) the following, "The administration has a plan for us to do Y assessment rather than X. How can we continue to do X and report about it in a way that meets the standards of Y?" Faculty know that assessment is just an elaborate exercise of whack-a-mole where they pop their head up long enough to be noticed but not so long as to get hit. Assessment, by substituting itself as the primary institutional goal, relegates educating others as secondary and makes one's ability to meet arbitrary measures paramount. Which, I suppose, makes sense: educating others seems so hard and ineffable—much better to have some numbers, narratives, or some other "evidence" that learning has occurred, even if such a determination is only based on the premise that your numbers are higher than someone else's. "We don't know what these numbers mean, but by God, our numbers are the highest numbers in all the land," says the witless rube determined to stay in the good graces of their superiors.

The second way that assessment teaches college position is by the department or faculty member's willingness to be a "good sport" and go along with the assessment plan. In some ways, it does not even matter how well one actually does on the assessment report as long as one expresses proper reverence for the ritual and a properly servile attitude toward the so-called "improvement plan." There is no greater example of this than a simple test—find a department where students are learning, faculty are happy, and the culture is functional and non-toxic. Now, take that department and have them stop doing assessment. Even if they continue their trajectory of success (or, more likely, experience even more success), their unwillingness to acquiesce to the culture of assessment will put them on the radar of every bureaucrat who believes that "the things that matter should be measured." Likewise, those departments that struggle with the goal of educating students can go for years, if not decades, camouflaging their failures within the cloak of institutional jargon, improvement plans, and half-baked interventions.

Assessment teaches faculty that their passions are only important insofar as it translates into greater institutional gains vis-à-vis their competitors (e.g., other instructors, departments, or universities). Within this mindset, there is no learning that is meaningful if it is not measured, and no measurement is important unless it is weighted, scored, and compared to others. And, the system of rewards and punishments that enforces this culture ensures that faculty will continue to play the game as long as they think that they can win it. That is, if they or their department/university is winning the game, then there is little impulse to change the system. In fact, they are most likely its most ardent defenders of the system since they realize that their success on the assessment tools marks them for special privileges and rewards.

3. Indifference and Fatigue

The worker becomes all the poorer the more wealth he produces, the more his production increases in power and size. The worker becomes an ever cheaper commodity the more commodities he creates (Marx 1844, para. 7).

The never-ending carousel of assessment has another result—indifference and fatigue. Faculty are given a set of assessment tools, told that the tools are the latest and greatest, and after three years (a proper time to begin mastering the assessment system) are told that the system will be changed by yet another paradigm-shifting set of assessment tools. *Ad nauseum, ad infinitum.* Each time the assessment plan becomes more convoluted, arcane, and specialized, even when the outcomes are really the same every year—is the university recruiting, retaining, and graduating students at a rate that is economically sustainable enough for administrators to continue robbing the university for six or seven figure salaries? Faculty, in turn, are pressured to ever greater feats of the production of nonsense that justifies this obscene Ponzi-scheme.

One of the fashionable phrases that I hear in relation to assessment that I believe contributes to this volume of assessment foisted on faculty, and the burnout they experience as a result, is *continuous improvement initiatives.* Continuous improvement is a concept imported from the corporate sector, whose goal is always to achieve greater profits. In higher education, it relies on the idea that every year faculty should achieve more than the year before. This is an unsustainable model, whose harms are disproportionately felt by faculty. There are three parts of continuous growth approaches to assessment

338   *C. Kyle Rudick*

that are symptomatic of either ignorance or malice on the part of administrators, special interest groups, and legislators.

First, the continuous growth model assumes that growth is infinite. For growth to be infinite, one of two things must be true: 1) that resources are infinite (i.e., there is always more money, time, resources to use to make something better) or 2) that costs can always be minimized (i.e., there always a more efficient way to do the same task). Neither of these beliefs is true in the abstract (there is not an unlimited amount of people, money, or time) or for higher education (there are less full-time faculty per pupil than ever before and teaching someone takes about the same amount of resources now as it did 3,000 years ago). There is no way that faculty can create the same educational outcomes for students when they are given the same (or less) resources to teach, research, or serve but now have to also document all of those activities.

Second, the continuous growth model assumes that achieving the same goal is failure. I have heard administrators (and more than a few faculty) state that "there is always room for improvement." First, if an instructor, department, or university is achieving excellence, then it has achieved excellence. Full stop. Making arbitrary goals that have no basis in reality other than "It's better than this year" is akin to my saying, "I want to earn a million dollars because I didn't do that this year." It is a goal. It is an improvement. But, it is not based in a rational understanding of the limits of my present circumstances or the ways to pursue it. Second, even if one can say there is "always room for improvement" one has to weigh the cost of improvement against the investment of resources. If the investment into gaining a couple of points of a test is to hire new faculty or academic staff, then most universities will not do it. As a result, the effort needed to improve (even when no improvement is necessary) means that the university must squeeze existing faculty to produce more.

Finally, the continuous growth model of assessment is anti-faculty. Because resources are not infinite, and investment into achieving growth is not grounded in reality, what happens is that upper administration (backed by a million mindless mid-level puppets) demand ever more faculty time to address assessment concerns. This process diverts faculty away from their true purpose of teaching, research, and service in the guise that filling out forms or sitting on committees of "continuous improvement" will somehow achieve those goals. Want to revamp your class? Too bad! You need to rewrite this rubric scale so next year we can justify our assertion that students are doing better! Want time to think through a research manuscript? Too bad! You need to fill out these forms defending why too many students are passing your exams! Want to create a new university-community partnership? Too bad! You need to write this report showing how your department will achieve a 100 percent retention rate and a 100 percent increase in recruitment next year and how you plan to exceed those goals every year for the next ten years! In short, every year more and more faculty time is diverted from their true purpose to engage in an exercise of banality whose power lies in its seductive glibness (i.e. "there's always room for improvement!")—not reality.

Assessment teaches faculty that to count anything as important, worthwhile, or good, then the institution must create a committee, to create a process, to a create a taskforce, to a create a rubric for assessment, and then engage in the same process to gather a departmental group that can use the rubric and another at the university level to monitor each department group. All of this work is completed, and yet, one rarely (if ever) sees such work produce changes in the university system or culture. It is an endless series of spinning one's wheels in mud—the higher your RPMs, the quicker you bury your axle into the ground. There is nothing on the other side of assessment that justifies the sheer amount of time and attention it takes to do it. In my experience, this process produces senior colleagues who are so jaded and cynical that even good ideas are met with resistance and suspicion. And, it creates an institutional culture that increasingly relies on the naiveté of junior colleagues and/or the economically precarious position of faculty in contingent positions to ensure that institutional work is done. Guess what happens to these latter groups? They eventually turn into the former.

4. Emotional Dependency

> The more the worker expends himself in work the more powerful becomes the world of objects which he creates in face of himself, the poorer he becomes in inner life, and the less he belongs to himself (Marx 1844, para. 10).

Assessment teaches faculty to place the happiness of others above their own. Want higher student evaluations? Offer students chocolate chip cookies before conducting their assessment (Hessler et al. 2018). Want administrators to be happy? Sit in the front row, bright eyed and mouth agape, at the wonders of Pearson, McGraw-Hill, or Cengage's new online assessment program that administrators adopted without faculty input for the paltry sum of ten million dollars over the next five years (Oh, and did I mention we are now in a hiring freeze? Budgets are so hard to balance!). Regardless, the happiness of others is always paramount and faculty members' emotional and psychological health is rarely discussed and hardly ever the subject of ongoing, systematic support from the university.

The amount of assessment that occurs within the institution may be inversely related to its usefulness but is positively correlated to how it encourages a sense of precarity on the part of faculty. Take, as an example, how my institution handles the assessment of faculty for tenure. Every year, for six years, I catalog my work completed over the course of a year, grouping my labor according to the sacred trinity of the academy: teaching, research, and service. My (1) teaching folder consists of syllabi, assignments, rubrics, and student evaluations; (2) research folder documents my publications, journal statistics (e.g., acceptance/rejection rates), and grants; and the (3) service folder shows the committees, journal review boards, and community activities I serve and support. Each year my fellow peers spend countless hours watching me teach, writing letters for my files, reading my tenure documents, and guiding me in the process, putting together a complete, shiny, and beautiful tenure dossier.

And yet, at the end of this process, my tenure determination was based on my narrative of teaching philosophy essay (three pages) and CV. *None* of my catalogued work was read beyond the departmental level. That is, the only people who spent the time to read my documentation were other, just as harried and harassed, faculty members. And, while I do not have direct experience with adjunct work, my understanding is that at my institution many of my adjunct colleagues replicate a great deal of this work for even less institutional recognition and no guarantee of job security. That I spent countless hours, not just gathering and showing my documentation, but making sure that every "i" was dotted and "t" crossed to make sure the dossier matched the organizational criteria of the university (even when it changed numerous times) was not an exercise to test my intellect, passion, or creativity. Rather, it served primarily to make me feel uneasy: "Am I doing enough to achieve tenure? And, if I am doing enough, is that 'enough' showcased in such a fashion as to be met with approval by the faceless, capricious gods who will judge my tenure case?"

Assessment initiatives, whether tenure, student evaluations, grades, or some other index of institutional fit(ness) cultivates a sense of emotional precarity that is then weaponized by the administrators in their efforts to force faculty to expend ever-increasing amounts of their resources on institutional prerogatives (e.g., assessment initiatives). Administrators who are interpersonally harmonious are not doing so because they have a nice personality or because they care about faculty, it is a feature of a type of administrative governmentality that cultivates an emotional connection to make it easier to advance institutional goals. One way this occurs is when faculty members are vocal in their disagreement or critique of administrative decision making. Watch how administrators use a variety of emotional appeals to personalize disagreements, how they cajole, threaten, emotionally blackmail, and flatter, all in an attempt to create a culture where dissent is so interpersonally unpleasant and face-threatening that faculty members shy away from protecting themselves or their students. And, central to this, is to identify those faculty members who do not acquiesce to this system, isolate them as troublemakers through (non)verbal communication in meetings (e.g., roll eyes, huff, sigh, or address their concern while making eye contact with a sycophant faculty member who will quickly agree with the administrator). The truth is that many administers may care about faculty in the abstract, they may even have some favorite faculty members, but it is the sort of benign paternalism that characterizes the way someone might treat a stable full of prize horses—with love and affection until one is no longer running fast enough or kicks someone and then it is time to turn it into dog food and glue. Assessment conditions faculty to acquiesce to this system and attach their emotional well-being to the promises and whims of people who often will cash out and leave the institution after five years of "work" as the continue their trajectory of failing upward through the system.

5. Political Constraint

A few days in my old man's factory have sufficed to bring me face to face with this beastliness, which I had rather overlooked. . . . It is impossible to carry on communist propaganda on a large scale and at the same time engage in huckstering and industry (Engels 1845, para. 8).

Faculty, by virtue of their training and disposition, often see themselves through meritocratic, individualistic lenses. Organizing instructors based on their labor, whether in a union or a strong faculty senate, is an incredibly rare and difficult task. Doing so requires working with each other to realize that faculty specialty areas, publication records, accolades, and other forms of demarcations are (more or less) mystifications created to encourage them to see each other as different (i.e., better) than one another and reduce solidarity and organizing.

The endless flood of assessment, and the committees, workshops, reading groups, and improvement meetings that accompany it, fill up the hours of the week. Although there is little empirical research about faculty workload, Ziker's (2014) suggests that faculty work an average of approximately 61 hours a week with over 30 percent (or 20 hours) spent in course administration, meetings, and writing reports. Imagine what one could do with another 20 hours a week. Without assessment, faculty would have more time to meet each other, build relationships, and even (gasp!) exert influence or even control over the university where they work. The rise of assessment culture in higher education is inversely related to faculty members' autonomy, control, and pedagogical freedom.

Perhaps the most insidious part of this political constraint is how benign and depoliticized the language of assessment sounds. Who among us does not think that knowing what is going well or wrong and changing our actions accordingly is a good idea? And yet, the disconnect between assessment and institutional change suggests that its usefulness is not wholly, or even primarily, about informing classroom or institutional practice. Rather, one of its goals is to keep faculty so busy documenting the world around them that they are unable or unwilling to take the time to change it. The evil of assessment is that it teaches good people to document their labor instead of doing it, much less celebrating it. It beats faculty members down, obtaining through sheer boredom and monotony what often cannot be achieved by force: a harassed and therefore pliable professorate that is no longer able to acknowledge or care about the way that their passion and creativity has been channeled away from themselves and the communities they serve to an unfeeling and unsupportive institutional culture. Because assessment teaches faculty that their jobs are not about teaching students, creating scholarship, or serving others—it is about documenting those things. As such, faculty members' political and axiological horizons are constrained to the logics of effectiveness and retention, channeling their attention away (perhaps thankfully) from the true horror of their increasingly minimal role in the institutional structure.

6. Alienation and Disconnect from Society

> The *alienation* of the worker in his product means not only that his labor becomes an object, an *external* existence, but that it exists *outside him*, independently, as something alien to him, and that it becomes a power on its own confronting him. It means that the life which he has conferred on the object confronts him as something hostile and alien (Marx 1844, para. 10).

Professors are increasingly talked about as an "un-needed" profession. Sure, some people might talk about the need for professional integrity when it comes to making sure the student who got an "A" really deserved an "A," but it is increasingly rare to find places in society (e.g., the media) that promote the idea that there is a pressing, societal injunction for a trained professorate. Professors, like K–12 teachers before them, have been drained of any professional need, only to have that vacuum filled by vaguely benign credentialists who ensure some modicum of correspondence between student learning and employment trainability exists. Faculty members know and internalize this increasingly hostile, anti-intellectual culture and become intellectual strangers in their own land.

But the problem of assessment goes beyond the idea that it deskills instructors and drains them of their professional expertise. Rather, it gets to the heart of the difference between the living labor of faculty with the parasitic culture of work that the institution prizes (Bourassa, 2018). To labor is a natural human activity. All humans labor; it is as central to our identity as language and as fundamental to our physiology as our opposable thumbs and bipedal legs. Leave a human alone and they will build a shelter. Put five together, they will build a house. 500 gets a town. 5,000 a city. The point is that labor is part of humans' ontological vocation; it is not only something we do, it is fundamentally who we are. Work, on the other hand, is a perversion of labor. Work is based on a hierarchical relationship where one group of people dictates how one's labor is to be spent. When faculty members' labor is corralled, pinched, prodded, and pushed into assessment, then the product produced is fundamentally at odds with our ontological vocation.

The documentation of one's labor—whether through a tenure file, student evaluation, or assessment report—is not labor; rather, it is a perversion of one's labor changing it to the mind-numbing level of work. Certainly, most people know that creating an assessment report about learning will not, in the end, teach students anything. Teaching can only be achieved by, well, the act of teaching. However, the issue of assessment goes beyond just its ability to usurp faculty members' time and energy away from the labor they wish to perform. Rather, assessment codifies and contains faculty labor, creating an unnatural abomination that stares back at instructors as a mute reprimand of their life and career choices.

This is perhaps one of the most disastrous parts of the assessment regime: it teaches faculty to hate their jobs and, by extension, to hate ourselves. It takes our labor and constrains it in such a way as to make it appear a matter of technique and effectiveness rather than one of love and connection. It slices and cuts those parts of us that are unpalatable to the institution—our creativity, our curiosity, our passion—by reward or punishment until we are no longer willing, perhaps not even able, to see our own dehumanization. The most thoughtful essay is reduced to the journal's impact factor, the moment of "Eureka!" a student may have in the classroom is reduced to a student evaluation report, and the free class offered at the local senior center is reduced to the total attendance number. There is no labor that cannot be reduced to work, no good deed that goes uncatalogued and collated in triplicate, and no activity that is not bent toward the goal of supporting the institution's goals.

7. One Cannot Hide

And this life activity [the worker] sells to another person in order to secure the necessary means of life. . . . He works that he may keep alive. He does not count

344   C. Kyle Rudick

the labor itself as a part of his life; it is rather a sacrifice of his life. It is a commodity that he has auctioned off to another (Marx 1847, para. 8).

The final lesson that assessment teaches is that there is no place for faculty
to hide. The culture of assessment promises that either you will write about
others or you will be written about by others. Many faculty members conduct
research, grade homework (our form of student surveillance), and perform
countless other duties in our homes, at bars or coffee shops, or in other places
that are not attached to the institution. Although some may argue that this
flexibility of our work is a perk, the truth is that it extends the reach of the
institution into every conceivable part of our life worlds. How many professors have you met who proudly state how they are always thinking about
their teaching, research, or service obligations while on vacation, weekends,
or at their child's birthday party (a great place for ethnographic data!)? Now,
how many talk about the importance of their families or children, connection
with people who are not colleagues, or hobbies that have nothing to do with
scholarship? The problem with assessment is that it creates a pressure to
always do something and document that doing—even if that doing is banal,
artificial, or even harmful—because the act of doing something is better than
doing nothing and doing something is worth nothing if it is not documented
in proper form.

This part of assessment culture ties into the increasingly precariousness
of full-time employment within higher education. Professors are politically
on their back foot about the value of their work and are constantly seeking
to justify their so-called "summers off" and "numerous paid vacations." Assessment hucksters enter into the scene with assurances that faculty are not
doing bad work; rather, the problem is that they are not communicating about
their work to the public in a way that can be appreciated. Assessment reports,
faculty are told, are the way to take the complexity of faculty members' labor
and make it digestible, if not palatable, to the important public stakeholders
(e.g., donors). The promise of assessment is that eventually faculty members
will find the perfect way to communicate their worth to the public, who will
finally simply respect faculty for what they do, and instructors will no longer
have to engage in the dog and pony show of assessment.

The problem with this promise should be obvious to anyone familiar with
the politics of US education over the past forty years. Like the opium addicts
of yore could have told us, assessment will never catch the dragon of public
respect. There is not an assessment plan or report that will convince a largely
hostile, anti-intellectual culture that what professors do is worthwhile or
necessary. Just ask the public K–12 teachers about how their arguments for
professional autonomy and expertise have fared against the onslaught of anti-
intellectualism, religious fanaticism, and racism over the past forty years. For

some reason, though, it seems that professors are falling into the same trap, seeking to find the perfect form of assessment that will convince the public of the worth of their work. In doing so, faculty members unwittingly create, support, and (re)produce a vast panopticon of surveillance on ourselves by tacitly agreeing that there is a problem, and that a system needs to be in place to assess how to address it. As a result, our work is constantly scrutinized by administrators, accreditation organizations, and government bodies who have a vested interest in making sure that faculty can never meet all the criteria of assessment—if we did, then we would not need the bureaucrats!

Surveillance is an essential feature of any culture of control. Instructors are, by and large, some of the most highly educated, creative, and individualistic people in society. In other words, they are the absolute worst type of people to try to manage. Assessment secures faculty members' acquiescence, if not servility, by constantly reminding faculty that there is no part of their professional (and little of their personal) lives that cannot be invaded by the institution. Even worse, it creates systems that encourage faculty members to monitor and snitch on each other: "Did you know that Bob is only teaching toward four of the five learning objectives?" "Sally sent up an assessment report that didn't have the proper action verbs! She's making us all look bad!" "How can we convince the provost to give us money to expand the major if Loretta won't follow the university prescribed rubric?!" Faculty become so conditioned to the idea that their work should be evaluated that they then begin monitoring themselves and each other. It creates a toxic environment that makes it impossible for faculty to become fully-actualized, creative intellectuals.

SEVEN WAYS TO RESIST
THE CULTURE OF ASSESSMENT

The culture of assessment is toxic and should be resisted and refuted at every turn. All-to-often faculty members are seduced into assessment practices through the innocuous, seemingly-reasonable appeal that sounds something like this: "Don't you want to know how to improve your practice? And, really, this assessment will take so little time anyway. And, what you're doing in your class will address our assessment rubric anyway, so it's not like it would be extra work." As the wise Admiral Akbar once said: "It's a trap!" Learning occurred before there was assessment, and all assessment is a slippery slope toward acquiescing to the belief that institutional prerogatives are more valid or important than faculty expertise and connection with students.

As such, I offer seven ways to resist the culture of assessment. Before reading my advice, I caution my reader: I am a White, cis-gender, middle-class male. I inhabit a masculine, bourgeoisie way of being that makes the navigation of my advice easier relative to my colleagues from traditionally marginalized identities. My advice is not meant to be prescriptive in the sense that it should be followed unthinkingly; rather, I suggest readers build my advice into their set of repertoires of resistance to the culture of assessment. I will also say that I am giving supremely bad advice to the reader who wishes to become an administrator. The height that an administrator reaches in rank over their career is directly proportional to their ability to banish logic, common sense, and moral decency while expressing (and demanding others express) loyalty to the institution's primary goal: the continuation of the institution. If you have any designs of being any administrator above, say, the department head/chair rank, then you will want to stop reading now (if you have not already) and erase this chapter from your memory.

1. Do Not Assign Work that can be Assessed

I am amazed by faculty members who complain (or brag!) about how much grading they do. Who is forcing them to assign this work? Do they really think that high amounts of homework—work that they do not want to read, or students want to complete—has any positive effect on learning? It does not! Stop assigning work! Or, at least, stop assigning work that can be assessed in a way that you know is counter to your goals of educating students. Some of the best work I have seen from students is when I provide loose parameters for excellence, and then let students reach their own creative heights. It is true that some students, given this opportunity, would give very little effort. But, I would rather have five marginal efforts and five beautiful soul-filled accomplishments than have ten rubric-enforced projects turned into me by zombie-eyed students. Meet with students regularly, give them feedback, talk through their projects with them, and give them all an A or B or whatever you agree to with them. Do not make your life more difficult by assigning work that lends itself to the worst aspects of assessment culture.

2. Assess with Good Humor and Learned Helplessness

You have been assigned to assess multiple sections of a class or perhaps the entire department. What do you do? You may not be able to just refuse, and if you do so, then you will get the reputation as the malcontent. Instead, accept the job with good humor, talk about how much of a team player you want to be, and act as dumb as a box of rocks. If you do so long enough, then whatever administrator whose job it is to oversee the assessment initiative will most likely do the job themselves (or at least a good deal of it). They may act

The Seven Lesson Faculty Member   347

frustrated or exasperated with you. Hold firm. Again, the institution cultivates emotional dependency, and wants you to feel bad for not making administrators' lives easier. That is not your job. Your job is to teach, research, and serve your community—not fill out Jim's spreadsheets for him. Make sure, though, that you are offloading the work back onto the proper part of the bureaucracy. Often, administrators will find precarious faculty (often from marginalized identities) to pick up your slack. Do not let them. Jealously guard being an integral part of the assessment team and then jovially bungle it at every turn.

3. Never Volunteer

Do not volunteer for assessment programs or to create assessment initiatives. There is nothing that will come from them other than faculty ire. There are two exceptions to this rule. First, if you believe the assessment committee will be used to fire or downsize faculty, you should make sure to be on the assessment committee so you can sabotage it from within. Second, if you are a tenured professor and the alternative is that administration will foist the job on a junior colleague or contingent faculty member. In that case, you should always jump on the grenade. That is heroic shit and you will be memorialized forever for it.

4. Put in as much Work as the Report Minimally Demands

Sometimes faculty get excited with the belief that *this* assessment plan will be the one to put their department, college, or university back on track. They quickly become disillusioned, though, by the monotonous grind of the meetings, the lack of progress, and the absence of direction. Their problem? They believed assessment was about improving the institution. Faculty should put as much work into assessment as it requires to continue their actual job of teaching, research, and service. Show up to the first meeting prepared, bright-eyed, and jovial. Impress others with your willingness to contribute to discussion and enthusiasm for the report. Volunteer for something innocuous, like taking notes or something else that allows you to play on your computer while the meeting proceeds. As the meetings wear on, slowly pull back, pushing whatever administrator who heads the committee out to sea on the shrinking iceberg of their intentions. If asked about your lack of presence, vaguely but ominously mention "life circumstances are really challenging right now." If the report is to be made public, apologetically state that you do not feel comfortable (due to your lack of presence) to have your name associated with the report. If it is an internal, do not worry. No one reads those reports seriously anyway.

5. Ask Forgiveness

Sometimes you will be asked to be a part of the assessment project and then, suddenly, the dean will take a job in a different institution or the provost's ritualistic reading of chicken entrails will lead them to "change directions" and you will be left with a thirty-page report that no one wants. Therefore, anytime you are assigned to do assessment, a good rule is to see how long you can go without doing it. Wait until at least the first deadline has passed to see if someone will email you asking where the report it. If they do, it *may* be an indicator that the report is needed (for your professional security, if not anything else). In this case, follow advice in steps two and four. If they never email you for the report, then good news: you are scot free! Spend your time doing something worthwhile and meaningful (i.e., anything other than assessment).

6. Bog Down Assessment Committees

Assessment thrives on uniformity and predictability. Thankfully, these are relatively easy to undermine through committee. Bring in different plans of assessment, informed by a wide range of theories, and argue their relative merit, ensuring that one can never be chosen. Or, choose a pet theory and do not let the committee proceed without capitulating to it. Argue over definitions and other minutia at every turn, never letting any issue pass without unanimous consensus. This tactic is especially effective if you have others on the committee who will also engage in this type of resistance. In that case, coordinate with each other: pretend to get into arguments with each other in the committee, making everyone uncomfortable; never agree with each other unless it is something that will harm the mission of the committee; and generally make the entire affair insufferable. Make sure at the end of every day you are on the committee that you decompress with your accomplice over food and/or drinks.

7. Start or Join a Union (or Faculty Advocacy Group)

Despite all your individual ways of undermining assessment, there remains the issue of the institutional power to compel your performance. In these cases, it is imperative that you join or start a union as a way to create a pool of labor power that can stand against the institutionalized power of the bureaucracy. Faculty should not mistake individualized resistance as working toward liberatory goals; rather, they need to situate their everyday practices within a larger labor politic that seeks to recover the sanctity of their profession against those forces that would drain it of its professionalism, joy, and

The Seven Lesson Faculty Member   349

creativity. Unionization and labor activism provide the only tested method of creating ongoing, systematic change. Without labor activism, it becomes easy for administration to point out the "bad apples" of faculty and replace them with more economically precarious or emotionally compliant substitutions.

CONCLUSION

Faculty, from the moment they first stepped on campus, have been told that assessment is an important tool. But, we may ask, important for whom? Is it important to legislators who continually pull funding from higher education while lambasting faculty as liberal elites? Or is it important to corporations who refuse to pay taxes while outsourcing the costs of job training onto higher education? Or is it administrators who typically see faculty creativity and individuality as barriers to be crushed in their effort to create the perfect institution (i.e., a faculty-less university)? Or is it students whose learning is harmed by assessment and who see faculty as adversaries due to its implementation? What do faculty owe any of these groups?

Our experience and expertise are what secures our places as scholars, not our ability to acquiesce to the demands of people who neither know nor care about creating an educated citizenry. Faculty do not owe these groups their time, energy, or resources. They are not obligated to offer their emotional or intellectual labor to a process that is ultimately anti-faculty and anti-learning. And, they are certainly not responsible for finding a way for higher education to assess its way into relevance. The responsibility of a trained, experienced faculty is to come together with their colleagues to find the best way to fulfill their historic mission: educating society. That mission will only be realized when assessment is consigned to the same intellectual trash heap that houses leeching and astrology.

NOTES

1. I cannot recall how many times I have had a conversation with some assessment-loving, middle-managing pedant only to be told, "Oh, your problem is with grading not assessment" or "Your problem is with assessment, not evaluation" or "Your problem is with evaluation, not grading." *Ad nauseum, ad infinitum*. Whatever euphemism is created, whatever minutiae of detail is different from one concept to another, those differences are eclipsed by what makes these concepts similar—the prerogative of an institution to deem this as good or that as bad and the power to enforce that choice (however arbitrary or wrong) through rewards and punishments.

350   *C. Kyle Rudick*

2. Assessment is an act of violence because it makes the learning of material a matter of enforcement rather than one of free choice. If a student is interested in a subject, but it is outside of the learning objectives, then it is considered inconsequential, trivial, or even dangerous. At its most extreme, assessment makes the learning of some curriculum important no matter how erroneous it may be and promotes myths of nationalism, racism, and sexism as fact (Loewen 1995).

3. I am indebted to Gatto's (2005) "7 Lesson Schoolteacher" for this approach.

REFERENCES

Bennett, Michael, and Jacqueline Brady. 2014. A Radical Critique of the Learning Outcomes Assessment Movement. *Radical Teacher* 100, 146–152. doi:10.5195/rt.2014.171.

Blasco, Maribel. 2016. "Conceptualising Curricular Space in Busyness Education: An Aesthetic Approximation." *Management Learning* 47, 117–136. https://doi.org/10.1177/1350507615587448.

Bourassa, Gregory N. 2018. "Postschool Imaginaries: Educational Life after Neoliberalism." *Policy Future in Education.* https://doi.org/10.1177/1478210318765544.

Engels, Friedrich. 1845. *Engels to Marx in Paris.* Accessed December 15, 2019. https://marxists.catbull.com/archive/marx/works/1845/letters/45_01_20.htm.

Fassett Deanna L., and John T. Warren. 2007. *Critical Communication Pedagogy.* Thousand Oaks, CA: Sage.

Fassett, Deanna L., and C. Kyle Rudick. 2018. "Critical Communication Pedagogy: Toward "Hope in Action." In *Oxford Encyclopedia of Communication and Critical Studies (Vol. 2)*, edited by Dana Cloud. New York: Oxford University.

Gatto, John T. 2005. *Dumbing Us Down: The Hidden Curriculum of Compulsory Schooling.* Gabriola Island, Canada: New Society Publishers.

Giroux, Henry A. 2010. "Dumbing Down Teachers: Rethinking the Crisis of Public Education and the Demise of the Social State." *Review of Education, Pedagogy, and Culture* 32 (4–5): 339–381. https://doi.org/10.1080/10714413.2010.510346.

Guskey, Thomas R. 2011. "Five Obstacles to Grading Reform." *Educational Leadership* 69 (3): 16–21. http://www.ascd.org/publications/educational-leadership/nov11/vol69/num03/Five-Obstacles-to-Grading-Reform.aspx.

Guskey, Thomas R. 2002. *How's My Kid Doing? A Parent's Guide to Grades, Marks, and Report Cards.* San Francisco: Jossey-Bass.

Hessler, Michael, Pöpping, Daniel M., Hollstein, Hanna, Ohlenburg, Hendrik, Arnemann, Philip, H., Massoth, Christina, Seidel, Laura, Zarbock, Alexander, and Manuel Wenk. 2018. "Availability of Cookies During an Academic Course Session Affects Evaluation of Teaching." *Medical Education* 52, 1064–1072. https://doi.org/10.1111/medu.13627.

Kahl Jr., David H. 2013. "Critical Communication Pedagogy and Assessment: Reconciling Two Seemingly Incongruous Ideas." *International Journal of Communication* 7 (2013): 2610–2630. http://ijoc.org/index.php/ijoc/article/view/1897/1033.

Kohn, Alfie. 2011. "The Case Against Grades: When Schools Cling to Letter and Number Ratings, Students Get Stuck in a System that Undermines Learning." *Educational Leadership* 69 (3): 28–33. https://www.alfiekohn.org/article/case-grades/.

Kohn, Alfie. 1999. "From Degrading to De-Grading." High School Magazine. https://www.alfiekohn.org/article/degrading-de-grading/?print=pdf.

Loewen, James W. 1995. *Lies My Teacher Told Me: Everything Your American History Textbook Got Wrong.* New York: New Press.

Marx, Karl. 1887. *Capital: A Critical Analysis of Capitalist Production.* Berlin, Germany: Dietz Verlag.

Marx, Karl. 1844. *Estranged Labor.* Accessed January 5, 2010. https://www.marxists.org/archive/marx/works/1844/manuscripts/labour.htm.

Marx, Karl. 1847. *What are Wages? How are they Determined?* Accessed January 5, 2020. https://www.marxists.org/archive/marx/works/1847/wage-labour/ch02.htm.

Marx, Karl, and Friedrich Engels. 2004. *The German Ideology Part One with Selections from Parts Two and Three, Tougher with Marx's "Introduction to a Critique of Political Economy"* (Christopher John Arthur, ed.). New York: International Publishers.

Murtonen, Mari, Gruber, Hans, and Erno Lehtinen. 2017. "The Return of Behaviourist Epistemology: A Review of Learning Outcomes Studies." *Educational Research Journal* 22, 114–128. https://doi.org/10.1016/j.edurev.2017.08.001.

Rugg, H. O. 1918. "Teachers' Marks and the Reconstruction of the Marking System." *Elementary School Journal* 18 (9): 701–719. https://doi.org/10.1086/454643.

Starch, Daniel, and Edward C. Elliott. 1913. "Reliability of the Grading of High School Work in Mathematics. *School Review* 21, 254–259. https://doi.org/10.1086/436086.

Ziker, John. 2014. "The Long, Lonely Job of Homo Academicus: How Professors Use Their Time." *The Blue Review.* March 31, 2014. Accessed September 15, 2015. https://thebluereview.org/faculty-timeallocation.

Index

action learning, 137
activism, 135
activist education. *See* education
alternative grading systems. *See* grading
  systems
  anti-grading movement. *See* grades
Antioch College, 4
Anzaldúa, Gloria, 92
assessment:
activist assessment, 274
assessment culture, 10, 333
assessment design, 133
assessment industrial complex, 2, 10
collaborative assessment, 36, 97,
  164–65, 199, 212, 217, 234, 266
communication activism pedagogy
  assessment, 134, 146
continuous improvement initiatives,
  337
critical approaches to, 199
democratic methods of, 167
effect on faculty, 332–33
formative assessment, 79, 149
language of, 12, 342
Learning Outcomes Assessment
  (LOA) movement, 11
measurability bias, 11
metric fixation, 10–11
nepantla approach to, 92–95, 100–3

self-assessment, 20, 77, 164, 166,
  169,173–75, 188, 22, 244, 246,
  266–69, 283–85, 287–88
social justice-inspired approaches,
  212–28
standards movement, 11
summative assessment, 79
assignments:
critical selfie project, 172, 181–83
discussion forum, 103
exams, 5, 8, 16, 34, 61, 115, 117,
  119–20, 123, 127, 133, 146, 211
flash memoir, 168, 172, 181–84
group multimedia project, 168, 185–87
love letter, 174
memoir writing, 165
mentor letter, 138–45, 151–52
midterm reflection, 173–75, 188–89,
  325
photovoice, 101
portfolio, 166, 172–73, 175, 197,
  211–12, 229
presentation, 121–25
quizzes, 8, 115, 117, 119–20, 127,
  175, 195, 213, 215, 265, 268, 283
reflection essay, 102
revision, 78, 166, 168, 188, 190, 202,
  204, 208–9, 211–13, 213, 215–16,
  228–29, 235, 243, 266–68

354   *Index*

rubric, 20, 53–54, 81, 92, 120, 122,
  125, 147, 168, 171–73, 188, 249,
  270–71, 332, 338–40, 345–46
Twitter flash nonfiction exercise, 172
word bank, 64–65, 73, 81,
Association of American Colleges and
  Universities, 43
autohistoria-teoría, 92, 97

Bartesaghi, Mariaelena, 197, 211, 213
bell curve. *See* grading systems
Bennington College, 4,
bias, 26–28, 31, 46, 111, 118, 177,
  313–15
big questions, 168, 182
borderland subjectivities, 91
brave space, 169–71
Brown University, 4
Burke, Kenneth, 44
  scientistic terminology, 44
  dramatistic perspective, 47
Butler, Ruth, 21

Carnegie Foundation for the
  Advancement of Teaching, 112
collaborative assessment. *See*
  assessment
collaborative multimedia, 165
collaborative teaching, 163–66
communication activism for social
  justice, 274
communication activism pedagogy. *See*
  pedagogies
communication pedagogies. *See*
  pedagogies
Communication Scholars for
  Transformation. *See* National
  Communication Association
competency-based learning. *See* grading
  systems
contingent faculty. *See* employment
contract renewal. *See* employment
convivencia. *See* vivencia
courses:
  Chicanx identity formation, 100–2

business communication, 109
communication and social activism,
  134, 136–45
gender and communication, 275–88,
  320
group communication, 223
health communication, 102–3
honors program, 163
intercultural communication, 320
interpersonal communication, 211
introduction to communication, 110
media studies, 102–3
oral communication, 110, 123, 163
public speaking, 110, 166, 184
speech for business, 110
written and oral communication, 163
criterion-referenced grading systems.
  See grading systems
critical communication pedagogy. *See*
  pedagogies
critical pedagogy. *See* pedagogies
critical universal design for learning.
  See pedagogies
culturally sustaining pedagogy. *See*
  pedagogies
curve grading. *See* grading systems

Davidson, Carl, 43
dialogue, 21, 23, 24, 62, 77, 113, 143,
  147, 163, 182, 212, 235, 262, 267–
  68, 298, 302–6, 316, 323, 333
disability accommodations:
  Americans with Disabilities Act, 71
  Center for Applied Special
    Technology (CAST), 68–74
  disability technologies, 76
  social model of disability, 70
  standard disability accommodations,
    62
  students with disabilities (SWD), 61

education:
  activist education, 133
  banking model of education, 78, 117,
    311, 321

Index 355

business model, 196, 299
consumer model, 299
customer satisfaction/service model,
8, 299
democratic education, 136
market education, 146, 300
neoliberal education, 3, 12, 33, 51,
95, 146, 200, 298–302, 334
pointless education, 232
traditional education, 133, 146
employment:
contingent faculty, 33, 93, 111, 129,
298, 301, 305, 339, 347
contract renewal, 13, 233, 313, 326
faculty, 302, 305, 312, 316, 318, 321,
344
hiring, 13, 27, 48, 233, 313, 340
promotion, 13, 25, 177, 205, 233,
312–13, 321, 326–27
status, 91
student, 8, 112
success, 48
tenure, 13, 33, 51, 110, 177, 232–33,
298, 301, 303, 305, 313, 326, 340,
343, 347
ethical communication, 180
Evergreen College, 4
Every Student Succeeds Act, 74
evaluation of instruction. *See* evaluation
of teaching
evaluation of teaching, 13, 93, 165, 177–
80, 229–31, 301, 305, 309, 339
bias in teaching evaluations, 313–15
exams. *See* assignments

Family Educational Rights and Privacy
Act (FERPA), 45
formative assessment. *See* assessment
Freire, Paulo, 49, 66, 163, 167, 177,
181, 199, 201, 206, 302–4, 311,
313, 321–22
conscientization, 304

Galván, Trinidad, 93
Goddard College, 4, 196

grade appeal. *See* grades
grades:
anti-grading movement, 10
anxiety about, 165, 172
bias in grades, 26–28, 46, 118, 177
commodity model, 301
criteria, 53
democracy in, 18
E grade, 6
Eurocentric approaches to, 22
grade appeal, 1, 47
grade distribution data, 13, 51, 229
grade grievance. *See* grade appeal
grade inflation, 9, 16, 51, 55, 297, 317
gradeless movement, 19
grade point average (GPA), 4, 9, 20,
28, 48, 54–55, 57, 119, 165, 234
purpose of, 13
rhetoricity of, 44
rhetorical force of, 44
rigor, 13, 34, 64–65, 73–74, 81, 297,
300, 304, 317–18, 336
standardization of, 6
student identities, 14, 55, 114, 179, 232
grade hashtags:
#gradeless, 19
#nogrades, 19
#ungrading, 19
grade-orientation, 18, 51
grade point average (GPA). *See* grades
grading scales:
3-point scale, 6
5- point scale, 6
100-point scale, 6
grading systems:
100% participation / engagement
approach, 219–23
3-P's grading, 17
A-F grading system, 5–6, 50, 52, 204
alternative grading systems, 10,
16–17, 172
bell curve, 6, 53
competency-based learning, 165,
269–70
consensus grading, 22, 211

356   *Index*

criterion-referenced grading systems, 17, 128
curve grading, 6, 19
emotional appeals, 49
group-focused approach, 223–27
guaranteed 'B' approach, 213–17
hybrid contract grading, 201–3
labor-based grading, 208–11
mastery grading, 17, 269–70
minimum grading, 16
narrative evaluation systems, 17–18
non-traditional grading systems, 10, 212–28
no-grading, 16–17
no points grading, 17, 166, 232, 269, 271
norm-referenced grading, 6, 17
pass/fail systems, 17, 166
pick a grade plan, 217–19
point-by-point grading, 16
select-an-assessment plan, 227–28
self-reflective grading, 16
standards-based grading, 17, 269–70
traditional grading systems, 10, 14, 110–11, 165
un-grading, 16–17, 232, 272

Hampshire College, 4
Harvard University, 5
   Harvard University's Implicit Bias Project, 118
hegemony, 29, 51, 57, 201, 298–99, 302–3, 305
hiring. *See* employment
honors distinctions, 6
hooks, bell, 77, 109–10, 167, 199, 323
Human Restoration Project, 19–20, 272

implicit bias, 31, 111, 118, 315

justice. *See* social justice

Kohn, Alfie, 4, 18–19, 21, 32, 168, 234, 270–72, 331–32
Krishnamurti, 255–56, 260, 291–92

learning goal, 7, 118
learning-orientation, 18, 51
letter-writing. *See* assignments
Likert scale, 317, 334
linguistic resistencia, 99

memoir writing. *See* assignments
mental testing movement, 6
mindfulness, 92, 95, 99

nepantla. *See* assessment
National Academies of Sciences, Engineering, and Medicine, 112
National Communication Association, 24
   Activism and Social Justice Division, 25–26
   Communication Scholars for Transformation, 25
   CRTNET (Communication Research and Theory Network), 24
   Distinguished Scholar controversy, 25–26
neoliberalism, 8, 298–302, 305–6
New College of Florida, 4
No Child Left Behind, 74
no-grading. *See* grading systems
norm-referenced grading. *See* grading systems.

panopticon, 312, 345
Parate v. Isibor, 47
pass/fail grading. *See* grading systems
pedagogies:
   activism pedagogy, 133, 145
   applied activist/activism pedagogy, 136, 146–47
   applied critical pedagogy, 136
   awareness pedagogy, 235, 255, 264–69, 289–92
   Chicana feminist pedagogies, 96
   critical pedagogy, 126, 164, 167, 199, 321
   critical communication pedagogy, 2, 24, 44, 62, 65–66, 200, 269, 298, 301–6, 320, 333

Index

357

critical universal design for learning, 62, 66, 76–79
communication activism pedagogy, 23, 134–36, 145–46, 269
communication pedagogies, 3
contemplative pedagogy, 99–100, 198–99, 265–67, 269–70, 285
culturally relevant pedagogy, 66
culturally responsive pedagogy, 66
culturally sustaining pedagogy, 62, 66–67
decolonizing pedagogies, 94, 199, 265
democratic pedagogies, 77, 163
feminist pedagogy, 180, 200
pedagogies of the home, 94
pedagogies of survival, 94
process-based pedagogy, 195, 228
radical pedagogy, 167
social justice education/pedagogy, 126, 129
transformative pedagogies, 91
universal design for learning, 62, 68–74
performance goal, 7, 51, 301
portfolio. *See* assignments
promotion. *See* employment

quizzes. *See* assignments

Rate My Professors, 8, 314
revision. *See* assignments
rubric. *See* assignments

Sarah Lawrence College, 4
self-assessment. *See* assessment
Shor, Ira, 204-6, 208
social justice, 2, 4, 23–27, 64, 78–79, 110–11, 113–14, 126, 130, 135, 133–40, 145–46, 148–50, 170, 195, 199, 264–65, 272, 274, 303, 320

social justice sensibility, 264
social mobility, 27, 52
standardized grading. *See* traditional grading systems
student evaluations. *See* evaluations of teaching
student evaluations of teaching. *See* evaluations of teaching
Students for a Democratic Society, 43
summative assessment. *See* assessment
supervivencia. *See* pedagogies; pedagogies of survival

Teachers Going Gradeless, 19, 272
Teachers Throwing Out Grades, 19, 272
teaching effectiveness, 313, 319–20
tenure. *See* employment
testimonios, 97–98
token economy, 16

un-grading. *See* grading systems
universal design for learning (UDL). *See* pedagogies
University of South Florida, 211

vivencia, 91, 93
convivencia, 93
vivencia-convivencia approach, 95

Whiteness:
hashtags, 25
in communication pedagogy, 26
White standard, 27
White supremacy, 27
White supremacist capitalist patriarchy, 26, 110
William and Mary, 5
World Café, 260–64
writing identity into existence, 95

Yale University, 5

About the Contributors

Kristen C. Blinne (PhD, University of South Florida) is an associate professor of communication studies at the State University of New York College at Oneonta. Her scholarly commitments center on listening across differences as well as the study of consciousness with a focus on non-ordinary states of knowing experienced through a wide range of practices, rituals, and beliefs of varying cultural traditions. She is continuously called to explore the questions: *How can we better understand and negotiate cultural differences and how can individuals and communities teach and learn to engage more peacefully, nonviolently, and compassionately with each other?* To answer these questions, she utilizes a social justice lens as well as contemplative, creative, and critical pedagogies and methodologies such as performative writing, autoethnography, poetry, arts-based methods, and other cultural documentation practices, including field recording, audio ethnography, and performance, aimed at assisting individuals to more effectively intervene into unjust discourses to construct a more just world.

Allison D. Brenneise (PhD, Southern Illinois University) is a member of the teaching faculty at the Department of Communication Studies, University of Minnesota, Twin Cities. She uses her roles as researcher, teacher, parent, and friend to advocate and engage others on topics of communication and (dis)ability. She uses qualitative methods to listen to people with disabilities communicate about their lived experiences to better understand communication and to inform the development of many disability literacies. Her work at the updated for accuracy intersections of disability accommodation and critical communication pedagogy is recently featured in *Communication Education* and in Atay and Fassett's *Mediated Critical Communication Pedagogy*.

Mark Congdon, Jr. (PhD, University of Maine) is an assistant professor in the Department of Communication Studies at Sacred Heart University. He is a former special education teacher and department chair. Mark has worked with various community-engaged projects aimed at increasing educational and professional opportunities for students considered at-risk. His scholarship and pedagogy explore social justice teaching and learning practices that increase the civic engagement and career readiness of students. Mark's work has been published in *Communication Education, Communication Teacher, The Qualitative Report*, and *Partnerships: A Journal of Service-Learning and Civic Engagement*, among others.

Summer R. Cunningham (PhD, University of South Florida) is an assistant professor of communication and affiliate faculty in women's and gender studies at the State University of New York College at Oneonta. She is interested in social justice and transformation, relationality, and innovative inquiry as a means for discovering new possibilities for being together. Her work employs creative, performative, and experimental methods with the aim of garnering interest in social issues for which people are either disinterested or do not see themselves as stakeholders. In her classroom, you should expect to dance, to sing, and to question.

David Deifell (PhD, The University of Iowa) was an associate professor of communication at Clarke University until spring 2020. Broadly speaking, Deifell explores the rhetorical consequences of educational and political discourses, often with special attention to student activism. Deifell's scholarly interests stem from his own political advocacy, which started with his founding of an Amnesty International chapter in his high school in the late 1980s.

Sarah De Los Santos Upton (PhD, University of New Mexico) is an assistant professor in the Department of Communication at the University of Texas at El Paso. Her research and teaching explore nepantla identity, borderland pedagogy, and reproductive justice. She is the co-author of *Challenging Reproductive Control and Gendered Violence in the Américas: Intersectionality, Power, and Struggles for Rights*, winner of the 2018 NCA Feminist and Women's Studies Bonnie Ritter Book Award, and the co-editor of *Latino/a Communication Studies: Theories, Methods, and Practice*. Her research is published in the journals *Departures in Critical Qualitative Research, Women's Studies in Communication, Development in Practice, Action Research*, and *Frontiers in Communication* as well as various edited volumes.

About the Contributors 361

Leandra H. Hernández (PhD, Texas A&M University) is an assistant professor in the Department of Communication at Utah Valley University. She utilizes Chicana feminist approaches to study Latino/a health, Latina/o sexualities, Latina/o journalism/media representations, and Latina/o cultural identities. She is the co-editor of the books *This Bridge We Call Communication: Anzaldúan Approaches to Theory, Method, and Praxis*; *Latino/a Communication Studies: Theories, Methods, and Practice*; and *Military Spouses with Graduate Degrees: Interdisciplinary Approaches to Thriving Amidst Uncertainty*. Her co-authored book *Challenging Reproductive Control and Gendered Violence in the Americas* received the 2018 NCA Feminist and Women's Studies Bonnie Ritter Book Award. Her research on various health communication and media studies topics can be found in the journals *Communication Research, Health Communication, Journal of Media and Religion,* and *Women's Studies in Communication.*

David H. Kahl, Jr. (PhD, North Dakota State University) is associate professor of communication at Penn State Erie, The Behrend College. His research focuses on the application of critical communication pedagogy to uncover and examine subjugating communicative practices by hegemonic structures in society. Kahl has published articles in state, regional, national, and international journals and has authored a variety of book chapters. He is a frequent presenter at conferences in the communication discipline and has received awards for his scholarship at both the regional and national levels. Kahl is currently editor of the *National Communication Association* journal, *Communication Teacher.*

Londie T. Martin (PhD, University of Arizona) is an associate professor in the Department of Rhetoric and Writing at the University of Arkansas at Little Rock where her teaching focuses on digital nonfiction and multimodality. As a feminist rhetorician, her interdisciplinary research emphasizes the role of sensate engagement in new media and performance contexts, and her work has been published in *Rhetoric Review* and *Kairos: A Journal of Rhetoric, Technology, and Pedagogy*. She serves on the editorial board for *Feminist Formations*, a leading academic journal in women's, gender, and sexuality studies.

Kristen A. McIntyre (PhD, North Dakota State University) is a professor in the Department of Applied Communication at the University of Arkansas at Little Rock. She directs the ACOM 1300: Introduction to Communication program as well as the UA-Little Rock Communication Skill Center. Her

362 *About the Contributors*

co-authored publications in communication education can be found in *Communication Quarterly, Communication Teacher, The Communication Centers Movement in Higher Education, Best Practices in Experiential and Service Learning in Communication,* and *The Handbook of Communication Training: A Best Practices Framework for Assessing and Developing Competence.*

Juliane Mora (PhD, University of Utah) is an assistant professor of communication studies and liaison to the School of Engineering and Applied Science at Gonzaga University. She has taught communication across the curriculum in the humanities, sciences, engineering, and business for the last two decades at five different institutions, from California to Florida. Her research interests are in communication pedagogy at the college level, particularly the practices educators use to work for social justice through classroom instruction. She is also concerned with communication across the curriculum and the specific uses of communication in teaching the content of other disciplines, most especially as they work towards justice and equity. She is passionate about creative approaches to teaching and strives to instill that passion in others through collaborative workshops in partnership with the center for teaching and learning. In addition to research and teaching, she views working with students outside the classroom as another form of social justice engagement, through student organization events, professional development workshops, alternative break service trips, volunteering, and advising.

David L. Palmer (PhD, Bowling Green State University) is a professor in the School of Communication at the University of Northern Colorado (UNC), where he teaches graduate and undergraduate courses in social justice activism, communication education, critical theory, rhetorical theory, music as social commentary, and organizational and small group dynamics, and where he served for a decade as the school's liaison to UNC's Professional Teacher Education program. A longtime activist, primarily in the service of alter-globalization causes, his research seeks to establish how educational systems focused on developing students as activists can be vital instruments for social change. Palmer is co-editor (with Lawrence R. Frey) of the award-winning text *Teaching Communication Activism: Communication Education for Social Justice*; and his scholarship is featured in a variety of outlets, including *Communication Education, Quarterly Journal of Speech, College Teaching,* and the book *Communication Activism (Volume 1).* Palmer is the recipient of numerous teaching awards, and he has been an invited speaker and active member at scores of national and local activism events that promote democratic education and social justice causes.

C. Kyle Rudick (PhD, Southern Illinois University) is an associate professor in the Department of Communication Studies at the University of Northern Iowa in Cedar Falls, Iowa. He has published research in a number of journals including *Communication Education, Western Journal of Communication, Communication Reports*, and *Communication Quarterly*. He is a member of the United Faculty union at the University of Northern Iowa and he has recently completed a new book blending student activism and student success: *Engage and Activate: Navigating College and Beyond.*

Lightning Source UK Ltd.
Milton Keynes UK
UKHW011457200223
417320UK00006B/43